Speaking Out . . .

"The first problem for all of us, men and women, is not to learn, but to unlearn."—*Gloria Steinem*

"The single most impressive fact about the attempt by American women to obtain the right to vote is how long it took."—*Alice Rossi*

"If you can't be direct, why be?"—*Lily Tomlin*

"Small things amuse small minds."—*Doris Lessing*

"Security is when everything is settled, when nothing can happen to you; security is the denial of life."—*Germaine Greer*

"When people say: she's got everything, I've only one answer: I haven't had tomorrow."—*Elizabeth Taylor*

Volume Two
1900–the present

The Quotable Woman

AN ENCYCLOPEDIA OF
USEFUL QUOTATIONS

compiled and edited by
Elaine Partnow

PINNACLE BOOKS   LOS ANGELES

*This book is dedicated
in memoriam
to my mother
Jeanette Bernstein Partnow
1912–1973
who gifted me with the joy of reading*

THE QUOTABLE WOMAN: VOLUME TWO

Copyright © 1977 by Elaine Partnow

An original Pinnacle Books edition, published anywhere.

First printing, October 1980

ISBN: 0-523-40874-9

Printed in the United States of America

PINNACLE BOOKS, INC.
2029 Century Park East
Los Angeles, California 90067

Contents

Acknowledgments

The following have given their permission for inclusion of extracts from the works named; this permission is gratefully acknowledged.

Bantam Books, Inc. From *The Feminist Papers: From Adams to de Beauvoir.* Edited and with Introductory Essays by Alice S. Rossi. Copyright © 1973 by Alice S. Rossi. Published by Columbia University Press and Bantam Books, Inc. Reprinted by permission of Bantam Books, Inc.

Bouquet Music, United Artists Music, Mediarts, Inc. From *On My Way to Where* by Dory Previn. Copyright © 1971. Saturday Review Press. Used by permission.

Broadside Series Press. From *Prophets for a New Day* by Margaret Walker. Copyright © 1970. Used by permission.

Curtis Brown, Ltd. From "A Ballad of Anthologies" by Phyllis McGinley. Published in the *Saturday Evening Post,* December 20, 1941. Reprinted by permission of Curtis Brown, Ltd. Copyright © 1941 by Phyllis McGinley.

Cleveland Press. From *Collected Poems* by Dilys Laing. Copyright © 1967 by David Laing. Used by permission of Cleveland Press and Western Reserve University.

Thomas Y. Crowell Company, Inc. Reprinted from *Poems From the Hebrew* by Robert Mezey. Copyright © 1973 by Robert Mezey. With permission of Thomas Y. Crowell Co., Inc.

Doubleday & Company, Inc. From *Poems* by Barbara Guest. Copyright © 1962 by Doubleday & Co., Inc. Reprinted by permission of Doubleday & Company, Inc.

Dramatists Play Service, Inc. From *Slam the Door Softly* by Clare Boothe Luce. Copyright © 1970. Used by permission.

Farrar, Straus & Giroux, Inc. From *Play It As It Lays* by

Joan Didion. Copyright © 1970 by Joan Didion. Reprinted with the permission of Farrar, Straus & Giroux, Inc.

Grove Press, Inc. From *A Taste of Honey* by Shelagh Delaney. Reprinted by permission of Grove Press, Inc. Copyright © 1959 by Theatre Workshop (Pioneer Theatres, Ltd.).

Harcourt Brace Jovanovich, Inc. Bailey, Pearl, *The Raw Pearl* (1968); *Pearl's Kitchen* (1973). Bracken, Peg, *The I Hate to Cook Book* (1960). Craigin, Elizabeth, *Either Is Love* (1937, 1963). Davis, Adele, *Let's Eat Right to Keep Fit* (1954). Delmar, Viña, *The Becker Scandal* (1968); *A Time Remembered* (1968). Fox, Mary Virginia, *Lady for the Defense* (1975). Lanchester, Elsa, *Charles Laughton and I* (1938). Lindbergh, Anne Morrow, *North to the Orient* (1935); *The Wave of the Future* (1940); *The Steep Ascent* (1944); *Hour of Gold, Hour of Lead* (1973); *Locked Rooms and Open Doors: Diaries of Anne Morrow Lindbergh, 1933–1935* (1974). McCarthy, Mary, *The Group* (1954); *Vietnam* (1967); *Hanoi* (1968); *Birds of America* (1971). Nin, Anaïs, *Diary of Anaïs Nin*, Vols. I–V (1966–1974). O'Connor, Flannery, *A Good Man Is Hard to Find* (1955). Origo, Iris, *Images and Shadows* (1970). Struther, Jan, *Mrs. Miniver* (1940). Walker, Alice, *In Love and Trouble: Stories of Black Women* (1973). Welty, Eudora, *A Curtain of Green and Other Stories* (1936); *The Wide Net and Other Stories* (1943); *The Golden Apples* (1949); *The Ponder Heart* (1954). West, Jessamyn, *The Friendly Persuasion* (1945); *Love, Death, and the Ladies' Drill Team* (1955); *To See the Dream* (1956); *South of the Angels* (1960); *Hide and Seek* (1973).

Harper & Row, Publishers, Inc. From *The World of Gwendolyn Brooks* (1971) by Gwendolyn Brooks: "We Real Cool" copyright © 1959 by Gwendolyn Brooks; "Pete at the Zoo," copyright © 1960 by Gwendolyn Brooks; and about 46 lines of poetry, copyright © 1971 by Gwendolyn Brooks Blakely; by permission of Harper & Row, Publishers, Inc.

Excerpts from *Ariel* by Sylvia Plath. Copyright © 1965 by Ted Hughes. By permission of Harper & Row, Publishers, Inc.

Hereford Music. From "Laid Off," "Get Off Me Baby,"

x

REFERENCE SOURCES

The author wishes to express her indebtedness to the following reference works, catalogs, and indices for the invaluable aid they provided in compiling this book.

The Academic Who's Who, 1973–1974
American Architects Directory, 1970
American Authors and Books
The American Heritage Dictionary, 1969, 1970
American Men and Women of Science: Behavioral and Social Sciences, 12th ed.
American Psychological Association Directory, 1974
Bartlett's Familiar Quotations (several editions)
The Biographical Encyclopedia and Who's Who of the American Theater, 1966
Biography Index, Vols. 1–9 and Sept. 1973–Aug. 1975
Books in Print (several editions)
Brown University Library Catalog of American Poetry and Plays
Chamber's Biographical Dictionary, 1969
The Columbia Encyclopedia, 3rd ed., 1963
Contemporary Authors, Vols. 1–56
Current Biography, 1940–1975
Cumulative Book Index (several editions)
Dictionary of American Biography, Vols. 1–10, 1933
Dictionary of American Scholars
Dictionary of Authors
Dictionary of National Biography, Vols 1–22 and 1901–1960
Dictionary of North American Authors
Encyclopedia Britannica, 1953
Encyclopedia of American Biography, 1974
The Great Quotations, 1967
The Home Book of Quotations
Index to Literary Biographies, Vols. 1 & 2, 1975
Index to Women, 1970
International Directory of Psychologists, 1966
Leaders in Education
Los Angeles Public Library Catalog
National Cyclopedia of American Biography
National Faculty Directory, Vols. 1 & 2, 1975
National Union Catalog
New York Times Obituary Index
The Oxford Dictionary of Quotations, 2nd ed., 1955
The Penguin Book of Modern Quotations
Readers' Guide to Periodical Literature
Roget's International Thesaurus, 3rd ed., 1962
Southern California Answering Network
UCLA Card Catalog
USC Card Catalog
Webster's American Biographies, 1974

Webster's Biographical Dictionary, 1972
Webster's New Twentieth Century Dictionary, 2nd ed., unabridged, 1971
Webster's New World Thesaurus, 1974
Who Was Who in America, 1607–1973
Who's Who, 1897–1975
Who's Who in America, 38th ed.
Who's Who in American Education
Who's Who in American Politics, 4th ed.
Who's Who in American Women, 1974–1975
Who's Who in France, 12th ed.
Who's Who in Germany, 5th ed.
Who's Who in Government, 2nd ed.
Who's Who in the Theatre, 15th ed.
Who's Who in the World, 1974
World Book Encyclopedia, 1972
Writer's Dictionary

Introduction

What makes anyone quotable? To have been at some time in the public eye, to have had wit, a way with words, been able to make a cogent observation in few words, to have hit hard in wrath or fervor! The choice of such quotations is probably determined both by the prestige of the quoted person and by the intrinsic worth of the quotation itself.

The case of *The Quotable Woman* is something else. It bears witness to an exhaustive study of the thought of women in virtually every walk of life and in most of communicative society, selected and distilled; but the selection is not made on the basis of exterior criteria of relative values nor according to the preferences of the author of the book, Elaine Partnow. Her inclusiveness [in Volumes One and Two] takes us chronologically from Catharine Esther Beecher, born in 1800 to Denise M. Boudrot, 1952, and in diversity from Mme. Chiang Kai-Shek to Amelia Earhart, from Margaret Mead to Golda Meir, from Zsa Zsa Gabor to Simone de Beauvoir.

What Ms. Partnow has achieved over and above the standard guidelines of a *Bartlett's* kind of volume is to make the quotations representative of the *total* woman—at least that is the impression she conveys to me relative to the women I recognize and know in her list. I found only one important woman absent from her roster: Nathalie Sarraute, the French novelist who in her quiet way has revolutionized the modern novel, and who does not get involved in women's movements. No grandiose statements have come from her direction, yet in her book of critical writings, entitled *Era of Suspicion,* she has provided our time with a label that may become as memorable as W. H. Auden's "age of anxiety" which characterized an earlier period. [This infraction has been remedied in Volume Two.]

Ms. Partnow's international optic has included most other women of note by giving the reader telling excerpts from

xiv

their writings and communications; the space allotted to each and the length of the passage are determined, as far as I can judge, by the pertinence and strength of the remarks. There are perhaps too many movie stars—but that is the circle she is closest to, and if I do not find enough scholars and educators that is my own professional bias. All anthologies bear the imprint of the collector, and out of this one Ms. Partnow emerges with a great deal of good sense, a great deal of faith in women's wisdom, and approval of their positive thinking. Many of the current women's liberation leaders are represented but not to the exclusion of those of another age. We read with pleasure [in Volume One] Emma Goldman's comprehension of what real liberation is: "true emancipation begins neither at the polls nor in courts. It begins in woman's soul," in *Tragedy of Women's Emancipation*. We are encouraged by Helen Gahagan Douglas' conviction [in Volume Two]: "I know the force women can exert in directing the course of events." We wish *that* time would come sooner than it has!

The reader will realize, indeed, how many substantial women had distinguished careers as writers, artists, and publicists before the fanfare about the "new" woman. Hopefully, the availability of these volumes will encourage speechwriters to look for words of wisdom to quote from famous women as they do from men. As a matter of fact, one of the greatest disadvantages that women have suffered in gaining entry into the mainstream of public life, intellectually and socially, beyond the limits of quotas and tokenism, has been their inability to penetrate the consciousness and frame of reference of the central intelligence of society. *The Quotable Woman* should henceforth find its place next to *Webster's Dictionary* on executive desks of thinkers, writers, movers, and shakers.

Beginning with a cursory reading, quickly you become absorbed, and as you read on and on, and follow the passage of the years, you realize that women's concerns follow closely those of men, that interests are not determined by sex but by the human condition. According to Ms. Partnow's meticulous analytical subject index, the most numerous of quotable reflections concern the self, life, love, marriage, children, death, war, and God. Ms. Partnow has allowed the poets among the women to speak in verse. She has wisely avoided aphorisms, and when she extracts from speeches and essays she deftly averts fragmentation; she succeeds in providing the reader with a clear-cut unity of thoughts. She also whets the appetite and is apt to send us to library shelves for further reading from the women quoted.

Let us hope that preachers, commencement speakers, and political speech writers, along with government agencies and groups searching for women executives, college presidents, etc. will have recourse to this valuable guide to the mind and heart of modern woman, and that as a reference book it may turn into *the portable woman.*

—Anna Balakian

Anna Balakian is Professor of French and Comparative Literature at New York University, author of four books on surrealism and symbolism, and of over a hundred essays on modern literature, and is currently President of the American Comparative Literature Association.

Preface

There is some controversy over the very concept of anthology and abridgment. In her anthology *The Feminist Papers*, Alice Rossi says, "Abridgment of any published book or essay is an assault, a cutting or pruning by one mind of the work of another." A flip of the coin and we find Louise Imogen Guiney's opinion that "quotations . . . from the great old authors are an act of filial reverence," expressed in an article she wrote for *Scribner's*. Since the coin will probably land on its edge, perhaps one should go along with Elizabeth Janeway, who wrote in *The Writer's Book*: "As long as mixed grills and combination salads are popular, anthologies will undoubtedly continue in favor."

And so they have. One of the most popular forms of anthology has been books of quotations. In January of 1974 the idea for *The Quotable Woman* crystallized in my mind's eye—not as a feminist book, nor a book of feminists; not as a "woman's book," nor a book for women only—but a book of women, by women, for everyone.

For more than a hundred years now women have been "les frondeuses" for abolition, children's rights, unionism, and more. From their first embryonic struggles for suffrage to today's fight for the Equal Rights Amendment, woman's impact on society has been felt in all its spheres—the arts, politics, theater, literature; they've even altered the structure of the family. Yet, despite their impact, there has not been one single encyclopedic volume from which we could cull the contemplations, insights, and instructions of the daring women who have braved these good fights—at no uncertain risks, if not always of their lives, certainly of their reputations. Not one dusty offering have we from the patriarchal archives of our nation's libraries.

The staggering dearth of women in so many well-known books of quotations prompted me to compile the chart shown on the next page.

A few of the greats were there—Dickinson, Stein, Woolf—along with a few obscure poets who wrote of hearts and flowers, but that was it! Where were the great female revolutionaries, educators, and artists? The adventurers, the feminists, the Third World women? I was appalled—and determined to accomplish what I'd set out to do.

My ground rules for choosing the contributors were based on reputation, remarkability, quotability, and availability of their work. Also, the attempt was made to be as representative of as many professions and nations as possible, though writers and poets, American and English, do predominate.

BOOK	TOTAL CONTRIBUTORS	PERCENTAGE OF WOMEN	TOTAL QUOTES	PERCENTAGE OF WOMEN
Bartlett's Familiar Quotations	2,000	7½ %	117,000	½ %
The Oxford Book of Quotations	1,500	8½	40,000	1
The New Dictionary of Thoughts	1,800	10	20,000	2½
Home Book of Quotations*		10		5½
Contemporary Quotations*		16		
Best Quotations for All Occasions*		5		¾

* Random samples.

I used many standard guides to create my bibliography—the *Encyclopedia Britannica*, reputable anthologies—and many off-beat guides as well: small presses, feminist bibliographies, *Rolling Stone*.† I estimate having made use of some 3,500 books and innumerable periodicals.

The quotations were chosen for various reasons—some for their lyricism, some for their uniqueness and piquancy, some because they were revelatory of the author's character, some because they were memorable and pertinent. Considered were infamous quotations, celebrated quota-

† A list of all reference works used in my research can be found on page xiv.

tions, inventive quotations, and always, always usable quotations. A conscious effort was maintained to be as objective and eclectic as possible.

If usability was one of the criteria used in selecting the quotations, it was the only criterion used in compiling the Subject Index. Breaking from the tradition of indexing quotations by key words or phrases, I have attempted to synthesize the meaning of each quotation into one or more classifications.

If "Graceless, Pointless, Feckless and Aimless waited their turn to be milked" (from *Conference at Cold Comfort Farm* by Stella Gibbons) is indexed as "graceless" it gives little help to a reader who wants to illustrate a point. Indexing of this nature may amount to little more than a gargantuan vestigial organ. The same is true of the "by subject" method of indexing in which, for example, George Eliot's "An ass may bray a good while before he shakes the stars down" will be placed under the heading of "fool." Somewhat helpful, yes, but not nearly so much as indexing it under "braggart" and "egotist."

I like an index that is practical and usable, one that tells the reader what the quotation is *about*. Of course, there are shortcomings to this type of index. The reader searching for that favorite old quotation whose author is forgotten must try to duplicate my thinking processes to find "Graceless and Pointless . . ." classified under "cows" (of necessity) as well as under "passivity," the point of the phrase. One might object—no, no "idleness" is more to the point. I can only ask the reader to use her/his imagination and/or thesaurus, as I did. To have indexed all possible synonymous meanings as well as multiple meanings would have produced an elephantine index. Still, most quotations are classified under at least two different subjects, and some under three or four.

This Subject Index is not meant, however, to categorically pigeonhole the thoughts expressed in the quotations—simply to serve as a guide. There is a not so subtle philosophical difference in this approach which ironically makes the index both more arbitrary and more useful while implying—with some justification—that the key word/phrase method tends to serve the book, not the reader.

It seemed propitious to present the contributors chronologically, to project a sense of history and give the reader a perspective on where women in general have been and where they are going. It offers insight into changes in ideas, language (original spellings and idiosyncrasies of speech have been maintained), the use of newly gained freedoms—even in the popularity of first names. Thus, the chronological order is one more useful tool.

The frustration of tracking down biographical data on "lost" women was at times maddening. Scores of letters were sent to women in care of publishers, agents, and various organizations. Information was sought in the biographies of a contributor's husband, son, brother, or great-grandnephew. Years of birth were most elusive. Occasionally, when faced with a missing chink in the biographical or bibliographical armor, I included the woman or quotation anyway. Rather than lose fine contributors and good quotations to be true to form, I chose to be true to the women.

Through all this sleuthing I have come to feel that the public regards women in past and current history very much like fine character actors—we recognize them but do not know their names; we need them but do not pay them homage; we make demands on them but do not document their contributions. I hope that the quotations garnered here will counteract some of those lapses, that they will stimulate reading and study, that they will help retrieve "lost" women and help "found" women get some of their own back.

The most difficult part of an impossible task was, simply, to stop. This is—and probably always will be—an unfinished work. For every woman included, five, ten, twenty more could be added. Among those most frequently missing are non-English speaking women. The highly prolific Marie von Ebner-Eschenbach, for example, is sorely underrepresented because so few English translations of her works could be found. I even had difficulty finding translations of George Sand! But at least these women are represented—there were dozens more I wanted to include, but I could find nothing by them available in English. Helplessly, I was forced to eliminate one woman after another.

Many talented and deserving women whose works were collaborations with male partners also had to be ignored. And several distinguished scientists and mathematicians were left out because, though the women were/are memorable, I could find nothing "quotable"—at least nothing most of us could understand. And quotability is the principal measure for inclusion in *The Quotable Woman*.

As this is a book of learning and sharing, I'd like to take some space to thank the people who contributed to its making:

To the women who worked as my assistants and co-workers, who went beyond the tasks asked of them, working golden time for grey wages: Janine Watson, Paula Gray, Krista Michaels, Hazel Medina and, most especially, Georgia Griggs, my right—and left—hand;

To the one who saw me through it all, and held me up a good part of the time: Turner Browne, my friend, my husband;

To family, friends, and associates who supported me and advised me: Al and Sylvia Partnow, Judith and Herb Hyman, Susan Partnow, Barry Ganapol, Alejandro Grattan, Aniko Klein, Stanley Corwin, Marcy Posner, Beth Sue Rose, and all the staff at Corwin Books, Bob Garfield, Beverly Iser, Annett H. Welles, Gilda Cohen, Michele Kort, Robin Pearl, Ann and Burt Witkovsky, and Connell Cowan;

To the librarians and information service of the Los Angeles City Public Library's Main Branch, and to the Graduate Reserve Desk and general facilities of UCLA's Research Library;

To all of them—a hearty and keenly felt thanks.

But most of all I am indebted to the women who made this book possible—the contributors. Thank you, sisters.

Elaine Partnow
Los Angeles

How to Use This Book

The women quoted are presented in chronological order according to the year of their birth, beginning with the year 1800, and alphabetically within each year. Each has been given a contributor number; these numbers appear in the headings for each page in the Quotations section, and are used in the Biographical and Subject Indices rather than page numbers.

Firm birth and/or death dates are not known for every woman. When it was possible to make an accurate guess, a date followed by a question mark is given. If this was not possible, the women were given "flourished" decade dates (e.g., fl. 1950s), meaning that as near as can be figured they were most active in a certain decade. Such women are grouped together at the beginning of that decade's entries. If it is not known when a woman died but it is probable that she is no longer living, there is a question mark instead of a death date. Women who are presumably still alive and active but for whom, despite all efforts, no birth date could be found are grouped together at the end of the Quotations section, following a "Contemporary/No Date" subhead.

The quotations for each woman are presented chronologically according to the copyright date or publication date of the source. If the source was published after a woman's death, it is followed by a "p" (e.g., 1973p), indicating that it is posthumous. If only an approximate year of publication is known, the date is preceded by "c" for circa (e.g., c.1943). Parenthetical dates within a source indicate the time at which the quotation was originally spoken or written, whereas dates appearing in quotation marks indicate chapter or section titles in the sources.

In some cases no date could be found for a quotation (especially true for some poems and essays); these quotations follow the dated sources, separated from them by three asterisks across the column, and are listed alphabetically, by the first word of each new quotation.

When possible, the location of the quotation within the source is given—that is, the part, chapter, act, scene, etc. If, however, a quote was derived from somewhere other than the source itself—for example, from a book review—and the precise location is not known, it precedes those quotations that are more specifically designated. Of course, many books have no chapter or part numbers or headings, and so locations cannot be specified for these.

Abbreviations used in source citations are: Vol.—volume; Pt.—part; Bk.—book; Ch.—chapter; St.—stanza; Sec.—section; No.—number; Sc.—scene; l.—line; c.—circa; p.—posthumous; ed.—editor.

When a quotation was taken from a book, article, or any work by a writer other than our contributor, it is indicated by the words "quoted in" followed by the source and its author. In the instance of anthological works "quoted in" is not used, but editors are indicated.

Quote marks around a quotation indicate that it is from dialogue spoken by a character in a work of fiction. Except for changes of dialogue, original paragraphing is not indicated.

For information concerning the Biographical and Subject Indices, see notes preceding each index.

I would venture to guess that Anon,
who wrote so many poems without signing
them, was often a woman.
                    —*Virginia Woolf*

American women are not the only people
in the world who manage to lose track
of themselves, but we do seem to
mislay the past in a singularly
absent-minded fashion.
                    —*Elizabeth Janeway*

The signals of the century
Proclaim the things that are to be—
The rise of woman to her place,
The coming of a nobler race.
                    —*Angela Morgan*

The Quotations

704. Lena Guilbert Ford
(fl. early 1900s–1916?)

1 Keep the home fires burning,
  While your hearts are yearning,
  Though your lads are far away
  They dream of home.
  There's a silver lining
  Through the dark cloud shining:
  Turn the dark cloud inside out,
  Till the boys come home.
  "Keep the Homes Fires Burning"   *1915*

705. Eva Lathbury
(fl. early 1900s)

1 The fall, like the serpent, was mythical: the apple was
  sound and Eve hysterical.
  Mr. Meyer's Pupil   *1907*

2 I can't help it . . . that's what we all say when we
  don't want to exert ourselves.
  Ibid.

706. Moira O'Neill
(fl. early 1900s)

1 Youth's for an hour,
  Beauty's a flower,
  But love is the jewel that wins the world.
  "Beauty's a Flower," *Songs of the
  Glens of Antrim*   *1901*

2 The memory's fairly spoilt on me
  Wid mindin' to forget.
  Ibid., "Forgettin'," St. 5

2

707. Lady Troubridge
(fl. early 1900s–1946)

1 A bad woman always has something she regards as a curse—a real bit of goodness hidden away somewhere.
The Millionaire   1907

2 If I had had a pistol I would have shot him—either that or fallen at his feet. There is no middle way when one loves.   Ibid.

3 It is far easier to love a woman in picturesque rags than in the common place garments of respectability.
Ibid.

4 A girl can't analyze marriage, and a woman—daren't.
Ibid.

708. Grace Adams
(1900–   )

1 Whenever serious intellectuals, psychologists, sociologists, practicing physicians, Nobel prize novelists take time off from their normal pursuits to scrutinize and appraise the Modern American Woman, they turn in unanimously dreary reports.
"American Women Are
Coming Along," *Harper's*   1939

709. Polly Adler
(1900–1962)

1 Too many cooks spoil the brothel.
A House Is Not a Home   1953

2 . . . I am one of those people who just can't help getting a kick out of life—even when it's a kick in the teeth.
Ibid., Ch. 1

3 The degree to which a pimp, if he's clever, can confuse and delude a prostitute is very nearly unlimited.
Ibid., Ch. 4

4 "My home is in whatever town I'm booked."

Ibid., Ch. 9

5 What it comes down to is this: the grocer, the butcher, the baker, the merchant, the landlord, the druggist, the liquor dealer, the policeman, the doctor, the city father and the politician—these are the people who make money out of prostitution, these are the real reapers of the wages of sin.

Ibid.

6 The women who take husbands not out of love but out of greed, to get their bills paid, to get a fine house and clothes and jewels; the women who marry to get out of a tiresome job, or to get away from disagreeable relatives, or to avoid being called an old maid—these are whores in everything but name. The only difference between them and my girls is that my girls gave a man his money's worth.

Ibid., Ch. 10

710. Dorothy Arzner
(1900–   )

1 It is my theory that if you have authority, know your business and know you have authority, you have the authority.

Quoted in *The New York Times*
June 15, 1972

2 I was led by the grace of God to the movies. I would like the industry to be more aware of what they're doing to influence people. . . .

Quoted in *Popcorn Venus*
by Marjorie Rosen   1973

711. Taylor Caldwell
(1900–   )

1 "Honest men live on charity in their age; the almhouses are full of men who never stole a copper penny. Honest men are the fools and the saints, and you and I are neither."

Dynasty of Death, Bk. I, Ch. 12   1938

2 ". . . I knew you would not betray us. Not because of—honor. But profit. And profits are not bedfellows of honor.

Ibid.

3 "Protestantism forgets that men are men, and that there are appetites that it is better to wink at, provided that certain duties are observed. We don't strain at a gnat and swallow a camel, nor swim in an ocean and drown in a puddle."

Ibid., Bk. II, Ch. 70

4 Men who retain irony are not to be trusted, thought Ernest. They can't always resist an impulse to tickle themselves.

Ibid., Ch. 78

5 "He that hath no rule over his own spirit is like a city that is broken down and without walls."

This Side of Innocence, Pt. I, Ch. 5   1946

6 A civilization based purely on agriculture was a civilization which never went hungry. But a raucous and ruthless civilization, dependent on the churning of the "devil machines" within brick walls, was vulnerable to every sensitive wind that blew from Wall Street.

Ibid., Pt. III, Ch. 43

7 Despair, Philip thought, is sometimes the great energizer of the mind, though sometimes its flowering may be sterile.

Ibid., Ch. 45

8 Why, hadn't Pa often told him that no one could understand a person who had a gift? They lived in a world of their own, beyond criticism, beyond the knowing of other men. . . . "In Germany we understand these things, these geniuses," Mr. Enger had often told Edward dolefully. "But not in America. America has no soul."

The Sound of Thunder,
Pt. I, Ch. 1   1957

9 "Learning," he would say, "should be a joy and full of excitement. It is life's greatest adventure; it is an illustrated excursion into the mind's noble and learned men, not a conducted tour through a jail. So its surroundings should be as gracious as possible, to complement it."

Ibid., Ch. 9

5

10 "Shakespeare speaks of 'lean and hungry men,' but he never seemed to notice that a lot of women are lean and hungry, too, and much more vulturous than many men."

The Late Clara Beame, Ch. 16   1963

11 "It never pays to complicate a woman's mind too much."   Ibid.

12 But what was a body? Dust, dung, urine, itches. It was the light within which was important, and it was not significant if that light endured after death, or if the soul was blinded eternally in the endless night of the suspired flesh.

Great Lion of God, Pt. I, Ch. 1   1970

13 One, if one is sensible, blames government, not the servers of the government, not those entangled in their governments.

Ibid., Ch. 10

14 Every object . . . burned with a blinding radiance as if each were being consumed by the sun. A very holocaust of flaming scintillation hovered over all things, appeared to emanate even from the pebbles of the paths. And the heat mounted.

Ibid., Pt. II, Ch. 24

15 ". . . it is not always wise to appear singular."

Ibid., Pt. III, Ch. 35

16 Is it not deplorable that a few heedless zealots can bring calamity to their law-abiding fellows?

Ibid., Ch. 43

17 The old [Roman] gods understood that life was reasonable and favors were exchanged for favors, and that is how it should be.   Ibid., Ch. 53

18 At the end—and as usual—God had betrayed the innocent and had left them comfortless.

Captains and the Kings,
Pt. I, Ch. 1   1972

19 It was business, and none of them had allegiances or attachments or involvements with any nation, not even their own. . . . Joseph immediately called them "the gray and deadly men," and did not know why he detested them, or why he found them the most dangerous of all among the human species.   Ibid., Ch. 21

6

20 "Once power is concentrated in Washington—admittedly not an immediate prospect—America will take her place as an empire and calculate and instigate wars, for the advantage of all concerned. We all know, from long experience, that progress depends on war."

Ibid.

21 "Mankind is the most selfish species this world has ever spewed up from hell, and it demands, constantly, that neighbors and politicians be 'unselfish,' and allow themselves to be plundered—for its benefit. Nobody howls more against 'public selfishness,' or even private selfishness, as much as a miser, just as whores are the strongest supporters of public morality, and robbers of the people extol philanthropy. I've lived a long time, but my fellow man baffles me more and more, which no doubt is naïve of me."

Ibid., Pt. II, Ch. 13

712. Helen Gahagan Douglas
(1900–1980)

1 The Eleanor Roosevelt I shall always remember was a woman of tenderness and deep sympathy, a woman with the most exquisite manners of anyone I have known—one who did what she was called upon to do with complete devotion and rare charm.

The Eleanor Roosevelt We Remember   1963

2 Would Eleanor Roosevelt have had to struggle to overcome this tortuous shyness if she had grown up secure in the knowledge that she was a beautiful girl? If she hadn't struggled so earnestly, would she have been so sensitive to the struggles of others? Would a beautiful Eleanor Roosevelt have escaped from the confinements of the mid-Victorian drawing room society in which she was reared? Would a beautiful Eleanor Roosevelt have wanted to escape? Would a beautiful Eleanor Roosevelt have had the same need to be, to do?

Ibid.

3 I know the force women can exert in directing the course of events.

Ibid.

4 If the national security is involved, *anything goes*. There are no rules. There are people so lacking in roots

about what is proper and what is improper that they don't know there's anything wrong in breaking into the headquarters of the opposition party.

Quoted in "Helen Gahagan Douglas"
by Lee Israel, *Ms*.   *October, 1973*

5   . . . the first step toward liberation for *any* group is to use the power in hand. . . . And the power in hand is the vote.

Ibid.

6 If I go to Congress, it won't be to spar with anybody, man or woman. I'm not a wit. I'm not a fencer. I don't enjoy that kind of thing. It's all nonsense and an insult to the intelligence of the American people.

Ibid., News Item (1944)

7 Such pip-squeaks as Nixon and McCarthy are trying to get us so frightened of Communism that we'll be afraid to turn out the lights at night.

Ibid., Speech (1950)

713. Queen Elizabeth
(1900–   )

1 The children will not leave unless I do. I shall not leave unless their father does, and the King will not leave the country in any circumstances whatever.

Attributed   *1940*

2 I'm glad we've been bombed [Buckingham Palace]. It makes me feel I can look the East End in the face.

Attributed   *1940*

714. Joanna Field
(1900–   )

1 I used to trouble about what life was for—now being alive seems sufficient reason.

A Life of One's Own (June 8)   *1934*

2 I feel we have picked each other from the crowd as fellow-travellers, for neither of us is to the other's personality the end-all and the be-all.

Ibid. (September 20)

8

3 . . . as soon as you are happy enjoying yourself, something hunts you on—the hounds of heaven—you think
you'll be lost—damned, if you are caught. . . .

Ibid. (October 10)

4 I came to the conclusion then that "continual mindful-
ness" . . . must mean, not a sergeant-major-like drill-
ing of thoughts, but a continual readiness to look and
readiness to accept whatever came.

Ibid.

5 I began to suspect that thought, which I had always
before looked on as a cart-horse to be driven, whipped
and plodding between shafts, might be really a Pegasus,
so suddenly did it alight beside me from places I had
no knowledge of.

Ibid.

6 . . . the growth of understanding follows an ascending
spiral rather than a straight line.

Ibid. (Undated)

715. Zelda Fitzgerald
(1900–1948)

1 Women, despite the fact that nine out of ten of them go
through life with a death-bed air either of snatching-
the-last-moment or with martyr-resignation, do not die
tomorrow—or the next day. They have to live on to
any one of many bitter ends.

"Eulogy on the Flapper," *Metropolitan
Magazine   June, 1922*

2 Most people hew the battlements of life from compromise, erecting their impregnable keeps from judicious
submissions, fabricating their philosophical drawbridges
from emotional retractions and scalding marauders in
the boiling oil of sour grapes.

Save Me the Waltz, Ch. 1   *1932*

3 Possessing a rapacious, engulfing ego, their particular
genius swallowed their world in its swift undertow and
washed its cadavers out to sea. New York is a good
place to be on the up-grade.

Ibid., Ch. 2

4 Women sometimes seem to share a quiet, unalterable
dogma of persecution that endows even the most so-

phisticated of them with the inarticulate poignancy of the peasant.

Ibid.

5 "Lives aren't as hard as professions," she gasped.
Ibid., Ch. 3

6 Wasn't any art the expression of the inexpressible? And isn't the inexpressible always the same, though variable—like the *Time* in physics?
Ibid.

7 "Oh, the secret life of man and woman—dreaming how much better we would be than we are if we were somebody else or even ourselves, and feeling that our estate has been unexploited to its fullest. I have reached the point where I can only express the inarticulate, taste food without taste, smell whiffs of the past, read statistical books, and sleep in uncomfortable positions."
Ibid., Ch. 4

8 "By the time a person has achieved years adequate for choosing a direction, the die is cast and the moment has long since passed which determined the future."
Ibid.

9 ". . . We grew up founding our dreams on the infinite promise of American advertising. I *still* believe that one can learn to play the piano by mail and that mud will give you a perfect complexion."
Ibid.

10 "It's very expressive of myself. I just lump everything in a great heap which I have labelled 'the past,' and, having thus emptied this deep reservoir that was once myself, I am ready to continue."
Ibid., Ch. 4

11 . . . I don't want to live—I want to love first, and live incidentally. . . .
Letter to F. Scott Fitzgerald (1919),
Quoted in Zelda by Nancy Milford
1970p

12 Don't you think I was made for you? I feel like you had me ordered—and I was delivered to you—to be worn—I want you to wear me, like a watch-charm or a button hole boquet [sic]—to the world.
Ibid.

13 Home is the place to do the things you want to do. Here we eat just when we want to. Breakfast and luncheon are extremely moveable feasts. It's terrible to allow conventional habits to gain a hold on a whole household; to eat, sleep and live by clock ticks.
Ibid., Interview in the *Baltimore Sun* (1923)

14 I don't seem to know anything appropriate for a person of thirty. . . .
Ibid., Letter to F. Scott Fitzgerald (1930)

15 Your entire life will soon be accounted for by the toils we have so assiduously woven—your leisure is eaten up by habits of leisure, your money by habitual extravagance, your hope by cynicism and mine by frustration, your ambition by too much compromise.
Ibid. (Undated)

16 A vacuum can only exist, I imagine, by the things which enclose it.
Ibid., Journal (1932)

17 . . . I have often told you that I am that little fish who swims about under a shark and, I believe, lives indelicately on its offal. Anyway, that is the way I am. Life moves over me in a vast black shadow and I swallow whatever it drops with relish, having learned in a very hard school that one cannot be both a parasite and enjoy self-nourishment without moving in worlds too fantastic for even my disordered imagination to people with meaning.
Ibid., Letter to F. Scott Fitzgerald (1932)

18 I wish I could write a beautiful book to break those hearts that are soon to cease to exist: a book of faith and small neat worlds and of people who live by the philosophies of popular songs. . . .
Ibid., Letter to Dr. Rennie (May, 1934)

19 I take a sun bath and listen to the hours, formulating, and disintegrating under the pines, and smell the resiny hardi-hood of the high noon hours. The world is lost in a blue haze of distances, and the immediate sleeps in a thin and finite sun.
Ibid., Journal (1938)

716. Lisa Gardiner
(1900–1956)

1 And remember, expect nothing and life will be velvet.
> Quoted in *Don't Fall Off the
> Mountain* by Shirley MacLaine
> *1970p*

717. Elizabeth Goudge
(1900–   )

1 Her birthdays were always important to her; for being a born lover of life, she would always keep the day of her entrance into it as a very great festival indeed. . . .
> *Green Dolphin Street*, Bk. I,
> Pt. II, Ch. 1   *1944*

2 His hatred of his wife horrified him. It was the first hatred of his life, it was growing in bitterness and intensity day by day, and he had no idea what to do about it.
> Ibid., Bk. II, Pt. III, Ch. 1

3 The elements were "seeking" each other in rage and confusion, and in the fury of the conflict boastful man was utterly humiliated, sucked down, drowned.
> Ibid., Ch. 2

4 She had a deep sense of justice and sometimes this made her feel as uncomfortable in her spirit if she deserved a whipping and did not get it as she felt in her body if she did get it, and of the two she preferred to suffer in body.
> *The Child from the Sea*,
> Bk. I, Ch. 1   *1970*

5 Peace, she supposed, was contingent upon a certain disposition of the soul, a disposition to receive the gift that only detachment from self made possible.
> Ibid., Ch. 7

6 . . . the butterflies. . . . Yet not quite birds, as they were not quite flowers, mysterious and fascinating as are all indeterminate creatures.
> Ibid., Pt. II, Ch. 1

12

7 ". . . The travail of creation of course exaggerates the importance of our work while we are engaged in it; we know better when the opus is finished and the lion is perceived to be only a broken-backed mouse. . . ."

Ibid., Pt. III, Ch. 2

8 "All true glory, while it remains true, holds it. It is the maintaining of truth that is so hard."

Ibid.

9 "All we are asked to bear we can bear. That is a law of the spiritual life. The only hindrance to the working of this law, as of all benign laws, is fear."

Ibid., Ch. 17

718. Helen Hayes
(1900–   )

1 An actress's life is so transitory—suddenly you're a building.*   News Item   *November, 1955*

2 One has to grow up with good talk in order to form the habit of it.

A Gift of Joy, with Lewis Funke,
Introduction 1965

3 We rely upon the poets, the philosophers, and the playwrights to articulate what most of us can only feel, in joy or sorrow. They illuminate the thoughts for which we only grope; they give us the strength and balm we cannot find in ourselves. Whenever I feel my courage wavering I rush to them. They give me the wisdom of acceptance, the will and resilience to push on.

Ibid.

4 Actors cannot choose the manner in which they are born. Consequently, it is the one gesture in their lives completely devoid of self-consciousness.

On Reflection, with Sandford Dody, Ch. 1   *1968*

5 When I was very young, I half believed one could find within the pages of these [biographical] memoirs the key to greatness. It's rather like trying to find the soul in the map of the human body. But it is enlightening— and it does solve some of the mysteries.   Ibid., Ch. 6

---

* Referring to a New York theater named for her.

6 Yes, I have doubted. I have wandered off the path. I have been lost. But I always returned. It is beyond the logic I seek. It is intuitive—an intrinsic, built-in sense of direction. I seem always to find my way home. My faith has wavered but has saved me.

Ibid., Ch. 15

719. Laura Z. Hobson
(1900–   )

1 It was the rhythm of all living, apparently, and for most people. Happiness, and then pain. Perhaps then happiness again, but now, with it, the awareness of its own mortality.

Gentlemen's Agreement, Ch. 1   1946

2 Did it never occur to one of them to write about a fine guy who was Jewish? Did each one feel some savage necessity to pick a Jew who was a swine in the wholesale business, a Jew who was a swine in the movies, a Jew who was a swine in bed?

Ibid., Ch. 3

3 Where did ideas come from, anyway? This one had leaped at him when he'd been exhausted, AWOL from his search.

Ibid., Ch. 4

4 We are born in innocence. . . . Corruption comes later. The first fear is a corruption, the first reaching for a something that defies us. The first nuance of difference, the first need to feel better than the different one, more loved, stronger, richer, more blessed—these are corruptions.

Ibid., Ch. 6

5 The anti-Semite offered the effrontery—and then the world was ready with harsh yardsticks to measure the self-control and dignity with which you met it. You were insensitive or too sensitive; you were too timid or too bellicose; they gave you at once the wound and the burden of proper behavior toward it.

Ibid., Ch. 8

6 What trouble it was to be young! At sixty you grieved for the world; in youth you grieved for one unique creature.   Ibid., Ch. 13

7 What was it, this being "a good father"? To love one's sons and daughters was not enough; to carry in one's bone and blood a pride in them, a longing for their growth and development—this was not enough. One had to be a ready companion to games and jokes and outings, to earn from the world this accolade. The devil with it.

The First Papers, Pt. I, Ch. 2   1964

8 If she began to imagine that he would be grateful for any understanding she gave him, she would launch herself on the long stony road of disappointment.

Consenting Adult   1975

9 She forced herself to stop thinking. . . . She was disciplined enough to do this nonthinking for short stretches, during the daytime at least. She had done it in other crises of her life; at times it was the only way to manage.

Ibid.

10 Why didn't children ever see that they could damage and harm their parents as much as parents could damage and harm children?

Ibid.

11 It was all happening in a great, swooping free fall, irreversible, free of decision, in the full pull of gravity toward whatever was to be.

Ibid.

12 "Dear Mama. . . . I have something to tell you that I guess I better not put off any longer . . . you see, I am a homosexual. I have fought it off for months and maybe years, but it just grows truer. . . ."

Ibid.

720. Kathryn Hulme
(1900–   )

1 I saw more of them [concentration-camp brands] on that first day. I saw so many that I was sure my memory was branded forever and that never again would I be able to think of mankind with that certain friendly ease which characterizes Americans like a birthright.

The Wild Place, Ch. 2   1953

2 Interior silence, she repeated silently. That would be her Waterloo. How without brain surgery could you quell the rabble of memories? Even as she asked herself the question, she heard her psychology professor saying quite clearly across a space of years, "No one, not even a saint, can say an *Ave* straight through without some association creeping in; this is a known thing."

The Nun's Story, Ch. 1   1956

3 "You must never lose the awareness that in yourself you are nothing, you are only an instrument. An instrument is nothing until it is lifted."

Ibid., Ch. 8

4 Her defeat had so many facets, she could not define it all at once, but only her scorching shame for being a hypocrite in the religious life, for wearing the garb of obedience while flaunting the Holy Rule, and the Cross of Christ above a heart filled with hate.

Ibid., Ch. 18

5 "I believe, Father," she said, "that even the smallest gesture of charity made in the world, with joy, would be ten times more pleasing to God than all the work I do here under the Holy Rule I only pretend to obey."

Ibid.

6 Then there had been the inspection of their child from head to toe as he watched Annie undress the baby before bedtime. The tiny perfect fingernails and toenails astonished him the most. They were like the small pink shells you scuffed up in the sands of tropical beaches, he whispered, counting them. And, for the twentieth time, he exclaimed, "I don't know *how* you did it all alone!" His admiration for her bravery sent a glow of happiness through her. It was a new kind of tribute from him. It was a payment in full for all the terrors of her lonely ordeal.

Annie's Captain, Ch. 9   1961

7 Their fright seemed to turn them into children.

Ibid., Ch. 18

8 Annie clung to life like a shipwrecked soul on a slender spar adrift in an ocean of pain. She denied the pains but the doctor guessed them when she began refusing all medicines for fear he would slip in the morphine he had promised not to give until she herself asked. Her

fortitude surpassed anything he had ever encountered and it turned him into a cursing madman every time he came downstairs. "She'd go through hell to keep her wits clear until *he* comes," he groaned. "God damn that bloody old scow!"

Ibid.

721. Loran Hurnscot
(1900?–1970)

1 There are times when I feel I can no longer bear that grey room where I go once a week or fortnight in order to discover (presumably) how to turn from one sort of person into another sort of a person.

A Prison, a Paradise, Vol. II   *1959*

2 It came over me, blindingly, for the first time in my life, that suicide was a wrong act, was indeed "Mortal sin." In that moment, God stopped me. I did not want my life, but I knew I was suddenly forbidden by something outside myself to let it go.   Ibid. (July 9, 1939)

3 It had always been pride that had held me off from Him. Now it was broken the obstacle was gone. One is never simple enough, while things go well.   Ibid.

4 And suddenly I was swept out of myself—knowing, knowing, knowing. Feeling the love of God burning through creation, and an ecstasy of bliss pouring through my spirit and down into every nerve.

Ibid. (October 4, 1939)

722. Guion Griffis Johnson
(1900–   )

1 Government existed for the best people—the intelligent, educated and wealthy. In a society where all are equally free and share alike in political privileges, there are some more fit for the exercise of good government than others.

"Southern Paternalism Toward
Negroes Atfer Emancipation,"
The Journal of Southern History
November, 1957

2 It was always the responsibility of the strong, so ran the benevolent paternalist's argument, to bear the burden of the weak. The strong race by virtue of its superior intelligence, culture, and wealth was the national protector of the Negro.

Ibid.

3 The argument against mixing in the schools stresses again the concept of superior and inferior races and the obligation of the superior to give the inferior equal but separate facilities so that the Negro may have the opportunity to rise within his own social system. In this way, God's plan will be carried out, for He separated the races and it is a violation of His will for blacks and whites to be mixed in educational facilities.

Ibid.

723. Wilhelmina Kemp Johnstone
(1900–)

1 But how glad I am, how very glad and grateful for that window looking out upon the sea!

"My Window," Bahamian Jottings 1973

2 Pride, we are told, my children, "goeth before a fall," and oh, the pride was there and so the fall was not far away!

Ibid., "The Old Ship's Story"

3 The dawn artist was already out, tipping the clouds with glory, and transforming the sky into a glow of wonder.

Ibid., "Our Trip to Green Cay"

724. Meridel Le Sueur
(1900–)

1 In the mid-centre of America a man can go blank for a long, long time. There is no community to give him life; so he can go lost as if he were in a jungle. No one will pay any attention. He can simply be as lost as if he had gone into the heart of an empty continent. A sensitive child can be lost too amidst all the emptiness and ghostliness. I am filled with terror when I think of the emptiness and ghostliness of mid-America. The rigors

18

of conquest have made us spiritually insulated against human values. No fund of instinct and experience has been accumulated, and each generation seems to be more impoverished than the last.

"Corn Village" (1930), *Salute to Spring*   1940

2 "I put my hand where you lie so silently. I hope you will come glistening with life power, with it shining upon you as upon the feathers of birds. I hope you will be a warrior and fierce for change, so all can live."

Ibid., "Annunciation"

3 Every generation must go further than the last or what's the use in it? A baker's son must bake better bread—a miner's son—each generation a mite further.

Ibid., "The Dead in Steel"

4 "They can kill the bodies of Sacco and Vanzetti but they can't kill what they stand for—the working class. It is bound to live. As certainly as this system of things, this exploitation of man by man, will remain, there will always be this fight, today and always until . . .'"

Ibid., "Farewell"

5 Hard times ain't quit and we ain't quit.

Ibid., "Salute to Spring"

6 Now I have always cried to these forebears and cried to them for answers, for compasses, and seen their deeds, their actions, solid and muscular. . . . Now, in a moment of crisis and cold, they point out where the warm ash of the old fires can give you warmth, where strength is cached. I can even catch their heraldic voices in the wind of struggle.

Crusaders   1955

7 . . . there is only one force that creates value and that is labor, and one manner of expropriation of wealth, the exploitation of labor and the natural resources.

Ibid.

8 . . . the history of an oppressed people is hidden in the lies and the agreed-upon myth of its conquerors.

Ibid., Ch. 3

9 . . . for there is no cruelty like that of the oppressor who fells his loss of the bit on those it has been his gain to oppress.

Ibid.

10 Security seemed to be something you had more of by being true to your beliefs. A house was only a house—it was nothing you gave your life to have, or sacrificed an idea to protect; the same with a job.

Ibid., Ch. 5

11 Memory in America suffers amnesia.

Ibid., Ch. 6

12 The funeral has long been an instrument also of conveying history that has become hidden, of subtly informing the young, and of mining and blowing the mineral of collective poetry and courage.   Ibid.

13 For none shall die who have the future in them.

Ibid.

14 Money is only money, beans tonight and steak tomorrow. So long as you can look yourself in the eye.

Ibid., Ch. 7

725. Margaret Mitchell
(1900–1949)

1 "I'm tired of everlastingly being unnatural and never doing anything I want to do. I'm tired of acting like I don't eat more than a bird, and walking when I want to run and saying I feel faint after a waltz, when I could dance for two days and never get tired. I'm tired of saying, 'How wonderful you are!' to fool men who haven't got one-half the sense I've got and I'm tired of pretending I don't know anything, so men can tell me things and feel important while they're doing it. . . ."

Gone with the Wind, Pt. I, Ch. 5   1936

2 "Until you've lost your reputation, you never realize what a burden it was or what freedom really is."

Ibid., Pt. II, Ch. 9

3 "What most people don't seem to realize is that there is just as much money to be made out of the wreckage of a civilization as from the upbuilding of one."   Ibid.

4 "Fighting is like champagne. It goes to the heads of cowards as quickly as of heroes. Any fool can be brave on a battle field when it's be brave or else be killed."

Ibid., Pt. IV, Ch. 31

5 "Southerners can never resist a losing cause."

Ibid., Ch. 34

6 "The Irish . . . are the damnedest race. They put so much emphasis on so many wrong things."

Ibid.

7 Now he disliked talking business with her as much as he had enjoyed it before they were married. Now he saw that she understood entirely too well and he felt the usual masculine indignation at the duplicity of women. Added to it was the usual masculine disillusionment in discovering that a woman has a brain.

Ibid., Ch. 36

8 If! If! If! There were so many ifs in life, never any certainty of anything, never any sense of security, always the dread of losing everything and being cold and hungry again. Ibid., Ch. 38

9 "Death and taxes and childbirth! There's never any convenient time for any of them!" Ibid.

10 "Everybody's mainspring is different. And I want to say this—folks whose mainsprings are busted are better dead."

Ibid., Ch. 40

11 "You kin polish a mule's feets an' shine his hide an' put brass all over his harness an' hitch him ter a fine cah'ige. But he a mule jes' de same. He doan fool nobody." Ibid., Ch. 48

12 "My pet, the world can forgive practically anything except people who mind their own business."

Ibid.

13 "Life's under no obligation to give us what we expect. We take what we get and are thankful it's no worse than it is."

Ibid., Pt. V, Ch. 53

14 "I won't think of it now. I can't stand it if I do. I'll think of it tomorrow at Tara. Tomorrow's another day."

Ibid., Ch. 57

15 "You're so brutal to those who love you, Scarlett. You take their love and hold it over their heads like a whip."

Ibid., Ch. 63

16 "What is broken is broken—and I'd rather remember it
as it was at its best than mend it and see the broken
places as long as I lived."

Ibid.

726. Barbara Morgan
(1900–   )

1 The Navajo and Pueblo Indian tribes who danced the
rituals . . . as partners in the cosmic process, attuned
me to the universally primal—rather than to either the
"primitive" or the "civilized."

Quoted in *The Woman's Eey*
by Anne Tucker   *1973*

2 . . . as the life style of the Space Age grows more
inter-disciplinary, it will be harder for the "one-track"
mind to survive. . . . I see simultaneous intake,
multiple-awareness, and synthesized comprehension as
inevitable, long before the year 2000 A.D.

Ibid.

727. Louise Nevelson
(1900–   )

1 The freer that women become, the freer will men be.
Because when you enslave someone—you *are* enslaved.
Quoted in *AFTRA*   Summer, 1974

728. Martha Ostenso
(1900–1963)

1 Fire overhead sounded a voluminous prolonged cry,
like a great trumpet call. Wild geese flying still farther
north, to a region beyond human warmth . . . beyond
even human isolation.

Wild Geese, Ch. 1   *1925*

2 The garden cost Amelia no end of work and worry; she
tended the delicate tomato vines as though they were
new born infants, and suffered momentary sinking of
the heart whenever she detected signs of weakness in
any of the hardier vegetables. She was grateful for the

toil in which she could dwell as a sort of refuge from deeper thought.

> Ibid., Ch. 7

3 Wherever the wind was bound, Elsa thought, there the whole world seemed to be going.

> *The Mad Carews*, Ch. 4   *1927*

4 Some clear intuition bade her fight the emotions which his coming stirred within her. It was a fight against that irresistible force which sought ever to turn back to the earth that which was the earth's; a struggle to evade the trap which would close her forever within Elder's Hollow.

> Ibid., Ch. 6

5 She was especially happy in the violence, the stride of the great, obstreperous city [Chicago], the fierce roar of the wind that was its voice, the white-green tumult of the waves breaking on the shore of Lake Michigan, its soul.

> Ibid., Ch. 21

6 "You have stirred the soil with your plow, my friend. It will never be the same again."

> *O River, Remember*, Ch. 4   *1943*

7 It came to him sharply then that his mother had gradually discarded every vestige of her immigrant past, while his father was still—well, what *was* his father? Surely an American now, but with the best, the most vigorous and honest and spiritually simple qualities of the old land giving something to the new.

> Ibid., Ch. 8

* * *

8 Pity the Unicorn,
Pity the Hippogriff,
Souls that were never born
Out of the land of If!

> "The Unicorn and the Hippogriff," St. 1

729. Vijaya Lakshmi Pandit
(1900–   )

1 I feel torn in two between my duty to the children and the other duties of serving the country which, in our case, has come to mean long months of imprisonment.

> *Prison Days* (March 17, 1943)   *1946*

2 It [political imprisonment] is a slow daily sacrifice which can be so much more deadly than some big heroic gesture made in a moment of emotional upheaval. . . .

Ibid. (May 3, 1943)

3 When my public activities are reported it is very annoying to read how I looked, if I smiled, if a particular reporter liked my hair style.

Quoted in *The Scotsman* (Glasgow)
August 29, 1955

4 You know, what happens to anybody who has been in these two places [Moscow and Washington, D.C.] and looked at them objectively, is the horrifying thought—if I may use that word in quotes—that they are so similar. . . . Take that passion for science—they're both absolutely dedicated to the machine, they are both extroverts, they both function in much the same way. . . .

Ibid.

5 It has simply been taken for granted that men and women are equal [in India] and even though some centuries separated the period when woman functioned as a free citizen in her own right and her re-emergence after India's independence, the theoretical acceptance of equality has always remained.

"The Second Sex," *Punch*   *May 16, 1962*

6 Difficulties, opposition, criticism—these things are meant to be overcome, and there is a special joy in facing them and in coming out on top. It is only when there is nothing but praise that life loses its charm and I begin to wonder what I should do about it.

Quoted in *The Envoy Extraordinary*
by Vera Brittain   *1965*

7 The Indian temperament exceeds in emotionally worded epistles, which keep one in suspense as to what the aim of the writer is, until one has waded through a sea of beautiful metaphors to the final paragraph.

Ibid. (c.1963)

8 Freedom is not for the timid. If one wishes to be in politics, one must be ready to face all eventualities.

Ibid. (c. 1964)

730. Malvina Reynolds
(1900–1978)

1 Where are you going, my little one, little one,
Where are you going, my baby, my own?
Turn around and you're two,
Turn around and you're four,
Turn around and you're a young girl going out of my
     door.
                              "Turn Around"   *1958*

2 Everybody thinks my head's full of nothing,
Wants to put his special stuff in,
Fill the space with candy wrappers,
Keep out sex and revolution,
But there's no hole in my head,
Too bad.   "No Hole in My Head"   *1965*

3 While that baby is a child it will suffer from neglect,
Be picked upon and pecked, run over and wrecked,
And its head will be crowned with the thorn,
But while it's inside her it must remain intact,
And it cannot be murdered till it's born.
                              "Rosie Jane"   *1973*

731. Nathalie Sarraute
(1900–   )

1 Those who live in a world of human beings can only
retrace their steps.
               "From Dostoievski to Kafka" (October,
                    1947), *The Age of Suspicion*   *1956*

2 Neither reproaches nor encouragements are able to revive a faith that is waning.
                         Ibid., *The Age of Suspicion*
                              (February, 1950)

3 . . . it might be said that, since Impressionism, all pictures have been painted in the first person . . .
                                        Ibid.

4 As for the novel, before it has even exhausted all the
advantages offered by the story told in the first person,

or reached the end of the blind alley into which all techniques necessarily lead, it has grown impatient and, in order to emerge from its present difficulties, is looking about for other ways out.

Ibid.

5 Suspicion . . . is one of the morbid reactions by which an organism defends itself and seeks another equilibrium.

Ibid.

6 For several years now interest in "the dark places of psychology"* has waned. This twilight zone in which, hardly thirty years ago, we thought we saw the gleam of real treasures, has yielded us very little, and we are obliged to acknowledge that, when all is said and done, this exploration, however bold and well carried out it may have been, however extensive and with whatever elaborate means, has ended in disappointment.

Ibid., "Conversation and Sub-conversation"
(January–February, 1956)

7 . . . the moderns displaced the essential interest of the novel. . . . For them it no longer lies in the enumeration of situations and characters, or in the portrayal of manners and customs, but in the revelation of a new psychological subject matter.

Ibid.

8 . . . what is hidden beneath the interior monologue: an immense profusion of sensations, images, sentiments, memories, impulses, little larval actions that no inner language can convey, that jostle one another on the threshold of consciousness, gather together in compact groups and loom up all of a sudden, then immediately fall apart, combine otherwise and reappear in new forms; while unwinding inside us, like the ribbon that comes clattering from a telescriptor slot, is an uninterrupted flow of words.

Ibid.

9 "We're swallowed up only when we are willing for it to happen."

The Planetarium, tr. Maria Jolas   1959

* Quoting from Virginia Woolf.

10 "But there are no more holy of holies, no more sacred places, no more magic, no more mirages for the thirsty, no more unsatisfied desires . . ."   *Ibid.*

11 Familiar images of a homeland revisited . . . tenderness radiates from them, security flows from them . . . Toward them leans the traveler returned from barbarous lands, the prisoner back from captivity . . .
    The Golden Fruits, tr. Maria Jolas   *1963*

12 "There are people we should not allow to come near us, not for anything. Parasites who devour our very substance. . . . Microbes that settle on us . . ."
                    Ibid.

13 In fact it would be better to proscribe, destroy once and for all those uselessly complicated, stupefying constructions, conceived by ignoramuses for the use of ignoramuses like themselves . . . all those pieces that have been exhumed, inspected, tagged and classified according to which rules, consigned in which textbooks, taught by which rustic pedagogues?
    Fools Say, tr. Maria Jolas   *1976*

732. Christina Stead
(1900?–   )

1 "I know your breed; all your fine officials debauch the young girls who are afraid to lose their jobs: that's as old as Washington."
    The Man Who Loved Children, Ch. 4   *1940*

2 "There are so many ways to kill yourself, they're just old-fashioned with their permanganate: do you think I'd take permanganate? I wouldn't want to burn my insides out and live to tell the tale as well; idiots! It's simple. I'd drown myself. . . . Why be in misery at the last?"
                    Ibid., Ch. 5

3 "Anyone would think a thin stick like me, weak and miserable, would go down with everything: do you think I get more than my old cough every winter? I bet I live till ninety, with all my aches and pains. To think that's fifty more years of the Great I-Am."
                    Ibid.

4 "I do not want to go to heaven; I want my children, forever children, and other children, stalwart adults, and a good, happy wife, that is all I ask, but not paradise; earth is enough for me: it is because I believe earth is heaven, Naden, that I can overcome all my troubles and face down my enemies."

Ibid., Ch. 7

5 "A mother! What are we worth really? They all grow up whether you look after them or not. That poor miserable brat of his is growing up, and I certainly licked the hide off her; and she's seen marriage at its worst, and now she's dreaming about 'supermen' and 'great men.' What is the good of doing anything for them?"

Ibid., Ch. 10

6 A cat and dog life it was; we didn't think we'd be able to stick it out. Eh, what a bloody egotist, love. . . .

Dark Places of the Heart   1966

7 "It's all bourgeois waste and caprice anyway. Someone taking the ideas of some Frenchman, great blocks of flats with angles and courtyards, a brick prison, it won't suit England; no fireplaces, no chimney and everything laid on from a center. . . . With this Corbusier there'll be no relaxing and no dreaming; only a soulless measured-off engineer's world with no place for us."

Ibid.

8 "Ye want to tell the plain truth all your life, woman, and speak straight and see straight; otherwise ye get to seein' double."

Ibid.

9 "Loneliness is a terrible blindness."   *Ibid.*

733. Opal Whiteley
(1900?–   )

1 The mamma where I love
  says I am a new sance.
  I think it is something grown-ups
  don't like to have around.

The Story of Opal   *1920*

* Written between the ages of five and twelve.

2 It is such a comfort to have a friend near.
   when lonesome feels do come.

                                        Ibid.

3 Potatoes are very interesting folks
   I think they must see a lot
   of what is going on in the earth
   They have so many eyes.

                                        Ibid.

4 And this I have learned
   grown-ups do not know the language
      of shadows.   *Ibid.*

5 Some days are long.
   Some days are short.
   The days that I have to stay in the
      house
   are the most long days of all.   *Ibid.*

734. Frances Winwar
(1900–   )

1 In her [Eleonora Duse] intellectual acquisitiveness she
   selected people as a bee chooses its flowers, for what
   they had to offer. Her lack of formal education made
   her the eternal disciple.
                 Wingless Victory, Ch. 14   1956

735. Yocheved Bat-Miriam
(1901–   )

1 Singing like a hope, shining like a tear,
    Silent, the echo of what will befall.
                 "Parting," St. 1, *Poems from the
                 Hebrew*, Robert Mezey, ed.   1973

2 I shall put on my dead face with a silence free
   Of joy and of pain forevermore,
   And dawn will trail like a child after me
   To play with shells on the shore.

                                        Ibid., St. 5

3 Not to be, to be gone—I pray for this
   At the gates of infinity, like a fey child.
                 Ibid., "Distance Spills Itself," St. 5

736. Miriam Beard
(1901–)

1   "Haven't you some small article I could send her, very attractive—typically American?"

    The sales expert looked depressed. . . . "American, you say? . . . Why, my dee-ur, *we* don't carry those *Colonial* goods. All *our* things are *imported*."

        Realism in Romantic Japan, Ch. 1   *1930*

2 A country honeycombed with agitation and a life made vivid by unending clash and controversy—that is what the traveler finds in Japan to-day.

                           Ibid., Ch. 5

737. Doris Fleeson
(1901–1970)

1 It is occasionally possible to charge Hell with a bucket of water but against stupidity the gods themselves struggle in vain.

        Newspaper Column   *February 17, 1964*

738. Elinor Hays
(1901?–)

1 It was not only childbearing that wore away women's lives. There were slower erosions.

         Morning Star, Pt. I, Ch. 1   *1961*

2 Those most dedicated to the future are not always the best prophets.

                Ibid., Pt. IV, Ch. 29

739. Gertrude Lawrence
(1901–1952)

1 In London I had been by terms poor and rich, hopeful and despondent, successful and down-and-out, utterly miserable and ecstatically dizzily happy. I belonged to

London as each of us can belong to only one place on this earth. And, in the same way, London belonged to me. *A Star Danced*, Ch. 1 *1945*

2 "So this is America!" I exclaimed. "Look at that bath, will you? Feel that delicious warmth. Central heating, my girl. No wonder they call this the most luxurious country on earth."

Ibid., Ch. 11

3 Perhaps you have to be born an Englishwoman to realize how much attention American men shower on women and how tremendously considerate all the nice ones among them are of a woman's wishes.

Ibid., Ch. 12

740. Margaret Mead
(1901–1978)

1 The negative cautions of science are never popular. If the experimentalist would not commit himself, the social philosopher, the preacher, and the pedagogue try the harder to give a short-cut answer.

Coming of Age in Samoa, Ch. 1 *1928*

2 The Samoan background which makes growing up so easy, so simple a matter, is the general casualness of the whole society. For Samoa is a place where no one plays for very high stakes, no one pays very heavy prices, no one suffers for his convictions or fights to the death for special ends. . . . No one is hurried along in life or punished harshly for slowness of development. Instead, the gifted, the precocious, are held back, until the slowest among them have caught the pace. And in personal relations, caring is as slight.

Ibid., Ch. 13

3 A society which is clamouring for choice, which is filled with many articulate groups, each urging its own brand of salvation, its own variety of economic philosophy, will give each new generation no peace until all have chosen or gone under, unable to bear the conditions of choice. The stress is in our civilization. . . .

Ibid., Ch. 14

4 And while every culture has in some way institutionalized the roles of men and women, it has not necessarily

been in terms of contrast between the prescribed personalities of the two sexes, nor in terms of dominance or submission.

Sex and Temperament in Three Primitive Societies 1935

5 The knowledge that the personalities of the two sexes are socially produced is congenial to every programme that looks forward towards a planned order of society. It is a two-edged sword. . . .

Ibid.

6 Just as the difference in height between males is no longer a realistic issue, now that lawsuits have been substituted for hand-to-hand encounters, so the difference in strength between men and women is no longer worth elaboration in cultural institutions.

Ibid.

7 To insist that there are no sex-differences in a society that has always believed in them and depended upon them may be as subtle a form of standardizing personality as to insist that there are many sex-differences.

Ibid.

8 The insistence . . . that the woman as a mother prevails over the woman as a citizen at least puts a slight drag upon agitation for war. . . .

Ibid.

9 The removal of all legal and economic barriers against women's participating in the world on an equal footing with men may be in itself a standardizing move towards the wholesale stamping-out of the diversity of attitudes that is such a dearly bought product of civilization.

Ibid.

10 Just as a festive occasion is the gayer and more charming if the two sexes are dressed differently, so it is in less material matters.

Ibid.

11 An occupation that has no basis in sex-determined gifts can now recruit its ranks from twice as many potential artists.

Ibid.

12 If we are to achieve a richer culture, rich in contrasting values, we must recognize the whole gamut of human potentialities, and so weave a less arbitrary social fabric, one in which each diverse human gift will find a fitting place.

Ibid.

13 . . . we may say that many, if not all, of the personality traits which we have called masculine or feminine are as lightly linked to sex as are the clothing, the manners, and the form of headdress that a society at a given period assigns to either sex.

Ibid.

14 We must recognize that beneath the superficial classifications of sex and race the same potentialities exist, recurring generation after generation, only to perish because society has no place for them.

From the South Seas   1939

15 We know of no culture that has said, articulately, that there is no difference between men and women except in the way they contribute to the creation of the next generation. . . .

Male and Female   1948

16 If little boys have to meet and assimilate the early shock of knowing that they can never create a baby with the sureness and incontrovertibility that is a woman's birthright, how does that make them more creatively ambitious, as well as more dependent upon achievement?

Ibid.

17 Living in the modern world, clothed and muffled, forced to convey our sense of our bodies in terms of remote symbols like walking sticks and umbrellas and handbags, it is easy to lose sight of the immediacy of the human body plan.

Ibid.

18 Furthermore, the little girl learns that she will have a baby not because she is strong or energetic or initiating, not because she works and struggles and tries, and in the end succeeds, but simply because she is a girl and not a boy, and girls turn into women, and in the end—if they protect their femininity—have babies.

Ibid.

33

19 Man's role is uncertain, undefined, and perhaps unnecessary. By a great effort man has hit upon a method of
   compensating himself for his basic inferiority.

   Ibid.

20 Women, it is true, make human beings, but only men
   can make men.

   Ibid.

21 It is of very doubtful value to enlist the gifts of women
   if bringing women into fields that have been defined as
   male frightens the men, unsexes the women, muffles
   and distorts the contribution women could make. . . .

   Ibid.

22 When we stopped short of treating women as people
   after providing them with all the paraphernalia of education and rights, we set up a condition whereby men
   also became less than full human beings and more nar-
   rowly domestic.

   "American Man in a Woman's World,"
   The New York Times Magazine
   February 10, 1957

23 Women want mediocre men, and men are working to
   be as mediocre as possible.

   Quoted in *Quote Magazine*   *May 15, 1958*

24 Early domesticity has always been characteristic of
   most savages, of most peasants and of the urban poor.
   Quoted in "New Look at Early
   Marriages," *U.S. News & World
   Report*   *June 6, 1960*

25 Why have we returned, despite our advances in technology, to the Stone Age picture? . . . In this retreat
   into fecundity, it is not the individual woman who is to
   blame. It is the climate of opinion that developed in
   this country.

   "American Women: The Changing
   Image," *Saturday Evening Post*
   March 3, 1962

26 A tribal people will be jealous of their women, or will
   offer them to male visitors in ways that are hard to
   resist, but tribal women do not fear that a woman an-
   thropologist will take their men.

   *Field Work in the Pacific
   Islands, 1925–1967*   *1967*

27 . . . most people prefer to carry out the kinds of experiments that allow the scientist to feel that he is in full control of the situation rather than surrendering himself to the situation, as one must in studying human beings as they actually live.

Blackberry Winter   *1972*

28 She was unquestionably female—small and dainty and pretty and wholly without masculine protest or femininist aggrievement.

Ibid.

29 . . . I had no reason to doubt that brains were suitable for a woman. And as I had my father's kind of mind— which was also his mother's—I learned that the mind is not sex-typed.

Ibid.

30 We are living beyond our means. As a people we have developed a life-style that is draining the earth of its priceless and irreplaceable resources without regard for the future of our children and people all around the world.

"The Energy Crises—Why Our World
Will Never Again Be the Same,"
Redbook   *April, 1974*

31 The contempt for law and the contempt for the human consequences of lawbreaking go from the bottom to the top of American society.

Ibid., Quoted in "Impeachment?" by
Claire Safran

741. Grace Moore
(1901–1947)

1 There, in repressed defiance, lies the natural instinct to tell the world where to get off: an instinct, alas, that too often takes itself out in the tardy retort framed *sotto voce*, or the year-in, year-out threat mumbled to oneself, "Just wait till I write that book!"

You're Only Human Once, Ch. 1   *1944*

2 I think that to get under the surface and really appreciate the beauty of any country, one has to go there poor.

Ibid., Ch. 4

742. Ruth Rowland Nichols
(1901–1961)

1 Many newspaper articles . . . discussed the supposed
rivalry between Amelia Earhart and me. I have no hesitation in stating that they were exaggerated or slanted
or untrue. . . . We were united by common bond of
interest. We spoke each other's language—and that was
the language of pioneer women of the air.
Wings for Life   1957

2 It was a great source of concern, to put it mildly, when
I finally had reached my altitude peak and discovered
that I was down to my last five gallons of gasoline.
Quoted in *The American Heritage*
History of Flight, Ch. 7   1960

743. Laura Riding
(1901–   )

1 We must distinguish better
Between ourselves and strangers.
There is much that we are not.
There is much that is not.
There is much that we have not to be.
"The Why of the Wind,"
Collected Poems   1938

2 I met God.
"What," he said, "you already?"
"What," I said, "you still?"   Ibid., "Then Follows"

3 You have pretended to be seeing.
I have pretended that you saw.
Ibid., "Benedictory"

4 Conversation succeeds conversation,
Until there's nothing left to talk about
Except truth, the perennial monologue,
And no talker to dispute it but itself.
Ibid., "The Talking World"

5 The mercy of truth—it is to be truth.
Ibid., "The Last Covenant"

6 I do not doubt you.
   I know you love me.
   It is a fact of your indoor face. . . .

   Ibid., "In Due Form"

7 In our unwilling ignorance we hurry to listen to stories
   of old human life, new human life, fancied human life,
   avid of something to while away the time of unanswered curiosity.

   "The Telling," *The Telling*   1967

8 Until the missing story of ourselves is told, nothing besides told can suffice us: we shall go on quietly craving
   it.

   Ibid.

9 May our Mayness become All-embracing. May we see
   in one another the All that was once All-one rebecome
   One.

   Ibid.

10 There can be no literary equivalent to truth.

   Ibid., "Extracts from Communications"

11 To a poet the mere making of a poem can seem to
   solve the problem of truth. . . . but only a problem of
   art is solved in poetry.

   Selected Poems: In Five Sets,
   Preface   1975

12 Art, whose honesty must work through artifice, cannot
   avoid cheating truth.

   Ibid.

744. Cornelia Otis Skinner
(1901–   )

1 I can enjoy flowers quite happily without translating
   them into Latin. I can even pick them with success and
   pleasure. What, frankly, I can't do is arrange them.

   "Floral Piece," *Dithers and Jitters*   1937

2 There are compensations for growing older. One is the
   realization that to be sporting isn't at all necessary. It is
   a great relief to reach this stage of wisdom.

   Ibid., "Bonnie Boating Weather"

3 It's not that I don't want to be a beauty, that I don't
   yearn to be dripping with glamor. It's just that I can't

see how any woman can find time to do to herself all the things that must apparently be done to make herself beautiful and, having once done them, how anyone without the strength of mind of a foreign missionary can keep up such a regime.   Ibid., "The Skin-Game"

4 We were young enough still to harbor the glad illusion that organized forms of get-together were commendable.

> *Our Hearts Were Young and Gay,*
> with Emily Kimbrough   1942

5 One of the most incongruous facets of the nature of *homo* not so *sapien* is the delight with which he wallows in temporary orgies of utter misery.
> "Crying in the Dark," *Bottoms Up!*   1950

6 That food has always been, and will continue to be, the basis for one of our greater snobbisms does not explain the fact that the attitude toward the food choice of others is becoming more and more heatedly exclusive until it may well turn into one of those forms of bigotry against which gallant little committees are constantly planning campaigns in the cause of justice and decency.
> Ibid., "Your Very Good Health"

7 It is disturbing to discover in oneself these curious revelations of the validity of the Darwinian theory. If it is true that we have sprung from the ape, there are occasions when my own spring appears not to have been very far.
> "The Ape in Me," *The Ape in Me*   1959

8 Courtesy is fine and heaven knows we need more and more of it in a rude and frenetic world, but mechanized courtesy is as pallid as Pablum . . . in fact, it isn't even courtesy. One can put up with "Service with a Smile" if the smile is genuine and not mere compulsory tooth-baring. And while I am hardly advocating "Service with a Snarl," I find myself occasionally wishing for "Service with a Deadpan," or just plain Service, executed with efficiency and minus all the Charm School garnish.   Ibid., "Production-Line Courtesy"

9 . . . that amenity which the French have developed into a great art . . . conversation.
> *Elegant Wits and Grand Horizontals,*
> Ch. 4   1962

10 These were clever and beautiful women, often of good
background, who through some breach of the moral
code or the scandal of divorce had been socially ostracized but had managed to turn the ostracism into profitable account. Cultivated, endowed with civilized
graces, they were frankly—kept women, but kept by
one man only, or, at any rate, by one man at a time.

Ibid., Ch. 8

* * *

11 Woman's virtue is man's greatest invention.

Quoted in *Paris '90*

745. Edith Mendel Stern
(1901–)

1 The role of the housewife is, therefore, analogous to
that of the president of a corporation who would not
only determine policies and make over-all plans but
also spend the major part of his time and energy in
such activities as sweeping the plant and oiling the machines. . . . For a woman to get a rewarding sense of
total creation by way of the multiple monotonous
chores that are her daily lot would be as irrational as
for an assembly line worker to rejoice that he had created an automobile because he tightened a bolt.

"Women Are Household Slaves,"
American Mercury   *January, 1949*

746. Jan Struther
(1901–1953)

1 It took me forty years on earth
  To reach this sure conclusion:
There is no Heaven but clarity,
  No Hell except confusion.

"All Clear," *The Glass Blower and
Other Poems*   1940

2 She saw every personal religion as a pair of intersecting
circles. . . . Probably perfection is reached when the
area of the two outer crescents, added together, is exactly equal to that of the leaf-shaped piece in the middle. On paper there must be some neat mathematical
formula for arriving at this; in life, none.

Mrs. Miniver   1940

747. Edith Summerskill
(1901–   )

1 The breach of promise . . . I can think of no action more basically insincere than one conducted with the maximum publicity, for damages for a broken heart by a young woman who must already loathe the man who has rejected her.

A Woman's World, Ch. 4   1967

2 I learned that economics was not an exact science and that the most erudite men would analyze the economic ills of the world and derive a totally different conclusion. . . . [Yet] governments still pin their faith to some new economic nostrum which is produced periodically by some bright young man. Only time proves that his alleged magic touch is illusory.

Ibid., Ch. 5

3 Prize-fighting is still accepted as a display worthy of a civilized people despite the fact that all those connected with it are fully aware it caters to the latent sadistic instincts.   Ibid., Ch. 12

4 The practice of abortion is as old as pregnancy itself. . . . [But] historically the opposition to abortion and birth control, like the laws of Moses, which were concerned with elementary hygiene and the safe preparation of food, stemmed from the urgency of the need to decrease the mortality and morbidity rates and to increase the population. . . . Today, literate people of the space age, in well-populated countries, are not prepared to accept taboos without question; and in the matter of abortion the human rights of the mother with her family must take precedence over the survival of a few weeks' old foetus without sense or sensibility.

Ibid., Ch. 19

5 There are those who believe that a divorce is better than subjecting a child to frequent scenes and quarrels but I am not among them. According to the report of some Judges sitting in custody, it is at the moment of the break-up of the home that the child shows signs of serious deterioration in bad behaviour and speech defects.   Ibid., Ch. 20

748. Marian Anderson
(1902–   )

1 Now I understand, if the good Lord doesn't like to behold the misery on the earth, He takes the clouds and covers it from His sight; but where human beings dwell there is always a dark shadow.

Quoted in Marian Anderson,
a Portrait by Kosti Vehanen
1941

2 Where there is money, there is fighting.

Ibid.

3 As long as you keep a person down, some part of you has to be down there to hold him down, so it means you cannot soar as you otherwise might.

Interview on CBS-TV
December 30, 1957

4 I had gone to Europe . . . to reach for a place as a serious artist, but I never doubted that I must return. I was—and am—an American.

Quoted in "Marian Anderson,"
Famous American Women
by Hope Stoddard   1970

5 I could see that my significance as an individual was small. . . . I had become, whether I liked it or not, a symbol, representing my people. I had to appear. . . . I could not run away from this situation.

Ibid.

749. Barbara Cartland
(1902?–   )

1 What did we in our teens realize of war? Only that we were unsatisfied after our meals, bored, in the selfishness of youth, with mourning and weeping, sick of being told plaintively that the world would "never be the same again."

The Isthmus Years, Ch. 1   1942

2 I have always found women difficult. I don't really understand them. To begin with, few women tell the

truth. I always say what I think and feel—it's got me into a lot of trouble but only with women. I've never had a cross word with a man for speaking frankly but women don't like it—I can't think why, unless it's natural love of subterfuge and intrigue.

Ibid., Ch. 8

3 Only through freedom will man find salvation, only through freedom can civilization survive and progress. We shall win, I am as sure of that as I am that England with all her faults, her mistakes, her snobbery and her social injustices is worth any individual sacrifice—this England which means far more in the sum total of human existence than a small green island surrounded by blue seas.

Ibid., Epilogue

750. Stella Gibbons
(1902–   )

1 Graceless, Pointless, Feckless and Aimless waited their turn to be milked.

Conference at Cold Comfort Farm,
Ch. 3   *1932*

2 Something nasty in the woodshed.

Ibid., Ch. 8

751. Madeline Gray
(1902–   )

1 Sex, as I said, can be summed up in three P's: procreation, pleasure, and pride. From the long-range point of view, which we must always consider, procreation is by far the most important, since without procreation there could be no continuation of the race. . . . So female orgasm is simply a nervous climax to sex relations . . . and as such it is a comparative luxury from nature's point of view. It may be thought of as a sort of pleasure-prize like a prize that comes with a box of cereal. It is all to the good if the prize is there, but the cereal is valuable and nourishing if it is not.

The Normal Woman   *1967*

752. Elsa Lanchester
(1902–   )

1 If I can't be a good artist without too much pain, then I'm damned if I'll be an artist at all.
Charles Laughton and I   1938

2 Comedians on the stage are invariably suicidal when they get home.   Ibid.

3 Every artist should be allowed a few failures.   Ibid.

4 Perhaps the beginning of our interest in each other was first shown by the fact that although we are both the kind of people who can usually express ourselves and our ideas with great ease in conversation, we were practically dumb when we were alone together. . . .
Ibid., Ch. 3

5 One has to let slimmers act of their own free will. If you wag a finger and say: "Now, now, you must not eat cake," it is quite enough to make anyone immediately eat a cake.   Ibid., Ch. 11

6 To complain too bitterly of the load of mischief that notoriety brings with it would mean that you are unsuited to the position you have made for yourself.
Ibid., Ch. 20

7 As the film actor is seen by thousands of people simultaneously all over the world he is, compared to the stage actor, relatively independent of the critics. His fame depends upon something much less secure than the opinion of one man or the approval of one town; it depends on his capacity to keep up with public taste.
Ibid., Ch. 21

753. Iris Origo
(1902–   )

1 But one resource is still left to man: a brotherly love and solidarity, a fearless recognition of the truth, untainted by praise or blame, which alone will render him capable of facing the insensibility of nature.
Leopardi, Ch. 13   1935

2 It is only comparatively seldom that the so-called "turning points" in a country's history—so convenient to the historian—are actually observable by those present at the time.

War in Val d'Orcia (February 2, 1943)   *1947*

3 We are being governed by the dregs of the nation—and their brutality is so capricious that no one can feel certain that he will be safe tomorrow.

Ibid. (November 28, 1943)

4 It is odd how used one can become to uncertainty for the future, to a complete planlessness, even in one's most private mind. What we shall do and be, and whether we shall, in a few months' time, have any home or possessions, or indeed our lives, is so clearly dependent on events outside our own control as to be almost restful.

Ibid. (February 9, 1944)

5 What fraction of even that small part of us of which we are fully aware have we ever succeeded in communicating to any other human being?

A Measure of Love, Introduction   *1957*

6 A life-sentence can be pronounced in many ways; and there are as many ways of meeting it. What is common to all who have received it—the consumptive, the paralyzed, the deaf, the blind—is the absence of a fixed point on the mind's horizon.

Ibid.

7 All of my past life that has not faded into mist has passed through the filter, not of my mind, but of my affections.

Images and Shadows   *1970*

8 It is the extreme concreteness of a child's imagination which enables him, not only to take from each book exactly what he requires—people, or genii, or tables and chairs—but literally to furnish his world with them.

Ibid., Pt. II, Ch. 6

9 I write because, exacting as it may be to do so, it is still more difficult to refrain, and because—however conscious of one's limitations one may be—there is always at the back of one's mind an irrational hope that this

next book will be different: it will be the rounded achievement, the complete fulfillment. It never has been: yet I am still writing.

Ibid., Ch. 8

754. Leni Riefenstahl
(1902–)

I only know how happy it makes me when I meet good men, simple men. But it repulses me so much to find myself faced with false men that it is a thing to which I have never been able to give artistic form.

Quoted by Michel Delahaye in
Cahiers du Cinema, No. 5   1966

I state precisely: it is *film-verité*. It reflects the truth that was then, in 1934, history. It is therefore a documentary. Not a propaganda film. Oh! I know very well what propaganda is. That consists of recreating certain events in order to illustrate a thesis or, in the face of certain events, to let one thing go in order to accentuate another.

Ibid.

There must be movement. Controlled movement of successive highlight and retreat, in both the architecture of the things filmed and in that of the film.

Ibid.

Whatever is purely realistic, slice-of-life, what is average, quotidian, doesn't interest me. Only the unusual, the specific, excites me.

Ibid.

Little by little, I discovered that the constraints imposed at times by the event could often serve me as a guide. The whole thing lay in knowing when and how to respect or violate those constraints.

Ibid.

My life became a tissue of rumors and accusations through which I had to beat a path. . . .

Ibid.

755. Marya Zaturenska
(1902–   )

* * *

1 Once they were flowers, and flame, and living bread
  Now they are old and brown and all but dead.
  "Spinners at Willowsleigh"

756. Bettina Ballard
(1903–1961)

1 Steichen had a talent for making people drop their af
  fectations and pretensions so that what came throug
  on his film were true portraits, whether that was wha
  the sitter wanted or not. Steichen himself was incapabl
  of pretense.
  In My Fashion, Ch. 1   196

2 None of the people I wrote about were as exciting i
  reality as I imagined them to be.
  Ibid., Ch. .

3 The feeling about time and what to do with it ha
  changed. What has become of those long hours whe
  we brushed our hair, fooled with our nails, tried for th
  most effective place of a beauty spot? Fashion is one o
  the great sacrifices of the jet age—there just isn't tim
  to play at it.
  Ibid., Ch. 2

4 Fashion is sold by loud-voiced barkers who clain
  magic claims for their wares; the superlatives mount t
  a higher pitch with each season. There is no privacy t
  fashion—no exclusivity.
  Ibid

5 Fashions are born and they die too quickly for anyon
  to learn to love them.
  Ibid

757. Tallulah Bankhead
(1903–1968)

I have three phobias which, could I mute them, would make my life as slick as a sonnet, but as dull as ditch water: I hate to go to bed, I hate to get up, and I hate to be alone.

Tallaulah, Ch. 1   *1952*

It's one of the tragic ironies of the theatre that only one man in it can count on steady work—the night watchman.   Ibid.

I'm the foe of moderation, the champion of excess. If I may lift a line from a die-hard whose identity is lost in the shuffle, "I'd rather be strongly wrong than weakly right."

Ibid., Ch. 4

Here's a rule I recommend. Never practice two vices at once.   Ibid.

I've been called many things, but never an intellectual.
Ibid., Ch. 15

758. Dorothy Dow
(1903–   )

Shall I tremble at a gray hair. . . .
"Unbeliever," *Time and Love*   *1942*

Things that are lovely
    Can tear my heart in two—
Moonlight on still pools,
    You.   Ibid., "Things"

759. Barbara Hepworth
(1903–   )

. . . I rarely draw what I see. I draw what I feel in my body.

Quoted by A. M. Hammersmith in the
World of Art Series   *1968*

760. Clare Boothe Luce
(1903–   )

1 MRS. MOREHEAD. Time comes when every man's got to feel something new—when he's got to feel young again, just because he's growing old. . . . A man has only one escape from his old self: to see a different self—in the mirror of some woman's eyes.

The Women, Act I   1936

2 JANE. Why does she get so mad every time he says they've got to consider the child? If children ain't the point of being married what is?

Ibid., Act II

3 MAGGIE. Marriage is a business of taking care of a man and rearing his children. . . . It ain't meant to be no perpetual honeymoon.

Ibid.

4 MISS WATTS. I relieve him of a thousand foolish details. I remind him of things he forgets, including, very often these days, his good opinion of himself. I never cry and I don't nag. I guess I *am* the office-wife. And a lot better off than Mrs. Haines. He'll never divorce me!

Ibid.

5 MIRIAM. Two kinds of women, Sylvia, owls and ostriches. To the feathered sisterhood.

Ibid.

6 MARY. Reno's full of women who all have their pride.

Ibid.

7 MARY. Love has pride in nothing—but its own humility.

Ibid.

8 LITTLE MARY. You know, that's the only good thing about divorce; you get to sleep with your mother.

Ibid., Act III

9 EDITH. Always remember, Peggy, it's matrimonial suicide to be jealous when you have a really good reason.

Ibid.

10 If "poor Germany" with eight million unemployed, ringed around with a wall of steel, could physically

conquer half of Europe and rock the other half with her pagan, immoral, revolutionary ideas . . . what could we not do with our greater brains and greater initiative and all the raw materials and the greatest productive plants in the world out of which, as you have already announced, we are determined to create the greatest army on earth? I ask again what shall we do with that army? *Quo vadis?*

Europe in the Spring, Ch. 12   1940

11 You see few people here in America who really care very much about living a Christian life in a democratic world.

Ibid.

12 Much of what Mr. [Vice-President Henry] Wallace calls his global thinking is, no matter how you slice it, still Globaloney.

Speech, U.S. House of Representatives
February 9, 1943

13 To put a woman on the ticket would challenge the loyalty of women everywhere to their sex, because it would be made to seem that the defeat of the ticket meant the defeat for a hundred years of women's chance to be truly equal with men in politics.

Quoted in *New York World-Telegram*   June 28, 1948

14 I am for lifting everyone off the social bottom. In fact, I am for doing away with the social bottom altogether.

Quoted in *Time*   February 14, 1964

15 BLACK WOMAN'S VOICE. There's no human being a man can buy anymore—except a woman.

Slam the Door Softly   1970

16 NORA. But if God had wanted us to think with our wombs, why did He give us a brain?

Ibid.

17 NORA. When a man can't explain a woman's actions, the first thing he thinks about is the condition of her uterus.

Ibid.

18 NORA. Know what Freud wrote in his diary when he was 77? "What do women want? My God, what do they want?" Fifty years this giant brain spends analyz-

49

ing women. And he still can't find out what they want. So this makes him the world's greatest expert on female psychology?

19 In our free-enterprise system, the resources of the nation . . . all turn the wheels of industry. But public confidence greases the axles. And the lack of confidence is the sand that can temporarily stall the machinery.

"A Call to Women," *Ladies' Home Journal*   March, 1974

20 . . . the American woman is the key—the utterly essential key—to consumer confidence. . . . Confidence, like charity, begins at home . . . begins with women.

Ibid.

21 The American Republic is now almost 200 years old, and in the eyes of the law women are still not equal with men. The special legislation which will remedy that situation is the Equal Rights Amendment. Its language is short and simple: *Equality of rights under the law shall not be abridged in the United States or by any state on account of sex.*

Quoted in the *Bulletin of the Baldwin School,* Pennsylvania   September, 1974

22 Childhood is a blissful time of play and fantasizing, of uninhibited sensual delight.

Ibid.

23 Endless commercials and television programs show the lovable woman as a cuddly, soft, yielding girl-child sex object, with hair that bounces, lips that invite deep kisses, a body that smells like heavenly spring.

Ibid.

24 A man's home may seem to be his castle on the outside; inside, it is more often his nursery.

Ibid.

25 To be a liberated woman is to renounce the desire of being a sex object or a baby girl. It is to acknowledge that the Cinderella-Prince Charming story is a child's fairy tale.

Ibid.

26 In politics women . . . type the letters, lick the stamps, distribute the pamphlets and get out the vote. Men get elected.

Quoted in Saturday Review/World
September 15, 1974

27 Male supremacy has kept woman down. It has not knocked her out.

Ibid.

28 The oppressed never free themselves—they do not have the necessary strengths.

Ibid.

29 Women can't have an honest exchange in front of men without having it called a cat fight.

Television Interview   April 1, 1975

761. Virginia Moore
(1903–   )

* * *

1 Suspicion is the badge of base-born minds,
And calculation never understands.

"Tragic Conclusions"

762. Empress Nagako
(1903–   )

1 We have always been trained in the past to a life of service and I am afraid that as these new changes come about there may be a loss of real values.

Meeting with Eleanor Roosevelt
(1953), Quoted in Eleanor: The Years
Alone by Joseph P. Lash   1972

763. Anaïs Nin
(1903–1977)

1 Mystical geometry. The arithmetic of the unconscious which impelled this balancing of events.

Winter of Artifice   1945

2 The imagination is far better at inventing tortures than life because the imagination is a demon within us and it knows where to strike, where it hurts. It knows the vulnerable spot, and life does not, our friends and lovers do not, because seldom do they have the imagination equal to the task.

Ibid.

3 . . . all elegant women have acquired a technique of weeping which has no . . . fatal effect on the make-up.

Ibid.

4 She could not believe in that which she wanted others to believe in—in a world made as one wanted it, an ideal world.

Ibid.

5 He wove a veritable spider web about himself. No man was ever more completely installed in the realm of possessions. . . . He had prepared a fortress against need, war and change.

Ibid.

6 He had a mania for washing and disinfecting himself. . . . For him the only danger came from the microbes which attacked the body. He had not studied the microbe of conscience which eats into the soul.

Ibid.

7 This enthusiasm which must be held in check was a great burden for a child's soul. . . . to restrain meant to kill, to bury.

Ibid.

8 Ice and Silence. Then I heard voices, first talking too fast for me to understand. A curtain was parted, the voices still tripped over each other, falling fast like a waterfall, with sparks, and cutting into my ears.

"Birth," *Under a Glass Bell* 1948

9 He wants to interfere with his instruments, while I struggle with nature, with myself, with my child and with the meaning I put into it all, with my desire to give and to hold, to keep and to lose, to live and to die.

Ibid.

10 There is blood in my eyes. A tunnel. I push into this tunnel, I bite my lips and push. There is a fire and flesh

ripping and no air. Out of the tunnel! All my blood is spilling out. Push! Push! Push! It is coming! It is coming! I feel the slipperiness, the sudden deliverance, the weight is gone.

Ibid.

11 She hated him because she could not remain detached. . . .

Ibid.

12 I thought we were above questions of good and evil. I am not saying you are bad. That does not concern me. I am saying only that you are *false* with me.

Ibid.

13 I stopped loving my father a long time ago. What remained was the slavery to a pattern.

Ibid.

14 When one is pretending the entire body revolts.

Ibid.

15 Certain gestures made in childhood seem to have eternal repercussions.

Ibid.

16 No need to hate. No need to punish. . . . The little girl in her was dead. . . . The woman was saved. And with the little girl died the need of a father.

Ibid.

17 She* is bizarre, fantastic, nervous, like someone in a high fever. Her beauty drowned me. . . . I feel she does not know what to do when confronted with these legends which are born around her face and body; she feels unequal to them.

The Diary of Anaïs Nin, Vol. I
(December 30, 1931)   *1966*

18 She lacks confidence, she craves admiration insatiably. She lives on the reflections of herself in the eyes of others. She does not dare to be herself.

Ibid.

19 I want the firsthand knowledge of everything, not fiction, intimate experience only. . . . I don't care for films, newspapers, "reportages," the radio. I only want to be involved while it is being lived. *Ibid.*

* Referring to Henry Miller's wife, June.

20 I worship that courage to hurt which she has, and I am willing to be sacrificed.

Ibid.

21 I was so filled with love for her I did not notice my effect on her.

Ibid.

22 Too much awareness, without accompanying experience, is a skeleton without the flesh of life.

The Diary of Anaïs Nin, Vol. II
(February, 1937) *1967*

23 Analysis does not take into account the creative products of neurotic desires.

Ibid.

24 Perhaps a child, like a cat, is so much inside of himself that he does not see himself in the mirror.

Ibid. (March, 1937)

25 I can remember what I did but not the reflection of what I did.

Ibid.

26 The face is masklike. It does not smile. It does not want to charm the mirror, or deceive the mirror, or flirt with it and gain a false answer. . . . You can never catch the face alive, laughing or loving.

Ibid.

27 To make history or psychology alive I personify it. . . . Myself . . . is an instrument to connect life and the myth.

Ibid. (August, 1937)

28 I am not interested in fiction. I want faithfulness.

Ibid.

29 Woman does not forget she needs the fecundator, she does not forget that everything that is born of her is planted in her.

Ibid.

30 The art of woman must be born in the womb-cells of the mind. She must be the link between synthetic products of man's mind and the elements. Ibid.

31 For the womb has dreams. It is not as simple as the good earth.

Ibid.

32 The crowd is a malleable thing, it can be dominated, dazzled, it's a public, it is faceless. This is the opposite of relationship.

                                    Ibid. (October, 1937)

33 Electric flesh-arrows . . . traversing the body. A rainbow of color strikes the eyelids. A foam of music falls over the ears. It is the gong of the orgasm.

                                    Ibid.

34 Inner chaos, like those secret volcanoes which suddenly lift the neat furrows of a peacefully plowed field, awaited behind all disorders of face, hair and costume, for a fissure through which to explode.

               A Spy in the House of Love   1968

35 Secrets. Need to disguise. The novel was born of this.
               The Diary of Anaïs Nin, Vol. III
                    (January, 1943)   *1969*

36 Those who live for the world . . . always lose their personal, intimate life.

                                    Ibid.

37 What I consider my weaknesses are feminine traits: incapacity to destroy, ineffectualness in battle.

                                    Ibid.

38 What I cannot love, I overlook. Is that real friendship?
               "San Francisco," *The Diary of
                    Anaïs Nin,* Vol. V   *1974*

39 Illusion. First there is the illusion of perfect accord, then revelation by experience of the many differences, and then I come upon a crossroad, and unless there is a definite betrayal, I finally accept the complete person.
                                    Ibid.

40 . . . we cannot cure the evils of politics with politics.
. . . Fifty years ago if we had gone the way of Freud (to study and tackle hostility within ourselves) instead of Marx, we might be closer to peace than we are.
                              Ibid., Letter to Geismar

41 A trite word is an overused word which has lost its identity like an old coat in a second-hand shop. The familiar grows dull and we no longer see, hear, or taste it.   Ibid.

42 Memory is a great betrayer.   Ibid.

43 If we are unable to make passion a relationship of duration, surviving the destruction and erosions of daily life, it still does not divest passion of its power to transform, transfigure, transmute a human being from a rather limited, petty, fearful creature to a magnificent figure reaching at moments the status of a myth.

Ibid.

44 How wrong it is for women to expect the man to build the world she wants, rather than set out to create it herself.

Ibid.

45 Anxiety is love's greatest killer, because it is like the strangle hold of the drowning.

Ibid.

46 The alchemy of fiction is, for me, an act of embalming.
Ibid., "Sierra Madre"

47 I will not be just a tourist in the world of images, just watching images passing by which I cannot live in, make love to, possess as permanent sources of joy and ecstasy.

Ibid.

48 The drugs, instead of bringing fertile images which in turn can be shared with the world . . . have instead become a solitary vice, a passive dreaming which alienates the dreamer from the whole world, isolates him, ultimately destroys him.

Ibid.

49 This year I finally achieved objectivity, very difficult for a romantic.

Ibid., Letter to Geismar

50 I don't need to be published. I only need to continue my personal life . . . and to do my major work. . . . I merely forgot for a few years what I had set out to do.

Ibid.

51 When you make a world tolerable for yourself you make a world tolerable for others.   Ibid.

52 One handles truths like dynamite. Literature is one vast hypocrisy, a giant deception, treachery. All writers have concealed more than they revealed.   Ibid.

53 The role of the writer is not to say what we can all say but what we are unable to say.

Ibid.

764. Nelly Ptaschkina
(1903–1920)

1 Youth does not know how to concentrate, and, on the other hand, does not want to confide in others. Hence the diary. The old work out everything in themselves.

The Diary of Nelly Ptaschkina
(January 23, 1918)   *1923p*

2 I am mentally short-sighted because, after all, I am but a child. . . .

Ibid. (January 25, 1918)

3 Whatever I neglect now I shall have to pay for later.

Ibid. (January 26, 1918)

4 It seems to me that man at birth does not represent a lump of clay, which can be shaped at will: for instance, either he is born intelligent or he is born stupid. Goodness can, on the other hand, be acquired.

Ibid.

5 I shall drive away my thoughts as soon as they touch upon dangerous ground. I . . . I shall *deceive myself.*

Ibid. (March 5, 1918)

6 Give women scope and opportunity, and they will be no worse than men.

Ibid. (October 1, 1918)

7 Marriage is slavery. . . . Human personality must develop quite freely. Marriage impedes this development; even more than that, it often drives one to "moral crimes," not only because forbidden fruit is sweet, but because the new love, which could be perfectly legitimate, becomes a crime.

Ibid. (October 25, 1918)

8 . . . love must and can only be an appendix to life, it certainly must not form its substance.

Ibid. (April 21, 1919)

9 Yes, one must renounce that which is too emotional. There is no need for these moods, this longing, these *attendrissements.* . . . Work is waiting for us.

Ibid. (May 27, 1919)

765. Teng Ying-Ch'ao
(1903–)

1 . . . in order to fight the Japanese we must study Japanese!

Quoted in *Women in Modern China*
by Helen Foster Snow   *1967*

766. Thyra Samter Winslow
(1903–1961)

1 Platonic love is love from the neck up.

Quoted by James Simpson in
Interview   *August 19, 1952*

767. Marguerite Yourcenar
(1903–)

1 The worst examples of savage ferocity only harden the auditor that much more, and since the human heart has about as much softness as a stone anyhow I see no need for going further in that direction. Our men were certainly not lacking in invention either, but so far as I was concerned I preferred to deal out death without embellishment, as a rule. Cruelty is the luxury of those who have nothing to do, like drugs or racing stables. In the matter of love, too, I hold for perfection unadorned.

Coup de Grâce   *1939*

2 There is so little basic difference between total innocence and complete degradation. . . .

Ibid.

3 The successive phases of love follow a monotonous course; what they still seem to me to resemble the most are the endless but sublime repetitions and returns in Beethoven's Quartets.

Ibid.

4 This morning it occurred to me for the first time that my body, my faithful companion and friend, truly bet-

ter known to me than my own soul, may be after all
only a sly beast who will end by devouring his master.
"Animula Vagula Blandula,"
Memoirs of Hadrian   1954

5 I have often thought that men who care passionately
for women attach themselves at least as much to the
temple and to the accessories of the cult as to their
goddess herself. . . . I should have desired more: to
see the human creature unadorned, alone with herself
as she indeed must have been at least sometimes, in
illness or after the death of a first-born child, or when a
wrinkle began to show in her mirror. A man who
reads, reflects, or plans belongs to his species rather
than to his sex; in his best moments he rises above the
human.
Ibid., "Varius Multiplex Multi Formis"

6 I have done much rebuilding. To reconstruct is to col-
laborate with time gone by, penetrating or modifying
its spirit, and carrying it toward a longer future. Thus
beneath the stones we find the secret of the springs.
Ibid., "Tellus Stabilita"

7 The memory of most men is an abandoned cemetery
where lie, unsung and unhonored, the dead whom they
have ceased to cherish. Any lasting grief is reproof to
their forgetfulness.
Ibid., "Saeculum Aureum"

8 Nothing seemed simpler: a man has the right to decide
how long he may usefully live. . . . [But] sickness
disgusts us with death, and we wish to get well, which
is a way of wishing to live. But weakness and suffering,
with manifold bodily woes, soon discourage the invalid
from trying to regain ground: he tires of those respites
which are but snares, of that faltering strength, those
ardors cut short, and that perpetual lying in wait for
the next attack.   Ibid., "Patientia"

768. Margery Allingham
(1904–1966)

1 Lying, they say, is a new modern art of the enemy's,
but telling the truth is not easy.
The Oaken Heart, Preface   1941

2 We—he and thee and the parson and all the other lads of the village—constitute the public, and the politicians are our servants. They apply for the job (often rather obsequiously, we notice with instant suspicion), we give it to them, we pay them in honours or cash, and we judge them solely by results.

Ibid., Ch. 1

3   "Do you know it occurred to me when I was listening to him that both in a past and in a future age this tremendous insistence of ours upon the nice importance of manners and breeding may well have seemed and still seem again to be absurd."

. . . "Fashion!" he repeated, as if the word had annoyed him. "I'll wager it goes far deeper than fashion."

"Few things go deeper than fashion," objected Castor.

Ibid., Ch. 8

4 It is always difficult to escape from youth; its hopefulness, its optimistic belief in the privileges of desire, its despair, and its sense of outrage and injustice at disappointment, all these spring on a man inflicting indelicate agony when he is no longer prepared.

Ibid., Ch. 21

5 Normally he was the happiest of men. He asked so little of life that its frugal bounty amazed and delighted him. . . . He believed in miracles and frequently observed them, and nothing astonished him. His imagination was as wild as a small boy's and his faith ultimate. In ordinary life he was, quite frankly, hardly safe out.

The Tiger in the Smoke, Ch. 2   1952

6 Chemists employed by the police can do remarkable things with blood. They can find it in shreds of cloth, in the interstices of floor boards, on the iron of a heel, and can measure it and swear to it and weave it into a rope to hang a man.

Ibid., Ch. 9

7 "Because nobody wants a prosaic explanation of fraud and greed."

The Villa Marie Celeste   1960

769. Elaine Frances Burton
(1904–   )

A woman in authority is often unpopular, only because she is efficient.   *What of the Women?*   *1941*

If you get a good woman, you get the finest thing on earth.   Ibid.

770. Eve Curie
(1904–   )

Let's face it: however old-fashioned and out of date and devaluated the word is, we like the way of living provided by democracy.

> Address, American Booksellers
> Association, New York
> *April 9, 1940*

We discovered that peace at any price is no peace at all. . . . We discovered that life at any price has no value whatever; that life is nothing without the privileges, the prides, the rights, the joys which make it worth living, and also worth giving. And we also discovered that there is something more hideous, more atrocious than war or than death; and that is to live in fear.   Ibid.

Public opinion waged the war. Statesmen, diplomats, government officials waged the war. To beat the Axis, it was not enough to win battle in the field, to kill millions of men. We also had to kill ideas that knew no frontiers and spread like disease.

> *Journey Among Warriors*, Pt. V, Ch. 26
> *1943*

771. Lilly Daché
(1904–   )

When I was six I made my mother a little hat—out of her new blouse.

> Newspaper Interview   *December 3, 1954*

2 Glamour is what makes a man ask for your telephone number. But it also is what makes a woman ask for the name of your dressmaker.

Quoted in *Woman's Home Companion*   July, 195

772. Adelle Davis
(1904–1974)

1 Nutrition is a young subject; it has been kicked around like a puppy that cannot take care of itself. Food faddists and crackpots have kicked it pretty cruelly. . . . They seem to believe that unless food tastes like Socrati hemlock, it cannot build health. Frankly, I often wonder what such persons plans to do with good health i case they acquire it.

Let's Eat Right to Keep Fit, Ch. 195

2 When the blood sugar is extremely low, the resulting irritability, nervous tension, and mental depression are such that a person can easily go berserk. . . . Add few guns, gas jets, or razor blades, and you have the stuff murders and suicides are made of. The American diet has become dangerous in many more ways than one.

Ibid., Ch.

3 Thousands upon thousands of persons have studied disease. Almost no one has studied health.

Ibid., Ch. 2

4 If this country is to survive, the best-fed-nation myth had better be recognized for what it is: propaganda designed to produce wealth but not health.

Ibid., Ch. 3

5 You can't eat well and keep fit if you don't shop well

Quoted in "The Great Adelle Davis Controversy" by Danie Yergin, *The New York Time Magazine*   May 20, 197.

6 Nutritional research, like a modern star of Bethlehem brings hope that sickness need not be a part of life.

Ibid

People in nutrition get the idea that they are going to live to be a hundred and fifty. And they never do.

Ibid.

773. Marlene Dietrich
(1904–   )

The average man is more interested in a woman who is interested in him than he is in a woman—any woman—with beautiful legs.

News Item   December 13, 1954

Latins are tenderly enthusiastic. In Brazil they throw flowers at you. In Argentina they throw themselves.

Quoted in Newsweek   August 24, 1959

774. Margaret Fishback
(1904–   )

* * *

The same old charitable lie
Repeated as the years scoot by
Perpetually makes a hit—
"You really haven't changed a bit!"

"The Lie of the Land"

775. Marya Mannes
(1904–   )

"I think funerals are barbaric and miserable. Everything connected with them—the black, the casket, the shiny hearse, the sepulchral tones of the preacher—is destructive to true memory."

"The First Days," Message
from a Stranger   1948

Promiscuous. . . . That was a word I had never applied to myself. Possibly no one ever does, for it is a sordid word, reducing many valuable moments to nothing more than dog-like copulation.

Ibid., "The Second Month"

3 They had no serenity, for true serenity comes after knowledge of pain. They had only the stillness of spiritual inertia. They were half alive.

Ibid., "The Seventh Month"

4 Who's kidding whom? What's the difference between Giant and Jumbo? Quart and *full* quart? Two-ounce and *big* two-ounce? What does Extra Long mean? What's a *tall* 24-inches? And what busy shopper can tell?

"New Bites by a Girl Gadfly,"
Life   June 12, 1964

5 The art of flirtation is dying. A man and woman are either in love these days or just friends. In the realm of love, reticence and sophistication should go hand in hand, for one of the joys of life is discovery.

Ibid.

6 What I call the destructive anxieties are not the growth of women's minds and powers, but quite the contrary: the pressures of society and the mass media to make woman conform to the classic and traditional images in men's eyes.

"The Roots of Anxiety in Modern
Women," Journal of Neuropsychiatry
May, 1964

7 The real demon is success—the anxieties engendered by this quest are relentless, degrading, corroding. What is worse, there is no end to this escalation of desire. . . .

Ibid.

8 Affluent as it was for the majority, the society we had produced was not admirable. It might be better than others, but it was nowhere near what it should have been. It was, in fact, going rotten. The private gain had for so long triumphed over the public need that the cities had become unlivable, the country desecrated, the arteries choked, and pollution—of air, of water, yes, of spirit too—a daily, oppressive, fact. And who else but our generation (if not ourselves) had made it so?

Them   1968

9 "Well, my theory has always been," said Lev, "that if each of our senses—sight, hearing, touch, smell, taste— was developed to its utmost capacity we would then

have attained not only total physical awareness, as in animals, but total spiritual development, as in man. Ideal man. Everything," pursued Lev, "atrophies without use."

Ibid.

10 Timing and arrogance are decisive factors in the successful use of talent. The first is a matter of instinct, the second part carapace and part self-hypnosis; the shell that protects, the ego that assumes, without question, that the talent possessed is not only unique but important, the particular vision demanding to be shared.

Out of My Time, Preface   *1971*

11 While the young fight the official barbarism of unsentient power—the insanities of war and the ruinous priorities imposed by leaders and organizations in the *name* of reason, perhaps our last duty is to fight for the civilization *of* reason.

Ibid., Ch. 9

12 The barbarian weapon is fission: the splitting asunder. It has been perfected for death. Our only weapon is fusion: an imperfect process still, though designed for life.

Ibid.

776. Nancy Mitford
(1904–1973)

1 "I simply don't see the point of getting up at six all the time you are young and working eighteen hours a day in order to be a millionaire, and then when you are a millionaire still getting up at six and working eighteen hours a day. . . . What does it all mean?"

Pigeon Pie, Ch. 1   *1940*

2 "Always remember, children, that marriage is a very intimate relationship. It's not just sitting and chatting to a person; there are other things, you know."

Love in a Cold Climate,
Pt. I, Ch. 14   *1949*

3 An aristocracy in a republic is like a chicken whose head has been cut off: it may run about in a lively way, but in fact it is dead.

Noblesse Oblige   *1956*

4 Americans relate all effort, all work, and all of life itself to the dollar. Their talk is of nothing but dollars. The English seldom sit happily chatting for hours on end about pounds. In England, public business is its own reward, nobody would go into Parliament in order to become rich, neither do riches bring public appointments.

Ibid.

5 All the heat there was seemed to concentrate in the Hons' cupboard, which was always stifling. Here we would sit, huddled up on the slatted shelves, and talk for hours about life and death.
The Pursuit of Love, Ch. 2   *1957*

777. Virgilia Peterson
(1904–1966)

1 Before Eve did bite into the apple, she had first to be alone with Adam under the tree where the apple grew.
A Matter of Life and Death   *1961*

2 In Reno, there is always a bull market, never a bear market, for the stocks and bonds of happiness.

Ibid.

3 Perhaps it is the expediency in the political eye that blinds it.

Ibid.

4 A lady, that is an enlightened, cultivated, liberal lady— the only kind to be in a time of increasing classlessness—could espouse any cause: wayward girls, social diseases, unmarried mothers, and/or birth control with impunity. But never by so much as the shadow of a look should she acknowledge her own experience with the Facts of Life.

Ibid.

5 European society . . . automatically assumes its superiority to Americans whether they have money or not, but money tends to blur the sharpness of the distinction.

Ibid.

778. Anne Roe
(1904–   )

1 Nothing in science has any value to society if it is not communicated. . . .
The Making of a Scientist, Ch. 1   *1952*

2 Freedom breeds freedom. Nothing else does.
Ibid., Ch. 16

779. Sally Stanford
(1904–   )

1 No, no one sets out to be a madam; but madams answer the call of a well-recognized and very basic human need. Their responsibilities are thrust upon them by the fundamental nitwittedness and economic shortsightedness of most hustling broads. And they become tempered and sharpened and polished to the highest degree of professional awareness by constant intercourse with men devoutly dedicated to the policy of getting something for nothing.
The Lady of the House, Prologue   *1966*

2 Well, there's a Book that says we're all sinners and I at least chose a sin that's made quite a few people happier than they were before they met me, a sin that's left me with very little time to consider other extremely popular moral misdemeanors, like usury, intolerance, bearing false tales, extortion, racial bigotry, and the casting of that first stone. And, I might add, a hell of a lot worse.

Ibid., Ch. 4

3 No man can be held throughout the day by what happens throughout the night.

Ibid., Ch. 13

4 Romance without finance is a nuisance. Few men value free merchandise. Let the chippies fall where they may.
Ibid.

780. Charlotte Wolff
(1904–)

1 I have no doubt that lesbianism makes a woman virile
and open to *any* sexual stimulation, and that she is
more often than not a more adequate and lively partner
in bed than a "normal" woman.

Love Between Women   1972

2 A niggling feeling of discomfort and unease follows
masturbation, even in those who do not feel guilty
about it.

Ibid.

781. Jane Ace
(1905–1974)

1 I'm a ragged individualist.

Quoted in *The Fine
Art of Hypochondria* by
Goodman Ace   1966

2 Well, time wounds all heels.

Ibid.

782. Shulamit Aloni
(1905–)

1 Thus the Israeli woman, like her American counterpart, pushes aside all youthful enthusiasm and ambition
to develop an active personality and instead copies the
model with which she is presented—an agreeable beautiful doll and cheap servant. One day, when the children have grown up, she comes face to face with the
emptiness and looks for fulfillment in language courses,
ceramics and art circles, volunteer work and charity,
wrapped around a cup of coffee watching a fashion
show.

Article in *Israel Magazine*   *April, 1971*

2 According to civil law, women are equal to men. But I have to go to a religious court as far as personal affairs are concerned. Only men are allowed to be judges there—men who pray every morning to thank God He did not make them women. You meet prejudice before you open your mouth. And because they believe women belong in the home, you are doubly discriminated against if you work.

> Quoted in "Women in Israel"
> (November, 1973), *Crazy Salad*
> by Nora Ephron   *1975*

783. Ilka Chase
(1905–   )

1 She thought of all foreign lands as lands of promise, and with the same yearning that so many Europeans had for America.

> *I Love Miss Tilli Bean*, Ch. 1   *1946*

2 She knew that no human being is immune to sorrow and she wanted me to be tough, the way a green branch is tough, and to be independent, so that if anything happened to her I would be able to take hold of my own life and make a go of it. Besides, she had a lot of respect for the human spirit; she never thought one person owned another.

> Ibid., Ch. 6

3 People are subject to moods, to temptations and fears, lethargy and aberration and ignorance, and the staunchest qualities shift under the stresses and strains of daily life. Like liberty, they are not secured for all time. They are not inevitable.

> *Free Admission*, Ch. 1   *1948*

4 There are various theories as to what characteristics, what combination of traits, what qualities in our men won the war. The democratic heritage is highly thought of; the instinctive mechanical know-how of thousands of our young men is frequently cited; the church and Coca-Cola, baseball, and the movies all come in for their share of credit; but, speaking from my own observation of our armed forces, I should say the war was won on coffee.

> Ibid., Ch. 10

5 The very fact that we make such a to-do over golden
weddings indicates our amazement at human endurance. The celebration is more in the nature of a reward
for stamina. . . .

Ibid., Ch. 15

784. Viña Delmar
(1905–   )

1 It must be true that whenever a sensational murder is
committed there are people who—though they are,
quite properly, of no interest to law enforcers, attor-
neys, or newspaper reporters—weep, lie sleepless, and
realize at last that their lives have been changed by a
crime in which they played no part.

The Becker Scandal   1968

2 "We have strict orders on how to teach. There are certain methods that must be employed. Your way is easier to learn, but it hasn't been approved by the school
board for use in the classroom."

Ibid.

3 . . . her plumpness was so neat and firm that she was
rather like one of the better apples that are purchased
for fruit-bowl display.

Ibid.

785. Frances Frost
(1905–1959)

1 I am the keeper of wall and sill,
I kneel on the hearth to a tempered fire:
(Flesh that was wild can learn to be still,
But what of a heart that was born to briar?)

"Capture," St. 4, *Hemlock Wall*   1929

2 But the trees that lost their apples
In the early windy year—
Hard-cheeked little apples,
Round and green and clear,—
They have nothing more to lose
And nothing more to fear.

Ibid., "Loss," St. 2

3 Grow, white boy! Drink deep of living,
  Deeper yet of mirth,
  For there is nothing better than laughter
  Anywhere on earth!

  Ibid., "White Boy," St. 3

786. Greta Garbo
(1905–)

1 There are many things in your heart you can never tell
  to another person. They are you, your private joys and
  sorrows, and you can never tell them. You cheapen
  yourself, the inside of yourself, when you tell them.

  Quoted in The Story of Greta Garbo
by Bruce Biery   1928

2 I never said, "I want to be alone." I only said, "I want
  to be left alone." There is all the difference.

  Quoted in Garbo by John
Bainbridge   1955

3 Why can't we avoid being followed and examined? It is
  cruel to bother people who want to be left in peace.
  This kills beauty for me.

  Ibid., Newspaper Interview, Naples (1938)

787. Ethel Jacobson
(1905?–)

1 Behind every man who achieves success
  Stand a mother, a wife and the IRS.

  Quoted in Reader's Digest   April, 1973

788. Adelaide Johnson
(1905–1960)

1 The neurotic needs of the parent . . . are vicariously
  gratified by the behavior of the child.

  "The Genesis of Antisocial Acting
Out in Children and Adults,"
Psychoanalytic Quarterly, Vol. 21
1952

2 Firmness bespeaks a parent who has learned . . . how all of his major goals may be reached in some creative course of action. . . .

Ibid.

789. Maggie Kuhn
(1905–   )

1 We want to give old folks a new sense of power and worth. We've been brainwashed by the youth cult to keep up youthful appearances, and to be ashamed of our age.

Quoted in "Profile of a Gray Panther"
by Carol Offen, Retirement Living
December, 1972

2 Ageism is any discrimination against people on the basis of chronological age—whether old or young. It's responsible for an enormous neglect of social resources.

Ibid.

3 Our [old people's] citizenship is not served when we take ourselves out of the mainstream of society and consign ourselves to a life of play. . . . Arbitrary retirement at a fixed age ought to be negotiated and decided according to the wishes of the people involved. Mandatory retirement ought to be illegal.

Ibid.

4 One reason our society has become such a mess is that we're isolated from each other. The old are isolated by government policy. So we have all sorts of stereotypes floating around about blacks, old people, and women.

Quoted in "How to Forget Age Bias,"
Ms.   June, 1975

5 Power should not be concentrated in the hands of so few, and powerlessness in the hands of so many.

Ibid.

790. Erika Mann
(1905–   )

1 "I want the child to become a human being, a good and decent man who knows the difference between lies

and truth, aware of liberty and dignity and true reason, not the opportunistic reason 'dictated by policy' which turns black white if it's useful at the moment. I want the boy to become a decent human being—a man and not a Nazi!"   *School for Barbarians,*
                                     Prologue   *1938*

2 But the Hitler Youth organization, that third circle around the child, is the most expansive, most important, and by far the most comprehensive of his influences.   Ibid., "The State Youth"

3 "There's absolutely no discipline in the democracies. The other day our propaganda minister said that the democracies strike him as being a collection of comical old fogies. But I've got to say it myself; they're rotten and corrupt to the marrow."
                    "The City," *The Lights Go Down*   *1940*

4 Music, the theatre, the beauty of men and things, a fine day, a child, an attractive animal—from all these he [Thomas Mann] drew much pleasure, provided he was getting on with his work. Without work—that is, without active hope—he would not have known how to live.

> *The Last Year of Thomas Mann, a*
> *Revealing Memoir by His Daughter*
> *1958*

5 The nightmare dreamer is delivered up to the horror he himself has created, and derives not the slightest relief from the neutral world, such as would be granted by feeling that it is hot or windy, that other people are present, or that the day or the night is coming to an end. The dreamer knows and perceives nothing but the horror of his dream.   Ibid.

791. Phyllis McGinley
(1905–   )

1 Oh, shun, lad, the life of an author.
    It's nothing but worry and waste.
Avoid that utensil,
The laboring pencil,
    And pick up the scissors and paste.
                    "A Ballad of Anthologies,"
                    A Ballad of Anthologies   *1941*

2 Mere wealth, I am above it.
It is the reputation wide,
The playwright's pomp, the poet's pride
  That eagerly I covet.

Ibid.

3 Forever that Ode on the Urn, sir,
  Has headed the publisher's list.
But the name isn't Keats
On the royalty sheets
  That go out to the anthologist,
My lad,
  The sedulous anthologist.   *Ibid.*

4 Compromise? Of course we compromise. But compromise, if not the spice of life, is its solidity. It is what makes nations great and marriages happy and Spruce Manor the pleasant place it is.
"Suburbia, of Thee I Sing,"
The Province of the Heart *1959*

5 It's this no-nonsense side of women that is pleasant to deal with. They are the real sportsmen. They don't have to be constantly building up frail egos by large public performances like over-tipping the hat-check girl, speaking fluent French to the Hungarian waiter, and sending back the wine to be recooled.
Ibid., "Some of My Best Friends . . ."

6 Nothing fails like success; nothing is so defeated as yesterday's triumphant Cause.
Ibid., "How to Get Along with Men"

7 Sin . . . has been made not only ugly but passé. People are no longer sinful, they are only immature or under privileged or frightened or, more particularly, sick.
Ibid., "In Defense of Sin"

8 We have not owned our freedom long enough to know exactly how it should be used.
Ibid., "The Honor of Being a Woman"

9 Yet who could deny that privacy is a jewel? It has always been the mark of privilege, the distinguishing feature of a truly urbane culture.
Ibid., "A Lost Privilege"

10 Buffet, ball, banquet, quilting bee,
  Wherever conversation's flowing,

Why must I feel it falls on me
  To keep things going?

"Reflections at Dawn," St. 3,
Times Three: 1932–1960   1960

11   . . . "I am he
Who champions total liberty—
Intolerance being, ma'am, a state
No tolerant man can tolerate.

Ibid., "The Angry Man," St. 2

12 I'm a middle-bracket person with a middle-bracket
     spouse
And we live together gaily in a middle-bracket house.
We've a fair-to-middlin' family; we take the middle
     view;
So we're manna sent from heaven to internal revenue.

Ibid., "The Chosen Peoples," St. 1

13 Oh! *do* you remember Paper Books
     When paper books were thrilling,
When something to read
Was seldom Gide
Or Proust or Peacock
Or Margaret Mead
     And seldom Lionel Trilling?

Ibid,, "Dirge for an Era," St. 4

14 Pressed for rules and verities,
All I recollect are these:
Feed a cold to starve a fever.
Argue with no true believer.
Think too-long is never-act.
Scratch a myth and find a fact.

Ibid., "A Garland of Precepts," St. 2

15 Senor Dali,
     Born delirious,
Considers it folly
     To be serious. . . .   Ibid., "Spectators' Guide to
                                        Contemporary Art," St. 3

16 The thing to remember about fathers is, they're men.

Ibid., "Girls-Eye View of Relatives," St. 3

17 These are my daughters, I suppose.
But where in the world did the children vanish?

Ibid., "Ballade of Lost Objects"

18 Time is the thief you cannot banish.   Ibid., St. 4

75

19 Though doubtless now our shrewd machines
    Can blow the world to smithereens
      More tidily and so on,
Let's give our ancestors their due.
Their ways were coarse, their weapons few.
But ah! how wondrously they slew
      With what they had to go on.

                Ibid., "The Conquerors," St. 5

20 We might as well give up the fiction
    That we can argue any view.
For what in me is pure Conviction
    Is simple Prejudice in you.

                Ibid., "Note to My Neighbor"

21 When blithe to argument I come,
    Though armed with facts, and merry,
May Providence protect me from
    The fool as adversary,
Whose mind to him a kingdom is
    Where reason lacks dominion,
Who calls conviction prejudice
    And prejudice opinion.

                Ibid., "Moody Reflections," St. 1

22 For the wonderful thing about saints is that they were
human. They lost their tempers, got hungry, scolded
God, were egotistical or testy or impatient in their
turns, made mistakes and regretted them. Still they
went on doggedly blundering toward heaven.

    "Running to Paradise," *Saint-Watching*   *1969*

23 History must always be taken with a grain of salt. It is,
after all, not a science but an art. . . .

                Ibid., "Aspects of Sanctity"

24 We live in the century of the Appeal. . . . One ap-
plauds the industry of professional philanthropy. But it
has its dangers. After a while the private heart begins
to harden. We fling letters into the wastebasket, are ab-
rupt to telephone solicitations. Charity withers in the
incessant gale.

                Ibid.

25 Wit is not the prerogative of the unjust, and there is
truly laughter in holy places.

                Ibid.

* * *

26 Always on Monday morning the press reports
   God as revealed to his vicars in various disguises—
   Benevolent, stormy, patient, or out of sorts.
   God knows which God is the God God recognizes.
                                       "The Day After Sunday"

27 Few friends he has that please his mind.
      His marriage failed when it began,
   Who worked unceasingly for mankind
      But loathed his fellowman.
                                       "The Old Reformer"

28 Meek-eyed parents hasten down the ramps
   To greet their offspring, terrible from camps.
                                "Ode to the End of Summer"

29 We never sit down to our pottage,
   We never go calm to our rest,
   But lo! at the door of our cottage,
   The knock of the guest.
                        "Elegy of a Country Dooryard," St. 3

792. Eileen O'Casey
(1905?–   )

1 I was liberated but not too liberated. I was Catholic,
   you see, and my conscience always bothered me.
         Quoted in "Eileen O'Casey Remembers" by Lee
      Grant, *Los Angeles Times*   *November 13, 1974*

2 Unless it's right next door, people don't notice killing
   and bloodshed. We take it in like the sun shines and
   the rain falls.

                                                    Ibid.

3 I feel very sorry commercialism has gone so far.

                                                    Ibid.

793. Gretta Brooker Palmer
(1905–1953)

* * *

1 Happiness is a by-product of an effort to make someone else happy.

                                       Permanent Marriage

77

794. Ivy Baker Priest
(1905–1975)

1 We women ought to put first things first. Why should we mind if men have their faces on the money, as long as we get our hands on it?

Green Grows Ivy, Ch. 1   *1958*

2 My father had always said that there are four things a child needs—plenty of love, nourishing food, regular sleep, and lots of soap and water—and after those, what he needs most is some intelligent neglect.

Ibid., Ch. 11

3 We seldom stop to think how many peoples' lives are entwined with our own. It is a form of selfishness to imagine that every individual can operate on his own or can pull out of the general stream and not be missed.

Ibid., Ch. 18

795. Ayn Rand
(1905–)

1 You came as a solemn army to bring a new life to men. You tore that life you knew nothing about, out of their guts—and you told them what it had to be. You took their every hour, every minute, every nerve, every thought in the farthest corners of their souls—and you told them what it had to be. You came and you forbade life to the living.

We the Living   *1936*

2 "Civilization is the progress toward a society of privacy. The savage's whole existence is public, ruled by the laws of his tribe. Civilization is the process of setting man free from men."

The Fountainhead   *1943*

3 "Creation comes before distribution—or there will be nothing to distribute."

Ibid.

4 "We praise an act of charity. We shrug at an act of achievement."

Ibid.

5 Every form of happiness is private. Our greatest moments are personal, self motivated, not to be touched. The things which are sacred or precious to us are the things we withdraw from promiscuous sharing.

Ibid.

6 "Every major horror of history was committed in the name of an altruistic motive. Has any act of selfishness ever equalled the carnage perpetrated by disciples of altruism?"

Ibid.

7 Great men can't be ruled.

Ibid.

8 He didn't want to be great, but to be thought great. He didn't want to build, but to be admired as a builder. He borrowed from others in order to make an impression on others.

Ibid.

9 If you learn how to rule one single man's soul, you can get the rest of mankind.

Ibid.

10 "Independence is the only gauge of human virtue and value. What a man is and makes of himself; not what he has or hasn't done for others. There is no substitute for personal dignity. There is no standard of personal dignity except independence."

Ibid.

11 Kill reverence and you've killed the hero in man.

Ibid.

12 "The world is perishing from an orgy of self-sacrificing."

Ibid.

13 "Throughout the centuries there were men who took first steps down new roads armed with nothing but their own vision. Their goals differed, but they all had this in common: that the step was first, the road new, the vision unborrowed, and the response they received—hatred. The great creators—the thinkers, the

artists, the scientists, the inventors—stood alone against the men of their time."

Ibid.

14 We can divide a meal among many men. We cannot digest it in a collective stomach.

Ibid.

15 "We are one in all and all in one.
There are no men but only the great WE,
One, indivisible and forever."

Anthem, Ch. 1   *1946*

16 It is forbidden, not to be happy. For, as it has been explained to us, men are free and the earth belongs to them; and all things on earth belong to all men; and the will of all men together is good for all; and so all men must be happy.

Ibid., Ch. 2

17 My happiness is not the means to any end. It is the end. It is its own goal. It is its own purpose. Neither am I the means to any end others may wish to accomplish. I am not a tool for their use. I am not a servant of their needs. I am not a bandage for their wounds. I am not a sacrifice on their altars.

Ibid., Ch. 9

18 The word which can never die on this earth, for it is the heart of it and the meaning and the glory. The sacred word: EGO.

Ibid., Ch. 12

19 It was an immense betrayal—the more terrible because he could not grasp what it was that had been betrayed.

Atlas Shrugged, Pt. I, Ch. 1   *1957*

20 "Disunity, that's the trouble. It's my absolute opinion that in our complex industrial society, no business enterprise can succeed without sharing the burden of the problems of other enterprises."

Ibid., Ch. 3

21 He could not stop the thing in his mind that went on throwing words at him; it was like trying to plug a broken hydrant with his bare hands.   Ibid., Ch. 6

22 "What you think you think is an illusion created by your glands, your emotions and, in the last analysis, by the content of your stomach. . . . That gray matter

you're so proud of is like a mirror in an amusement park which transmits to you nothing but distorted signals from a reality forever beyond your grasp.

Ibid., Pt. II, Ch. 1

23 "The entire history of science is a progression of exploded fallacies, not of achievements."

Ibid.

24 "That which you see is the first thing to disbelieve."

Ibid.

25 "To demand 'sense' is the hallmark of nonsense. Nature does not make sense. Nothing makes sense."

Ibid.

26 Questions of right have no bearing on human existence.

Ibid., Ch. 4

27 The day of the hero is past.

Ibid.

28 "People don't look for *kinds* of work any more, ma'am," he answered impassively. "They just look for work."

Ibid., Ch. 10

29 "If my fellow men believe that the force of the combined tonnage of their muscles is a practical means to rule me—let them learn the outcome of a contest in which there's nothing but brute force on one side, and force ruled by a mind, on the other."

Ibid., Pt. III, Ch. 2

30 "It has long been conceded by all progressive thinkers that there are no entities, only actions—and no values, only consequences."

Ibid., Ch. 3

31 They did not know . . . that the same force that had made him tolerant, was now the force that made him ruthless—that the justice which would forgive miles of innocent errors of knowledge, would not forgive a single step taken in conscious evil.

Ibid., Ch. 6

32 The modern mystics of muscle who offer you the fraudulent alternative of "human rights" versus "property rights," as if one could exist without the other, are making a last, grotesque attempt to revive the doctrine

81

of soul versus body. Only a ghost can exist without material property; only a slave can work with no right to the product of his effort.

Ibid., Ch. 7

33 . . . those ages when . . . a sunset put an end to human activity.

Ibid., Ch. 10

34 . . . "society" may do anything it pleases, since "the good" is whatever it chooses to do *because* it chooses to do it. And—since there is no such entity as "society," since society is only a number of individual men . . . *some* men (the majority or any gang that claims to be its spokesman) are ethically entitled to pursue any whim (or any atrocities) they desire to pursue, while *other* men are ethically obliged to spend their lives in the service of that gang's desires.

Speech, "Ethics in Our Time,"
University of Wisconsin   *February 9, 1961*

35 If we ask our intellectual leaders what *are* the ideals we should fight for, their answer is such a sticky puddle of stale syrup—of benevolent bromides and apologetic generalities about brotherlove, global progress and universal prosperity at America's expense—that a fly would not die *for* it or *in* it.

For the New Intellectual   *1961*

36 Man's unique reward, however, is that while animals survive by adjusting themselves to their background, man survives by adjusting his background to himself.

Ibid.

37 Morality is a code of values to guide man's choices and actions; when it is set to oppose his own life and mind, it makes him turn against himself and blindly act as the tool of its own destruction.

Ibid.

38 Professional intellectuals are the voice of a culture and are, therefore, its leaders, its integrators and its bodyguards.

Ibid.

39 Integrity does not consist of loyalty to one's subjective whims, but of loyalty to rational principles. A "compromise" (in the unprincipled sense of that word) is not a breach of one's comfort, but a breach of one's

convictions. A "compromise" does not consist of doing something one dislikes, but of doing something one knows to be evil.

"Doesn't Life Require Compromise?"
(July, 1962), *The Virtue of Selfishness*   1964

40 Love and friendship are profoundly personal, selfish values: love is an expression and assertion of self-esteem, a response to one's own values in the person of another. One gains a profoundly personal, selfish joy from the mere existence of the person one loves. It is one's own personal, selfish happiness that one seeks, earns and derives from love.

Ibid., "The Ethics of Emergencies" (1963)

41 Ever since Kant divorced reason from reality, his intellectual descendants have been diligently widening the breach.

"The Cashing-In: The Student
'Rebellion,'" *The New Left*   1968

42 If a dramatist had the power to convert philosophical ideas into real, flesh-and-blood people and attempted to create the walking embodiment of modern philosophy—the result would be the Berkeley rebels.

Ibid.

43 The hippies were taught by their parents, their neighbors, their tabloids and their college professors that faith, instinct and emotion are superior to reason—and they obeyed. They were taught that material concerns are evil, that the State or the Lord will provide, that the Lilies of the Field do not toil—and they obeyed. They were taught that love, indiscriminate love, for one's fellow-men is the highest virtue—and they obeyed. They were taught that the merging of one's self with a herd, a tribe or a community is the noblest way for men to live—and they obeyed. There isn't a single basic principle of the Establishment which they do not share—there isn't a belief which they have not accepted.

Ibid., "Apollo and Dionysus"

796. Mary Renault
(1905–   )

1 Miss Searle had always considered boredom an intellectual defeat.

North Face, Ch. 1   1948

2 It was pleasant to talk of these things again: but, as he reminded himself, to her it was all a kind of keepsake, like the flower her grandmother might have pressed in a book. Exchanging ideas with women was always an illusion; they tagged everything on to some emotion, they were all incapable of the thing in itself.

Ibid., Ch. 5

3 Which of youth's pleasures can compare with the making ready for one's first big war?

The King Must Die, Bk. II, Ch. 3   1958

4 Man born of woman cannot outrun his fate. Better then not to question the Immortals, nor when they have spoken to grieve one's heart in vain. A bound is set to our knowing, and wisdom is not to search beyond it. Men are only men.

Ibid., Bk. V, Ch. 2

5 "Go with your fate, but not beyond. Beyond leads to dark places."

"Marathon," *The Bull from the Sea*   1958

6 I thought of my life, the good and evil days; of the gods, and fate; how much of a man's life and of his soul they make for him, how much he makes for himself. . . . Fate and will, will and fate, like earth and sky bringing forth the grain together; and which the bread tastes of, no man knows.

Ibid., "Skyros"

797. Anna F. Trevisan
(1905–   )

1 MRS. BRENTA. When they're grown up, you might just as well not have them. They come home and they go out. This is like a railroad station and a restaurant.

Easter Eve   1946

2 ELZA. Some things are very important and some are very unimportant. To know the difference is what we are given life to find out. . . .

Ibid.

3 ELZA. The mother! She is what keeps the family intact. . . . It is proved. A fact. Time and time again. The father, no matter how good . . . a father cannot keep the family intact.

MRS. BRENTA. They scatter when the mother dies.

ELZA. True. In almost every instance.

Ibid.

4 ANNIE. How was they to know the ould war would take them so soon and last so long?
In the Valley of the Shadow   1946

5 ANNIE. Give me first the courage and the strength to bear my lot. And all the mothers the world over, who have sons acrost the seas.

Ibid.

6 BARRY. He'll be ruined tied to yer apron and yer teachin's. Pamperin' and pettin', pettin' and pamperin'.

Ibid.

7 MRS. GRISWOLD. The world is exhausted.

Ibid.

798. Margaret Webster
(1905–   )

1 When an actor says a line, he makes his point and his thought moves on to the next; but a singer has to repeat the same words over a dozen times, the emotional shading varying with the music, the thought progressing only in terms of sound.
Don't Put Your Daughter on the Stage   1972

2 Revivals at the Met are unmitigated torture for the stage director and an almost total waste from his point of view.

Ibid.

799. Hannah Arendt
(1906–1975)

1 Against the egalitarian order of persuasion stands the authoritarian order, which is always hierarchical. If authority is to be defined at all, then, it must be in contradistinction to both coercion by force and persuasion through arguments.

Nomos I: Authority,
Carl J. Frederich, ed. *1958*

2 With the loss of tradition we have lost the thread which safely guided us through the vast realms of the past, but this thread was also the chain fettering each successive generation to a predetermined aspect of the past. It could be that only now will the past open up to us with unexpected freshness and tell us things that no one as yet had ears to hear.

Ibid.

3 Culture relates to objects and is a phenomenon of the world; entertainment relates to people and is a phenomenon of life. An object is cultural to the extent that it can endure; its durability is the very opposite of functionality, which is the quality which makes it disappear again from the phenomenal world by being used and used up. The great user and consumer of objects is life itself, the life of the individual and the life of society as a whole. Life is indifferent to the thingness of an object; it insists that everything must be functional, fulfill some needs. *Daedalus* *1960*

4 Our tradition of political thought had its definite beginning in the teachings of Plato and Aristotle. I believe it came to a no less definite end in the theories of Karl Marx. *Between Past and Future,* Ch. 1 *1961*

5 Only beginning and end are, so to speak, pure or unmodulated; and the fundamental chord therefore never strikes its listeners more forcefully and more beautifully than when it first sends its harmonizing sound into the world and never more irritatingly and jarringly than when it still continues to be heard in a world whose sounds—and thought—it can no longer bring into harmony.

Ibid.

6 Immortality is what nature possesses without effort and without anybody's assistance, and immortality is what the mortals must therefore try to achieve if they want to live up to the world into which they were born, to live up to the things which surround them and to whose company they are admitted for a short while.

Ibid., Ch. 2

7 Eichmann, much less intelligent and without any education to speak of, at least dimly realized that it was not an order but a law which had turned them all into criminals. The distinction between an order and the Führer's word was that the latter's validity was not limited in time and space, which is the outstanding characteristic of the former.

Eichmann in Jerusalem, Ch. 8 *1963*

8 It is true that totalitarian domination tried to establish these holes of oblivion into which all deeds, good and evil, would disappear, but . . . holes of oblivion do not exist. . . . One man will always be left alive to tell the story. . . . For the lesson of such stories is simple and within everybody's grasp. Politically speaking, it is that under conditions of terror most people will comply but *some people will not*. . . . Humanly speaking, no more is required, and no more can reasonably be asked, for this planet to remain a place fit for human habitation.

Ibid., Ch. 14

9 It is quite gratifying to feel guilty if you haven't done anything wrong: how noble! Whereas it is rather hard and certainly depressing to admit guilt and to repent.

Ibid., Ch. 15

10 It is in the very nature of things human that every act that has once made its appearance and has been recorded in the history of mankind stays with mankind as a potentiality long after its actuality has become a thing of the past. No punishment has ever possessed enough power of deterrence to prevent the commission of crimes. On the contrary, whatever the punishment, once a specific crime has appeared for the first time, its reappearance is more likely than its initial emergence could ever have been.

Ibid., Epilogue

11 The trouble with Eichmann was precisely that so many were like him, and that the many were neither per-

verted nor sadistic, that they were, and still are, terribly and terrifyingly normal. From the viewpoint of our legal institutions and of our moral standards of judgment, this normality was much more terrifying than all the atrocities put together, for it implied—as had been said at Nuremberg over and over again by the defendants and their counsels—that this new type of criminal, who is in actual fact *hostis generis humani*, commits his crimes under circumstances that make it well-nigh impossible for him to know or to feel that he is doing wrong.

> Ibid.

12 Wars and revolutions . . . have outlived all their ideological justifications. . . . No cause is left but the most ancient of all, the one, in fact, that from the beginning of our history has determined the very existence of politics, the cause of freedom versus tyranny.

> *On Revolution,* Introduction   1963

13 It may be a truism to say that liberation and freedom are not the same; that liberation may be the condition of freedom but by no means leads automatically to it; that the notion of liberty implied in liberation can only be negative, and hence that even the intention of liberating is not identical with the desire for freedom. Yet if these truisms are frequently forgotten, it is because liberty has always loomed large and the foundation of freedom has always been uncertain, if not altogether futile.

> Ibid., Ch. 1

14 From this he [Marx] concluded that freedom and poverty were incompatible. His most explosive and indeed most original contribution to the cause of revolution was that he interpreted the compelling needs of mass poverty in political terms as an uprising, not for the sake of bread or wealth, but for the sake of freedom as well.

> Ibid., Ch. 2

15 . . . without the presence of misfortune, pity could not exist, and it therefore has just as much vested interest in the existence of the unhappy as thirst for power has a vested interest in the existence of the weak. Moreover, by virtue of being a sentiment, pity can be enjoyed for its own sake, and this will almost automatically lead

to a glorification of its cause, which is the suffering of others.

Ibid.

16 Why should the vice that covered up vices become the vice of vices? Is hypocrisy then such a monster? . . . What makes it so plausible to assume that hypocrisy is the vice of vices is that integrity can indeed exist under the cover of all other vices except this one. Only crime and the criminal, it is true, confront us with the perplexity of radical evil; but only the hypocrite is really rotten to the core.

Ibid.

17 . . . [America's] own failure to remember that a revolution gave birth to the United States and that the republic was brought into existence by no "historical necessity" and no organic development, but by a deliberate act: the foundation of freedom. . . . When we were told that by freedom we understood free enterprise, we did very little to dispel this monstrous falsehood. . . . Wealth and economic well-being, we have asserted, are the fruits of freedom, while we should have been the first to know that this kind of "happiness" . . . has been an unmixed blessing only in this country, and it is a minor blessing compared with the truly political freedoms, such as freedom of speech and thought, of assembly and association, even under the best conditions. Economic growth may one day turn out to be a curse rather than a good, and under no conditions can it either lead into freedom or constitute a proof for its existence.

Ibid., Ch. 6

18 In this system the opinions of the people are indeed unascertainable for the simple reason that they are nonexistent. Opinions are formed in a process of open discussion and public debate, and where no opportunity for the forming of opinions exists, there may be moods—moods of the masses and moods of individuals, the latter no less fickle and unreliable than the former—but no opinion.

Ibid.

19 Secrecy—what diplomatically is called "discretion," as well as the *arcana imperii*, the mysteries of government—and deception, the deliberate falsehood and the outright lie used as legitimate means to achieve politi-

89

cal ends, have been with us since the beginning of recorded history. Truthfulness has never been counted
among the political virtues, and lies have always been
regarded as justifiable tools in political dealings.

"Lying in Politics," *Crises of*
the Republic   1972

20 For the trouble with lying and deceiving is that their
efficiency depends entirely upon a clear notion of the
truth that the liar and deceiver wishes to hide. In this
sense, truth, even if it does not prevail in public, possesses an ineradicable primacy over all falsehoods.

Ibid.

21 Disobedience to the law, civil and criminal, has become
a mass phenomenon in recent years, not only in America, but also in a great many other parts of the world.
The defiance of established authority, religious and secular, social and political, as a world-wide phenomenon
may well one day be accounted the outstanding event
of the last decade.

Ibid., "Civil Disobedience"

22 There is all the difference in the world between the
criminal's avoiding the public eye and the civil disobe-
dient's taking the law into his own hands in open defiance. This distinction between an open violation of the
law, performed in public, and a clandestine one is so
glaringly obvious that it can be neglected only by prejudice or ill will.

Ibid.

23 Man's urge for change and his need for stability have
always balanced and checked each other, and our current vocabulary, which distinguishes between two fac-
tions, the progressives and the conservatives, indicates
a state of affairs in which this balance has been thrown
out of order. No civilization—the man-made artifact to
house successive generations—would ever have been
possible without a framework of stability, to provide
the wherein for the flux of change. Foremost among
the stabilizing factors, more enduring than customs,
manners and traditions, are the legal systems that regu-
late our life in the world and our daily affairs with each
other.

Ibid.

24 Promises are the uniquely human way of ordering the future, making it predictable and reliable to the extent that this is humanly possible.

Ibid.

25 The ceaseless, senseless demand for original scholarship in a number of fields, where only erudition is now possible, has led either to sheer irrelevancy, the famous knowing of more and more about less and less, or to the development of a pseudo-scholarship which actually destroys its object.

Ibid., "On Violence"

26 Power and violence are opposites; where the one rules absolutely, the other is absent. Violence appears where power is in jeopardy, but left to its own course it ends in power's disappearance.

Ibid.

800. Margaret Bourke-White
(1906–1971)

1 Usually I object when someone makes overmuch of men's work versus women's work, for I think it is the excellence of the results which counts.

Portrait of Myself   1963

2 . . . war correspondents . . . see a great deal of the world. Our obligation is to pass it on to others.

Quoted in *The Woman's Eye*
by Anne Tucker   1973p

3 . . . to understand another human being you must gain some insight into the conditions which made him what he is.

Ibid.

4 What makes Soviet Russia the new land of the machine are the new social relationships of the men and women around the machine. The new man . . . and with him, on an equal footing, the new woman—operating drill presses, studying medicine and engineering—are integral parts of a people working collectively toward a common goal.

Ibid.

801. Jacqueline Cochran
(1906?–   )

1 I can cure your men of walking off the program. Let's put on the girls.

> Quoted in *The American Heritage History of Flight*, Ch. 8   *1962*

802. Catherine Cookson
(1906–   )

1 "Catholic, be damned! They tell 'em to have bairns, but do they bloody well keep them?"

> *The Fifteen Streets*, Ch. 1   *1952*

2 God knew there was no happiness came out of a mixed marriage. With a Church of England one it would be bad enough, but with a Spiritualist! . . . And yet . . . what was the obstacle of class?

> Ibid., Ch. 7

3 "It's no good saying one thing and thinking another."

> Ibid., Ch. 8

803. Anna Roosevelt Halsted
(1906–1975)

1 There are so many indignities to being sick and helpless. . . .

> Letter to David Gray (November 1, 1962), Quoted in *Eleanor: The Years Alone* by Joseph P. Lash   *1972*

804. Lillian Hellman
(1906–   )

1 MRS. MORTAR. But the cinema is a shallow art. It has no—no—no fourth dimension.

> *The Children's Hour*, Act I   *1934*

2 MRS. TILFORD. I have seen too many people, out of pride, act on that pride. In the end they punish themselves.

Ibid., Act II, Sc. 1

3 MARTHA. I look forward all day to that bath. It's my last touch with the full life. It makes me feel important to know that there's one thing ahead of me, one thing I've *got* to do.

Ibid., Act III

4 CARDIN. Karen, there are a lot of people in this world who have had bad trouble in their lives. We're three of those people. We could sit around the rest of our lives and exist on that trouble, until in the end we had nothing else and we'd want nothing else.

Ibid.

5 KAREN. So you've come here to relieve your conscience? Well, I won't be your confessor. It's choking you, is it? And you want to stop the choking, don't you? You've done a wrong and you have to right that wrong or you can't rest your head again. You want to be "just," don't you, and you wanted us to help you be just?

Ibid.

6 HANNAH. Lucy, there were people made to think and people made to listen. I ain't sure either you or Lundee were made to do either.

Days to Come, Act I   1936

7 EASTER. When you got nothin' to do, we can't do it for you.

Ibid., Act II, Sc. 1

8 ANDREW. Lonely. I always thought loneliness meant alone, without people. It means something else.

JULIE. That's a late discovery. You're lucky.

ANDREW. Why do people always think it's lucky to find out the simple things long after one should have known them?

JULIE. Because each year you can put off knowing about them gives you one more year of peace.

ANDREW. I don't think so. Unless you can put it off forever.   *Ibid.*

9 WHALEN. Didn't anybody ever tell you that Christians aren't supposed to act like Christians?

Ibid., Sc. 2

10 WHALEN. When you don't feel yourself anything, I mean any part of anything, that's when you get scared.

Ibid.

11 WHALEN. Do you think you can love the smell that comes from dirty skin, or the scum on dishes, or the holes in the floor with the bugs coming through—or the meanness and the cowardice that comes with poverty? I hate the poor, Mrs. Rodman. But I love what they could be.

Ibid.

12 WILKIE. You're a noble lady, and I am frightened of noble ladies. They usually land the men they know in cemeteries.

Ibid., Sc. 3

13 ANDREW. Polite and blind, we lived.

Ibid., Act III

14 ANDREW. Murder is worse than lost love. Murder is worse than a broken heart.

Ibid.

15 Cynicism is an unpleasant way of saying the truth.

The Little Foxes, Act I   *1939*

16 God forgives those who invent what they need.

Ibid.

17 Fashions in sin change.

Watch on the Rhine   *1941*

18 It doesn't pay well to fight for what we believe in.

Ibid., Act I

19 Years ago I heard somebody say that being a Roumanian was not a nationality, but a profession.

Ibid., Act III

20 KARP. But I will tell you this: when the end is on its way, no amount of noise will help. If you act noisy, you lose face with yourself.

The North Star   *1943*

21 KURIN. A famous doctor comes back to his village. To write. To write a history of our village. Who cares

about our village? What has ever happened here? Wars, revolutions—that's in everybody's life. It would be better if you wrote a nice cookbook. History people make themselves; cooking they have to learn.

Ibid.

22 RODION. It is not modest to think one has the key to everything.

Ibid.

23 GRISHA. Those who are clumsy in the body are often clumsy in the head.

Ibid.

24 KOLYA. The brightest of women are not bright.

Ibid.

25 KOLYA. You are what you are. It is my opinion the trouble in the world comes from people who do not know what they are, and pretend to be something they're not.

Ibid.

26 VON HARDEN. If you wish to be a warrior, Doctor Richter, you must take chances with your life.

Ibid.

27 KURIN. The civilized men who are sorry . . . to me *you* are the real filth. Men who do the work of Fascists and pretend to themselves they are better than those for whom they work. Men who do murder while they laugh at those who order them to do it.

Ibid.

28 MARCUS. Carry in your own valise, son. It is not seemly for a man to load his goods on other men, black or white.

Another Part of the Forest, Act I   1946

29 PENNIMAN. The judgement of music, like the inspiration for it, must come slow and measured, if it comes with truth.

Ibid., Act II

30 MARCUS. Your people deserved to lose their war* and their world. It was a backward world, getting in the way of history. Appalling that you still don't realize it. Really, people should read more books.

Ibid.

---

* Referring to the Civil War.

31 BIRDIE. You lose your manners when you're poor.

> Ibid.

32 MARCUS. A dead man, a foolish man, an empty man from an idiot world. A man who wants nothing but war, any war, just a war. A man who believes in nothing, and never will. A man in space. . . .

> Ibid.

33 LAVINIA. Imagine taking money for other people's misery.

> Ibid., Act III

34 LAVINIA. But maybe half a lie is worse than a real lie.

> Ibid.

35 LAVINIA. I'm not going to have any Bibles in my school. That surprise you all? It's the only book in the world but it's just for grown people, after you know it don't mean what it says.

> Ibid.

36 I am not willing, now or in the future, to bring bad trouble to people who, in my past association with them, were completely innocent of any talk or any action that was disloyal or subversive. . . . I cannot and will not cut my conscience to fit this year's fashions, even though I long ago came to the conclusion that I was not a political person and could have no comfortable place in any political group.

> Letter to the House Committee on
> Un-American Activities, *The Nation*
> May 31, 1952

37 CARRIE. Not like the country. My. I never heard anybody say a thing like that before. It takes courage to just up and say you don't like the country. Everybody likes the country.

> *Toys in the Attic*, Act I   1959

38 JULIAN. . . . success isn't everything but it makes a man stand straight. . . .

> Ibid.

39 LILY. Because I must ask truth, and speak truth, and act with truth, now and forever.

ALBERTINE. Do you think this is the proper climate? So hot and damp. Puts mildew on the truth.

> Ibid., Act II

40 LILY. I don't want to be wise, ever, Mama, ever. I'm in love.

Ibid.

41 ALBERTINE. People don't want other people to guess they never knew what they wanted in the first place.

Ibid.

42 ALBERTINE. You do too much. Go and do nothing for a while. Nothing.

Ibid.

43 CARRIE. I read in a French book that there was nothing so abandoned as a respectable young girl.

Ibid.

44 ANNA. The leaf came in the spring, stayed nice on the branch in the autumn until the winter winds would blow it in the snow. Mama said that in that little time of holding on, a woman had to make ready for the winter ground where she would lie the rest of her life.

Ibid., Act III

45 CARRIE. There are lives that are shut and should stay shut. . . .

Ibid.

46 ANNA. Well, people change and forget to tell each other. Too bad—causes so many mistakes.

Ibid.

47 . . . he was a man of great force, given, as she was given, to breaking the spirit of people for the pleasure of exercise.

An Unfinished Woman   1969

48 I didn't know what she was saying when she moved her lips in a Baptist church or a Catholic cathedral or, less often, in a synagogue, but it was obvious that God could be found anywhere. . . .

Ibid.

49 Mama seemed to do only what my father wanted, and yet we lived the way my mother wanted us to live.

Ibid.

50 I was taught, also, that if you gave, you did it without piety and didn't boast about it.

Ibid.

51 . . . the first sexual stirrings of little girls, so masked, so complex, so foolish as compared with the sex of little boys.

Ibid.

52 My father was often angry when I was most like him.
Ibid.

53 . . . if you are willing to take the punishment, you are halfway through the battle. That the issue may be trivial, the battle ugly, is another point.

Ibid.

54 By the time I grew up, the fight for the emancipation of women, their rights under the law, in the office, in bed, was stale stuff.

Ibid.

55 Dashiell Hammett used to say I had the meanest jealousy of all. I had no jealousy of work, no jealousy of money. I was just jealous of women who took advantage of men, because I didn't know how to do it.

Quoted in "A Star Is Born," *Crazy Salad*
by Nora Ephron   *1973*

805. Mirra Komarovsky
(1906–   )

1 It is possible, of course, that the only effect of . . . sheltering is to create in women a generalized dependency which will then be transferred to the husband and which will enable her all the more readily to accept the role of wife in a family which still has many patriarchal features.

"Functional Analysis of Sex Roles,"
American Sociological Review
August, 1950

2 What are we educating women for? To raise this question is to face the whole problem of women's role in society. We are uncertain about the end of women's education precisely because the status of women in our society is fraught with contradictions and confusion.

Women in the Modern World   *1953*

3 Today the survival of some . . . stereotypes is a psychological strait jacket for both sexes.   Ibid.

4 What is important to a relationship is a harmony of emotional roles and not too great a disparity in the general level of intelligence.

Ibid.

5 A social order can function only because the vast majority have somehow adjusted themselves to their place in society and perform the functions expected of them.

Ibid.

6 With new and old patterns both in the air, it is all too human for each partner to reach out for the double dose of privileges, those of the old and those of the new role, leaving to the mate the double dose of obligation.

Ibid., Ch. 3

7 For an interest to be rewarding, one must pay in discipline and dedication, especially through the difficult or boring stages which are inevitably encountered.

Ibid., Ch. 4

8 Were our knowledge of human relationships a hundredfold more reliable than it is now, it would still be foolish to seek ready-made solutions for problems of living in the index of a book.

Ibid., Ch. 6

9 The most elusive knowledge of all is self-knowledge and it is usually acquired laboriously through experience outside the classroom.

Ibid.

10 The price of concentration on home-making involves the sacrifice of other instruction.

Ibid., Ch. 7

11 The greatest danger of traditional education is that learning may remain purely verbal. Words are learned and placed in dead storage in one part of the mind while life is lived unilluminated and unguided by this learning. Such a danger is inherent in the very nature of education.

Ibid.

12 Controversy both within and between disciplines is an inevitable feature of scientific development. . . . But not all intellectual controversy is equally beneficial. Pseudo-issues produced by verbal or logical ambiguities are much too frequent and waste our resources. They

are usually occasioned by the failure to discern the tacit assumption of the contending positions.

Common Frontiers of the Social Sciences, Introduction   *1957*

806. Dilys Laing
(1906–1960)

1 Proud inclination of the flesh,
most upright tendency, salute
in honor of the secret wish.
        "Villanelle," St. 1, *Collected Poems*   *1967p*

2 . . . memory is a storm I can't repel.
                    Ibid., "Venus Petrified," St. 3

3 The woman took a train
away away from herself.
                    Ibid., "The Double Goer," St. 1

4   and I
grow younger as I leave
my me behind.
                                    Ibid., St. 2

5 She faced the crowd and cried:
I love you all but one:
the one who wears my face.
She is the one I fled from.
                                    Ibid., St. 6

6 I was a child who clutched the amulet
of childhood in a terror of time. I saw
archangels, worshipped trees, expected God.
                    Ibid., "The Little Girls," St. 2

7 Time is illumined with inverted light:
the past all whole, the present weird with fault.
                    Ibid., "Lot's Daughter," St. 3

8 Vague, submarine, my giant twin
swims under me, a girl of shade
who mimics me.

                                    Ibid., "Ego"

9 Women receive
the insults of men
with tolerance,

having been bitten
in the nipple
by their toothless gums.

Ibid., "Veterans"

10 The end will be, perhaps, the end of me,
which will, I humbly guess, be his beginning.

Ibid., "Private Entry in the Diary of a
Female Parent"

11   To be a woman and a writer
is double mischief, for
the world will slight her
who slights "the servile house," and who would rather
make odes than beds.

Ibid., "Sonnet to a Sister in Error," St. 2

807. Anne Morrow Lindbergh
(1906–   )

1 Travelers are always discoverers, especially those who
travel by air. There are no signposts in the sky to show
a man has passed that way before. There are no channels marked. The flier breaks each second into new un-
charted seas.

North to the Orient, Ch. 1   1935

2 Rivers perhaps are the only physical features of the
world that are at their best from the air.

Ibid., Ch. 17

3 One can never pay in gratitude; one can only pay "in
kind" somewhere else in life. . . .

Ibid., Ch. 19

4   . . . the fundamental magic of flying, a miracle that
has nothing to do with any of its practical purposes—
purposes of speed, accessibility, and convenience—and
will not change as they change.

Ibid., Ch. 23

5 The wave of the future is coming and there is no fighting it.

The Wave of the Future   1940

6 Somehow the leaders in Germany, Italy and Russia
have discovered how to use new economic forces. . . .

They have felt the wave of the future and they have leapt upon it.

Ibid.

7 Lost time was like a run in a stocking. It always got worse.

The Steep Ascent, Ch. 3　　1944

8 There is no harvest for the heart alone;
The seed of love must be
Eternally
Resown.

"Second Sowing," St. 4, *The Unicorn*
and Other Poems　　1948

9 Perhaps middle-age is, or should be, a period of shedding shells; the shell of ambition, the shell of material accumulations and possessions, the shell of the ego.

Gift from the Sea　　1955

10 One cannot collect all the beautiful shells on the beach.

Ibid.

11 It isn't for the moment you are struck that you need courage, but for the long uphill climb back to sanity and faith and security.

Hours of Gold, Hours of Lead　　1973

12 Ideally, both members of a couple in love free each other to new and different worlds.

Ibid., Introduction

13 But total freedom is never what one imagines and, in fact, hardly exists. It comes as a shock in life to learn that we usually only exchange one set of restrictions for another. The second set, however, is self-chosen, and therefore easier to accept.

Ibid.

14 The loneliness you get by the sea is personal and alive. It doesn't subdue you and make you feel abject. It's a stimulating loneliness.

Ibid., Letter to Charles Lindbergh (March 17, 1929)

15 Fog is very terrible. It comes about you before you realize and you are suddenly blind and dumb and cold. It really does seem like death. . . .

Ibid., Letter to Mother, Mrs. Charles
Long Cutty (September 7, 1929)

16 Is there *anything* as horrible as *starting* on a trip? Once you're off, that's all right, but the last moments are earthquake and convulsion, and the feeling that you are a snail being pulled off your rock.

Ibid. (January 2, 1930)

17 For miles out in the China Sea you see mud from the Yangtze river, then suddenly you are on China, and you gasp at the flat fields stretching as far as you can see, the great flat river. . . . There is something magnificent about it. A feeling of its grandeur and age. . . .

Ibid. (September 26, 1931)

18 . . . suffering . . . no matter how multiplied . . . is always individual.

Quoted by Dorothea Lange in
The Woman's Eye by Anne Tucker
1973

19 Love is a force. . . . It is not a result; it is a cause. It is not a product; it produces. It is a power, like money, or steam or electricity. It is valueless unless you can give something else by means of it.

Locked Rooms and Open Doors   1974

20 People talk about love as though it were something you could give, like an armful of flowers.

Ibid.

808. Maria Goeppert Mayer
(1906–1972)

1 No one has ever seen, nor probably ever will see, an atom, but that does not deter the physicist from trying to draw a plan of it, with the aid of such clues to its structure as he has.

"The Structure of the Nucleus,"
Scientific American   March, 1951

2 Of course my father always said I should have been a boy. He said, Don't grow up to be a woman, and what he meant by that was, a housewife . . . without any interests.

Quoted in "Maria Goeppert-Mayer,"
A Life of One's Own
by Joan Dash   *1973p*

3 Mathematics began to seem too much like puzzle solving. Physics is puzzle solving, too, but of puzzles created by nature, not by the mind of man.

Ibid.

809. Rita Boumy Pappas
(1906–   )

1 I did not let them nail my soul
as they do butterflies.

"Roxane M."   *1975*

2 My fine days? Oh, a few fleeting birds,
I had no other treasure than my tears.
That is why, none of those who tortured me
have seen me weep.

Ibid.

810. Ting Ling
(1906–   )

1 In the Chinese family system, there is superficial quiet and calmness and quarreling is frowned upon, but in reality all is in conflict.

Quoted in *Women in Modern China*
by Helen Foster Snow   *1967*

2 I wanted to escape from love but didn't know how.

Ibid.

3 The Red Army soldiers are a totally new type that cannot be found anywhere else in China. They have never known anything but revolution. Because they originally lived in the Sovietized areas, they had no ideology of private property and no domestic ideas. No unhappiness ever comes to mind. They think only of how to overcome the difficulties of their work and never of their troubles.

Ibid.

811. Dorothy Baker
(1907–1968)

1 In the first place maybe he shouldn't have got himself mixed up with Negroes. It gave him a funny slant on

things and he never got over it. It gave him a feeling
for undisciplined expression, a hot, direct approach, a
full-throated ease that never did him any final good in
his later dealings with those of his race, those whom
civilization has whipped into shape, those who can contain themselves and play what's written.

> *Young Man with a Horn,*
> Bk. I, Ch. 1   1938

2 It left him a little fluttery in the stomach, things like
that are so close. You're thrown out for insubordina-
tion or else you aren't, and where the actual line of
demarcation stands out clear, God Himself only can
know. . . . All he knew was that recognition, that
sweet thing, had been given to him because he had
been doing some good playing. It's a simple formula:
do your best and somebody might like it.

> *Ibid., Bk. III, Ch. 2*

3 Fortune, in its workings, has something in common
with the slot-machine. There are those who can bait it
forever and never get more than an odd assortment of
lemons for their pains; but once in a while there will
come a man for whom all the grooves will line up, and
when that happens there's no end to the showering
down.

> *Ibid., Bk. IV, Ch. 2*

4 "Now, the easy thing to say is that they wrote great
poetry because they had these weaknesses. . . . It's
much too easy. We could make a grand tour of all the
jails right now, and find a thousand drug addicts and
homosexuals who never wrote a line of poetry in their
lives and never will. It isn't because of these things that
her poems were great, it's in spite of them."

> *Trio   1945*

5 And you've tried to make me believe we were something we weren't and that we lived on a higher plane
and saw everything clearer and freer than anybody
else. . . . Well, I've been through it all now. I've
learned everything you wanted me to learn. . . . I
know what higher morality's like, and no decent person
would be caught dead with me.   *Ibid.*

6 "She wastes herself, she drifts, all she wants to do with
her life is lose it somewhere."

> *Cassandra at the Wedding   1962*

7 "Same thing everywhere I'd looked. Large amounts of safety, very few risks. Let nothing endanger the proper marriage, the fashionable career, the nonirritating thesis that says nothing new and nothing true."

Ibid.

812. Rachel Carson
(1907–1964)

1 The ocean is a place of paradoxes.
"Under Sea," *Atlantic Monthly*   *September, 1937*

2 All the people of a country have a direct interest in conservation. . . . Wildlife, water, forests, grasslands—all are part of man's essential environment; the conservation and effective use of one is impossible except as the others are also conserved.
"Guarding Our Wildlife Refuge,"
Conservation in Action   1946

3 Like the resource it seeks to protect, wildlife conservation must be dynamic, changing as conditions change, seeking always to become more effective.

Ibid.

4 Beginnings are apt to be shadowy and so it is with the beginnings of that great mother of life, the sea.
The Sea Around Us, Pt. I, Ch. 1   1951

5 Spring moves over the temperate lands of our Northern Hemisphere in a tide of new life, of pushing green shoots and unfolding buds, all its mysteries and meanings symbolized in the northward migration of the birds, the awakening of sluggish amphibian life as the chorus of frogs rises again from the wet lands, the different sound of the wind which stirs the young leaves where a month ago it rattled the bare branches.
Ibid., Ch. 3

6 For the sea lies all about us. . . . In its mysterious past it encompasses all the dim origins of life and receives in the end, after, it may be, many transmutations, the dead husks of that same life. For all at last return to the sea—to Oceanus, the ocean river, like the everflowing stream of time, the beginning and the end.
Ibid., Pt. III, Ch. 14

7 Always the edge of the sea remains an elusive and indefinable boundary. The shore has a dual nature, changing with the swing of the tides, belonging now to the
land, now to the sea.

"The Marginal World,"
The Edge of the Sea   1955

8 The rested waters, the cold wet breath of the fog, are of
a world in which man is an uneasy trespasser; he punc-
tuates the night with the complaining groan and grunt
of a foghorn, sensing the power and menace of the sea.
Ibid., "The Enduring Sea"

9 The discipline of the writer is to learn to be still and
listen to what his subject has to tell him.
Speech, American Association of
University Women   *June 22, 1956*

10 In every outthrust headland, in every curving beach, in
every grain of sand there is a story of the earth.
"Our Ever-Changing Shore,"
Holiday   *July, 1958*

11 As cruel a weapon as the cave man's club, the chemical
barrage has been hurled against the fabric of life.
The Silent Spring   1962

12 No witchcraft, no enemy action had silenced the rebirth of new life in this stricken world. The people had
done it themselves.

Ibid., Ch. 1

13 For the first time in the history of the world, every
human being is now subjected to contact with dangerous chemicals, from the moment of conception until
death.

Ibid., Ch. 3

14 If we are going to live so intimately with these chemicals—eating and drinking them, taking them into the
very marrow of our bones—we had better know something about their nature and their power.

Ibid.

15 In an age when man has forgotten his origins and is
blind even to his most essential needs for survival, water along with other resources has become the victim of
his indifference.

Ibid., Ch. 4

16 Our attitude toward plants is a singularly narrow one. If we see any immediate utility in a plant we foster it. If for any reason we find its presence undesirable or merely a matter of indifference, we may condemn it to destruction forthwith.

Ibid., Ch. 6

17 Under the philosophy that now seems to guide our destinies, nothing must get in the way of the man with the spray gun.

Ibid., Ch. 7

18 Over increasingly large areas of the United States, spring now comes unheralded by the return of the birds, and the early mornings are strangely silent where once they were filled with the beauty of bird song.

Ibid., Ch. 8

19 Who has decided . . . that the supreme value is a world without insects, even though it be also a sterile world ungraced by the curving wing of a bird in flight? The decision is that of the authoritarian temporarily entrusted with power. . . .

Ibid.

20 The battle of living things against cancer began so long ago that its origin is lost in time. But . . . man, alone of all forms of life, can *create* cancer producing substances. . . .

Ibid., Ch. 14

21 If Darwin were alive today the insect world would delight and astound him with its impressive verification of his theories of the survival of the fittest. Under the stress of intensive chemical spraying the weaker members of the insect populations are being weeded out. . . . Only the strong and fit remain to defy our efforts to control them.

Ibid., Ch. 16

22 The "control of nature" is a phrase conceived in arrogance, born of the Neanderthal age of biology and the convenience of man.

Ibid., Ch. 17

813. Daphne Du Maurier
(1907–)

1 These things were permanent, they could not be dissolved. They were memories that cannot hurt. All this I resolved in my dream, while the clouds lay across the face of the moon, for like most sleepers I knew that I dreamed.

Rebecca, Ch. 1   *1938*

2 We can never go back again, that much is certain. The past is still too close to us. The things we have tried to forget and put behind us would stir again, and that sense of fear, of furtive unrest . . . might in some manner unforeseen become a living companion, as it had been before.

Ibid., Ch. 2

3 We were like two performers in a play, but we were divided, we were not acting with one another. We had to endure it alone, we had to put up this show, this miserable, sham performance for the sake of all these people I did not know and did not want to see again.

Ibid., Ch. 17

4 Forgotten the lies, the deceit, the sudden bursts of temper. Forgotten the wild extravagance, the absurd generosity, the vitriolic tongue. Only the warmth remained, and the love of living.

Mary Anne, Pt. I, Ch. 1   *1954*

5 She could not separate success from peace of mind. The two must go together; her observation pointed to this truth. Failure meant proverty, poverty meant squalor, squalor led, in the final stages, to the smells and stagnation of Bowling Inn Alley.   Ibid., Ch. 10

6 One second's hesitation. Tears, or laughter? Tears would be an admission of guilt, so laughter was best.
Ibid., Pt. II, Ch. 7

7 "Corruption continues with us beyond the grave," she said, "and then plays merry hell with all ideals. . . ."
Ibid., Ch. 11

8 All courtiers gossip madly, it's part of their business.
Ibid., Pt. III, Ch. 5

9 The pair were playing a game that defied intervention, they were matched like reel and rod and there was no unwinding. They juggled in jargon, dabbled in *double-entendres*, wallowed in each other's witticisms, and all at the expense of the Defendant.

Ibid., Pt. IV, Ch. 2

10 How replace the life of a loved lost child with a dream?
Don't Look Now   1970

11 . . . the little festive atmosphere of strangeness, of excitement, that only a holiday bedroom brings. This is ours for the moment, but no more. While we are in it we bring it life. When we have gone it no longer exists, it fades into anonymity.

Ibid.

12 "The trouble is," said Laura, "walking in Venice becomes compulsive once you start. Just over the next bridge, you say, and then the next one beckons."

Ibid.

814. Edith Head
(1907–   )

1 The subjective actress thinks of clothes only as they apply to her; the objective actress thinks of them only as they affect others, as a tool for the job.

The Dress Doctor, with
Jane Kesner Ardmore   *1959*

815. Zora Neale Hurston
(1907–1960)

1 Ships at a distance have every man's wish on board. For some they come in with the tide. For others they sail forever on the horizon, never out of sight, never landing, until the Watcher turns his eyes away in resignation, his dreams mocked to death by Time. That is the life of men. Now, women forget all those things they don't want to remember, and remember everything they don't want to forget. The dream is the truth. Then they act and do things accordingly.

Their Eyes Were Watching God, Ch. 1   *1937*

110

2 She had the misfortune to be too good-looking and too available for women to take to her, but not pretty enough for any man to excuse her generosity and want to protect her. Nor had she the avarice nor the hardness to turn her position to profit.

Seraph on the Suwanne, Ch. 15   1948

3 "I'll bet you when you get down on them rusty knees and get to worrying God, He goes in His privy-house and slams the door. That's what he thinks about *you* and *your* prayers."

Ibid.

4 "You love like a coward. Don't take no steps at all. Just stand around and hope for things to happen outright. Unthankful and unknowing like a hog under an acorn tree. Eating and grunting with your ears hanging over your eyes, and never even looking up to see where the acorns are coming from."

Ibid., Ch. 23

5 "Don't you realize that the sea is the home of water? All water is off on a journey unlessen it's in the sea, and it's homesick, and bound to make its way home someday."

Ibid., Ch. 27

816. Violette Leduc
(1907–1972)

1 I was and I always shall be hampered by what I think other people will say.

La Bâtarde   1965

2 "She is killing me and there's nothing I can accuse her of."

Ibid.

3 The pearl wanted what I wanted. I was discovering the little male organ we all of us have. A eunuch taking heart again.

Therese and Isabelle   1968

4 To give oneself, one must annihilate oneself.

Ibid.

5 To write is to inform against others.

Mad in Pursuit   1971

6 "Will you sell your sex for the sake of your pen? . . .
I would sell everything for greater exactness."

Ibid.

7 "I desire, am only able to desire, myself."

Ibid.

8 "I walk without flinching through the burning cathedral of the summer. My bank of wild grass is majestic
and full of music. It is a fire that solitude presses
against my lips." Ibid.

817. Elsa Schiaparelli
(1907?–   )

1 So fashion is born by small facts, trends, or even politics, never by trying to make little pleats and furbelows,
by trinkets, by clothes easy to copy, or by the shorten-
ing or lengthening of a skirt.
Shocking Life, Ch. 9   *1954*

2 Courtesans used to know more about the soul of men
than any philosopher. The art is lost in the fog of
snobbism and false respectability.

Ibid., Ch. 21

3 A good cook is like a sorceress who dispenses happiness. Ibid.

4 The moment that people stop copying you, it means
that you are no longer any good, and that you have
ceased to be news. Ibid.

5 Eating is not merely a material pleasure. Eating well
gives a spectacular joy to life and contributes immensely to goodwill and happy companionship. It is of
great importance to the morale. Ibid.

818. Helen Foster Snow
(1907–   )

1 To be a Marxist does not mean that one becomes a
Communist party member. There are as many varieties
of Marxists as there are of Protestants.
"Women and Kuomintang,"
Women in Modern China   *1967*

2 The war between the artist and writer and government or orthodoxy is one of the tragedies of humankind. One chief enemy is stupidity and failure to understand anything about the creative mind. For a bureaucratic politician to presume to tell any artist or writer how to get his mind functioning is the ultimate in asininity. The artist is no more able to control his mind than is any outsider. Freedom to think requires not only freedom of expression but also freedom from the threat of orthodoxy and being outcast and ostracized. Ibid.

3 . . . one can judge a civilization by the way it treats its women. Ibid., "Bound Feet and Straw Sandals"

819. Barbara Stanwyck
(1907–   )

1 Sponsors obviously care more about a ninety-second commercial and *want* to pay you more than any guest star gets for a ninety-minute *acting* performance.
Quoted in *McCall's* March, 1965

2 There is a point in portraying surface vulgarity where tragedy and comedy are very close.
Quoted in *Starring Miss Barbara Stanwyck* by Ella Smith 1974

3 They don't seem to write . . . comedy anymore—just a series of gags.
Ibid., Interview with Hedda Hopper (1953)

4 My only problem is finding a way to play my fortieth fallen female in a different way from my thirty-ninth.
Ibid.

5 I marvelled at the pioneers. The real people who went into the wilderness with little other than their courage.
Ibid., *New York Journal-American* (1965)

820. Jessamyn West
(1907–   )

1 "No human would enjoy my singing . . . only maybe an old house that can't be choosy."
"Lead Her Like a Pigeon,"
The Friendly Persuasion 1945

2 "After a good heart," she said, "the least a woman can do is pick a face she fancies. Men's so much alike and many so sorry, that's the very least. If a man's face pleasures thee, that doesn't change. That is something to bank on."

Ibid.

3 She intended to forgive. Not to do so would be un-Christian; but she did not intend to do so soon, nor forget how much she had to forgive.

Ibid., "The Buried Leaf"

4 . . . but time for a woman was no such pliable commodity as it was for a man; time for a woman was rigid, and marked with names of duties.

Ibid., "A Likely Exchange"

5 "Men ain't got any heart for courting a girl they can't pass—let alone catch up with."

Ibid.

6 Eliza's face got pink. She'd never learned to take a compliment—and she'd had two a day for forty years. They made her feel uneasy—as if she weren't taken for granted like sun and moon.

Ibid., "The Illumination"

7 Old fool, Jess thought. Why's the old got to ladle out their past to the young? Got to say, I's a frolicsome sprout if ever there was one? If youngness is what we want here it is under our noses, not second-hand, not warmed over. Live in that. The young's got no time to travel back seventy-five years, watch thee sashay in and out of duck ponds, Jess Birdwell.

Ibid., "Homer and the Lilies"

8 "It's better to learn to say good-by early than late. . . ."
"Learn to Say Good-by,"
Love, Death, and the Ladies'
Drill Team   1955

9 She had been conscious throughout her girlhood of the eyes of all the potential lovers and husbands upon her, approving, disapproving. From those eyes, not knowing a thing about either lovers or husbands. . . . She had lived a hypothetical life. Nothing real, and the unreality she had conjured up was not really suitable, as it turned out, for the life she had been imagining.

Ibid., "Foot-Shaped Shoes"

114

10 Writing is so difficult that I often feel that writers, having had their hell on earth, will escape all punishment hereafter.

To See the Dream, Ch. 1   1956

11 My upbringing was such that I cannot easily converse with men as though they were normal human beings. They are too special for that. God knows how much knowledge and insight and sense and nonsense I've missed because of this.

Ibid., Ch. 2

12 Being consistent meant not departing from convictions already formulated; being a leader meant making other persons accept these convictions. It was a narrow track, and one-way, but a person might travel a considerable distance on it. A number of dictators have.

Ibid., Ch. 7

13 She thought God could put up with a married couple's making love—after all, it was His own idea for providing babies—but she supposed He considered worship one thing and love-making another. She did, certainly. Nevertheless, she was continually getting them mixed up.

South of the Angels, Bk. I, Ch. 2   1960

14 Continence is a habit more compelling than tomcatting. Enough tomcatting sooner or later acts as its own cure. Continence does not cure continence. There are more reformed rakes than reformed celibates.

Ibid., Bk. II, Ch. 5

15 The thoughtful California rain, which had fallen intermittently during the night, eased off toward daylight, and by ten had stopped altogether. Tha rain was also thoughtful enough not to scare people into thinking, when so much more was needed, that it had finished for good.

Ibid., Bk. IV, Ch. 2

16 March days, ending at six-thirty, with apricot skies and a soft wind off the ocean, a little blade-sized blower with only strength enough to move the grass at your feet, provided exactly as much day as a human being could stand.

Ibid., Ch. 4

17 We want the facts to fit the preconceptions. When they
don't, it is easier to ignore the facts than to change the
preconceptions.

The Quaker Reader, Introduction   *1962*

18 Friends [Quakers] refused to take legal oaths, since by
doing so they acquiesced in the assumption that, unless
under oath, one was not obliged to tell the truth.

Ibid.

19 It is particularly important, it seems to me, in an era of
ever increasing departmentalization and specialization,
to make the attempt occasionally to see wholes and to
understand what lies behind the exterior manifestations.

Ibid.

20 A religious awakening which does not awaken the
sleeper to love has roused him in vain.

Ibid.

21 Fiction reveals truths that reality obscures.

Quoted in *Reader's Digest*   *April, 1973*

22 "He should have put his wife to work. That's the way
doctors and lawyers pay for their education nowadays."

Hide and Seek, Ch. 1   *1973*

23 Visitors to Los Angeles, then and now, were put out
because the residents of Los Angeles had the inhospita-
ble idea of building a city comfortable to live in, rather
than a monument to astonish the eye of jaded travelers.

Ibid., Ch. 22

821. Anne Anastasi
(1908–   )

1 . . . it is apparent that we cannot speak of inferiority
and superiority, but only of specific differences in apti-
tudes and personality between the sexes. These differences are largely the result of cultural and other expe-
riential factors. . . .

Differential Psychology   *1937*

822. Harriette Arnow
(1908–   )

1 "If a religion is unpatriotic, it ain't right."
The Dollmaker, Ch. 4   *1954*

2 "I've been readen th Bible an a hunten God fer a long
while—off an on—but it ain't so easy as picken up a
nickel off th floor."
Ibid., Ch. 15

3 "Who inu hell," I said to myself, "wants to try to make
pies like Mother makes when it's so much simpler to
let Mother make um inu first place?"
Ibid., Ch. 28

4 "You never did see them ads an signs an letters beggen
all th people back home to come up here an save democracy fer you all. They done it ina last war, too.
Now you can git along without us, so's you cain't git
shet a us quick enough. Want us to go back home an
raise another crop a youngens at no cost to you an
Detroit, so's they'll be all ready to save you when you
start another war—huh?"
Ibid., Ch. 33

5 There was something frantic in their blooming, as if
they knew that frost was near and then the bitter cold.
They'd lived through all the heat and noise and stench
of summertime, and now each widely opened flower
was like a triumphant cry, "We will, we will make seed
before we die."
Ibid., Ch. 34

6 Christ had had no money, just his life. Life and money:
could a body separate the two? What had Judas done
for his money? Whispered a little, kept still as she did
now.
Ibid., Ch. 37

7 "Supposen the rebels lose. They'll try again. Supposen
they win? How can they ever stick together in one nation? They'll be jarren and fighten around over slavery,
trade and a lot of other things. Right now the East
don't want the West, and the North is a different world
from the South. And they've got Spain on their door-
step. But supposen they do clean out Spain, kill every

117

Indian, plow up every acre a ground from the Atlantic to the Pacific? They'll still have their wars."

The Kentucky Trace   1974

823. Sylvia Ashton-Warner
(1908–   )

1 When I teach people, I marry them.

Teacher   1963

2 Love interferes with fidelities.

Ibid.

3 When love turns away, now, I don't follow it. I sit and suffer, unprotesting, until I feel the tread of another step.

Ibid.

4 Ah, the simple rapture of fulfillment at my work being understood that cold morning. What unutterable reward for my labor.

Ibid.

5 I've got to relearn what I was supposed to have learned.

Myself (February, 1941)   1967

6 I'm not one of these people who were born for nothing.

Ibid.

7 I'll follow them into their own minds and fraternize there. . . .

Ibid.

8 I flung my tongue round like a cat-o'-nine-tails so that my pleasant peaceful infant room became little less than a German concentration camp as I took out on the children what life should have got.

Ibid. (August, 1941)

9 I am my own Universe, I my own Professor.   Ibid.

10 "The intellect is the tool to find the truth. It's a matter of sharpening it."   Ibid. (March 22, 1942)

11 "Your work means more to me than my own does to me because your work involves your contentment and that comes before my work with me."   Ibid.

12 "The *need* to study, to do, to make, to think, *arises* from being married. I need to be married to work."

Ibid.

13 Love has the quality of informing almost everything—even one's work.

Ibid. (November 12, 1942)

14 In mind I lay a hand on his arm but only in mind. That would be revealing a feeling, an offense against London.

Three   1970

15 As the blackness of the night recedes so does the nadir of yesterday. The child I am forgets so quickly.

Ibid.

16 I'm happy, not because I'm coming home to welcome and warmth but because I'm not. I have no home and am better off without one.

Ibid.

17 "Women are so illogical. They find their baking going wrong and blame the baking powder but they haven't read the directions. They can't see a thing objectively. They react subjectively. They don't act, they react."

Ibid.

18 "God, the illogic! The impossibility of communication in this house. The sheer operation alone of getting something through to somebody."

Ibid.

19 "Quite nice women suddenly have to wear this title with the stigma on it and a crown of thorns. We're so frightened of it that we change our nature to avoid it and in so doing we end up the classical mother-in-law we feared in the first place; so gravely have we twisted ourselves."   Ibid.

20 What can be heavier in wealth than freedom?   Ibid.

824. Simone de Beauvoir
(1908–   )

1 But between the past which no longer is and the future which is not yet, this moment when he exists is nothing.   *The Ethics of Ambiguity*, Ch. 1   1948

2 Existence asserts itself as an absolute which must seek its justification within itself and not suppress itself, even though it may be lost by preserving itself. To attain his truth, man must not attempt to dispel the ambiguity of his being but, on the contrary, accept the task of realizing it. He rejoins himself only to the extent that he agrees to remain at a distance from himself.

Ibid.

3 In the face of an obstacle which it is impossible to overcome, stubbornness is stupid.

Ibid.

4 In order for the artist to have a world to express he must first be situated in this world, oppressed or oppressing, resigned or rebellious, a man among men.

Ibid., Ch. 3

5 And, furthermore, technic itself is not objectively justified; if it sets up as absolute goals the saving of time and work which it enables us to realize and the comfort and luxury which it enables us to have access to, then it appears useless and absurd, for the time that one gains can not be accumulated in a storehouse; it is contradictory to want to save up existence, which, the fact is, exists only by being spent, and there is a good case for showing that airplanes, machines, the telephone, and the radio do not make men of today happier than those of former times. But actually it is not a question of giving men time and happiness, it is not a question of stopping the movement of life; it is a question of fulfilling it.

Ibid.

6 A man would never get the notion of writing a book on the peculiar situation of the human male.

The Second Sex   *1953*

7 For him she is sex—absolute sex, no less. She is defined and differentiated with reference to man and not he with reference to her; she is the incidental, the inessential as opposed to the essential. He is the Subject, he is the Absolute—she is the Other.

Ibid.

8 The couple is a fundamental unity with its two halves riveted together, and the cleavage of society along the line of sex is impossible.

Ibid.

9 . . . the present enshrines the past. . . .

Ibid.

10 How is it that this world has always belonged to the men . . . ?

Ibid.

11 . . . no one is more arrogant toward women, more aggressive or scornful, than the man who is anxious about his virility.

Ibid.

12 But it is doubtless impossible to approach any human problem with a mind free from bias.

Ibid.

13 . . . the only public good is that which assures the private good of the citizens. . . .

Ibid.

14 It is not clear just what the word *happy* really means and still less what true values it may mask. . . . In particular those who are condemned to stagnation are often pronounced happy on the pretext that happiness consists in being at rest.

Ibid.

15 There is no justification for present existence other than its expansion into an indefinitely open future.

Ibid.

16 Alain said that magic is spirit drooping down among things; an action is magical when, instead of being produced by an agent, it emanates from something passive.

Ibid.

17 Refusal to make herself the object is not always what turns women to homosexuality; most lesbians, on the contrary, seek to cultivate the treasures of their femininity. . . .

Ibid.

18 Between women love is contemplative. . . . There is no struggle, no victory, no defeat; in exact reciprocity each is at once subject and object, sovereign and slave; duality becomes mutuality.

Ibid.

19 Anger or revolt that does not get into the muscles remains a figment of the imagination. Ibid.

121

20 . . . humanity is something more than a mere species: it is a historical development.

Ibid.

21 Society, being codified by man, decrees that woman is inferior: she can do away with this inferiority only by destroying the male's superiority.

Ibid.

22 All oppression creates a state of war.

Ibid.

23 . . . what man and woman loathe in each other is the shattering frustration of each one's own bad faith and baseness.

Ibid.

24 What time and strength he squanders in liquidating, sublimating, transferring complexes, in talking about women, in seducing them, in fearing them! He would be liberated himself in their liberation.

Ibid.

25 Woman has to learn that exchanges—it is a fundamental law of political economy—are based on the value the merchandise offered has for the buyer, and not for the seller: she has been deceived in being persuaded that her worth is priceless.

Ibid.

26 . . . justice can never be done in the midst of injustice.

Ibid.

27 . . . the effort to inhibit all sex curiosity and pleasure in the child is quite useless; one succeeds only in creating repressions, obsessions, neuroses.

Ibid.

28 . . . those interested in perpetuating present conditions are always in tears about the marvelous past that is about to disappear, without having so much as a smile for the young future.

Ibid.

29 Let us not forget that our lack of imagination always depopulates the future; for us it is only an abstraction; each one of us secretly deplores the absence there of the one who was himself.

Ibid.

30 I fail to see . . . that liberty ever creates uniformity.
. . . It is institutions that create uniformity.

Ibid.

31 . . . when we abolish the slavery of half of humanity,
together with the whole system of hypocrisy that it implies, then the "division" of humanity will reveal its
genuine significance and the human couple will find its
true form.   *Ibid.*

32 "Ah! if only there were two of me," she thought, one
who spoke and the other who listened, one who lived
and the other who watched, how I would love myself!
I'd envy no one."
     All Men Are Mortal, Ch. 1, Prologue   *1955*

33   "Once I was able to hold my breath for sixty years.
But as soon as someone tapped me on the shoul-
der . . ."
     "Sixty years!"
     "Sixty seconds, if you like," he said. "What's the dif-
ference? There are moments when time stands still."
He looked at his hands for what seemed a long while.
"Moments when you're beyond life and yet still see.
And then time begins flowing again, your heart beats,
you stretch out your arms, you take a step forward.
You still know, but you no longer see."

Ibid.

34 This stale taste of my life will never change. Always the
same past, the same feelings, the same rational
thoughts, the same boredom. For thousands of years!
Never will I escape from myself!   *Ibid., Bk. III*

35 It was for them to decide. Why live, if living is merely
not dying? But to die in order to save one's life, is not
that the greatest dupery of all?   *Ibid., Bk. V*

36 We would walk the streets, talking about our lives and
about Life; adventure, unseen but ever-present, rubbed
shoulders with us everywhere.
     Memoirs of a Dutiful Daughter, Pt. III   *1959*

37 She was trying to get rid of a religious hangover.
                                              Ibid., Pt. IV

38 "Never talk about what you are not familiar with," said
Mlle. Houchet. But in that case you would never open
your mouth.   *Les Belles Images*, Ch. 1   *1966*

39 "There won't be a war. The gap between the capitalist
and socialist countries will soon be done away with.
Because now we're in the great twentieth-century revolution: producing is more important than possessing."

Ibid.

40 Whatever the country, capitalist or socialist, man was
everywhere crushed by technology, made a stranger to
his own work, imprisoned, forced into stupidity. The
evil all arose from the fact that he had increased his
needs rather than limited them; instead of aiming at an
abundance that did not and perhaps never would exist,
he should have confined himself to the essential mini-
mum, as certain very poor communities still do. . . .
As long as fresh needs continued to be created, so new
frustrations would come into being. When had the decline begun? The day knowledge was preferred to wisdom and mere usefulness to beauty. . . . Only a moral
revolution—not a social or a political or a technical
revolution—only a moral revolution would lead man
back to his lost truth.

Ibid., Ch. 3

41 It's frightening to think that you mark your children
merely by being yourself. . . . It seems unfair. You
can't assume the responsibility for everything you do—
or don't do.

Ibid.

42 I find it absurd to assume that all coitus is rape. By
saying that, one agrees to the masculine myth that a
man's sex is a sword, a weapon.

Quoted in "The Radicalization of
Simone de Beauvoir" by Alice
Schwarzer, *The First Ms. Reader*,
Francine Klagsbrun, ed.   *1972*

43 Abolishing capitalism will not mean abolishing the patriarchal tradition as long as the family is preserved.

Ibid.

44 Since it is the Other within us who is old, it is natural
that the revelation of our age should come to us from
outside—from others. We do not accept it willingly.

The Coming of Age, Pt. II, Ch. 5   *1972*

45 For human reality, existing means existing in time: in
the present we look towards the future by means of

124

plans that go beyond our past, in which our activities fall lifeless, frozen and loaded with passive demands. Age changes our relationship with time: as the years go by our future shortens, while our past grows heavier.

Ibid., Ch. 6

46 . . . it is old age, rather than death, that is to be contrasted with life. Old age is life's parody, whereas death transforms life into a destiny: in a way it preserves it by giving it the absolute dimension—"As into himself eternity changes him at last." Death does away with time.

Ibid., Conclusion

47 One is not born a genius, one becomes a genius.

Quoted in *The Woman's Eye*
by Anne Tucker   1973

48 I tore myself away from the safe comfort of certainties through my love for truth; and truth rewarded me.

All Said and Done   1974

49 He was not ready to receive what I had to bring.

Ibid.

50 . . . the torment that so many young women know, bound hand and foot by love and motherhood without having forgotten their former dreams.

Ibid.

825. Bette Davis
(1908–   )

1 I have always been driven by some distant music—a battle hymn no doubt—for I have been at war from the beginning. I've never looked back before. I've never had the time and it has always seemed so dangerous. To look back is to relax one's vigil.

The Lonely Life, Ch. 1   1962

2 The male ego with few exceptions is elephantine to start with.   *Ibid.*, Ch. 9

3 The sweetness of first love. It still clings like ivy to the stone walls of this institution called Bette Davis. Stonewall Davis! Alma Mater! You can't mortar bricks with treacle but I tried.   *Ibid.*

125

4 Discipline is a symbol of caring to a child. He needs guidance. If there is love, there is no such thing as being too tough with a child. A parent must also not be afraid to hang himself. If you have never been hated by your child, you have never been a parent.

Ibid., Ch. 19

5 Love is not enough. It must be the foundation, the cornerstone—but not the complete structure. It is much too pliable, too yielding.

Ibid.

6 I was always eager to salt a good stew. The trouble was that I was expected to supply the meat and potatoes as well.

Ibid., Ch. 20

7 The act of sex, gratifying as it may be, is God's joke on humanity. It is man's last desperate stand at superintendency.

Ibid.

8 The weak are the most treacherous of us all. They come to the strong and drain them. They are bottomless. They are insatiable. They are always parched and always bitter. They are everyone's concern and like vampires they suck our life's blood.

Ibid.

9 But my biggest problem all my life was men. I never met one yet who could compete with the image the public made out of Bette Davis.

Quoted in "Bette Davis,"
Conversations in the Raw
by Rex Reed   1969

10 This became a credo of mine . . . attempt the impossible in order to improve your work.

Mother Goddamn, Ch. 10   1974

* * *

11 I am a woman meant for a man, but I never found a man who could compete.

Newspaper Interview

826. Agnes De Mille
(1908–   )

1 I learned three important things in college—to use a
library, to memorize quickly and visually, to drop
asleep at any time given a horizontal surface and fifteen
minutes. What I could not learn was to think creatively
on schedule.

Dance to the Piper   1952

2 With the smell of iris and budding acacia coming
through the windows, the sound of scholasticism filling
my dreams with a reassuring hum, I sank deeper and
deeper into a kind of cerebral miasma as I postponed
all vital decisions.

Ibid.

3 There was no use in apologizing for the way I looked.
Nobody looked the way I did who expected to be seen
by anyone else.

Ibid.

4 No trumpets sound when the important decisions of
our life are made. Destiny is made known silently.

Ibid.

5 Dancing is not taught as an art in any university. There
it is still in the gymnasium.

Ibid.

6 A good education is usually harmful to a dancer. A
good calf is better than a good head.

News Item   *February 1, 1954*

7 Theater people are always pining and agonizing because they're afraid that they'll be forgotten. And in
America they're quite right. They will be.

Quoted in "The Grande Dame of
Dance" by Jane Howard, *Life*
November 15, 1963

8 The truest expression of a people is in its dances and its
music. Bodies never lie.

"Do I Hear a Waltz?," *The New York
Times Magazine*   *May 11, 1975*

827. Sheilah Graham
(1908?–   )

1 I think people still want to marry rich. Girls especially. . . . [It's] simple. Don't date poor boys. Go
where the rich are. . . . You don't have to be rich to
go where they go.

Quoted in "Sheilah Graham:
Still Upwardly, Verbally
Mobile" by Kathleen Hendrix,
Los Angeles Times   *October 13, 1974*

2 . . . you have to really drink a lot to enjoy parties.

Ibid.

3 You just never know when you're going into eternity.

Ibid.

828. Nancy Hale
(1908–   )

1 "Your father used to say, 'Never give away your work.
People don't value what they don't have to pay for.'"

"Eyes or No Eyes, or The Art of
Seeing," *The Life in the Studio*   *1957*

2 She could never get used to the idea that most people
don't use their eyes except to keep from running into
things.

Ibid.

3 After my mother's death I began to see her as she had
really been. . . . It was less like losing someone than
discovering someone.

Ibid., "A Good Light"

4 Like all real artists', her objective had been to create
riches with modest means; squandering seemed to her a
kind of stupidity. Since she never had but one standard,
perfection—which in the nature of things fits art better
than life—she often gave a misleading impression of
Yankee parsimony.

Ibid.

5 . . . this mysterious thing, artistic talent; the key to so
much freedom, the escape from so much suffering.

Mary Cassatt: A Biography of the
Great American Painter, Pt. I, Ch. 4
1975

6 . . . the cynicism of the young about society is as
nothing to the cyncism of young artists for the art establishment.

Ibid.

7 An artist's originality is balanced by a corresponding
conservatism, a superstitiousness, about it; which might
be boiled down to "What worked before will work
again."   Ibid., Pt. II, Ch. 6

8 The best work of artists in any age is the work of innocence liberated by technical knowledge. The laboratory experiments that led to the theory of pure color
equipped the impressionists to paint nature as if it had
only just been created.   Ibid., Ch. 7

9 I had wanted to say then to the young man, "Painting
one picture—even a mediocre picture—is more important than collecting a hundred." I'd wanted to say,
"You couldn't have any collections at all unless you
first had pictures."   Ibid., Epilogue

829. Amy Johnson
(1908?–1941)

1 Had I been a man I might have explored the Poles or
climbed Mount Everest, but as it was my spirit found
outlet in the air. . . .

Essay in *Myself When Young*,
Margot Asquith, ed.   *1938*

830. Madeline Mason-Manheim
(1908–   )

1 How shall you speak of parting?
How shall the bands be loosened
That Friendship fastened round you?
"Parting," St. 3, *Hill Fragments*   *1925*

I share the heart-ache of the traveler
Who would retrace his steps
And find the way he came.

Ibid., "Aspiration"

3   Know you Silence, my friend?
It is the dumbness of the tongue when the heart would
    be heard;
It is the muteness of the lips when the spirit speaks
    loudest.
It is the uttering of the unutterable.

Ibid., "Silence," St. 1

4 My heart sings while I weep.
My heart knows
That Sorrow is a trail of dreams
To farther worlds.

Ibid., "Compensation," St. 3

5 Your destiny, O River,
It is even as the destiny of man.
O, ye are brethren,
Souls unharboured,
Seeking to regain the Sea.

Ibid., "The River"

6 Sleep, companion of Silence, walks in her garden;
Walks 'midst her deathless poppies and gathers them to
    her breast.

Ibid., "Sleep"

7 They call you barren
Who, unseeing, gaze upon you.
Yet Time's most secret thoughts,
The jewels of the ages
Are buried in your breast
As in your loneliness you lie
Beneath the everlasting heights.

Ibid., "The Desert," St. 1

8 Yours the voice
Sounding ever in my ears.

Ibid., "To My Mother," St. 1

831. Alice Neel
(1908–   )

1 But we are all creatures in a way, aren't we? And both men and women are wretched.

> Quoted in "Alice Neel: Portraits of
> Four Decades" by Cindy Nemser, *Ms.*
> *October, 1973*

2 You can't leave humanity out. If you didn't have humanity, you wouldn't have anything.   Ibid.

832. Ann Ronell
(1908–   )

1 Who's afraid of the big bad wolf?

> "Who's Afraid of the Big Bad Wolf?"
> from Walt Disney's *Three Little Pigs*
> *1933*

833. Amy Vanderbilt
(1908–1974)

1 Ceremony is really a protection, too, in times of emotional involvement, particularly at death. If we have a social formula to guide us and do not have to extemporize, we feel better able to handle life. If we ignore ceremony entirely, we are not normal, warm human beings. Conversely, if we never relax it, if we "stand on ceremony" in all things, we are rigid. We must learn which ceremonies may be breached occasionally at our convenience and which ones may never be if we are to live pleasantly with our fellow man.

> *New Complete Book of Etiquette,*
> Pt. I, Introduction   *1963*

2 Good manners have much to do with the emotions. To make them ring true, one must feel them, not merely exhibit them.   Ibid., Pt. II, Introduction

3 One face to the world, another at home makes for misery.   Ibid., Pt. VI, Introduction

4 The civilian once under the mantle of officialdom, wherever it may be, is subject to the rules governing civilian behavior under official circumstances.

Ibid., Pt. VIII, Introduction

834. Yang Ping
(1908–)

1 That I should think, even now, of wanting to continue to exist only as the vessel of a chemical experimentation heartlessly, inexorably formulating itself within me! And against my will! . . . And yet I love this little life! With all the pain of it, I long for the wonderful thing to happen, for a tiny human creature to spring from between my limbs bravely out into the world. I need it, just as a true poet *needs* to create a great undying work.

"Fragment from a Lost Diary," *Fragment from a Lost Diary and Other Stories,* Naomi Katz and Nancy Milton, eds. *1973*

2 Only when the beat of life is lifted to this pitch, this fury, and this danger, only when destiny (here in my case it is but a wayward sperm carrying its implacable microscopic chromosomes, but nevertheless it is a form of destiny!) poses the choice between irreconcilable desires at a given moment, only when a human being feels the necessity of ignoring personal feeling in the decision taken—only then can one talk of a revolutionary awakening!

Ibid.

3 Women and revolution! What tragic, unsung epics of courage lie silent in the world's history!

Ibid.

835. Amalia Fleming
(1909?–)

1 So much sorrow should certainly not come to a man who has given so much of value to humanity.

Letter to Ben May (November 5, 1949), Quoted in *The Life of Sir Alexander Fleming* by André Maurois *1959*

2 Alec is very well. I think he has a good wife! . . . I
am working on a problem which fascinates me but I
keep failing to do what I try. Still there is an end even
to failures.

Ibid. (December, 1954)

3 He, too, I thought, possesses, like Pasteur, and in the
highest degree, the art of choosing the crucial experiment and of grasping the capital importance of a
chance observation. . . . But . . . for Fleming there
was a wide world lying beyond the confines of his lab.
The appearance of a new flower in his garden was as
interesting to him as the work he might be engaged
on. . . . [He] felt himself to be an infinitesimal part
of nature, and from that feeling was born his refusal to
indulge in self-importance and his dislike of big words.
It was almost possible to say that he was a genius in
spite of himself, and reluctantly.

Ibid., Ch. 16

4 I respect every ideology, including communism, provided they are not trying to impose their will through
force. I am against any totalitarian regime.

Quoted in *Newsweek*   *October 11, 1971*

5 The innocent people who have nothing to say are tortured the most because when a prisoner admits something, the torture stops.

Quoted in "Greece: Survival of the
Shrewdest" by Susan Margolis, *Ms.*
October, 1973

836. Anne Fremantle
(1909–   )

1 Among the most truly responsible for all people are
artists and revolutionaries, for they most of all are prepared to pay with their lives.

Introduction to *Woman as
Revolutionary,* Fred. C. Griffin, ed.
1973

2 The revolutionary attempts a secular denial of mortality, the artist a spiritual one.

Ibid.

837. Katharine Hepburn
(1909–   )

1 I can remember walking as a child. It was not customary to say you were fatigued. It was customary to complete the goal of the expedition.

> Quoted in "Hepburn: She Is the Best,"
> *Los Angeles Times*   *November 24, 1974*

2 It's such a cuckoo business. And it's a business you go into because you're egocentric. It's a very embarrassing profession.

> Ibid.

3 Television, which sank the picture industry, has turned the Academy Awards into a big television show. I think it should be an intimate honor.

> Ibid.

4 To keep your character intact you cannot stoop to filthy acts. It makes it easier to stoop the next time.

> Ibid.

5 Trying to be fascinating is an asinine position to be in.

> Dick Cavett Show, ABC-TV   *April 2, 1975*

6 Without discipline, there's no life at all.

> Ibid.   *April 4, 1975*

7 You never feel that you have fame. It's always in back of you.

> Ibid.

8 To be loved is very demoralizing.

> Ibid.

9 As for me, prizes mean nothing. My prize is my work.

> Quoted in *Kate* by Charles Higham   *1975*

10 I always wear slacks because of the brambles and maybe the snakes. And see this basket? I keep everything in it. So I look ghastly, do I? I don't care—so long as I'm comfortable.

> Ibid.

11 . . . plain women know more about men than beautiful ones do.

> Ibid.

838. Queen Juliana
(1909–   )

1 You people of the United States of America have the wonderfully farseeing conception of being Democracy's material and spiritual arsenal, to save the world's highest values from annihilation.

Radio Address, NBC   *April 13, 1941*

2 I want to emphasize that for a queen the task of being a mother is just as important as it is for every other Netherlands woman.

Inauguration Address, Amsterdam
September 6, 1948

3 Though previous generations were also inspired by the fervent will to improve the world, they failed because they did not call a final halt to the forces of destruction. To do this is precisely the task of the present generation. . . .

Address, University of Paris
May 25, 1950

839. Gabrielle Roy
(1909–   )

1 The city was made for couples, not for four or five silly girls with their arms interlaced, strolling up St. Catherine Street, stopping at every shop-window to admire things they would never own.

The Tin Flute, Ch. 1   *1947*

2 When there was enough money for their needs, the ties between them had been strong, but once the money was lacking, what a strain was put on their love!

Ibid., Ch. 32

3 The Christian Scientists held that it was not God Who wanted sicknesses, but man who puts himself in the way of suffering. If this were the case, though, wouldn't we all die in perfect health?

The Cashier, Ch. 3   *1955*

4 How clearly he realized that men did not like what they called love. That most embarrassing of subjects

between men they approached with half-utterances, with false carelessness, or else with a vulgar leer, never easily and comfortably.

Ibid., Ch. 8

5 Oh! The matchless release of the man asleep! Who has not realized through experience that sleep tells the truth about us? In sleep a human being is finally brought back to himself, having sloughed off everything else. Bound hand and foot, fettered with fatigue, he at last drifts toward the cavern of the unknown. Some men have returned therefrom with poems fully written, or with equations solved.

Ibid., Ch. 12

840. Eudora Welty
(1909–   )

1 He did not like illness, he distrusted it, as he distrusted the road without signposts.

"Death of a Travelling Salesman,"
*A Curtain of Green and Other
Stories   1936*

2 This time, when his heart leapt, something—his soul—seemed to leap too, like a little colt invited out of a pen.

Ibid.

3 I have been sick and I found out, only then, how lonely I am. Is it too late?

Ibid.

4 Come and stand in my heart, whoever you are, and a whole river would cover your feet and rise higher and take your knees in whirlpools, and draw you down to itself, your whole body, your heart too.

Ibid.

5 These people cherished something here that he could not see, they withheld some ancient promise of food and warmth and light. Between them they had a conspiracy.

Ibid.

6 How itensified, magnified, really vain all attempt at expression becomes in the afflicted!

Ibid., "The Key"

7 Radio, sewing machine, book ends, ironing board and that great big piano lamp—peace, that's what I like. Butterbean vines planted all along the front where the strings are.

> Ibid., "Why I Live at the P.O."

8 "No, babe, it ain't the truth. . . . Truth is something worse, I ain't said what, yet. It's something hasn't come to me, but I ain't sayin' it won't."

> Ibid., "Powerhouse"

9 His memory could work like the slinging of a noose to catch a wild pony.

> "First Love," *The Wide Net and Other Stories* 1943

10 "We're walking along in the changing-time," said Doc. "Any day now the change will come. It's going to turn from hot to cold. . . . Old Jack Frost will be pinching things up. Old Mr. Winter will be standing in the door. Hickory tree there will be yellow. Sweet-gum red, hickory yellow, dogwood red, sycamore yellow. . . . Persimmons will all git fit to eat, and the nut will be dropping like rain all through the woods here. And run, little quail, run, for we'll be after you too."

> Ibid., "The Wide Net"

11 "I rather a man be anything, than a woman be mean."

> Ibid., "Livvie"

12 She was calm the way a child is calm, with never the calmness of a spirit. But like distant lightning that silently bathes a whole shimmering sky, one awareness was always trembling about her: one day she would be free to come and go. . . .

> Ibid., "At the Landing"

13 There was a need in all dreams for something to stay far, far away, never to torment with the rest, and the bright moon now was that.

> Ibid.

14 Haven't you noticed it prevail, in the world in general? Beware of a man with manners.

> *The Golden Apples,* Ch. 1 1949

15 She yearned for her heart to twist. But it didn't, not in time.

> Ibid., Ch. 4

16 He spoke with no sign of pain. Just that edge of competition was in his voice. He was ever the most ambitious fool. To me ambition's always been a mystery. . . .

Ibid., Ch. 5

17 Attrition was their wisdom.

Ibid., Ch. 7

18 He loved being happy! He loved happiness like I love tea.

The Ponder Heart   1954

19 She was dead as a doornail. And she'd died laughing. I could have shaken her for it. She'd never laughed for Uncle Daniel before in her life. And even if she had, that's not the same thing as smiling; you may think it is, but I don't.

Ibid.

20 "Never think you've seen the last of anything. . . ."
The Optimist's Daughter, Pt. I, Ch. 1   *1969*

21 "I'm afraid my [minister] husband's running a little late. You know people like *this* don't die every day in the week. He's sitting home in his bathrobe now, tearing his hair, trying to do him justice."

Ibid., Pt. II, Ch. 2

22 All they could see was sky, water, birds, light and confluence. It was the whole morning world. And they themselves were a part of the confluence. Their own joint act of faith had brought them here at the very moment and matched its occurrence, and proceeded as it proceeded. Direction itself was made beautiful, momentous. They were riding as one with it, right up front.

Ibid., Pt. IV

841. Gale Wilhelm
(1909–   )

1 "I'm going to turn on the light and we'll be two people in a room looking at each other and wondering why on earth they were afraid of the dark."

We Too Are Drifting   1935

842. Bertha Adams Backus
(fl. 1910s)

1 Build for yourself a strong-box,
   Fashion each part with care;
  When it's strong as your hand can make it,
   Put all your troubles there.
                          "Then Laugh," St. 1   *1911*

843. Janet Begbie
(fl. 1910s)

* * *

1 Carry on, carry on, for the men and boys are gone,
   But the furrow shan't lie fallow while the women carry
   on.
                                        "Carry On"

844. Esther Lilian Duff
(fl. 1910s)

1 Some of the roofs are plum-color,
  Some of the roofs are gray,
  Some of the roofs are silverstone,
  And some are made of clay;
  But under every gabled close
  There's a secret hid away.
     "Not Three, But One," *Bohemian Glass*   *1916*

845. Hsiang Chin-yu
(fl. 1910s–1927)

1 . . . the emancipation of women can only come with a
change in the social structure which frees men and
women alike.

              Quoted in *Women in Modern China*
              by Helen Foster Snow   *1967p*

846. Annie Kenney
(fl. 1910s)

1 I was once told that the lesson I had to learn in life was patience. If that is true, I can only say I began life very badly indeed!

Memoirs of a Militant 1924

2 . . . Paradise would be there once the vote was won! I honestly believed every word I said. I had yet to learn that Nature's works are very slow but very sure. Experience is indeed the best though the sternest teacher.

Ibid.

3 Prison. It was not prison for me. Hunger-strikes. They had no fears for me. Cat and Mouse Act. I could have laughed. A prison cell was quiet—no telephone, no paper, no speeches, no sea sickness, no sleepless nights. I could lie on my plank bed all day and all night and return once more to my day dreams.

Ibid.

847. Myrtie Lillian Barker
(1910–   )

1 The idea of strictly minding our own business is moldy rubbish. Who could be so selfish?

I Am Only One 1963

848. Mary Ingraham Bunting
(1910–   )

1 When her last child is off to school, we don't want the talented woman wasting her time in work far below her capacity. We want her to come out running.

Quoted in *Life* *January 13, 1961*

849. Hilda Conkling
(1910–   )

* * *

1 Poems come like boats
  With sails for wings;
  Crossing the sky swiftly
  They slip under tall bridges
  Of cloud.

"Poems"

2 The hills are going somewhere;
  They have been on the way a long time.
  They are like camels in a line
  But they move more slowly.

"Hills"

3 The world turns softly
  Not to spill its lakes and rivers.

"Water"

850. Margaret Halsey
(1910–   )

1 . . . she blushed like a well-trained sunrise.
  With Malice Toward Some   1938

2 These people . . . talk simply because they think
  sound is more manageable than silence.

Ibid.

3 The boneless quality of English conversation, . . . so
  far as I have heard it, is all form and no content. Listening to Britons dining out is like watching people
  play first-class tennis with imaginary balls.

Ibid.

4 . . . it takes a great deal to produce ennui in an En-
  glishman and if you do, he only takes it as convincing
  proof that you are well-bred.

Ibid.

5 The attitude of the English . . . toward English history reminds one a good deal of the attitude of a Hollywood director toward love.   Ibid.

141

6 Living in England, provincial England, must be like being married to a stupid but exquisitely beautiful wife.

Ibid.

7 American interiors tend to have no happy medium between execrable taste and what is called "good taste" and is worn like a wart.

Ibid.

8 Humility is not my forte, and whenever I dwell for any length of time on my own shortcomings, they gradually begin to seem mild, harmless, rather engaging little things, not at all like the staring defects in other people's characters.

Ibid.

9 Such leaping to foot, such opening of doors, such lightning flourishes with matches and cigarettes—it is all so heroic, I never quite get over the feeling that someone has just said, "To the lifeboats!"

Ibid.

10 . . . the English think of an opinion as something which a decent person, if he has the misfortune to have one, does all he can to hide.

Ibid.

11 All of Stratford, in fact, suggests powdered history— add hot water and stir and you have a delicious, nourishing Shakespeare.

Ibid.

12 . . . in England, having had money . . . is just as acceptable as having it, since the upperclass mannerisms persist, even after the bankroll has disappeared. But never having had money is unforgivable, and can only be atoned for by never trying to get any.

Ibid.

13 Father is also, in our country, The Boy We Left Behind Us.

The Folks at Home　1952

14 The whole flavor and quality of the American representative government turns to ashes on the tongue, if one regards the government as simply an inferior and rather second-rate sort of corporation.

Ibid.

15 . . . there is not enough loving-kindness afloat in the continental United States to see a crippled old lady across an Indian trail.

Ibid.

16 What I know about money, I learned the hard way—by having had it.

Ibid.

17 The role of a do-gooder is not what actors call a fat part.

Ibid.

851. Jacquetta Hawkes
(1910–   )

1 . . . we do in fact maintain our fragile lives on a wafer balanced between a hellish morass and unlimited space.

A Land   1952

2 The young are now kinder than they were and are more tender towards old age, more aware perhaps with the growth of self-consciousness that it will come also to them.

Ibid.

3 We live in a world made seemingly secure by the four walls of our houses, the artificiality of our cities, and by the four walls of habit. Volcanoes speak of insecurity, of our participation in process. They are openings not any longer into a properly appointed hell, but into an equally alarming abysm of thought.

Ibid.

4 . . . the universe is substantially homogeneous, and shooting stars are chips from globes very much like our own. They are, as the label in the Geological Museum soberly states, "fragments of former worlds."

Ibid.

852. Mary Keyserling
(1910–   )

1 Occupationally women are relatively more disadvantaged today than they were twenty-five years ago. . . .

This deterioration has occurred despite the increase in women's share of total employment over the same period and the rising number of women who enroll in and graduate from institutions of higher education.

Windows on Day Care 1972

2 There shouldn't be a single little child in America left alone to fend for himself.

Ibid., Ch. 2

3 Our ultimate goal as a nation should be to make available comprehensive, developmental child-care services to all families that wish to use them.

Ibid., Ch. 9

853. Alicia Markova
(1910–)

1 . . . glorious bouquets and storms of applause. . . . These are the trimmings which every artist naturally enjoys. But to *move* an audience in such a role, to hear in the applause that unmistakable note which breaks through good theatre manners and comes from the heart, is to feel that you have won through to life itself. Such pleasure does not vanish with the fall of the curtain, but becomes part of one's own life.

Giselle and I, Ch. 18 1960

854. Mother Teresa
(1910–)

1 . . . the poor are our brothers and sisters. . . . [They are the] people in the world who need love, who need care, who have to be wanted.

Quoted in "Saints Among Us," *Time*
December 29, 1975

2 Our work brings people face to face with love.

Ibid.

3 Loneliness and the feeling of being unwanted is the most terrible poverty.

Ibid.

4 Our intellect and other gifts have been given to be used for God's greater glory, but sometimes they become the

very god for us. That is the saddest part: we are losing our balance when this happens. We must free ourselves to be filled by God. Even God cannot fill what is full.

Ibid.

5 To keep a lamp burning we have to keep putting oil in it.

Ibid.

855. Simone Weil
(1910–1943)

1 Just as a person who is always asserting that he is too good-natured is the very one from whom to expect, on some occasion, the coldest and most unconcerned cruelty, so when any group sees itself as the bearer of civilization this very belief will betray it into behaving barbarously at the first opportunity.

"Hitler and Roman Foreign Policy,"
Nouveaux Cahiers   *January 1, 1940*

2 I would suggest that barbarism be considered as a permanent and universal human characteristic which becomes more or less pronounced according to the play of circumstances.

Ibid.

3 There is something else which has the power to awaken us to the truth. It is the works of writers of genius. . . . They give us, in the guise of fiction, something equivalent to the actual density of the real, that density which life offers us every day but which we are unable to grasp because we are amusing ourselves with lies.

"Morality and Literature,"
Cahiers du Sud   *January, 1944p*

4 If I ever was afraid, it was then. I can still feel the way it was in the metal shop, the presses, the ten-hour-day, and the brutal foremen, and the missing fingers, and the heat, and the headaches, and. . . .

La Condition Ouvrière   *1951p*

5 Obvious and inexorable oppression that cannot be overcome does not give rise to revolt but to submission.

Ibid.

6 You take the risk of becoming the arbiter of another human existence. My conclusion (which I offer only as

145

a suggestion) is not that it is necessary to flee from love, but that one should not go looking for it, especially not when one is very young.

Ibid., Letter to a Girl Student

7 The human soul never ceases to be modified by its encounter with might, swept on, blinded by that which it believes itself able to handle, bowed beneath the power of that which it suffers. . . . Might is that which makes a thing of anybody who comes under its sway.

La Source Grecque   1952p

8 The vocation of each of the peoples of antiquity: a view of divine things (all but the Romans). Israel: God in one person. India: assimilation of the soul with God in mystical union. China: God's own method of operation, fullness of action which seems inaction, fullness of presence which seems absence, emptiness and silence. Egypt: immortality, salvation of the virtuous soul after death by assimilation with a suffering God, dead and resurrected, Charity toward one's neighbour. Greece (which greatly felt the influence of Egypt): the wretchedness of man, the distance and transcendence of God.

Ibid.

9 A right is not effectual by itself, but only in relation to the obligation to which it corresponds. . . . An obligation which goes unrecognized by anybody loses none of the full force of its existence. A right which goes unrecognized by anybody is not worth very much.

"L'Enracinement," Pt. I (1949),
The Need for Roots   1952p

10 One of the indispensable foods of the human soul is liberty. Liberty, taking the word in its concrete sense, consists in the ability to choose.

Ibid.

11 Punishment must be an honour. It must not only wipe out the stigma of the crime, but must be regarded as a supplementary form of education, compelling a higher devotion to the public good. The severity of the punishment must also be in keeping with the kind of obligation which has been violated, and not with the interests of public security.

Ibid.

12 Money destroys human roots wherever it is able to penetrate, by turning desire for gain into the sole motive. It easily manages to outweigh all other motives, because the effort it demands of the mind is so very much less. Nothing is *so* clear *and so* simple as a row of figures.

Ibid., Pt. II

13 Propaganda is not directed towards creating an inspiration: it closes, seals up all the openings through which an inspiration might pass; it fills the whole spirit with fanaticism.

Ibid., Pt. III

14 Evil becomes an operative motive far more easily than good; but once pure good has become an operative motive in the mind, it forms there the fount of a uniform and inexhaustible impulsion, which is never so in the case of evil.

Ibid.

15 Death and labour are things of necessity and not of choice.

Ibid.

16 The idea of a snare set for man by God is also the meaning of the myth of the labyrinth . . . that path where man, from the moment he enters upon it, loses his way and finds himself equally powerless, at the end of a certain time, to return upon his steps or to direct himself anywhere. He errs without knowing where, and finally arrives at the place where God waits to devour him.

Intimations of Christianity,
Elisabeth Chase Geissbuhler, ed.
1957p

17 If we want to traverse this somber age in manly fashion, we shall refrain, like the Ajax of Sophocles, from letting empty hopes set us afire.

"Revolution Proletarienne"
(August 25, 1933), *Oppression and Liberty*   *1957p*

18 But not even Marx is more precious to us than the truth.

Ibid.

19 War, which perpetuates itself under the form of preparation for war, has once and for all given the State an important role in production.

Ibid.

20 Technical progress seems to have gone bankrupt, since instead of happiness it has only brought the masses that physical and moral wretchedness in which we see them floundering. . . .

Ibid., "Reflections Concerning the
Causes of Liberty and Social
Oppression" (1934)

21 The word "revolution" is a word for which you kill, for which you die, for which you send the labouring masses to their death, but which does not possess any content.

Ibid.

22 . . . the time has come to give up dreaming of liberty, and to make up one's mind to conceive it.

Ibid.

23 . . . man alone can enslave man.

Ibid.

24 The inversion of the relation between means and end—an inversion which is to a certain extent the law of every oppressive society—here becomes total or nearly so, and extends to nearly everything. The scientist does not use science in order to manage to see more clearly into his own thinking, but aims at discovering results that will go to swell the present volume of scientific knowledge. Machines do not run in order to enable men to live, but we resign ourselves to feeding men in order that they may serve the machines. Money does not provide a convenient method for exchanging products; it is the sale of goods which is a means for keeping money in circulation. Lastly, organization is not a means for exercising a collective activity, but the activity of a group, whatever it may be, is a means for strengthening organization.

Ibid.

25 The majority of human beings do not question the truth of an idea without which they would literally be unable to live.

Ibid., "Is There a Marxist Doctrine?" (1943)

26 He [Marx] labelled this dream "dialectical materialism." This was sufficient to shroud it in mystery. These
two words are of an almost impenetrable emptiness. A
very amusing game—though rather a cruel one—is to
ask a Marxist what they mean.

Ibid.

27 The payment of debts is necessary for social order. The
non-payment is quite equally necessary for social order.
For centuries humanity has oscillated, serenely unaware, between these two contradictory necessities.

"On Bankruptcy" (1937), *Selected
Essays: 1934–1953*   *1962p*

28 Imagination is always the fabric of social life and the
dynamic of history. The influence of real needs and
compulsions, of real interests and materials, is indirect
because the crowd is never conscious of it.

Ibid., "A Note on Social Democracy" (1937)

29 . . . when a man's life is destroyed or damaged by
some wound or privation of soul or body, which is due
to other men's actions or negligence, it is not only his
sensibility that suffers but also his aspiration toward the
good. Therefore there has been sacrilege towards that
which is sacred in him.

Ibid., "Draft for a Statement of
Human Obligation" (1943)

30 The needs of a human being are sacred. Their satisfaction cannot be subordinated either to reasons of state,
or to any consideration of money, nationality, race, or
colour, or to the moral or other value attributed to the
human being in question, or to any consideration whatsoever.

Ibid.

31 At the bottom of the heart of every human being from
earliest infancy until the tomb, there is something that
goes on indomitably expecting, in the teeth of all experience of crimes committed, suffered, and witnessed,
that good and not evil will be done to him. It is this
above all that is sacred in every human being.

Ibid., "Human Personality" (1943)

32 To us, men of the West, a very strange thing happened
at the turn of the century; without noticing it, we lost
science, or at least the thing that had been called by

that name for the last four centuries. What we now have in place of it is something different, radically different, and we don't know what it is. Nobody knows what it is.

> "Classical Science and After"
> (1941), *On Science, Necessity,
> and the Love of God,* Richard
> Rees, ed.   *1968p*

33 The future is made of the same stuff as the present.

> Ibid., "Some Thoughts on the
> Love of God" (October, 1940–
> May, 1942)

34 . . . if we are suffering illness, poverty, or misfortune, we think we shall be satisfied on the day it ceases. But there too, we know it is false; so soon as one has got used to not suffering one wants something else.

> Ibid.

35 Evil is neither suffering nor sin; it is both at the same time, it is something common to them both. For they are linked together; sin makes us suffer and suffering makes us evil, and this indissoluble complex of suffering and sin is the evil in which we are submerged against our will, and to our horror.

> Ibid.

36 How could we search for God, since He is above, in a dimension not open to us? . . . We must only wait and call out.

> Ibid., "Some Reflections on the Love
> of God" (October 1940–May, 1942)

37 Physical love and labour.
labour: to feel with one's whole self the existence of the world
love: to feel with one's whole self the existence of another being?

> "The Pre-War Notebook," *First and
> Last Notebooks,* Richard Rees, ed.
> *1970p*

38 Life does not need to mutilate itself in order to be pure.

> Ibid.

39 Lesson of the work of art: it is forbidden to touch things of beauty. The artist's inspiration is always *Platonic.* Thus art is the symbol of the two noblest human

150

efforts: to construct (work), and to refrain from destruction (love overcome). For all love is naturally sadistic; and modesty, respect, reserve, are the mark of the human. Not to seize possession of what one loves . . . not to change it in any way . . . refuse power. . . .

Ibid.

40 Learn to reject friendship, or rather the dream of friendship. To want friendship is a great fault. Friendship ought to be a gratuitous joy, like the joys afforded by art, or life (like aesthetic joys). I must refuse it in order to be worthy to receive it. . . .

Ibid.

41 Evil being the root of mystery, pain is the root of knowledge.

Ibid., "The New York Notebook" (1942)

42 To get power over is to defile. To possess is to defile.

Ibid.

43 Charity. To love human beings in so far as they are nothing. That is to love them as God does.

Ibid.

44 Nothing can have as its destination anything other than its origin. The contrary idea, the idea of progress, is poison.

Ibid.

45 Truth is not discovered by proofs but by exploration. It is always experimental. But necessity also is an object of exploration.

Ibid.

46 Joy fixes us to eternity and pain fixes us to time. But desire and fear hold us in bondage to time, and detachment breaks the bond.

Ibid.

47 The proper method of philosophy consists in clearly conceiving the insoluble problems in all their insolubility and then in simply contemplating them, fixedly and tirelessly, year after year, without any hope, patiently waiting.

Ibid., "London Notebook" (1943)

48 There is very profound truth in the Greek sophisms proving that it is impossible to learn. We understand little and badly. We need to be taught by those who

understand more and better than ourselves. For example, by Christ. But since we do not understand anything, we do not understand them either. How could we know that they are right? How could we pay them the proper amount of attention, to begin with, which is necessary before they can begin to teach us? That is why miracles are needed.

Ibid.

49 Why is it that reality, when set down untransposed in a book, sounds false?

Ibid.

856. Virginia Mae Axline
(1911–   )

1 Out again into the night where the dulled light obscures the decisive lines of reality and casts over the immediate world a kindly vagueness. . . . The darkened sky gives growing room for softened judgments, for suspended indictments, for emotional hospitality. What *is*, seen in such light, seems to have so many possibilities that definitiveness becomes ambiguous.

Dibs: In Search of Self, Ch. 2   1965

2 "So much to say. And so much not to say! Some things are better left unsaid. But so many unsaid things can become a burden."

Ibid., Ch. 8

3 Asking questions in therapy would be so helpful if anyone ever answered them accurately. But no one ever does.

Ibid., Ch. 12

857. Lucille Ball
(1911–   )

1 Luck? I don't know anything about luck. I've never banked on it, and I'm afraid of people who do. Luck to me is something else: hard work—and realizing what is opportunity and what isn't.

Quoted in *The Real Story of Lucille Ball*, by Eleanor Harris, Ch. 1   1954

2 I think knowing what you can *not* do is more important than knowing what you can do. In fact, that's good
taste.

Ibid., Ch. 7

858. Elizabeth Bishop
(1911–   )

1 It is like what we imagine knowledge to be:
dark, salt, clear, moving, utterly free,
drawn from the cold hard mouth
of the world, derived from the rocky breast
forever, flowing and drawn, and since
our knowledge is historical, flowing, and flow.
"At the Fishhouses," *A Cold Spring*   1955

2 The Seven Wonders of the World are tired
and a touch familiar, but the other scenes,
innumerable, though equally sad and still, are foreign.
Ibid., "Over 2000 Illustrations
and a Complete Concordance"

3 Icebergs behoove the soul
(Both being self-made from elements least visible)
to see themselves: fleshed, fair, erected indivisible.
"The Imaginary Iceberg," *North
and South*   1955

4 Time is an *Etoile*; the hours diverge
so much that days are journeys round the suburbs,
circles surrounding stars, overlapping circles.
Ibid., "Paris, 7 A.M."

5 We stand as still as stones to watch
    the leaves and ripples
while light and nervous water hold
    their interview.

Ibid., "Quai d'Orleans"

6 Brazilians are very quick, both emotionally and physically. Like the heroes of Homer, men can show their
emotions without disgrace.

Brazil, Ch. 1   1962

7 The masses of poor people in the big cities, and the
poor and not-so-poor of the "backlands," love their
children and kill them with kindness by the thousands.

153

The wrong foods, spoiled foods, warm medicines, sleeping syrups—all exact a terrible toll. . . .

Ibid.

8 Democracy in the contemporary world demands, among other things, an educated and informed people. Up until now, Brazil has not had one. Illiteracy, slow communication, and a consequent lack of awareness among the people have made it possible for determined groups of men to control the affairs of the country without the general consent—even the knowledge—of the Brazilian people as a whole.

Ibid., Ch. 9

859. Hortense Calisher
(1911–   )

1 A happy childhood can't be cured. Mine'll hang around my neck like a rainbow, that's all, instead of a noose.
Queenie, Pt. I   1971

2 Every sixteen-year-old is a pornographer, Miss Piranesi. We had to know what was open to us.

Ibid.

3 On dirt—as Mrs. O. bitchily points out—there are still divisions among us between the ones who wash under their armpits and in all the private places presumably, no matter how fiercely street-stained their feet are— "and the ones who stink all through for the sake of whatever revolution is for today." Like any stool pigeon, she's half right.

Ibid.

4 But now, even to be anything anti-anti, you still have to do it with the body; anything purely mental is insincere. And I agree, oh, I agree—but why can I only do it mentally?

Ibid.

5 . . . the circulation of money is different from the circulation of the blood. Some eras obscure that; now it was nakedly appearing. I began to understand why the banker had jumped. A circulatory failure.

Herself, Pt. I   1972

6 An *oeuvre* is a body of work which, like a true body, interacts with itself, and with its own growth. We here in America are not allowed the sweet sense of growing them while in life; even after death, the obituary quickly picks over the works for "what will last." Yet if a writer's work has a shape to it—and most have a repetition like a heartbeat—the *oeuvre* will begin to construct him.

Ibid., Pt. II

7 She [Colette] is no more essentially feminine as a writer than any man is essentially masculine as a writer—certain notable attempts at the latter notwithstanding. She uses the psychological and concrete dossier in her possession as a woman, not only without embarrassment but with the most natural sense of its value, and without any confusion as to whether the sexual balance of her sensitivity need affect the virility of her expression when she wants virility there. Reading her, one is reminded that art—whether managed as a small report on a wide canvas, or vice versa—is a narrow thing in more senses than one, and that the woman writer, like any other, does her best to accept her part in the human condition, and go on from there.

Ibid.

8 Every art is a church without communicants, presided over by a parish of the respectable. An artist is born kneeling; he fights to stand. A critic, by nature of the judgment seat, is born sitting.

Ibid., Pt. IV

9 When anything gets freed, a zest goes round the world. What is most evident is that the old dictionary distinction between "license" and "freedom" doesn't do any more. As the Jew had come to know—and the blacks and the queers are now showing us, inside literature and out—"Freedom" is what you are given—and its iron hand often remains on your shoulder. "License" is what you *take*.

Ibid.

10 When you come to the end of the past—no more peroration. Tolerate life—a poem which annoys when it falls into grandeur. The past will come round again.

Ibid., Pt. V

860. Leah Goldberg
(1911–1970)

1 There is a law of life in her hands milking,
For quiet seamen hold a rope like her.
> "Of Bloom," Pt. II, St. 2
> *Poems from the Hebrew,*
> Robert Mezey, ed.   *1973p*

2 Land of low clouds, I belong to you.
I carry in my heart your every drop of rain.
> Ibid., "Song of the Strange Woman,"
> Pt. III, St. 1

861. Mahalia Jackson
(1911–1972)

1 It's easy to be independent when you've got money.
But to be independent when you haven't got a thing—
that's the Lord's test.
> *Movin' On Up,* with Evan McLoud
> Wylie, Ch. 1   *1966*

2 Gospel music in those days of the early 1930s was
really taking wing. It was the kind of music colored
people had left behind them down south and they liked
it because it was just like a letter from home.
> Ibid., Ch. 5

3 Blues are the songs of despair, but gospel songs are the
songs of hope.
> Ibid., Ch. 6

4 Someday the sun is going to shine down on me in some
faraway place.
> Quoted in "Unforgettable Mahalia
> Jackson" by Mildred Falls, *Reader's
> Digest   March, 1973p*

5 The grass is still green. The lawns are as neat as ever.
The same birds are still in the trees. I guess it didn't
occur to them to leave just because we moved in.
> Ibid.

862. Ruth McKenney
(1911–   )

1 If modern civilization had any meaning it was displayed in the fight against Fascism.

> Letter to George Seldes, *The Great Quotations*, George Seldes, ed.   *1960*

2 Man has no nobler function than to defend the truth.

> Ibid.

863. Josephine Miles
(1911–   )

1 All our footsteps, set to make
Metric advance,
Lapse into arcs in deference
To circumstance.

> "On Inhabiting an Orange," St. 2,
> *Poems, 1930–1960*   *1960*

2 This weight of knowledge dark on the brain is never
To be burnt out like fever,

But slowly, with speech to tell the way and ease it,
Will sink into the blood, and warm, and slowly
Move in the veins, and murmur, and come at length
To the tongue's tip and the finger's tip most lowly
And will belong to the body wholly.

> Ibid., "Physiologus," Sts. 2–3

3 Where is the world? not about.
The world is in the heart
And the heart is clogged in the sea lanes out of port.

> Ibid., "Merchant Marine," St. 1

4 I chewed on a straw hoping it would get sweeter.
It got drier and drier
And gradually caught on fire.   Ibid., "Loser," St. 2

5 How conduct in its pride
Maintains a place and sits
At the head of the table at the head of the hall
At the head of the hosts and guests.

> Ibid., "Conduct," St. 1

6 My pride should affect your escape,
It carries every key.
It's own trusty, and a good chiseling trusty,
It can at its own price set everybody free.
Ibid., "Pride," St. 1

7 Little things make Germany a lovely place. . . .
"Germany," House and Home   1961

8 Accustomed as we are to change, or unaccustomed, we
think of a change of heart, of clothes, of life, with some
uncertainty. We put off the old, put on the new, yet say
that the more it changes the more it remains the same.
Every age is an age of transition.
Poetry and Change, Introduction   1974

9 True, translation may use the value terms of its own
tongue in its own time; but it cannot force these on a
truly alien text.
Ibid., Ch. 12

864. Anna Russell
(1911–   )

1 The reason that there are so few women comics is that
so few women can bear being laughed at.
Quoted in the Sunday Times
(London)   August 25, 1957

865. Rosalind Russell
(1911–1976)

1 . . . taste. You cannot buy such a rare and wonderful
thing. You can't send away for it in a catalogue. And
I'm afraid it's becoming obsolete.
Quoted in "Rosalind Russell: Screen's
Career Career Girl," Los Angeles
Times   March 31, 1974

2 The sex symbol always remains, but the sophisticated
woman has become old hat.
Ibid.

3 Sex for sex's sake on the screen seems childish to me,
but it's violence that really bothers me. I think it's de-

grading. It breeds something cancerous in our young people. We have a great responsibility to the future in what were're communicating.

Ibid.

866. Viola Spolin
(1911?–   )

1 We learn through experience and experiencing, and no one teaches anyone anything. This is as true for the infant moving from kicking to crawling to walking as it is for the scientist with his equations. If the environment permits it, anyone can learn whatever he chooses to learn; and if the individual permits it, the environment will teach him everything it has to teach.
   Improvisation for the Theater, Ch. 1   *1963*

2 In a culture where approval/disapproval has become the predominant regulator of effort and position, and often the substitute for love, our personal freedoms are dissipated.

Ibid.

3 It stands to reason that if we direct all our efforts towards reaching a goal, we stand in grave danger of losing everything on which we have based our daily activities. For when a goal is superimposed on an activity instead of evolving out of it, we often feel cheated when we reach it.

Ibid.

4 The audience is the most revered member of the theater. Without an audience there is no theater. . . . They are our guests, our evaluators, and the last spoke in the wheel which can then begin to roll. They make the performance meaningful.

Ibid.

5 It is the avant-garde teachers who . . . have come to realize that body release, not body control, is what is needed for natural grace to emerge, as opposed to artificial movement.

Ibid., Ch. 5

6 There are few places outside of his own play where a child can contribute to the world in which he finds himself. His world: dominated by adults who tell him

what to do and when to do it—benevolent tyrants who dispense gifts to their "good" subjects and punishment to their "bad" ones, who are amused at the "cleverness" of children and annoyed by their "stupidities."

Ibid., Ch. 13

7 Through spontaneity we are reformed into ourselves. Freed from handed-down frames of reference, spontaneity becomes the moment of personal freedom when we are faced with a reality, explore it, and act accordingly. It is the time of discovery, of experiencing, of creative expression.

Quoted in "Spolin Game Plan for
Improvisational Theater" by Barry
Hyams, Los Angeles Times   May 26, 1974

8 First teach a person to develop to the point of his limitations and then—pfft!—break the limitation.

Ibid.

9 One must be chary of words because they turn into cages.

Ibid.

10 The physical is the known; through it we may find our way to the unknown, the intuitive, and perhaps beyond that to man's spirit itself.

Ibid.

867. Madeleine Bingham
(1912–   )

1 In every country the organization of society is like a section of a rock face, with new layers and old layers built one upon the other. The decay of old ways of behaving and old laws does not take place within a few years; it is a gradual process of erosion.

Scotland Under Mary Stuart, Ch. 2   1971

2 Once the fervour has gone out of it, a revolution can turn out to be dull work for the ordinary people.

Ibid., Ch. 7

3 A country which is engaged in constant war, both internal and external, does not provide good ground in which the arts may flourish.

Ibid., Ch. 12

* * *

4 Too many cooks may spoil the broth, but it only takes one to burn it. *The Bad Cook's Guide*

5 There may be as many good fish in the sea as ever came out of it, but cooking them is even more difficult than catching them. *Ibid.*

868. Julia Child
(1912–   )

1 Sometimes . . . it takes me an entire day to write a recipe, to communicate it correctly. It's really like writing a little short story. . . .

Quoted in "The Making of a
Masterpiece" by Patricia Simon,
McCall's   October, 1970

2 Learn how to cook! That's the way to save money. You don't save it buying hamburger helpers, and prepared foods; you save it buying fresh foods in season or in large supply, when they are cheapest and usually best, and you prepare them from scratch at home. Why pay for someone else's work, when if you know how to do it, you can save all that money for yourself?

Julia Child's Kitchen, Introduction   *1975*

869. Lucille Fletcher
(1912–   )

1 Such amazing things happened to the female sex on an ocean cruise. The sea air acted like an aphrodisiac. Or maybe it was the motion. Or the carnival atmosphere. Whatever it was, and he had never seen it otherwise, the ladies, married or single, young or old, simply went to pieces aboard the *S.S. Columbia.* They toppled like tenpins—into bed.

The Girl in Cabin B54, Ch. 2   *1968*

2 "The brain, of course, is still an unknown country in many respects—like outer space. And as a psychologist, I myself can believe that certain people, extraordinarily sensitive people, may possess special mental equipment which can tune in, as it were, certain waves, vibrations, even imagery, which other people cannot sense at all." *Ibid.,* Ch. 8

870. Virginia Graham
(1912–   )

1 It will be the firm intention of your hosts to take you, as soon as possible, *away* from their homes. Remember, they do not know what on earth to do with you and have been arguing about it for weeks, so do not be difficult and announce that all you want to do is sit still and look at the view. They are irrevocably determined you should be entertained, and it is a matter of little importance whether you wish to be or whether you don't.

Say Please, Ch. 1   *1949*

2 As hunting takes place in the open air and is ever so English and ever so traditional, the word bitch can be frequently employed without offence, and indeed it is a rare pleasure for a lady to be able to look fearlessly into the eyes of another lady, even though she be on four legs, and say loudly and clearly, "Bitch!"

Ibid., Ch. 3

3 Good shot, bad luck and hell are the five basic words to be used in a game of tennis, though these, of course, can be slightly amplified.

Ibid., Ch. 8

4 Words, like fashions, disappear and recur throughout English history, and one generation's phraseology, while it may seem abominably second-rate to the next, becomes first rate to the third. . . .

Ibid., Ch. 14

5 In society it is etiquette for ladies to have the best chairs and get handed things. In the home the reverse is the case. That is why ladies are more sociable than gentlemen.

Ibid.

6 Be blind. Be stupid. Be British. Be careful.

Ibid., Ch. 25

871. Lady Bird Johnson
(1912–   )

1 Lyndon [Johnson] acts like there was never going to be a tomorrow.

Quoted in The New York Times
Magazine   November 29, 1964

2 It all began so beautifully. After a drizzle in the morning, the sun came out bright and clear. We were driving into Dallas. In the lead car were President and Mrs. Kennedy. . . .

A White House Diary
(November 22, 1963)   1970

3 As I record this several days later, I must say that being with President Truman those days has been one of the biggest pluses of this period of my life. It has been an insight into history for me, a joy to see a man who has lived through so much public rancor and condemnation and has emerged philosophic, salty, completely unembittered, a happy man—and vindicated by history on most of his major decisions.

Ibid. (March 12, 1964)

4 It's odd that you can get so anesthetized by your own pain or your own problem that you don't quite fully share the hell of someone close to you.

Ibid., (February 8, 1965)

5 This was one of those terrific, pummeling White House days that can stretch and grind and use you—even I, who only live on the periphery. So what must it be like for Lyndon!   Ibid. (March 14, 1968)

872. Dena Justin
(1912–   )

1 The earth as Mother, the womb from which all living things are born and to which all return at death, was perhaps the earliest representation of the divine in protohistoric religions.

"From Mother Goddess to Dishwasher,"
Natural History   February, 1973

2 It is remarkable how many legends survive among pre-
literate cultures of an earlier matriarchal period and a
violent uprising by men in which they usurped female
authority.

Ibid.

3 Mythologically speaking, the ancients scooped our
modern-day biologists by unknown thousands of years
in their recognition of the female principle as the primal creative force. And they too buried the truth, re-
structuring the myths to accommodate male ideology.

Ibid.

4 Although the witch, incarnate or in surrogate mother
disguise, remains a universal bogey, pejorative aspects
of the wizard, her masculine counterpart, have van-
ished over the patriarchal centuries. The term *wizard*
has acquired reverential status—wizard of finance, wizard of diplomacy, wizard of science.

Ibid.

873. Mary Lavin
(1912–   )

1 Her theme was happiness: what it was, what it was
not; where we might find it, where not; and how, if
found, it must be guarded. Never must we confound it
with pleasure. Nor think sorrow its exact opposite.

"Happiness," The New Yorker
December 14, 1968

2 "Take my own father! You know what he said in his
last moments? On his deathbed, he defied me to name
a man who had enjoyed a better life. In spite of the
dreadful pain, his face *radiated* happiness!" said
Mother, nodding her head comfortably. "Happiness
drives out pain, as fire burns out fire."

Ibid.

3 Our father, while he lived, had cast a magic over everything, for us as well as for her. He held his love up over
us like an umbrella and kept off the troubles that afterward came down on us, pouring cats and dogs!

Ibid.

4 "Life is a vale of tears," they said. "You are privileged
to find it out so young!" Ugh! After I staggered onto

my feet and began to take hold of life once more, they fell back defeated. And the first day I gave a laugh—pouf, they were blown out like candles. They weren't living in a real world at all; they belonged to a ghostly world where life was easy: all one had to do was sit and weep. It takes effort to push back the stone from the mouth of the tomb.   Ibid.

5 . . . a new noise started in her head; the noise of a nameless panic that did not always roar, but never altogether died down.

"Via Violetta," *A Memory and Other Stories*   1972

874. Mary McCarthy
(1912–   )

1 The American, if he has a spark of national feeling, will be humiliated by the very prospect of a foreigner's visit to Congress—these, for the most part, illiterate hacks whose fancy vests are spotted with gravy, and whose speeches, hypocritical, unctuous, and slovenly, are spotted also with the gravy of political patronage, these persons are a reflection on the democratic process rather than of it; they expose it in its underwear.

"America the Beautiful,"
Commentary   September, 1947

2 . . . freedom to criticize is held to compensate for the freedom to err—this is the American system. . . . One is assured, gently, that one has the freedom to criticize, as though this freedom, *in itself,* as it attaches to a single individual, counterbalanced the unjust law on the books. This sacred right of criticism is always invoked whenever abuses are mentioned, just as the free circulation of ideas and works of art is offered as evidence of basic cultural freedom.

"No News, or What Killed the Dog." *The Reporter*   July, 1952

3 Liberty, as it is conceived by current opinion, has nothing inherent about it; it is a sort of gift or trust bestowed on the individual by the state pending *good behavior.*

Speech, "The Contagion of Ideas"
Summer, 1952

4 . . . Elinor was always firmly convinced of other people's hypocrisy since she could not believe that they
noticed less than she did.

The Group, Ch. 1   1954

5 "You mustn't force sex to do the work of love or love
to do the work of sex."

Ibid., Ch. 2

6 Despite the fact that she had had no sexual experience,
she had a very clear idea of the male member, and she
could not help forming a picture of Put's as pale and
lifeless, in the coffin of his trousers, a veritable *nature
morte*.

Ibid., Ch. 6

7 "Medicine seems to be all cycles," continued Mrs.
Hartshorn. "That's the bone I pick with Sloan. Like
what's his name's new theory of history. First we
nursed our babies; then science told us not to. Now it
tells us we were right in the first place. Or were we
wrong then but would be right now? Reminds me of
relativity, if I understand Mr. Einstein."

Ibid., Ch. 10

8 She had tried to bind him with possessions, but he
slipped away like Houdini.

Ibid., Ch. 13

9 Sometimes she felt that he was postponing being a success till he could wear out her patience; as soon as she
gave up and left him, his name would mock her in
lights.

Ibid.

10 Labor is work that leaves no trace behind it when it is
finished, or if it does, as in the case of the tilled field,
this product of human activity requires still more labor,
incessant, tireless labor, to maintain its identity as a
"work" of man.

"The *Vita Activa*," *The New
Yorker*   October 18, 1958

11 There are no new truths, but only truths that have not
been recognized by those who have perceived them
without noticing.   Ibid.

12 . . . bureaucracy, the rule of no one, has become the
modern form of despotism.   Ibid.

13 When an American heiress wants to buy a man, she at once crosses the Atlantic.

On the Contrary   1961

14 . . . Americans do not dissemble what they are up to. They do not seem to feel the need, except through verbiage; *e.g.*, napalm has become "Incinderjell," which makes it sound like Jell-O. And defoliants are referred to as weed-killers—something you use in your driveway. The resort to euphemism denotes, no doubt, a guilty conscience or—the same thing nowadays—a twinge in the public-relations nerve.

"The Home Program," *Vietnam*   1967

15 In politics, it seems, retreat is honorable if dictated by military considerations and shameful if even *suggested* for ethical reasons. . . .

Ibid., "Solutions"

16 Anyway, it has to be acknowledged that in capitalist society, with its herds of hippies, originality has become a sort of fringe benefit, a *mere* convention, accepted obsolescence, the Beatnik model being turned in for the Hippie model, as though strangely obedient to capitalist laws of marketing.   Ibid., "Language"

17 In the Stalinist days, we used to detest a vocabulary that had to be read in terms of antonyms— "volunteers," denoting conscripts, "democracy," tyranny, and so on. Insensibly, in Vietnam, starting with the little word "advisors," we have adopted this slippery Aesopian language ourselves. . . .

Ibid.

18 He had never outgrown the feeling that a quest for information was a series of maneuvers in a game of espionage.

"Winter Visitors," *Birds of America*   1965

19 Maybe any action becomes cowardly once you stop to reason about it. Conscience doth make cowards of us all, eh, *mamma mia*? If you start an argument with yourself, that makes two people at least, and when you have two people, one of them starts appeasing the other.

Ibid., "Epistle from Mother Carey's Chicken"

20 Being abroad makes you conscious of the whole imitative side of human behavior. The ape in man.   Ibid.

875. Pat Nixon
(1912–   )

1 I have sacrificed everything in my life that I consider precious in order to advance the political career of my husband.

> Quoted in *Women at Work*
> by Betty Medsger   *1975*

876. Ann Petry
(1912–   )

1 It took me quite a while to realize that there were fashions in literary criticism and that they shifted and changed much like the fashions in women's hats.

> "The Novel as Social Criticism," *The Writer's Book*, Helen Hull, ed.
> *1950*

2 It seems to me that all truly great art is propaganda. . . .

> Ibid.

3 Time, that enemy of labels. . . .

> Ibid.

877. May Sarton
(1912–   )

1 The college was not founded to give society what it wants. Quite the contrary.

> *The Small Room*   *1961*

2 Excellence cost a great deal.

> Ibid.

3 "There was such a thing as women's work and it consisted chiefly, Hilary sometimes thought, in being able to stand constant interruption and keep your temper. . . ."

> *Mrs. Stevens Hears the Mermaids Singing*   *1965*

4 It's hard to be growing up in this climate where sex at its most crude and cold is O.K. but feeling is somehow indecent.

> Ibid.

5 The Lord is not my shepherd. I shall want.

> Ibid.

6 We are all monsters, if it comes to that, we women who have chosen to be something more and something less than women.

> Ibid.

7 Women's work is always toward wholeness.

> Ibid.

8 Women have moved and shaken me, but I have been nourished by men.

> Ibid.

9 We have to expiate for this cursed talent someone handed out to us, by mistake, in the black mystery of genetics.

> Ibid.

10 True feeling justifies, whatever it may cost.

> Ibid.

11 My faults too have been those of excess; I too have made emotional demands, without being aware of what I was asking; I too have imagined that I was giving when I was battering at someone for attention.

> *Journal of a Solitude*   1973

12 I would predicate that in all great works of genius masculine and feminine elements in the personality find expression, whether this androgynous nature is played out sexually or not.

> Ibid.

13 The strange effect of all these "lovers" is to make me feel not richer, but impoverished and mean.

> Ibid.

878. Barbara Tuchman
(1912–   )

1 Publicly his [the Kaiser's] performance was perfect; privately he could not resist the opportunity for fresh scheming.   *The Guns of August*, Ch. 1   1962

2 The Russian colossus exercised a spell upon Europe. On the chessboard of military planning, Russia's size

and weight of numbers represented the largest piece . . . the Russian "steam roller." . . . Although the defects of the Russian Army were notorious, although the Russian winter, not the Russian Army, had turned Napoleon back from Moscow, . . . a myth of its invincibility prevailed.

Ibid., Ch. 5

3 Alone in Europe Britain had no conscription. In war she would be dependent on voluntary enlistment. . . . [Therefore] it was a prime necessity for Britain to enter war with a united government.

Ibid., Ch. 7

4 Honor wears different coats to different eyes. . . .

Ibid.

5 The will to defend the country outran the means. . . . The Army marched in a chaos of improvisation. It marched also, or was borne along, on a crest of enthusiasm, haloed by a mist of illusion.

Ibid., Ch. 11

6 . . . out of the excited fancy produced by the fears and exhaustion and panic and violence of a great battle a legend grew. . . .

Ibid.

7 For one August in its history Paris was French—and silent.

Ibid., Ch. 20

8 So close had the Germans come to victory, so near the French to disaster, so great, in the preceding days, had been the astonished dismay of the world as it watched the relentless advance of the Germans and the retreat of the Allies on Paris, that the battle that turned the tide came to be known as the Miracle of the Marne.

Ibid., Afterword

9 Men could not sustain a war of such magnitude and pain without hope—the hope that its very enormity would ensure that it could never happen again and the hope that when somehow it had been fought through to a resolution, the foundations of a better-ordered world would have been laid. . . . When every autumn people said it could not last through the winter, and when every spring there was still no end in sight, only the

hope that out of it all some good would accrue to mankind kept men and nations fighting. When at last it was over, the war had many diverse results and one dominant one transcending all others: disillusion.

Ibid.

10 We're being made to look like Lolitas and lion tamers.
Quoted in The Beautiful People
by Marilyn Bender   1968

11 The core of the military profession is discipline and the essence of discipline is obedience. Since this does not come naturally to men of independent and rational mind, they must train themselves in the habit of obedience on which lives and the fortunes of battle may someday depend. Reasonable orders are easy enough to obey; it is capricious, bureaucratic or plain idiotic demands that form the habit of discipline.
Stilwell and the American Experience
in China: 1911–1945, Pt. I, Ch. 1
1970

12 Through all changing circumstances and conditions in the coming period this remained the purpose of American aid and it retained the original flaw: the American purpose was not the Chinese purpose.
Ibid., Pt. II, Ch. 9

13 China was a problem from which there was no American solution. The American effort to sustain the status quo could not supply an outworn government with strength and stability or popular support. It could not hold up a husk nor long delay the cyclical passage of the mandate of heaven. In the end China went her own way as if the Americans had never come.
Ibid., Ch. 20

14 . . . the deep-seated American distrust that still prevailed of diplomacy and diplomats. . . . Diplomacy means all the wicked devices of the Old World, spheres of influence, balances of power, secret treaties, triple alliances, and, during the interwar period, appeasement of Fascism.
"If Mao Had Come to Washington
in 1945," Foreign Affairs
October, 1972

15 Friendship of a kind that cannot easily be reversed to-morrow must have its roots in common interests and shared beliefs, and even between nations, in some personal feeling.

"Friendship with Foreign Devils,"
Harper's   December, 1972

16 In a country where misery and want were the foundation of the social structure, famine was periodic, death from starvation common, disease pervasive, thievery normal, and graft and corruption taken for granted, the elimination of these conditions in Communist China is so striking that negative aspects of the new rule fade in relative importance.

Notes from China, Ch. 1   1972

17 The farmer is the eternal China.

Ibid., Ch. 3

879. Charleszetta Waddles
(1912–   )

1 You can't give people pride, but you can provide the kind of understanding that makes people look to their inner strengths and find their own sense of pride.

Quoted in "Mother Waddles: Black Angel of the Poor" by Lee Edson, *Reader's Digest*   October, 1972

2 God knows no distance.

Ibid.

880. Eleanor Clark
(1913–   )

1 ". . . we've achieved what no nation ever has before in the world. *Saturation* ugliness! and all that goes with it, in the way of mental crack-up. Now we can sleep a while, and dream our pastures new."

Baldur's Gate, Pt. II, Ch. 2   1955

2 "He was the kind of man, if a mule kicked somebody down the street, he'd work till he gut it on his conscience."

Ibid., Pt. III, Ch. 2

3 "You can hang the wash without a line."

Ibid., Ch. 3

4 "We Occidentals have a congenital, it may even be a
fatal, need for good manners, or you might say ceremony, in our approach to meaning, I suppose to make
up for our crudeness in living."

Ibid.

881. Nathalia Crane
(1913–   )

* * *

1 But my heart is all aflutter like the washing on the line.
"The Flathouse roof," St. 1

2 Crumpling a pyramid, humbling a rose,
The dust has its reasons wherever it goes.

"The Dust"

3 Every gaudy color
Is a bit of truth.

"The Vestal," St. 5

4 Great is the rose
That challenges the crypt.
And quotes millenniums
Against the grave.

"Song from Tadmor"

5 He showed me like a master
That one rose makes a gown;
That looking up to Heaven
Is merely looking down.

"My Husbands"

6 He wooed the daunted odalisques,
He kissed each downcast nude;
He whispered that an angel's robe
Is mostly attitude.

"The First Reformer"

7 In the darkness, who would answer for the color of a
rose,
Or the vestments of the May moth and the pilgrimage
it goes?

"The Blind Girl," St. 1

8 The little *and*, the tiny *if*,
   The ardent *ahs* and *ohs*,
They haunt the lane of poesy,
   The boulevards of prose.

                          "Alliances"

9 There is a glory
In a great mistake.

                        "Imperfection"

10 You cannot choose your battlefield,
The gods do that for you,
But you can plant a standard
Where a standard never flew.

                      "The Colors"

882. Elizabeth Janeway
(1913–   )

1 Such simplicity cannot be taught. But it can be denied
and lost.

                 The Writer's Book, Ch. 1
                 Helen Hull, ed.   1950

2 For there is always this to be said for the literary profession—like life itself, it provides its own revenges and
antidotes.

                           Ibid., Ch. 24

3 . . . it is through the ghost [writer] that the great gift
of knowledge which the inarticulate have for the world
can be made available.

                           Ibid., Ch. 29

4 In this nadir of poetic repute, when the only verse that
most people read from one year's end to the next is
what appears on greeting cards, it is well for us to stop
and consider our poets. . . . Poets are the leaven in
the lump of civilization.

                           Ibid., Ch. 30

5 As long as mixed grills and combination salads are
popular, anthologies will undoubtedly continue in favor.   Ibid., Ch. 32

6 After all, every circle has a point for a center. The size
of the circle is determined by the energy with which it

is expanded, not by the magnificence of what it may or may not take off from.

Ibid., Ch. 40

7 After the city, where we had always lived, those country years were startling. . . . The surprise of animals . . . in and out, cats and dogs and a milk goat and chickens and guinea hens, all taken for granted, as if man was intended to live on terms of friendly intercourse with the rest of creation instead of huddling in isolation on the fourteenth floor of an apartment house in a city where animals occurred behind bars in the zoo.

"Steven Benedict," Accident   1964

8 The Goddamn human race deserves itself, and as far as I'm concerned it can have it.

Ibid., "Charles Benedict"

9 I admire people who are suited to the contemplative life, but I am not one of them. They can sit inside themselves like honey in a jar and just be. It's wonderful to have someone like that around, you always feel you can count on them. You can go away and come back, you can change your mind and your hairdo and your politics, and when you get through doing all these upsetting things, you look around and there they are, just the way they were, just being.

Ibid., "Elizabeth Jowett"

10 American women are not the only people in the world who manage to lose track of themselves, but we do seem to mislay the past in a singularly absent-minded fashion.

"Reflections on the History of Women,"
Women: Their Changing Roles
1973

11 Like their personal lives, women's history is fragmented, interrupted; a shadow history of human beings whose existence has been shaped by the efforts and the demands of others.

Ibid.

12 If every nation gets the government it deserves, every generation writes the history which corresponds with its view of the world.

Ibid.

13 Perhaps it is just a hangover from the past, but even those writers who declare that the importance of sex is its sheer pleasure do so with an evangelical zeal that is directive rather than permissive.

Between Myth and Morning 1974

14 . . . reaction isn't action—that is, it isn't truly creative.

Ibid.

15 We have to see, I think, that questioning the value of old rules is different from simply breaking them.

Ibid.

16 When dealing with adultery becomes a matter of private choice instead of public rules, middle-class morality, that bastion of social stability, has ceased to function.

Ibid.

17 Confronted with the possibility of public catastrophe, every tyrant will opt to let permissiveness rule in private. Besides, will not such permissiveness turn the attention of the people away from public problems to private pleasures? One can image a modern Machiavelli suggesting to his prince that sex would make a very good opiate for the people.

Ibid.

18 Young or old, skepticism about conventional wisdom can give way all too early to a relapse into credulity before the allurements of new certainties.

Ibid.

19 With the old rules for masculine superiority fading in the public sphere, how can men face the feminine superiority they have posited in the private world?

Ibid.

20 Poor engineer, hoist with his own petard! Ibid.

21 Love between women is seen as a paradigm of love between equals, and that is perhaps its greatest attraction. Ibid.

22 Sexual freedom? Nonsense! These are directions for the greedy use of freedom in old, manipulative ways in order to gain the traditional feminine "catch-a-man" goal.

Ibid.

23 Sex cannot be contained within a definition of physical pleasure, it cannot be understood as merely itself for it has stood for too long as a symbol of profound connection between human beings.

Ibid.

* * *

24 . . . it is almost shockingly delightful to read a book which could have been written by absolutely no one else in the world than the great and important figure whose name is signed to it. . . .

"This I Remember"

25 Unable to dedicate herself to her husband—why, we shall never be sure—she ended by dedicating herself to his work. . . . On the basis of an unusual if not unsatisfactory marriage was built an edifice of cooperation, of mutual aid and respect which was of immeasurable influence.

Ibid.

883. Margo Jones
(1913–1955)

1 Everything in life is theatre.

Quoted in *The New York Times*
July 26, 1955p

2 The theatre has given me a chance not only to live my own life but a million others. In every play there is a chance for one great moment, experience or understanding.

Ibid.

3 With imagination and a tremendous willingness for hard work, it is possible to create a great theatre, a vigorous and vital theatre, in the second half of the twentieth century.

"Theatre '50: A Dream Come True,"
Ten Talents in the American Theatre,
David H. Stevens, ed.   *1957p*

4 There are two kinds of theatre, good and bad. Much as I should like to see theatre in America, I would rather have no theatre than bad theatre. What we must strive for is perfection and come as close to it as is humanly possible.

Ibid.

5 We have seen too much defeatism, too much pessimism, too much of a negative approach. The answer is simple: if you want something very badly, you can achieve it. It may take patience, very hard work, a real struggle, and a long time; but it can be done. That much faith is a prerequisite of any undertaking, artistic or otherwise.

Ibid.

884. Dorothy Kilgallen
(1913–1965)

1 I am off on a race around the world—a race against time and two men. I know I can beat time. I hope I can beat the men.

Girl Around the World   1936

2 The chief product of Baghdad is dates . . . and sheiks.

Ibid.

3 The world is grand, awfully big and astonishingly beautiful, frequently thrilling. But I love New York.

Ibid.

885. Vivien Leigh
(1913–1967)

1 In Britain, an attractive woman is somehow suspect. If there is talent as well it is overshadowed. Beauty and brains just can't be entertained; someone has been too extravagant.

Quoted by Robert Ottaway in
Light of a Star by Gwen Robyns
1968p

2 I swing between happiness and misery and I cry easily. I'm a mixture of my mother's determination and my father's optimism. I'm part prude and part nonconformist and I must say what I think and I don't dissemble. I'm a mixture of French, Irish and Yorkshire, and perhaps that's what it all is.

Ibid.

886. Tillie Olsen
(1913–   )

1 And when is there time to remember, to sift, to weigh, to estimate, to total?

"I Stand Here Ironing" (1954),
Tell Me a Riddle   1960

2 Now suddenly she was Somebody, and as imprisoned in her difference as she had been in her anonymity.

Ibid.

3 My wisdom came too late.

Ibid.

4 It is destroying, dissolving him utterly, this helpless warmth against him, this feel of a child. . . .

Ibid., "Hey Sailor, What Ship?" (1955)

5 That's what I want to be when I grow up, just a peaceful wreck holding hands with other peaceful wrecks. . . .

Ibid.

6 There are worse words than cuss words, there are words that hurt.

Ibid.

7 In the beginning there had been youth and the joy of raising hell. . . . And later there were memories to forget, dreams to be stifled, hopes to be murdered.

Ibid.

8 . . . the Law and the Wall: only so far shall you go and no further, uptown forbidden, not your language, not your people, not your country.

Ibid.

9 "Not everybody feel religion the same way. Some it's in their mouth, but some it's like a hope in their blood, their bones."

Ibid., "O Yes" (1956)

10 It is a long baptism into the seas of humankind, my daughter. Better immersion than to live untouched. . . .

Ibid.

179

11 For forty-seven years they had been married. How deep back the stubborn, gnarled roots of the quarrel reached, no one could say—but only now, when tending to the needs of others no longer shackled them together, the roots swelled up visible, split the earth between them, and the tearing shook even the children, long since grown.

> Ibid., "Tell Me a Riddle," Ch. 1 (1960)

12 He could not, could not turn away from this desire: to have the troubling of responsibility, the fretting with money, over and done with; to be free, to be *care*free where success was not measured by accumulation. . . .

> Ibid.

13 The television is shadows. Mrs. Enlightened! Mrs. Cultured! A world comes into your house—and it is shadows. People you would never meet in a million lifetimes. Wonders.

> Ibid.

14 Like the hide of a drum shall you be, beaten in life, beaten in death.

> Ibid.

15 "Vinegar he poured on me all his life; I am well marinated; how can I be honey now?"

> Ibid.

16 Heritage. How have we come from the savages, now no longer to be savages—this to teach. To look back and learn what humanizes man—this to teach. To smash all ghettos that divide us—not to go back, not to go back—this to teach.

> Ibid., Ch. 2

17 "Remember your advice, easy to keep your head above water, empty things float. Float."

> Ibid., Ch. 3

18 ". . . life may be hated or wearied of, but never despised."

> Ibid., Ch. 4

19 Always roused by the writing, always denied. . . . My work died.

> *Silences: When Writers Don't Write*   1965

20 The mute inglorious Miltons: those whose waking hours are all struggle for existence; the barely edu-

cated; the illiterate; women—their silence the silence of centuries as to how life was, is, for most of humanity.

Ibid.

21 . . . the circumstances for sustained creation are almost impossible.

Ibid.

22 More than in any other human relationship, overwhelmingly more, motherhood means being instantly interruptible, responsive, responsible. . . .

Ibid.

23 It is distraction, not meditation, that becomes habitual; interruption, not continuity; spasmodic, not constant toil.

Ibid.

24 Time granted does not necessarily coincide with time that can be most fully used.

Ibid.

887. Rosa Parks
(1913–   )

1 My only concern was to get home after a hard day's work.*

Quoted in *Time*   *December 15, 1975*

888. Sylvia Porter
(1913–   )

1 We are into an "era of aspirations" in our economy. In this era, most of us will spend a shrinking share of our income on the traditional necessities of food, clothing, shelter, and transportation while we spend a steadily increasing share of our income for goods and services which reflect our hopes and wants.

Sylvia Porter's Money Book, Ch. 1   *1975*

2 The average family exists only on paper and its average budget is a fiction, invented by statisticians for the con-

---

* Referring to her refusal to give up her seat on a bus in Montgomery, Alabama, in 1955 to a white who was standing. From her act of defiance grew the Montgomery bus boycott and the leadership of Martin Luther King, Jr.

venience of statisticians. . . . There is no sense in attempting to fit into a ready-to-wear financial pattern which ignores your own personal wants and desires.

Ibid.

3 Money never remains just coins and pieces of paper. It is constantly changing into the comforts of daily life. Money can be translated into the beauty of living, a support in misfortune, an education, or future security. It also can be translated into a source of bitterness.

Ibid.

4 For millions, the retirement dream is in reality an economic nightmare. For millions, growing old today means growing poor, being sick, living in substandard housing, and having to scrimp merely to subsist. And this is the prospect not only for the one out of every ten Americans now over sixty-five . . . but also for the sixty-five million who will reach retirement age within the next thirty-three years.

Ibid., Ch. 19

889. Nancy Reeves
(1913–   )

1 Today the hemisphere of the public has been assigned to the male and the hemisphere of the private to the female. Each sex has become a symbol for its territory. The conflict between them can then be seen as a reflection of the longing of each to be part of the other's sphere, to link the public with the private in our schizoid world, to embrace the whole of life.

Womankind Beyond the Stereotypes   1971

890. Muriel Rukeyser
(1913–   )

1 Women and poets see the truth arrive,
Then it is acted out,
The lives are lost, and all the newsboys shout.

"Letter to the Front," Beast in View   1944

2 Women in drudgery knew
They must be one of four:
Whores, artists, saints, and wives.

Ibid., "Wreath of Women"

3 However confused the scene of our life appears,
however torn we may be who now do face that scene,
it can be faced, and we can go on to be whole.
The Life of Poetry   *1949*

4   . . . on second cry I woke
fully and gave to feed and fed on feeding.
"Night Feeding," St. 2,
Selected Poems   *1951*

5 The spies who wait for the spy at the deserted crossing,
a little dead since they are going to kill.
"Ann Burlak," St. 4, *Waterlily*
Fire: 1935–1962   *1962*

6 Those women who stitch their lives to their machines
and daughters at the symmetry of looms.
Ibid.

7 Years when the enemy is in our state,
and liberty, safe in the people's hands,
is never safe and peace is never safe.
Ibid.

8   . . . the seeking marvelous look
Of those who lose and use and know their lives.
Ibid., "Nine Poems for the Unborn Child," II

9 The strength, the grossness, spirit and gall of choice.
Ibid., VI, St. 1

10 You will enter the world which eats itself
Naming faith, reason, naming love, truth, fact.
Ibid., VII, St. 1

11 I have forgotten what it was
that I have been trying to remember.
"Woman as Market,"
The Speed of Darkness   *1968*

12 my lifetime
listens to yours.
Ibid., "Käthe Kollwitz," I, St. 1

13 the revolutionary look
that says   I am in the world
to change the world.
Ibid., St. 2

14 A theme may seem to have been put aside,
   but it keeps returning—
   the same thing modulated,
   somewhat changed in form.

Ibid., II, St. 2

15 I believe
         that bisexuality
   is almost   a necessary factor
   in artistic production. . . .

Ibid., St. 6

16 What would happen if one woman told the
      truth about her life?
         The world would split open

Ibid., III, St. 4

17 No more masks! No more mythologies!
Ibid., "The Poem as Mask," St. 3

18 Overtaken by silence

   But this same silence is become speech
   With the speed of darkness.
Ibid., "The Speed of Darkness," II

19 The universe is made of stories,
   not of atoms.

Ibid., IX, St. 2

20 Whatever we stand against
   We will stand feeding and seeding.
"Wherever," St. 3, *Breaking Open*   1973

21 Escape the birthplace; walk into the world
   Refusing to be either slave or slaveholder.
Ibid., "Secrets of American
Civilization," St. 3

22 The collective unconscious is the living history brought
   to the present in consciousness.
Quoted in "Rare Battered She-Poet"
by Louise Bernikow, *Ms.*   April, 1974

891. Honor Tracy
(1913–   )

1 He was a member of the eccentric race of fiscophobes,
Englishmen who would do anything and live anywhere,
no matter how bored and miserable they might be,
rather than stay at home and pay English taxes.

The Butterflies of the Province,
Ch. 1   *1970*

2 "Early upbringing," David moaned. "One struggles
against it in vain."

Ibid., Ch. 5

892. Julia de Burgos
(1914–1953)

1   You are the bloodless doll of social lies
And I the virile spark of human truth. . . .
"To Julia de Burgos," *The Nation*   *1972p*

2   You curl your hair and paint your face. Not I:
I am curled by the wind, painted by the sun.

Ibid.

893. Agnes "Sis" Cunningham
(1914–   )

1 We . . . were young radicals who felt that by singing
ideas straightforwardly we could get more said in five
minutes than in hours, or days, of talking.

"Songs of Hard Years," with
Madeline B. Rose, *Ms.*   *March, 1974*

* * *

2 Oh, it's good to be living and working
when we know the land's our own
To know that we have got a right to
all the crops we've grown.

"When We Know the Land's Our Own"

894. Gypsy Rose Lee
(1914–1970)

1 Mother, in a feminine way, was ruthless. She was, in her own words, a jungle mother, and she knew too well that in a jungle it doesn't pay to be nice. "God will protect us," she often said to June and me. "But to make sure," she would add, "carry a heavy club."
Gypsy, Ch. 1   *1957*

2 [He] often said I was the greatest no-talent star in the business.
Ibid.

895. Catherine Marshall
(1914–   )

1 Often God has to shut a door in our face, so that He can subsequently open the door through which He wants us to go.
A Man Called Peter, Ch. 2   *1951*

2 . . . truth could never be wholly contained in words. All of us know it: At the same moment the mouth is speaking one thing, the heart is saying another. . . .
Christy, Prologue   *1967*

3 So once I shut down my privilege of disliking anyone I chose and holding myself aloof if I could manage it, greater understanding, growing compassion came to me. . . .
Ibid., Ch. 12

4 Usually passion wants to grab and to yank.
Ibid., Ch. 33

5 . . . in rejecting secrecy I had also rejected the road to cynicism.
Ibid.

6 . . . I learned that true forgiveness includes total acceptance. And out of acceptance wounds are healed and happiness is possible again.
Ibid.

896. Hazel Brannon Smith
(1914–)

1 I've always been too interested in what is happening in the present and what is going to happen to be much concerned about the past.

> Quoted in "The 11-Year Siege of Mississippi's Lady Editor" by T. George Harris, *Look*   *November 16, 1965*

2 I ain't no lady. I'm a newspaperwoman.

> *Ibid.*

3 A crusading editor is one who goes out and looks for the wrongs of the world. I just try to take care of things as they come up. I try to make them a little better.

> *Ibid.*

4 I can't think of but one thing that's worse than being called a nigger-lover. And that's a nigger-hater!

> *Ibid.*

897. Barbara Ward
(1914–)

1 All archaic societies feel themselves bound to a "melancholy wheel" of endless recurrence. . . . No vision of reality as progressing forward to new possibilities, no sense of the future as better and fuller than the present, tempered the underlying fatalism of ancient civilization. It is only in the Jewish and Christian faith that a Messianic hope first breaks upon mankind.

> *The Rich Nations and the Poor Nations*, Ch. 1   *1962*

2 It is very much easier for a rich man to invest and grow richer than for the poor man to begin investing at all. And this is also true of nations.

> *Ibid.*

3 . . . there is no human failure greater than to launch a profoundly important endeavour and then leave it half done. This is what the West has done with its colonial system. It shook all the societies in the world loose

from their old moorings. But it seems indifferent whether or not they reach safe harbour in the end.

Ibid., Ch. 2

4 To me, one of the most vivid proofs that there is a moral governance in the universe is the fact that when men or governments work intelligently and far-sightedly for the good of others, they achieve their own prosperity too.

Ibid., Ch. 6

5 It is only when people begin to shake loose from their preconceptions, from the ideas that have dominated them, that we begin to receive a sense of opening, a sense of vision. . . . That is the sort of time we live in now. We . . . live in an epoch in which the solid ground of our preconceived ideas shakes daily under our uncertain feet.

"Only One Earth," *Who Speaks for Earth?*, Maurice F. Strong, ed. *1973*

6 . . . mankind must go beyond the limits of purely national government and begin to find out what the "post-national community" is like. . . . [But] it cannot, must not, mean a suppression of all variety and a civilization so standarized that we all end up hideously the same.

Ibid.

7 We can all cheat on morals. . . . But today the morals of respect and care and modesty come to us in a form that we cannot evade. We cannot cheat on DNA. We cannot get round photosynthesis. We cannot say I am not going to give a damn about phytoplankton. All these tiny mechanisms provide the preconditions of our planetary life. To say we do not care is to say in the most literal sense that "we choose death."

Ibid.

898. Babe Didrikson Zaharias
(1914–1956)

1 All my life I've always had the urge to do things better than anybody else. Even in school, if it was something like making up a current events booklet, I'd want mine to be the best in the class.

Quoted in " 'Babe' Didrikson Zaharias," *Famous American Women* by Hope Stoddard *1970p*

2 Boy, don't you men wish you could hit a ball like that!
Ibid.

3 All my life I've been competing—and competing to win. I came to realize that in its way, this cancer was the toughest competition I'd faced yet. I made up my mind that I was going to lick it all the way. I not only wasn't going to let it kill me, I wasn't even going to let it put me on the shelf.

Ibid.

899. Ingrid Bergman
(1915–)

1 . . . I saw my wrinkles in their wrinkles. You know, one looks at herself in the mirror every morning, and she doesn't see the difference, she doesn't realize that she is aging. But then she finds a friend who was young with her, and the friend isn't young anymore, and all of a sudden, like a slap on her eyes, she remembers that she, too, isn't young anymore.
Quoted in "Ingrid Bergman," *The Egotists* by Oriana Fallaci   1963

2 Things came to me asking to be done, and I did them—spontaneously, without asking whether it was wise or not. And the day after, I could say, "Maybe I shouldn't have done it." But years later, I always realized I was right in doing them.

Ibid.

3 I've never sought success in order to get fame and money; it's the talent and the passion that count in success.   Ibid.

900. Caroline Bird
(1915–)

1 The contraceptive pill may reduce the importance of sex not only as a basis for the division of labor, but as a guideline in developing talents and interests.
Born Female, Foreword   1968

2 We are destroying talent. The price of occupational success is made so high for women that barring excep-

tional luck only the unusually talented or frankly neurotic can afford to succeed. Girls size up the bargain early and turn it down.

Ibid.

3 A career woman who has survived the hurdle of marriage and maternity encounters a new obstacle: the hostility of men.

Ibid., Ch. 3

4 Secretaries may be specially prized, and the top secretaries exceptionally well paid, because they give men who can afford to pay well the subservient, watchful and admiring attention that Victorian wives used to give their husbands.

Ibid., Ch. 4

5 Equity speaks softly and wins in the end. But it is expedience, with its loud voice, that sets the time of victory.

Ibid., Ch. 10

6 Femininity appears to be one of those pivotal qualities that is so important no one can define it.

Ibid., Ch. 11

7 Are young women staying single because they have been influenced by women's liberation? Maybe. But I'm inclined to think that the causal relationship is the other way around. . . . Feminism has never been deader than it was during the 1950s, when the marriage rate hit a new high, the age of marriage a new low, and the ideal of universal, compulsory marriage boomed marriage counseling, psychiatric therapy and romantic portrayals of married life.

"The Case Against Marriage,"
New Woman   September, 1971

8 Predictable demography has caught up with the university empire builders. . . . To keep their mammoth plants financially solvent, many institutions have begun to use hard-sell, Madison-Avenue techniques to attract students. They sell college like soap. . . .

The Case Against College   1975

9 . . . just as society had systematically damaged women by insisting that their proper place was in the home, so we may be systematically damaging 18-year-olds by insisting that their proper place is in college.

Ibid.

10 Equalizing opportunity through universal higher education subjects the whole population to the intellectual
mode natural only to a few. It violates the fundamental
egalitarian principle of respect for the differences between people.

Ibid.

11 The big advantage of getting your college money in
cash now is that you can invest it in something that has
a higher return than a diploma.

Ibid.

12 In fact there is no real evidence that the higher income
of college graduates is due to college. College may simply attract people who are slated to earn more money
anyway: those with higher IQs, better family back-
grounds, a more enterprising temperament.

Ibid.

13 A liberal-arts education is supposed to provide you
with a value system, a standard, a set of ideas, not a
job. . . . The fact is, of course, that the liberal arts are
a religion in every sense of that term. . . . [And if]
the liberal arts are a religious faith, the professors are
its priests.

Ibid.

14 College, then, may be a good place for those few young
people who are really drawn to academic work, who
would rather read than eat, but it has become too ex-
pensive, in money, time, and intellectual effort, to serve
as a holding pen for large numbers of our young. We
ought to make it possible for those reluctant, unhappy
students to find alternative ways of growing up, and
more realistic preparation for the years ahead.

Ibid.

901. Janet Harris
(1915–   )

1 . . . with the beginnings of the middle years, we face
an identity crisis for which nothing in our past has prepared us.   *The Prime of Ms. America*   1975

2 We were brought up with the value that as we sow, so
shall we reap. We discarded the idea that anything we
did was its own reward.   *Ibid.*

3 Reared as we were in a youth- and beauty-oriented society, we measured ourselves by our ornamental value.
Ibid.

4 I'm the ultimate in the throwaway society, the disposable woman.

Ibid.

5 . . . one searches the magazines in vain for women
past their first youth. The middleaged face apparently
sells neither perfume nor floor wax. The role of the
mature woman in the media is almost entirely negative.
Ibid.

6 We are anonymous—graphed but not acknowledged, a
shadowy presence—hinted at, but never defined.

Ibid.

7 At its most basic root, the death or disintegration of
one's parents is a harsh reminder of one's own mortality.

Ibid.

8 We were born in an era in which it was a disgrace for
women to be sexually responsible. We matured in an
era in which it was an obligation.   *Ibid.*

9 Quite a few women told me, one way or another, that
they thought it was sex, not youth, that's wasted on the
young. . . .   *Ibid.*

902. Billie Holiday
(1915–1959)

1 Mama may have
Papa may have
But God bless the child that's got his own
That's got his own.
"God Bless the Child"   *1941*

2 And when you're poor, you grow up fast.
Lady Sings the Blues, with William
Dufty, Ch. 1   *1956*

3 You can be up to your boobies in white satin, with
gardenias in your hair and no sugar cane for miles, but
you can still be working on a plantation.

Ibid., Ch. 11

4 People don't understand the kind of fight it takes to record what you want to record the way you want to record it.

Ibid., Ch. 13

5 Sometimes it's worse to win a fight than to lose.

Ibid.

903. Ethel Rosenberg
(1915–1953)

1 Together we hunted down the answers to all the seemingly insoluble riddles which a complex and callous society presented. . . . And yet for the sake of these answers, for the sake of American democracy, justice and brotherhood, for the sake of peace and bread and roses, and children's laughter, we shall continue to sit here [in prison] in dignity and in pride—in the deep abiding knowledge of our innocence before God and man, until the truth becomes a clarion call to all decent humanity.

Letter to Julie Rosenberg, Sing Sing
(May 27, 1951), Death House Letters
of Ethel and Julius Rosenberg　1953p

2 Work and build, my sons, and build
a monument to love and joy,
to human worth, to faith we kept
for you, my sons, for you.

Ibid., "If We Die" (January 24, 1953)

3 . . . suffice it to say that my husband and I shall die innocent before we lower ourselves to live guilty! And nobody, not even you, whom we continue to love as our own true brother, can dictate terms to the Rosenbergs, who follow only the dictates of heart and soul, truth and conscience, and the God-blessed love we bear our fellows!

Ibid., Letter to Emanuel H.
Bloch, Defense Attorney
(January 30, 1953)

904. Natalie Shainess
(1915–   )

1 In the generally progressive alienation of our times, we are back to the laws of the jungle, but without the gratification of biologic fulfillment.

> "A Psychiatrist's View: Images of Woman—Past and Present, Overt and Obscured," *American Journal of Psychotherapy*   *January, 1969*

2 At a recent meeting devoted to the theme of dissent, a Negro analyst pointed to the analyst's blind spot, in studying only the dissenters, but not the people or ideas dissented against. How valid a perception!

> Ibid.

3 It seems that the rewards of an affluent society turn bitter as gall in the mouth.

> Ibid.

4 As we have become a thing-oriented, impulse-ridden, narcissistically self-preoccupied people, we are increasingly dedicated to the acquisition of things, and cultivate little else.

> Ibid.

905. Margaret Walker
(1915–   )

1 For my people thronging 47th Street in Chicago and Lenox
Avenue in New York and Rampart Street in New Orleans, lost disinherited dispossessed and happy people filling the cabarets and taverns and other people's pockets. . . .

> "For My People," St. 6, *For My People*   1942

2 Let a new earth rise. Let another world be born. Let a bloody
peace be written in the sky. Let a second generation full of courage issue forth;
let a people loving free-
dom come to growth.

> Ibid., St. 10

3 There were bizarre beginnings in old lands for the mak-
      ing
      of me.

> Ibid., "Dark Blood," St. 1

4 Now this here gal warn't always tough
   Nobody dreamed she'd turn out rough.

> Ibid., "Kissie Lee," St. 2

5 Old women working by an age-old plan
   to make their bread in ways as best they can.

> Ibid., "Whores," St. 1

6 Hurry up, Lucille, Hurry up
   We're Going to Miss Our Chance to go to Jail.

> "Street Demonstration," St. 2
> *Prophets for a New Day*   1970

7 I like it fine in Jail
   And I don't want no Bail.

> Ibid., "Girl Held Without Bail," St. 2

8   . . . the filthy
      privies marked "For Colored Only"
      and the drinking-soda-fountains
      tasting dismal and disgusting
      with a dry and dusty flavor
      of the deep humiliation. . . .

> Ibid., "Now"

9 Time to wipe away the slime.
   Time to end this bloody crime.

> Ibid.

10 Everything I have ever written or hoped to write is
   dedicated . . . to our hope of peace and dignity and
   freedom in the world, not just as black people, or as
   Negroes, but as free human beings in a world community.

> Quoted in *By a Woman Writt*,
> Joan Goulianos, ed.   *1974*

906. Helen Yglesias
(1915–   )

1 They never ask the patient. The patient is anesthetized
   on the operating table, cut open. They call in the husband. "We think it best to remove this precancerous

breast. Since this is your hunk of meat, do we have your permission, husband?"

How She Died, Ch. 1   1972

2 "Life is too short to understand God altogether, especially nowadays."

Ibid.

3 I wanted to pull him toward me and comfort him with my body as I had when he was a child, but that time was over. We could only be to each other what any two human beings might be, close or far, quick or dull, yielding or hard.

Ibid., Ch. 11

4 "I like to beat people at chess, and get better marks, and be elected to everything. It's disgusting to want those things. A person like that could do anything."

Ibid.

5 Listening was a three times a day ritual with her, the news made even more nightmarish in the repetition: the war, the official statements, the enemy's denial, the traffic deaths, conspiracy charges, abortion reform fights, kidnappings, terrorism, peace talks, negotiations of all kinds, hijackings, charges and countercharges of anti-Semitism, Panther trials, civilian massacre trials, murder trials, riots, demonstrations, flaring wars between nations in corners of the world that didn't seem to really exist, the nonsense item they always found to end each broadcast with—and then the weather, reported as if every dip of the wind was a judgment day warning.

Ibid., Ch. 16

907. Dorothy Salisbury Davis
(1916–   )

1 There are seasons in Washington when it is even more difficult than usual to find out what is going on in the government. Possibly it is because nothing is going on, although a great many people seem to be working at it.

Old Sinners Never Die, Ch. 1   1959

2 We are all at the mercy of God as well as of one another. And for that we can be grateful, He has so much more of it than we have.

Black Sheep Among White Lamb, Ch. 7   1963

3 She listened with the remote and somewhat smug solicitude that one bestows on other people's tragedies. . . .

"The Purple Is Everything," *Ellery Queen's Mystery Magazine*   1964

4 She dressed more severely than was her fashion, needing herringbone for backbone. . . .

Ibid.

5 "The business of this street is business," the [police] sergeant said, "and that's my business."

Ibid.

6 A curator perhaps, but she would not have called him a connoisseur. One with his face and disposition would always taste and spit out. . . .

Ibid.

7 But the discovery of the flaw does not in itself effect a cure; often it aggravates the condition.

Ibid.

8 The law is above the law, you know.
The Little Brothers, Ch. 8   1973

9 You know what truth is, gentlemen? Truth is self-justification. That is everybody's truth. . . .   Ibid.

908. Betty Furness
(1916–   )

1 You fellows have got to get this [phosphate-pollution problem] straightened out, because the laundry's piling up.

Quoted in *Bella!*, Mel Ziegler, ed.   1972

909. Natalia Ginzburg
(1916–   )

1 I haven't managed to become learned about anything, even the things I've loved most in life: in me they remain scattered images, which admittedly feed my life of memories and feelings, but fail to fill my empty cultural wasteland.

"He and I" (1963), *Italian Writing Today*, Raleigh Trevelyan, ed.   1967

2 . . . it hurts me not to love music, because I feel my spirit is hurt by not loving it. But there's nothing to be done about it; I shall never understand music, and never love it. If I occasionally hear music I like, I can't remember it; so how could I love a thing I can't remember?

Ibid.

3 My tidiness, and my untidiness, are full of regret and remorse and complex feelings.

Ibid.

4 He says they're all play-acting; and maybe he's right. Because, in the midst of my tears and his rages, I am completely calm. Over my real sorrows I never weep.

Ibid.

5 . . . sometimes I wonder if we were those two people nearly twenty years ago along via Nazionale; two people who talked so politely, so urbanely, in the sunset; who chatted about everything, and nothing; two pleasant talkers, two young intellectuals out for a walk; so young, so polite, so distracted, so ready to judge each other with absent kindliness, so ready to say goodbye for ever, in that sunset, on that street corner.

Ibid.

910. Françoise Giroud
(1916–   )

1 Are there still virgins? One is tempted to answer no. There are only girls who have not yet crossed the line, because they want to preserve their market value. . . . Call them virgins if you wish, these travelers in transit.

Quoted in Coronet   November, 1960

2 Childhood is something so close, so special. . . . It's something you ought to keep to yourself. The way you keep back tears.

I Give You My Word   1974

3 To live several lives, you have to die several deaths.

Ibid.

4 Nothing is more difficult than competing with a myth.

Ibid.

5 As soon as a woman crosses the border into male territory, the nature of professional combat changes.

Ibid.

6 . . . the present evolution of women . . . is to my mind the most profound revolution that highly developed societies will have to contend with. . . .

Ibid.

7 As though femininity is something you can lose the way you lose your pocketbook: hmm, where in the world did I put my femininity?

Ibid.

8 . . . I don't for one moment believe that over the centuries some universal plot has been hatched by men to keep women in a state of servitude.

Ibid.

9 . . . the history of humanity is a very long one, during which the division of labor between men and women was, like many other things, dictated by profound necessity. . . .

Ibid.

10 When mores are no longer founded on the law of civilization but on habit, then comes the revolt.

Ibid.

11 One sometimes has the impression that American women have a kind of dishwashing fixation.

Ibid.

12 All missionaries are my enemies, even when their cause is good.

Ibid.

13 To hold a man, or several men, was for her the epitome of female gamesmanship, the only thing that made life meaningful. What war is to men.

Ibid.

14 The more subversive ideas are, the more moderate the language ought to be in expressing them. . . . If you look closely at most of the ideas expressed with violence, you begin to see that, once you've scraped away the terminology, you're usually left with the worst platitudes.

Ibid.

15 When you are carrying on a struggle, you have to accept the notion that you will have enemies.

> Ibid.

911. Elizabeth Hardwick
(1916–   )

1 The curious modernity of the plot [*Hedda Gabler*] is that the workings of destiny have shrunk to yawning boredom.

> *Seduction and Betrayal: Women in Literature*   1974

2 Hedda [Gabler], rather than Nora [of *A Doll's House*], was the real prophecy.

> Ibid.

3 Women, wronged in one way or another, are given the overwhelming beauty of endurance, the capacity for high or low suffering, for violent feeling absorbed, finally tranquilized, for the radiance of humility, for silence, secrecy, impressive acceptance. Heroines are, then, heroic.

> Ibid.

4 You cannot seduce anyone when innocence is not a value. Technology annihilates consequence. Heroism hurts and no one easily consents to be under its rule.

> Ibid.

5 Stoicism . . . cannot be without its remaining uses in life and love; but if we read contemporary fiction we learn that improvisation is better.

> Ibid.

6 The raging productivity of the Victorians, shattered nerves and punctured stomachs, but it was a thing noble, glorious, awesome in itself.

> Ibid.

7 They [the F. Scott Fitzgeralds] had created themselves together, and they always saw themselves, their youth, their love, their lost youth and lost love, their failures and memories, as a sort of living fiction.

> Ibid.

912. Jane Jacobs
(1916–   )

1 But look what we have built . . . low-income projects
that become worse centers of delinquency, vandalism
and general social hopelessness than the slums they
were supposed to replace. . . . Cultural centers that
are unable to support a good bookstore. Civic centers
that are avoided by everyone but bums. . . .
Promenades that go from no place to nowhere and have
no promenaders. Expressways that eviscerate great cities. This is not the rebuilding of cities. This is the sack-
ing of cities.

> *The Death and Life of Great American
> Cities*, Introduction   1961

2 There is a quality even meaner than outright ugliness
or disorder, and this meaner quality is the dishonest
mask of pretended order, achieved by ignoring or suppressing the real order that is struggling to exist and to
be served.

> Ibid.

3 Streets and their sidewalks, the main public places of a
city, are its most vital organs. . . . If a city's streets
are safe from barbarism and fear, the city is thereby
tolerably safe from barbarism and fear. . . . To keep
the city safe is a fundamental task of a city's streets and
its sidewalks.

> Ibid., Pt. I, Ch. 2

4 Conventionally, neighborhood parks or parklike open
spaces are considered boons conferred on the deprived
populations of cities. Let us turn this thought around,
and consider city parks deprived places that need the
boon of life and appreciation conferred on *them*.

> Ibid., Ch. 5

5 The main responsibility of city planning and design
should be to develop—insofar as public policy and action can do so—cities that are congenial places for . . .
[a] great range of unofficial plans, ideas and opportunities to flourish, along with the flourishing of . . .
public enterprises.

> Ibid., Pt. III, Ch. 13

201

6 Innovating economies expand and develop. Economies that do not add new kinds of goods and services, but continue only to repeat old work, do not expand much nor do they, by definition, develop.

The Economy of Cities, Ch. 2   1969

7 A city that is large for its time is always an impractical settlement because size greatly intensifies whatever serious practical problems exist in an economy at a given time.

Ibid., Ch. 3

8 The only possible way to keep open the economic opportunities for new activities is for a "third force" to protect their weak and still incipient interests. Only governments can play this economic role. And sometimes, for pitifully brief intervals, they do. But because development subverts the status quo, the status quo soon subverts governments.

Ibid., Ch. 8

9 The bureaucratized, simplified cities, so dear to present-day city planners and urban designers, and familiar also to readers of science fiction and utopian proposals, run counter to the processes of city growth and economic development. Conformity and monotony, even when they are embellished with a froth of novelty, are not attributes of developing and economically vigorous cities. They are attributes of stagnant settlements.

Ibid.

913. Florynce R. Kennedy
(1916–   )

1 . . . there can be no really pervasive system of oppression, such as that in the United States, without the consent of the oppressed.

"Institutionalized Oppression vs. the Female," *Sisterhood Is Powerful,* Robin Morgan, ed.   1970

2 Oppressed people are frequently very oppressive when liberated.   Ibid.

3 Women are dirt searchers; their greatest worth is eradicating rings on collars and tables. Never mind real-

estate boards' corruption and racism, here's your soap-suds. Everything she is doing is peripheral, expendable, crucial, and nonnegotiable. Cleanliness is next to godliness.

Ibid.

4 Every form of bigotry can be found in ample supply in the legal system of our country. It would seem that Justice (usually depicted as a woman) is indeed blind to racism, sexism, war and poverty.

Ibid.

5 Being a mother is a noble status, right? Right. So why does it change when you put "unwed" or "welfare" in front of it?

Quoted in "The Verbal Karate of
Florynce R. Kennedy, Esq."
by Gloria Steinem, *Ms.*
March, 1973

6 Niggerization is the result of oppression—and it doesn't just apply to black people. Old people, poor people, and students can also get niggerized.

Ibid.

7 The biggest sin is sitting on your ass.

Ibid.

8 Don't agonize. Organize.

Ibid.

9 If men could get pregnant, abortion would be a sacrament.

Ibid.

10 My parents gave us a fantastic sense of security and worth. By the time the bigots got around to telling us we were nobody, we already *knew* we were somebody.

Ibid.

11 There are very few jobs that actually require a penis or vagina. All other jobs should be open to everybody.

Quoted in "Freelancer with No Time
to Write" by John Brady, *Writer's*
Digest   February, 1974

12 If you have a child, you know that when he gets quiet, that's when you start to worry. That's why the Establishment should be worried about the antiestablishmentarians—the women, the Blacks, the youth, the aged,

all the people who have no full part in the system, those I call the "niggers" of this country. They are planning campaigns in each legislative district. They are moving out of the streets and into the executive suites.

Quoted in "Impeachment?" by Claire
Safran, Redbook　　April, 1974

914. Patricia McLaughlin
(1916–　　)

1 Discoveries have reverberations. A new idea about one-self or some aspect of one's relations to others unsettles all one's other ideas, even the superficially related ones. No matter how slightly, it shifts one's entire orientation. And somewhere along the line of consequences, it changes one's behavior.

Quoted in American Scholar
Autumn, 1972

915. Cicely Saunders
(1916–　　)

1 It makes a difference as a very frightened lady drops into unconsciousness that I believe in a religion which speaks of a God who dies, and rises.

Quoted in "Saints Among Us," Time
December 29, 1975

916. Anya Seton
(1916–　　)

1 People in England seemed to think nothing of false teeth, even when they got them from the National Health.

Green Darkness, Pt. I, Ch. 1　　1972

2 "As I grew up I got cynical. I'd see Mother enthusiastic and involved with charlatans. Numerologists and astrologists who charged five hundred dollars for a 'reading' which was so vague you could twist the meaning

204

any way you wanted. And faith healers who couldn't seem to heal themselves, and a Yogi in California who preached purity, sublimity and continence, and then tried to seduce me one day while Mother was out."

Ibid., Ch. 2

3 "Truth is naturally universal," said Akananda, "and shines into many different windows, though some of them are clouded."

Ibid., Pt. III, Ch. 19

917. Frances Silverberg
(1916–   )

1 It was better not to speak, nor let your face or eyes show what you were feeling, because if people didn't know how you felt about them, or things, or maybe thought you had no feelings at all, they couldn't hurt you as much, only a little.

"Rebecca by Any Other Name,"
American Scene: New Voices,
Don Wolfe, ed.   <i>1963</i></div>

918. Annie Skau
(1916?–   )

1 The old Christian who has lived and walked with the Lord for many years is living in a treasure chamber.

Quoted in "Saints Among Us," Time
December 29, 1975

919. Hiltgunt Zassenhaus
(1916–   )

1 If they bomb my home in Hamburg, all I have left is what I can carry with me. . . . [But] there was something no suitcase could hold. It was intangible and the prisoners hungered for it. Only our minds and hearts could give truth and hope.

Walls: Resisting the Third Reich—
One Woman's Story   1974

920. Maeve Brennan
(1917–)

1 She had found that the more the child demanded of
her, the more she had to give. Strength came up in
waves that had their source in a sea of calm and uncon-
querable devotion. The child's holy trust made her
open her eyes, and she took stock of herself and found
that everything was all right, and that she could meet
what challenges arose and meet them well, and that she
had nothing to apologize for—on the contrary, she had
every reason to rejoice.

> "The Eldest Child," *The New Yorker*
> *June 23, 1968*

2 She . . . enjoyed the illusion that life had nothing to
teach her.

> *Ibid.*

3 He wished they could go back to the beginning and
start all over again, but the place where they had stood
together, where they had been happy, was all trampled
over and so spoiled that it seemed impossible ever to
make it smooth again.

> *Ibid.*

921. Gwendolyn Brooks
(1917–)

1 Abortions will not let you forget.
You remember the children you got that you did not
  get. . . .

> "The Mother," St. 1,
> *A Street in Bronzeville*   1945

2 To whatever you incline, your final choice here must
  be handling
Occasional sweet clichés with a dishonesty of deft tact.
For these people are stricken, they want none of your
  long-range messages,
Only the sweet clichés, to pamper them, modify fright.
> *Ibid.,* "The Funeral," St. 1

3 I hold my honey and I store my bread
In little jars and cabinets of my will.

I label clearly, and each latch and lid
I bid, Be firm till I return from hell.
I am very hungry. I am incomplete.
And none can tell when I may dine again.

> Ibid., "My dreams, my works,
> must wait till after hell"

4 People like definite decisions,
Tidy answers, all the little ravellings
Snipped off, the lint removed, they
Hop happily among their roughs
Calling what they can't clutch insanity
Or saintliness.

> "Memorial to Ed Blanc," St. 3,
> *Annie Allen*   1949

5 Maxie Allen always taught her
Stipendiary little daughter
To thank her Lord and lucky star
For eye that let her see so far,
For throat enabling her to eat
Her Quaker Oats and Cream-of-Wheat,
For tongue to tantrum for the penny,
For ear to hear the haven't-any,
For arm to toss
For leg to chance,
For heart to hanker for romance.

> Ibid., "Maxie Allen," St. 1

6 "Do not be afraid of no,
Who has so far, so very far to go". . . .

> Ibid., "Do not be afraid of no," St. 1

7 It is brave to be involved,
To be fearful to be unresolved.

> Ibid., St. 9

8 We do not want them to have less.
But it is only natural that we should think we have not
enough.
We drive on, we drive on.
When we speak to each other our voices are a little
gruff.

> Ibid., "Beverly Hills, Chicago," St. 8

9 To be cherished was the dearest wish of the heart of
Maude Martha Brown, and sometimes when she was
not looking at dandelions . . . it was hard to believe

that a thing of only ordinary allurements—if the allurements of any flower could be said to be ordinary—was
as easy to love as a thing of heart-catching beauty.
Maude Martha, Ch. 1   1953

10 What she wanted was to donate to the world a good
Maude Martha. That was the offering, the bit of art,
that could not come from any other. She would polish
and hone that.

Ibid., Ch. 6

11 But if the root was sour what business did she have up
there hacking at a leaf?

Ibid., Ch. 19

12 She had a tremendous impatience with other people's
ideas—unless those happened to be exactly like hers;
even then, often as not, she gave hurried, almost angry,
affirmative, and flew on to emphatic illumination of her
own.

Ibid., Ch. 23

13 I am scarcely healthy-hearted or human.
What can I teach my cheated Woman?
"My Little 'Bout-Town Gal," St. 2,
The Bean Eaters   1960

14 We real cool. We
Left school. We

Lurk late. We
Strike straight. We

Sing sin. We
Thin gin. We

Jazz June. We
Die soon.

Ibid., "We Real Cool"

15 I wonder if the elephant
Is lonely in his stall
When all the boys and girls are gone
And there's no shout at all,
And there's no one to stamp before,
No one to note his might.
Does he hunch up, as I do,
Against the dark of night?

Ibid., "Pete at the Zoo"

16 The man whose height his fear improved he
   arranged to fear no further.
   　　　　　"Medgar Evers," St. 1, *In the Mecca*　　1968

17 He opened us—
   who was a key,

   who was a man.
   　　　　　Ibid., "Malcolm X," Sts. 4–5

18 Does man love Art? Man visits Art, but squirms.
   Art hurts. Art urges voyages—
   and it is easier to stay at home,
   the nice beer ready.
   　　　　　Ibid., "The Chicago Picasso," St. 1

922. Barbara Deming
(1917–　　)

1 It is particularly hard on us as pacifists, of course, to
   face our own anger. It is particularly painful for us—
   hard on our pride, too—to have to discover in ourselves murderers.
   　　　　　"On Anger," *We Cannot Live
   Without Our Lives*　　1974

2 . . . not a bullying power, not the power to make people afraid. The power to make them see new things as
   possible.　　　　　Ibid.

3 If men put from them in fear all that is "womanish" in
   them, then long, of course, for that missing part in their
   natures, so seek to possess it by possessing us; and because they have feared it in their own souls seek, too,
   to dominate it in us—seek even to slay it—well, we're
   where we are now, aren't we?
   　　　　　Ibid., "Two Perspectives on Women's Struggles"

923. Phyllis Diller
(1917–　　)

1 Cleaning your house while your kids are still growing
   Is like shoveling the walk before it stops snowing.
   　　　　Phyllis Diller's Housekeeping Hints　　1966

2 Never go to bed mad. Stay up and fight.　　　　Ibid.

924. Indira Gandhi
(1917–   )

1 Peace we want because there is another war to fight against poverty, disease and ignorance. We have promises to keep to our people of work, food, clothing, and shelter, health and education.

> Radio Broadcast (January 26, 1966),
> Quoted in *Indira Gandhi*
> by Mithrapuram K. Alexander   *1968*

2 The young people of India must recognize that they will get from their country tomorrow what they give her today.

> Ibid.

3 You cannot shake hands with a clenched fist.

> Press Conference, New Delhi
> (October 19, 1971), Quoted in
> *Indira Speaks* by Dhiren Mullick   *1972*

4 Martyrdom does not end something; it is only the beginning.

> Ibid., Address to Parliament,
> New Delhi (August 12, 1971)

5 One cannot but be perturbed when fire breaks out in a neighbour's house.

> Ibid., Address in Kremlin,
> Moscow (September 28, 1971)

6 To natural calamities of drought, flood and cyclone has been added the man-made tragedy of vast proportions. I am haunted by tormented faces in our overcrowded refugee camps reflecting grim events, which have compelled exodus of these millions from East Bengal.

> Ibid., Meeting with Richard Nixon,
> Washington, D.C. (November 4, 1971)

7 No Government, no Head of Government can last if the people feel that this Government is not going to defend the security of the country.

> Ibid., Address, Columbia University
> (November 7, 1971)

8 The times have passed when any nation sitting three or four thousand miles away could give orders to Indians on the basis of their colour superiority to do as they wished. India has changed and she is no more a country of natives.

> Ibid., Address, Workers' Congress,
> New Delhi (December 2, 1971)

9 We know the true value of democracy, peace and freedom, since it was denied us for so long. . . . We have been slaves and will not allow others to make slaves of us again.

> Ibid., Address, New Delhi (December 12, 1971)

10 There are moments in history when brooding tragedy and its dark shadows can be lightened by recalling great moments of the past.

> Ibid., Letter to Richard Nixon
> (December 16, 1971)

11 There are many kinds of wars. One war has just ended but I do not know if peace has come.

> Ibid., Address, Ambala (December 24, 1971)

12 You must learn to be still in the midst of activity and to be vibrantly alive in repose.

> Quoted in "The Embattled Woman"
> by James Shepherd, *People* June 30, 1975

13 Is it possible, was it ever possible, to keep alive in India the beautiful dream of parliamentarian democracy the British imported along with five o'clock tea?

> Quoted in "Indira's Coup" by
> Oriana Fallaci, *New York Review*
> *of Books* September 18, 1975

14 My father [Pandit Jawaharlal Nehru] was a statesman, I'm a political woman. My father was a saint. I'm not.

> Ibid.

15 There exists no politician in India daring enough to attempt to explain to the masses that cows can be eaten.

> Ibid.

16 To bear many children is considered not only a religious blessing but also an investment. The greater their number, some Indians reason, the more alms they can beg.

> Ibid.

17 In a traditional society like India's, scandals are unavoidable. There is, in fact, the first consequence of the
most ancient of social diseases: corruption.

Ibid.

18 As for Western women, it seems to me that they have
often had to struggle to obtain their own rights. That
did not leave them much time to prove their abilities.
The time will come.

Quoted in "Conversation with
Indira Gandhi" by José-Luis de
Vilallonga, *Oui*   1975

19 I think that the highly industrialized Western world has
neglected to the utmost degree to leave room for man.
The infernal production-consumption cycle has completely dehumanized life. The individual has become a
tool. He hardly has any contact with nature anymore.
That is, with himself. He has lost his soul and is not
even trying to find it again.

Ibid.

925. Katharine Graham
(1917–   )

1 Common humor is very basic, isn't it? At both the
[Washington] *Post* and *Newsweek* there's a rather
great, healthy irreverence that makes working a lot of
fun.

Quoted in "The Power That Didn't
Corrupt" by Jane Howard, *Ms.*
October, 1974

2 If one is rich and one's a woman, one can be quite
misunderstood.

Ibid.

3 Bromidic though it may sound, some questions *don't*
have answers, which is a terribly difficult lesson to
learn.

Ibid.

4 So few grown women like their lives.

Ibid.

5 To love what you do and feel that it matters—how
could anything be more fun?   *Ibid.*

926. Fay Kanin
(1917?–   )

1 It's my feeling that the highest aspiration of the [screen] writer is to be a writer-executive in the sense that he goes on to control his material in one further aspect by producing or directing it. I believe every writer who can should try to accomplish that. Because it's the best way he can get his work done well.

> Quoted in "Fay Kanin," *The Screen-*
> *writer Looks at the Screenwriter*
> by William Froug   *1972*

2 While other crafts have to sit around chewing their fingernails waiting for a movie to be put together, writers have one great strength. They can sit down and generate their own employment and determine their own fate to a great extent by the degree of their disciplines, their guts, and their talents.

> Ibid.

3 For myself, I think the word auteur has been used, misused, paraded, fought over, intellectualized, and interpreted to the point of boredom. As I understand from my French, auteur means author. And I cannot see how someone is an author who, having a concept for a film, does not at some point sit down and write it. . . .

> Ibid.

4 Only an insatiable ego or an intolerable sense of inferiority could lead a director to ignore the basic creativity of the man or woman who thought it up, sweated it out, and delivered those precious pages into his hands.

> Ibid.

5 But in terms of the studio system, as I see it today, and as I knew it, it's as different as day and night. I see frightened people, unwilling to make a decision. Certainly not enjoying the making of the film because the end result is so perilous, so in question.

> Ibid.

6 But, in the end, I believe that to be a creative person and not to be able to express it in your own terms is difficult, and eventually intolerable, for any human being anywhere.

> Ibid.

927. Carson McCullers
(1917–1967)

1 "There are those who know and those who don't know.
And for every ten thousand who don't know there's
only one who knows. That's the miracle of all time—
that these millions know so much but don't know this."

The Heart Is a Lonely Hunter,
Pt. I, Ch. 2   *1940*

2 The inside room was a very private place. She could be
in the middle of a house full of people and still feel
like she was locked up by herself.

Ibid., Pt. II, Ch. 5

3 "Say a man died and left his mule to his four sons. The
sons would not wish to cut up the mule into four parts
and each take his share. They would own and work the
mule together. That is the way Marx says all of the
natural resources should be owned—not by one group
of rich people but by all the workers of the world as a
whole."

Ibid., Ch. 6

4 "Today we are not put up on the platforms and sold at
the courthouse square. But we are forced to sell our
strength, our time, our souls during almost every hour
that we live. We have been freed from one kind of slavery only to be delivered into another."

Ibid.

5 An army post in peacetime is a dull place. Things happen, but then they happen over and over again. . . .
But perhaps the dullness of a post is caused most of all
by insularity and by a surfeit of leisure and safety, for
once a man enters the army he is expected only to follow the heels ahead of him.

Reflections in a Golden Eye, Ch. 1   *1941*

6 Three words were in the captain's heart. He shaped
them soundlessly with his trembling lips, as he had not
breath to spare for a whisper: "I am lost." And having
given up life, the Captain suddenly began to live.

Ibid., Ch. 3

7 His preoccupation with the soldier grew in him like a disease. As in cancer, when the cells unaccountably rebel and begin the insidious self-multiplication that will ultimately destroy the body, so in his mind did the thoughts of the soldier grow out of all proportion to their normal sphere.

Ibid., Ch. 4

8 This was the summer when for a long time she had not been a member. She belonged to no club and was a member of nothing in the world. Frankie had become an unjoined person who hung around in the doorways, and she was afraid.

The Member of the Wedding, Pt. I   1946

9 This August she was twelve and five-sixths years old. She was five feet and three-quarter inches tall, and she wore a Number 7 shoe. . . . If she reached her height on her eighteenth birthday, she had five and one-sixth growing years ahead of her. Therefore, according to mathematics and unless she could somehow stop herself, she would grow to be over nine feet tall. And what would be a lady who was over nine feet high? She would be a Freak.

Ibid.

10 "I see a green tree. And to me it is green. And you would call the tree green also. And we would agree on this. But is the colour you see as green the same colour I see as green? Or say we both call a colour black. But how do we know that what you see as black is the same colour I see as black?"

Ibid., Pt. II, Ch. 2

11 "We all of us somehow caught. We born this way or that way and we don't know why. But we caught anyhow. . . . And maybe we wants to widen and bust free. But no matter what we do we still caught. Me is me and you is you and he is he. We each one of us somehow caught all by ourself."

Ibid.

12 F. Jasmine did not want to go upstairs, but she did not know how to refuse. It was like going into a fair booth, or fair ride, that once having entered you cannot leave until the exhibition or the ride is finished. Now it was the same with this soldier, this date. She could not leave until it ended.   *Ibid.*, Ch. 3

13 . . . the anodyne of time. . . .

> "The Sojourner," *The Ballad of*
> *the Sad Cafe*   1951

14 Sweet, casual intimacy, the soft-fleshed loveliness indisputably possessed.

> Ibid.

15 His own life seemed so solitary, a fragile column supporting nothing amidst the wreckage of the years.

> Ibid.

16 Was it indeed true that at one time he had called this stranger, Elizabeth, Little Butterduck during nights of love, that they had lived together, shared perhaps a thousand days and nights and—finally—endured in the misery of sudden solitude the fiber by fiber (jealousy, alcohol and money quarrels) destruction of the fabric of married love.

> Ibid.

17 The prelude was as gaily iridescent as a prism in a morning room.

> Ibid.

18 *"L'improvisation de la vie humaine,"* he said. "There's nothing that makes you so aware of the improvisation of human existence as a song unfinished. Or an old address book."

> Ibid.

19 Ferris glimpsed the disorder of his life: the succession of cities, of transitory loves; and time, the sinister glissando of the years, time always.

> Ibid.

928. Jessica Mitford
(1917–   )

1 Easier would it be, I thought, to recognize the individual faces of sheep on an Australian ranch than to match names and faces among this monotonous sea of seemingly unvaried human beings.

> *Hons and Rebels,* Ch. 11   1960

2 Things on the whole are much faster in America; people don't *stand for election,* they *run for office.* If a

person say he's *sick*, it doesn't mean regurgitating; it means *ill*. *Mad* means angry, not *insane*. Don't ask for the left-luggage; it's called a check-room. A nice joint means a good pub, not roast meat.

Ibid.

3 O death where is thy sting? O grave where is thy victory? Where, indeed? Many a badly stung survivor, faced with the aftermath of some relative's funeral, has ruefully conceded that the victory has been won hands down by a funeral establishment—in disastrously unequal battle.

The American Way of Death   1963

4 No doubt prison administrators sense that to permit the media and the public access to their domain would result in stripping away a major justification for their existence: that they are confining depraved, brutal creatures.

Kind and Unusual Punishment, Ch. 1   *1971*

5 What of homosexuality, recognized by everyone in Corrections as an inevitable consequence of long-term segregation of the sexes? Having driven them to it, why punish for it?

Ibid., Ch. 2

6 When is conduct a crime, and when is a crime not a crime? When Somebody Up There—a monarch, a dictator, a Pope, a legislator—so decrees.   *Ibid.*, Ch. 5

7 One of the nicest American scientists I know was heard to say, "Criminals in our penitentiary are fine experimental material—much cheaper than chimpanzees." I hope the chimpanzees don't come to hear of this.

Ibid., Ch. 9

8 No doubt like schools, old-age homes, mental hospitals, and other closed institutions that house the powerless, prisons afford a very special opportunity to employees at all levels for various kinds of graft and thievery.

Ibid., Ch. 10

9 Radical and revolutionary ideologies are seeping into the prisons. Whereas formerly convicts tended to regard themselves as unfortunates whose accident of birth at the bottom of the heap was largely responsible for their plight, today many are questioning the validity of the heap.   *Ibid.*, Ch. 13

10 Those of us on the outside [of prisons] do not like to think of wardens and guards as our servants. Yet they are, and they are intimately locked in a deadly embrace with their human captives behind the prison walls. By extension so are we. A terrible double meaning is thus imparted to the original question of human ethics: Am I my brother's keeper?

Ibid., Ch. 15

929. Estelle R. Ramey
(1917–   )

1 . . . what is human and the same about the males and females classified as *Homo sapiens* is much greater than the differences.

"Men's Monthly Cycles (They Have
Them Too, You know)," The First
Ms. Reader, Francine Klagsbrun, ed.
1972

2 In man, the shedding of blood is always associated with injury, disease, or death. Only the female half of humanity was seen to have the magical ability to bleed profusely and still rise phoenix-like each month from the gore.

Ibid.

3 Women's chains have been forged by men, not by anatomy.

Ibid.

4 I don't mind . . . the fun and games of being treated like a fragile flower. But as a physiologist working with the unromantic scientific facts of life, I find it hard to delude myself about feminine frailty.

Quoted in The Prime of Ms. America
by Janet Harris   1975

930. Christiane Rochefort
(1917–   )

1 CELINE. It's not only that you are killing grass and trees. . . . You are killing LIFE.

Les Stances à Sophie   1970

2 JULIA. Never argue with them. You're always forgetting you're a woman. They never listen to what you're
saying, they just want to listen to the music of your
voice.

> Ibid.

3 CELINE. Don't you read the paper? Don't you know
that men don't hit their wives any more?

> Ibid.

4 . . . when someone tells you that you're paranoic in a
situation that is not socialized yet, you feel you are.

> Quoted in "Les Stances à Sophie"
> by Annette Levy, *Women and Film*
> (Vol. I, Nos. 3 and 4)   *1973*

5 You can go to the hospital. If you don't go to the hospital, you can go to marriage. And if you don't go to
marriage you can go to the women's movement.

> Ibid.

931. Han Suyin
(1917–   )

1 What we loved best about England was the grass—the
short, clean, incredibly green grass with its underlying
tough, springy turf, three hundred years growing.

> *Destination Chungking*, Ch. 2   *1942*

2 The city hums with noise and work and hope. This is
Chungking, not dead Pompeii—five hundred thousand
Chinese with a will to withstand, to endure and build
again. Next year, next spring, the planes will lay it
waste again. Next autumn we shall be building. . . .

> Ibid., Ch. 12

3 "Your laws are ineffective," Wen declared. "Why? Because no system of control will work as long as most of
those administering the law against an evil have more
than a finger dipped into it themselves."

> Ibid., Ch. 13

4 "I'd sell my love for food any day. The rice bowl is to
me the most valid reason in the world for doing anything. A piece of one's soul to the multitudes in return
for rice and wine does not seem to me a sacrilege."

> *A Many-Splendoured Thing*, Preface   *1950*

5 Our feelings are very much governed by commonplace associations, and often influenced by that sort of short-term logic which renders steady thinking superfluous.
Ibid., Pt. II, Ch. 1

6 "For sages and wise men have been mute for many centuries, and their names are forgotten. But drunkards leave a resounding echo after them."
Ibid., Ch. 7

7 Foolish, mad, invulnerable in lunacy, having forgotten what I knew the winter before; that no one is invulnerable to repeated suggestion; that I was no different, no stronger, no more able to withstand reiteration than others. . . .
Ibid., Pt. II, Ch. 8

8 Afterwards, as happens when a man is safely dead, they sang his praise.
Ibid., Pt. IV

9 This is Malaya. Everything takes a long, a very long time, in Malaya. Things get done, occasionally, but more often they don't, and the more in a hurry you are, the quicker you break down.
And the Rain My Drink, Ch. 2   1956

10 Barbed wire fences the clearings where man survives, and outside it is the grey-green toppling surge, all-engulfing, of the jungle.   *Ibid.*, Ch. 8

11 "I'm nicely dead," she told Leo, and it was his turn to find nothing to say.
The Mountain Is Young,
Pt. I, Ch. 1   1958

12 She was plunged in this new consciousness where vision and hearing was all, in which there was total forgetting of self, the body moving without knowing itself in movement, wholly transported in this same ecstasy, the trance concentration which here made her one with all the thousands gathered.   *Ibid.*, Pt. II, Ch. 13

13 . . . all humans are frightened of their own solitude. Yet only in solitude can man learn to know himself, learn to handle his own eternity of aloneness. And love from one being to another can only be that two solitudes come nearer, recognize and protect and comfort each other.   *Ibid.*, Pt. V, Ch. 1

14 How few of us really try to find out what we're like, really, inside?

Winter Love   1962

15 The world needs the artist who records, with dispassionate compassion, more than the missionary who proclaims with virulence unreal crusades against reality, especially those who want to put the clock back to an ideal past that never was.

The Crippled Tree, Pt. I, Ch. 1   1965

16 For exploitation and oppression is not a matter of *race*. It is the system, the apparatus of world-wide brigandage called imperialism, which made the Powers behave the way they did. I have no illusions on this score, nor do I believe that any Asian nation or African nation, in the same state of dominance, and with the same system of colonial profit-amassing and plunder, would have behaved otherwise.

Ibid., Ch. 9

17 These ways to make people buy were strange and new to us, and many bought for the sheer pleasure at first of holding in the hand and talking of something new. And once this was done, it was like opium, we could no longer do without this new bauble, and thus, though we hated the foreigners and though we knew they were ruining us, we bought their goods. Thus I learned the art of the foreigners, the art of creating in the human heart restlessness, disquiet, hunger for new things, and these new desires became their best helpers.

Ibid., Ch. 15

18 A country is not truly betrayed to the enemy outside its gates unless there are also traitors within. For money, for power, these can be found.

Ibid., Ch. 17

19 Looking back now, with the hindsight of history, I can understand it so much better. But understanding is also effacement, a vagueness, which explains, but explains away the minute agonies, the grief that warps a life, which accepts, as a tree, crippled at its root by some voracious stabbing insect and for ever after bearing the mark of the beast upon its unfolding, is accepted in the landscape.

Ibid., Pt. II, Ch. 18

20 "Goldfish are flowers," said Papa, "flowers that move."

Ibid., Ch. 26

21 Pain occupies its verbal niche in a construction of words, building a life after it has been lived, for what is lived is encountered in a retrospect of sentences made to fit what happened shaped by what was.

Ibid., Ch. 30

22 On the railway. . . . beneficent dragons champing docile impatience on the iron tracks, insides of fire so still, hooting melody of the night proclaiming life, life roaring, life waiting to pounce.

Ibid.

932. Pearl Bailey
(1918–   )

1 When you're young, the silliest notions seem the greatest achievements.

The Raw Pearl, Ch. 1   1968

2 Vaudeville is a marvelous stepping stone to legit and movies. You learn to touch the audience, yet leave them alone, which no other part of the business teaches you so well. Sometimes a performer can become so much a part of the show business world that he loses touch with the people, the audiences, outside. It's good to be, as the Bible says, in the world but not of it.

Ibid., Ch. 5

3 What is really sad is when a legend starts to fade. I think about the cowboys who carved notches in their guns for every man they killed. Everything the person has done is right there. You can see the experience in them. But sometimes, though the gun still has bullets and the aim is still good, the world stops the carving of the notches. It is so sad to see a legendary performer cut off from his audiences, even though the basic talent is still there, seasoned by experience. Who throws away a beautiful old bottle of wine?

Ibid., Ch. 6

4 There's a period of life when we swallow a knowledge of ourselves and it becomes either good or sour inside.

Ibid., Ch. 13

5 The fact is that it takes more than ingredients and technique to cook a good meal. A good cook puts something of *himself* into the preparation—he cooks with enjoyment, anticipation, spontaneity, and he is willing to experiment.

Pearl's Kitchen, Preface   *1973*

6 My kitchen is a mystical place, a kind of temple for me. It is a place where the surfaces seem to have significance, where the sounds and odors carry meaning that transfers from the past and bridges to the future.

Ibid., "Sanctuary"

7 I cannot understand how we can put together all those programs for sending food across the oceans when at home we have people who are slowly starving to death. We could use less foreign aid and more home aid.

Ibid., Epilogue

8 Hungry people cannot be good at learning or producing anything, except perhaps violence.

Ibid.

933. Peg Bracken
(1918–   )

1 . . . unnecessary dieting is because everything from television to fashion ads have made it seem wicked to cast a shadow. This wild, emaciated look appeals to some women, though not to many men, who are seldom seen pinning up a *Vogue* illustration in a machine shop.

The I Hate to Cook Book   *1960*

934. Gertrude Louise Cheney
(1918–   )

1 All people are made alike.
They are made of bone, flesh and dinners.
Only the dinners are different.

"People"   *1927*

935. Betty Ford
(1918–   )

1 . . . I wouldn't be surprised [if her daughter had an affair]. I think she's a perfectly normal human being like all young girls. If she wanted to continue, I would certainly counsel and advise her on the subject. And I'd want to know pretty much about the young man . . . whether it was a worthwhile encounter. . . . She's pretty young to start affairs, [but] she's a big girl.

Interview, "60 Minutes,"
CBS-TV   *August 10, 1975*

936. Corita Kent
(1918–   )

1 There are so many hungry people that God cannot appear to them except in the form of bread.

"Enriched Bread" (silkscreen)   *1965*

2 One of the things Jesus did was to step aside from the organized religion of his time because it had become corrupt and bogged down with rules. Rules became more important than feeding the hungry.

Quoted in "A Time of Transition for
Corita Kent" by Lucie Kay Scheuer,
Los Angeles Times   *July 11, 1974*

3 Women's liberation is the liberation of the feminine in the man and the masculine in the woman.

Ibid.

* * *

4 The real circus
with acrobats, jugglers
and bareback riders =
also an empty field
transformed, and
in the tent artists and
freaks, children and
pilgrims and animals
are gathered in com-
munion = us

Poster, New York Urban Coalition, Inc.

937. Ann Landers
(1918–   )

1 Women complain about sex more often than men. Their gripes fall into two major categories: (1) Not enough. (2) Too much.

Ann Landers Says Truth Is Stranger . . . , Ch. 2   *1968*

2 What the vast majority of American children needs is to stop being pampered, stop being indulged, stop being chauffeured, stop being catered to. In the final analysis it is not what you do for your children but what you have taught them to do for themselves that will make them successful human beings.

Ibid., Ch. 3

3 All married couples should learn the art of battle as they should learn the art of making love. Good battle is objective and honest—never vicious or cruel. Good battle is healthy and constructive, and brings to a marriage the principle of equal partnership.

Ibid., Ch. 11

938. Ida Lupino
(1918–   )

1 And believe me, *Bring it in on time* is such a major factor in television that I'd sometimes get absolutely sick to my stomach days before-hand. . . . So any ladies who want to take over men's jobs—if that's what they really want—had better have strong stomachs.

Quoted in *Popcorn Venus* by Marjorie Rosen   *1973*

939. Anna Magnani
(1918–1973)

1 Great passions, my dear, don't exist: they're liars' fantasies. What do exist are little loves that may last for a short or a longer while.

Quoted in "Anna Magnani," *The Egotists* by Oriana Fallaci   *1963*

225

2 . . . I might use foul language, but I do hate bad breeding.

Ibid.

3 Movies, today, are made up of festivals, cannibalism, the idiocy they call lack of communication, intellectuals who always make out that they're teaching something and undervalue the public, forgetting that the public is composed—all right—of insecure individuals, but, put together, these insecure individuals become a miracle of intelligence. And intelligence won't put up with being led by the nose by imbeciles who preach from the pulpit.

Ibid.

4 Children are like puppies: you have to keep them near you and look after them if you want to have their affection.   Ibid.

940. Martha Mitchell
(1918–1976)

1 I'm not certain that we should have Democrats in the Cabinet.

Interview, "Today Show," NBC-TV
February 11, 1971

2 "I've never said I was against integration. It should have started right after the Civil War. But why single out the South? The South has been imposed on long enough. It's the orphan of the nation.

Quoted in Martha: The Mouth That
Roared by Charles Ashman and
Sheldon Engelmayer   1973

941. Penelope Mortimer
(1918–)

1 In all the years of her marriage, a long war in which attack, if not happening, was always imminent, she had learned an expert cunning. The way to avoid being hurt, to dodge unhappiness, was to run away. Feelings of guilt and cowardice presented no problems that couldn't be overcome by dreams, by games, by the gen-

tle sound of her own voice advising and rebuking her as she went about the house.

Daddy's Gone A-Hunting, Ch. 1   1958

2 "There is an obsessive tenderness and passion, an eating out of one's heart, a sense of longing, an affliction, which remains buried and unchanged from childhood, this is what is called falling in love. The longing is for reciprocation, the affliction is in knowing that reciprocation is forbidden."

Ibid., Ch. 5

3 "I thought I was supposed to lie on a couch and you wouldn't say a word. It's like the Inquisition or something. Are you trying to make me feel I'm wrong? Because I do that for myself."

The Pumpkin Eater, Ch. 1   1962

4 . . . some of my innocence, trust, stupidity, idealism has been stripped away from me like skins. I was smaller, uglier, more powerful than I had been before, and I felt bewitched by fear.   Ibid., Ch. 5

5 It was intensely boring, but they all made a great fuss over me and I began to think that perhaps it was better to be bored and admired than interested and miserable.

Ibid., Ch. 10

6 "What do your patients do while you're away? Commit suicide, murder their wives, or do they just sit and cry and take pills and think about what they told you last time? . . . If I'm sane enough to be left alone with my *thoughts* for two weeks then I'm too sane to need these futile, boring conversations—because my God, they bore me—at six guineas a time."   Ibid., Ch. 11

7   "I have arguments with myself."
     "About what?"
     "Between the part of me that believes in things, and the part that doesn't."
     "And which wins?"
     "Sometimes one. Sometimes the other."
     "Then stop arguing."   Ibid., Ch. 23

8 I was, and still am, running away from the person to whom . . . I had addressed my life.

Long Distance   1974

9 Grief is a very antisocial state. . . .   Ibid.

942. Muriel Spark
(1918–   )

1 "Being over seventy is like being engaged in a war. All our friends are going or gone and we survive amongst the dead and the dying as on a battlefield."
> *Memento Mori*, Ch. 4   *1959*

2 "If I had my life over again I should form the habit of nightly composing myself to thoughts of death. I would practise, as it were, the remembrance of death. There is no other practise which so intensifies life. Death, when it approaches, ought not to take one by surprise. It should be part of the full expectancy of life."
> Ibid., Ch. 11

3 There was altogether too much candour in married life; it was an indelicate modern idea, and frequently led to upsets in a household, if not divorce.
> Ibid., Ch. 12

4 "Give me a girl at an impressionable age, and she is mine for life."
> *The Prime of Miss Jean Brodie*, Ch. 1   *1961*

5 "One's prime is elusive. You little girls, when you grow up, must be on the alert to recognize your prime at whatever time of your life it may occur. You must then live it to the full."
> Ibid.

6 "Art and religion first; then philosophy; lastly science. That is the order of the great subjects of life, that's their order of importance."
> Ibid., Ch. 2

7 "To me education is a leading out of what is already there in the pupil's soul. To Miss Mackay it is a putting in of something that is not there, and that is not what I call education, I call it intrusion. . . ."
> Ibid.

8 It is not to be supposed that Miss Brodie was unique. . . . There were legions of her kind during the nineteen-thirties, women from the age of thirty and upward who crowded their war-bereaved spinsterhood

with voyages of discovery into new ideas and energetic practices in art or social welfare, education or religion.

Ibid., Ch. 3

9 Miss Brodie said: "Pavlova contemplates her swans in order to perfect her swan dance, she studies them. That is true dedication. You must all grow up to be dedicated women as I have dedicated myself to you."

Ibid.

10 "It is impossible to persuade a man who does not disagree, but smiles."

Ibid., Ch. 4

11 "Nothing infuriates people more than their own lack of spiritual insight, Sandy, that is why the Moslems are so placid, they are full of spiritual insight."

Ibid.

12 A house in which there are no people—but with all the signs of tenancy—can be a most tranquil good place.

"The Portobello Road," *Collected Stories: I*   1968

13 Kathleen, speaking from that Catholic point of view which takes some getting used to, said, "She was at Confession only the day before she died—wasn't she lucky?"

Ibid.

14 For some years she had been thinking she was not much inclined towards sex. . . . It is not merely a lack of pleasure in sex, it is dislike of the excitement. And it is not merely dislike, it is worse, it is boredom.

Ibid., "Bang-Bang You're Dead"

15 She did not know then that the price of allowing false opinions was the gradual loss of one's capacity for forming true ones.

Ibid.

16 Oh, the trifles, the people, that get on your nerves when you have a neurosis!

Ibid., "Come Along, Marjorie"

17 Now I realised the distinction between neurosis and madness, and in my agitation I half-envied the woman beyond my bedroom wall, the sheer cool sanity of her behaviour within the limits of her impracticable mania.

Ibid.

18 New York, home of the vivisectors of the mind, and of the mentally vivisected still to be reassembled, of those who live intact, habitually wondering about their states of sanity, and home of those whose minds have been dead, bearing the scars of resurrection. . . .

The Hothouse by the East River, Ch. 1   *1973*

19 "Sex," she says, "is a subject like any other subject. Every bit as interesting as agriculture."

Ibid., Ch. 4

943. Abigail Van Buren
(1918–   )

1 People who fight fire with fire usually end up with ashes.

"Dear Abby" Newspaper Column
March 7, 1974

2 Some people are more turned on by money than they are by love. . . . In one respect they're alike. They're both wonderful as long as they last.

Ibid.   *April 26, 1974*

3 Religion, like water, may be free, but when they pipe it to you, you've got to help pay for the piping. And the piper!   Ibid.   *April 28, 1974*

4 The best index to a person's character is (a) how he treats people who can't do him any good, and (b) how he treats people who can't fight back.

Ibid.   *May 16, 1974*

5 Psychotherapy, unlike castor oil, which will work no matter how you get it down, is useless when forced on an uncooperative patient.   Ibid.   *July 11, 1974*

944. Ella Grasso
(1919–   )

1 I'm opposed to abortion because I happen to believe that life deserves the protection of society.

Quoted in "Ella Grasso of
Connecticut" by Joseph B. Treaster, *Ms.*
October, 1974

2 I would not be President because I do not aspire to be President. But I'm sure that a woman will be President. When? I don't know. It depends. I don't think the woods are full of candidates today.

Quoted in *Newsweek*   *November 4, 1974*

3 In Connecticut I'm just an old shoe.

Quoted in *Time*   *November 18, 1974*

4 I keep my campaign promises, but I never promised to wear stockings.

Ibid.

945. Uta Hagen
(1919–   )

1 More than in the other performing arts the lack of respect for acting seems to spring from the fact that every layman considers himself a valid critic.

Respect for Acting, Pt. I, Introduction   *1973*

2 The American theatre poses endless problems for any actor who wants to call himself an artist, who wants to be part of an art form.

Ibid.

3 Talent is an amalgam of high sensitivity; easy vulnerability; high sensory equipment (seeing, hearing, touching, smelling, tasting—*intensely*); a vivid imagination as well as a grip on reality; the desire to communicate one's own experience and sensations, to make one's self heard and seen.

Ibid., Ch. I

4 Rebellion or revolt does not necessarily find its expression in violence. A gentle, lyric stroke may be just as powerful a means of expression.

Ibid.

5 To maintain one's ideals in ignorance is easy. . . .

Ibid.

6 We must overcome the notion that we must be *regular.* . . . It robs you of the chance to be extraordinary and leads you to the mediocre.   Ibid., Ch. 2

7 A great danger is to take the five senses for granted. Most people do. Once you become aware that the

sources which move in on you when you truly touch, taste, smell, see and hear are endless, you must also realize that self-involvement deadens the senses, and vanity slaughters them until you end up playing alone—and meaninglessly.

Ibid., Ch. 6

946. Pauline Kael
(1919–   )

1 Movies have been doing so much of the same thing—in slightly different ways—for so long that few of the possibilities of this great hybrid art have yet been explored.
"Movies as Opera,"
Going Steady, Pt. I   *1968*

2 Good movies make you care, make you believe in possibilities again.
Ibid., Pt. II, Ch. 1

3 Technique is hardly worth talking about unless it's used for something worth doing. . . .
Ibid., Ch. 2

4 The new tribalism in the age of the media is not necessarily the enemy of commercialism; it is a direct outgrowth of commercialism and its ally, perhaps even its instrument.   Ibid., Ch. 4

5 Unsupervised enjoyment is probably not the only kind there is but it may feel like the only kind. Irresponsibility is part of the pleasure of all art, it is the part the schools cannot recognize.   Ibid., Ch. 5

6 Art is still what teachers and ladies and foundations believe in, it's civilized and refined, cultivated and serious, cultural, beautiful, European, Oriental: it's what America isn't, and it's especially what American movies are not.   Ibid.

7 Trash has given us an appetite for art.   Ibid.

8 The lowest action trash is preferable to wholesome family entertainment. When you clean them up, when you make movies respectable, you kill them. The wellspring of their *art*, their greatness, is in not being respectable.   Ibid., Ch. 6

9 If big film directors are to get credit for doing badly what others have been doing brilliantly for years with no money, just because they've put it on a big screen, then businessmen are greater than poets and theft is art.   *Ibid.*, Ch. 8

10 The words "Kiss Kiss Bang Bang," which I saw on an Italian movie poster, are perhaps the briefest statement imaginable of the basic appeal of movies.

Kiss Kiss Bang Bang, Title Note   *1968*

11 What they think is creativity is simply the excitement of success, the exhilaration of power.   *Ibid.*, Pt. I

12 . . . banality and luxuriant wastefulness . . . are so often called the superior "craftsmanship" of Hollywood.   *Ibid.*

13 It seems likely that many of the young who don't wait for others to call them artists, but simply announce that they are, don't have the patience to make art.

Ibid.

14 Good liberal parents didn't want to push their kids in academic subjects but oohed and aahed with false delight when their children presented them with a baked ashtray or a woven doily. Did anyone guess or foresee what narcissistic confidence this generation would develop in banal "creativity"? Now we're surrounded, inundated by artists.   *Ibid.*

15 We try to protect ourselves as women by betraying other women. And, of course, women who *are* good writers succeed in betrayal but fail to save themselves.

Ibid., Pt. II

16 . . . advertising determines what is accepted as art.

Ibid., Pt. III

17 What makes movies a great popular art form is that certain artists can, at moments in their lives, reach out and unify the audience—educated and uneducated—in a shared response. The tragedy in the history of movies is that those who have this capacity are usually prevented from doing so.   *Ibid.*

18 We may be reaching the end of the era in which individual movies meant something to people. In the new era, movies may just mean a barrage of images.

Ibid., Pt. V

947. Elizabeth Duncan Koontz
(1919–   )

1 . . . like steel that has been passed through fire, the century will be stronger for having been tested.

Quoted in "Impeachment?" by Claire
Safran, Redbook   April, 1974

948. Isobel Lennart
(1919?–   )

1 FANNY. Look—suppose all you ever had for breakfast was onion rolls. All of a sudden one morning, in walks a bagel. You'd say, "Ugh! What's that?" Until you tried it. *That's* my trouble. I'm a bagel on a plate full of onion rolls!   *Funny Girl*, Act I, Sc. 3   *1964*

2 NICK. Success is something to enjoy—to flaunt! Otherwise, why work so hard to get it?   Ibid., Sc. 10

3 NICK. Fanny, would you say you were a woman of— wide experience? . . .

FANNY. . . . I've been too busy. What about you? *Hundreds* of girls, huh?

NICK. The count is in mere dozens. Of very minor entanglements. I like to feel free.

FANNY. You can get lonesome—being that free.

NICK. You can get lonesome—being that busy.

Ibid., Sc. 11

4 FANNY. It's wonderful to hear an audience applaud, but you can't take an audience home with you!

Ibid., Sc. 14

949. Doris Lessing
(1919–   )

1 . . . he went on to remark gently that some women seemed to imagine birth control was a sort of magic; if they bought what was necessary and left it lying in a

corner of a drawer, nothing more was needed. To this attitude of mind, he said, was due a number of births every year which would astound the public.

A Proper Marriage, Pt. I, Ch. 1   1952

2 Love had brought her here, to lie beside this young man; love was the key to every good; love lay like a mirage through the golden gates of sex.

Ibid.

3 "Is there any evidence whatsoever that a person educated in one way rather than another will have different qualities, different abilities? And is there any evidence that the mass of human beings are better than brutes!"

Ibid.

4 There is something in the word "meeting" which arouses an instinctive and profound distrust in the bosoms of British people at this late hour of their history.

Ibid., Pt. IV, Ch. 2

5 "If people dug up the remains of this civilization a thousand years hence, and found Epstein's statues and that man Ellis, they would think we were just savages."

Martha Quest, Pt. I, Ch. 1   1952

6 "Died of gas from the war, she says. Pity those War Office blokes never understood that people could be ill because of the war, and it only showed afterwards. He got no compensation, she says. Damned unfair."

Ibid., Pt. II, Ch. 2

7 "In university they don't tell you that the greater part of the law is learning to tolerate fools."

Ibid., Pt. III, Ch. 2

8 . . . she envied her lost capacity for making the most of time—that was how she put it, as if time were a kind of glass measure which one could fill or not.

Ibid., Pt. IV, Ch. 1

9 What of October, that ambiguous month, the month of tension, the unendurable month?   Ibid.

10 "Sometimes I look at a young man in the States who has a certain resemblance, and I ask myself: Perhaps he is my son? Yes, yes, my friend, this is a question that every man must ask himself, sometimes, is it not?"

The Habit of Loving, Ch. 3   1957

235

11 The smell of manure, of sun on foliage, of evaporating water, rose to my head; two steps farther, and I could look down into the vegetable garden enclosed within its tall pale of reeds—rich chocolate earth studded emerald green, frothed with the white of cauliflowers, jewelled with the purple globes of eggplant and the scarlet wealth of tomatoes.   Ibid., Ch. 9

12 Effort, after days of laziness, seemed impossible.
                                        Ibid., Ch. 15

13 Pleasure resorts are like film stars and royalty who—or so one hopes—must be embarrassed by the figures they cut in the fantasies of people who have never met them.
                                        Ibid., Ch. 17

14 . . . he hated her for his ineptitude.
                            "One Off the Short List,"
                    A Man and Two Women · 1958

15 . . . the rifle, justified by utility. . . .   Ibid.

16 "Small things amuse small minds. . . ."
                        Ibid., "A Woman on a Roof"

17 "Don't you think there's something awful in two grown people stuck together all the time like Siamese twins?"
                    Ibid., "A Man and Two Women"

18 Bed is the best place for reading, thinking, or doing nothing.
                                    Ibid., "A Room"

19 "There's nothing in sight, not one object or building anywhere, that is beautiful. Everything is so ugly and mean and graceless that it should be bulldozed into the earth and out of the memory of man."
                    Ibid., "England Versus England"

20 . . . she was thirty-nine. . . . No, she did not envy her eighteen-year-old self at all. But she did envy, envied every day more bitterly, that young girl's genuine independence, largeness, scope, and courage.
                            Ibid., "Between Men"

21 . . . the satisfied fervour of one who has at last pinned a label on a rare specimen: "She is, of course, one of your typical English spinsters." . . . "I suppose she has given up?" "Given up what?" I asked. . . .
                            Ibid., "Our Friend Judith"

22 They separated gently, but the movements both used
   . . . were more like a fitting together.

   Ibid., "Each Other"

23 Above all, intelligence forbids tears.

   Ibid., "To Room 19"

24 A high price has to be paid for the happy marriage
   with the four healthy children in the large white gar-
   dened house.

   Ibid.

25 Some people had to live with crippled arms, or stam-
   mers, or being deaf. She would have to live knowing
   she was subject to a state of mind she could not own.

   Ibid.

26 It seems to me like this. It's not a terrible thing—I
   mean it may be terrible, but it's not damaging, it's not
   poisoning to do without something one really wants. . . .
   What's terrible is to pretend that the second-rate is
   first-rate. To pretend that you don't need love when
   you do; or you like your work when you know quite
   well you're capable of better.

   The Golden Notebook 1962

27 After a certain age—and for some of us that can be
   very young—there are no new people, beasts, dreams,
   faces, events: it all has happened before . . . and everything is an echo and a repetition; and there is no
   grief even that it is not a recurrence of something long
   out of memory.

   Particularly Cats, Ch. 2 1967

28 If a fish is the movement of water embodied, given
   shape, then cat is a diagram and pattern of subtle air.

   Ibid.

29 Oh cat; I'd say, or pray: be-*ooo*tiful cat! Delicious
   cat! Exquisite cat! Satiny cat! Cat like a soft owl, cat
   with paws like moths, jewelled cat, miraculous cat! Cat,
   cat, cat, cat.

   Ibid.

30 What is charm then? The free giving of a grace, the
   spending of something given by nature in her role of
   spendthrift. . . . Charm is something extra, superfluous, unnecessary, essentially a power thrown away—
   given.

   Ibid., Ch. 9

31 ". . . that is what learning is. You suddenly understand something you've understood all your life, but in
a new way."

The Four-Gated City   1969

32 Thinking? She would not have said so. She was trying
to catch hold of something, or to lay it bare so she
could look and define; for some time now she had been
"trying on" ideas like so many dresses off a rack.

The Summer Before the Dark   1973

33 Laughter is by definition healthy.

Ibid.

34 "The way to learn a language is to breathe it in. Soak it
up! Live it!"

Ibid.

35 And what authority even the creases in a suit can convey. . . .

Ibid.

36 Nonsense, it was all nonsense: this whole damned out-
fit, with its committees, its conferences, its eternal talk,
talk, talk, was a great con trick; it was a mechanism to
earn a few hundred men and women incredible sums of
money.

Ibid.

37 This was a happy and satisfactory marriage because
both she and Michael had understood, and very early
on, that the core of discontent, or of hunger, if you
like, which is unfailingly part of every modern marriage . . . was fed and heightened by what people
were educated to expect of marriage, which was a very
great deal because the texture of ordinary life . . . was
thin and unsatisfactory. Marriage had had a load
heaped on it which it could not sustain.   Ibid.

38 . . . older woman, younger man! Popular wisdom
claims that this particular class of love affair is the
most poignant, tender, poetic, exquisite one there is, altogether the choicest on the menu.   Ibid.

39 . . . should one judge people by the attitudes expected
of them by virtue of the years they had lived, their
phase or stage as mammals, or as items in society?
Well, that is how most people have to be judged; only a
few people are more than that.   Ibid.

40 There was nothing to prevent one or all of us becoming
victims at any moment.
The Memoirs of a Survivor   *1975*

950. Iris Murdoch
(1919–   )

1   "What are you famous *for*?"
   "For nothing. I am just famous."
   The Flight from the Enchanter   *1955*

2 "We can only learn to love by loving. . . ."
                The Belt   *1958*

3 "Only lies and evil come from letting people off. . . ."
          A Severed Head   *1961*

4 "You cannot have both civilization and truth. . . ."
                       Ibid.

5 "To be a complete victim may be another source of
power."   *The Unicorn*   *1963*

6 Munching the substance of one's life as if it were a fruit
with a thin soft furry exterior and a firm sweet fleshy
inside.   *The Nice and the Good*   *1968*

7 One's most ordinary everyday mode of consciousness
being busy and lively and unconcerned with self. *Ibid.*

8 Love can't always do work. Sometimes it just has to
look into the darkness.   *Ibid.*

9 In its own element, in its own silence, indubitably physical, indubitably present, and yet Other.   *Ibid.*

10 He led a double life. Did that make him a liar? He did
not feel a liar. He was a man of two truths.
   The Sacred and Profane Love Machine   *1974*

951. Françoise Parturier
(1919–   )

1 To tell a woman using her mind that she is thinking
with a man's brain means telling her that she can't
think with her own brain; it demonstrates your ineradicable belief in her intellectual inadequacy.
         Open Letter to Men   *1968*

2 In general all curvaceousness strikes men as incompatible with the life of the mind.

Ibid.

3 You men can't stand the truth, sir, as soon as it embarrasses your interests or your pleasure. . . .

Ibid.

4 And the more deodorants there are in the drugstores, the worse [woman] smells in literature.

Ibid.

5 That the most intelligent, discerning and learned men, men of talent and feeling, should finally put all their pride in their crotch, as awed as they are uneasy at the few inches sticking out in front of them, proves how normal it is for the world to be crazy. . . .

Ibid.

6 . . . we've never been in a democracy; we've always been in a phallocracy!

Ibid.

7 A real woman is a young, pretty, sexy, tender woman who is no taller than five feet six who adores you.

Ibid.

8 You say being a housewife is the noblest calling in the world. . . . You remind me of those company executives who . . . praise the "little guys" of their organization in their speeches. . . .

Ibid.

952. Eva Perón
(1919–1952)

1 Our President [General Juan Perón] has declared that the only privileged person in our country are the children.

Speech, "My Labour in the
Field of Social Aid," American
Congress of Industrial Medicine
December 5, 1949

2 Almsgiving tends to perpetuate poverty; aid does away with it once and for all. Almsgiving leaves a man just where he was before. Aid restores him to society as an

240

individual worthy of all respect and not as a man with a grievance. Almsgiving is the generosity of the rich; social aid levels up social inequalities. Charity separates the rich from the poor; aid raises the needy and sets him on the same level with the rich.

Ibid.

953. Mary Carolyn Davies
(fl. 1920s)

* * *

1 As oft as on the earth I've lain
   I've died and come to life again.

"Out of the Earth"

2 A trap's a very useful thing:
   Nature in our path sets Spring.
   It is a trap to catch us two,
   It is planned for me and you.

"Traps"

3 If I had known what trouble you were bearing;
   What griefs were in the silence of your face;
   I would have been more gentle, and more caring,
   And tried to give you gladness for a space.

"If I Had Known"

4 Iron, left in the rain
       And fog and dew,
   With rust is covered. —Pain
       Rusts into beauty too.

"Rust"

5 May I forget
   What ought to be forgotten; and recall
   Unfailing, all
   That ought to be recalled, each kindly thing,
   Forgetting what might sting.

"A Prayer for Every Day"

6 Let me be joy, be hope! Let my life sing!

Ibid.

7 Men are the devil—they all bring woe.
   In winter it's easy to say just "No."
   Men are the devil, that's one sure thing,
   But what are you going to do in spring?

"Men Are the Devil"

8 The talking oak
  To the ancient spoke.
  But any tree
  Will talk to me.

                              "Be Different to Trees"

9 Three can laugh and doom a king,
  Three can make the planets sing.

                                        "Three"

10 Women are doormats and have been,
     The years these mats applaud—
   They keep the men from going in
     With muddy feet to God.

                                    "Door-Mats"

954. Mary J. Elmendorf
(fl. 1920s)

* * *

1 Beauty's the thing that counts
  In women; red lips
  And black eyes are better than brains.
                              "Beauty's the Thing"

955. Charlotte Hardin
(fl. 1920s)

1 I found many who were continually wishing for beauty.
  I went to them with a sunset and a spray of mist, but
  they had already contented themselves in a shop with
  little painted candlesticks.
                              Coins and Medals   *1921*

956. Edith Summers Kelley
(fl. 1920s–1956)

1 . . . the barnyard was an expression of something that
  was real, vital, and fluid, that . . . was of natural and
  spontaneous growth, that . . . turned with its surroundings, that . . . was a part of the life that offered
  itself to her.

                                    Weeds   *1923*

2 The only break in what would seem to an outsider an intolerable stretch of tedium was the dinner. This usually consisted of salt hog meat, fried or boiled potatoes and some other vegetable, followed by a heavy-crusted apple pie or a soggy boiled pudding.

Ibid.

957. Elazabeth Shane
(fl. 1920s)

* * *

1 But every road is rough to me
  That has no friend to cheer it.

"Sheskinbeg"

958. Margaret Turnbull
(fl. 1920s–1942)

1 No man is responsible for his father. That is entirely his mother's affair.

Alabaster Lamps　1925

2 When a man confronts catastrophe on the road, he looks in his purse—but a woman looks in her mirror.

The Left Lady　1926

959. Bella Abzug
(1920–　)

1 I am not elevating women to sainthood, nor am I suggesting that all women share the same views, or that all women are good and all men bad. Women have screamed for war. Women, like men, have stoned black children going to integrated schools. Women have been and are prejudiced, narrowminded, reactionary, even violent. *Some* women. They, of course, have a right to vote and a right to run for office. I will defend that right, but I will not support them or vote for them.

Speech, National Women's Political
Caucus, Washington, D.C.　*July 10, 1971*

2 I've been described as a tough and noisy woman, a prize fighter, a man-hater, you name it. They call me

Battling Bella, Mother Courage, and a Jewish mother with more complaints than Portnoy. There are those who say I'm impatient, impetuous, uppity, rude, profane, brash, and overbearing. Whether I'm any of those things, or all of them, you can decide for yourself. But whatever I am—and this ought to be made very clear at the outset—I am a very serious woman.

Bella!, Mel Ziegler, ed., Introduction *1972*

3 Liberals! They're not leaders! If they were real leaders they'd understand that their style of politicking and self-aggrandizement is what's destroying the capacity of any of us to get anywhere.

Ibid. (January 19, 1971)

4 But the establishment is made up of little men, very frightened.

Ibid. (May 5, 1971)

5 In Britain the government has to come down in front of Parliament every day to explain its actions, but here the President never answers directly to Congress.

Ibid. (June 17, 1971)

6 One thing that crystallized for me like nothing else this year is that Congress is a very *unrepresentative* institution. . . . These men in Congress . . . represent their *own* point of view—by reason of their sex, background, and class.   Ibid., Epilogue

7 She [a woman politician] will be challenging a system that is still wedded to militarism and that saves billions of dollars a year by underpaying women and using them as a reserve cheap labor supply.

"Bella's-Eye View of Her Party's
Future," *Ms.*   *April, 1974*

8 A thoughtful husband, the [candidate's] manual said, should squelch any rumors that his wife is running for office because their marriage is on the skids. (Why else would a woman want to be in Congress?)   Ibid.

9 You can't have a Congress that responds to the needs of the workingman when there are practically no people here who represent him. And you're not going to have a society that understands its humanity if you don't have more women in government.

Quoted in "Impeachment?" by Claire
Safran, *Redbook*   *April, 1974*

10 If we get a government that reflects more of what this country is really about, we can turn the century—and the economy—around.

Ibid.

11 . . . our time has come. We will no longer content ourselves with leavings and bits and pieces of the rights enjoyed by men . . . we want our equal rights, nothing more but nothing less. We want an equal share of political and economic power.

Quoted in *Gullible's Travels*
by Jill Johnston   1974

960. Rosemary Brown
(1920?–   )

1 I'm not committed to welfare measures. I don't think they get at the root of the problem. I'm committed to the eradication of all poverty, to its being wiped out. I'm not hung up on guaranteed incomes and that kind of thing, because I don't think that's the solution. We've got to change the system and make it impossible to be poor.

Quoted in "The Radical Tradition of
Rosemary Brown" by Sharon Batt,
Branching Out   July/August, 1975

2 We cannot swing our vote. We have to swing our party.

Ibid.

3 The feeling is that until men are comfortable working in some of these fields that are traditionally considered to be female . . . women end up doing two jobs, and the men are still doing just one.   Ibid.

4 The whole idea of the feminist struggle being a peripheral kind of thing that you do in your spare time is something that has to be changed.   Ibid.

961. Rosalind Franklin
(1920–1958)

1 This was my first continental holiday by car . . . and I confirmed my impression that cars are undesirable.

. . . Travelling around in a little tin box isolates one
from the people and the atmosphere of the place in a
way that I have never experienced before. I found myself eyeing with envy all rucksacks and tents.

Quoted in *Rosalind Franklin and DNA*
by Anne Sayre   *1975p*

962. Barbara Guest
(1920–   )

1 I wonder if this new reality is going to destroy me.
"The Hero Leaves His Ship," St. 1,
The location of Things   *1962*

2 I am talking to you
With what is left of me written off,
On the cuff, ancestral and vague,
As a monkey walks through the many fires
Of the jungle while the village breathes in its sleep.
Ibid., "Sunday Evening," St. 3

3 Then you took my hand. You told me that love
was a sudden disturbance of the nerve ends
that startled the fibers and made them new
again.
Ibid., "Sadness," St. 3

4 Where goes this wandering blue,
This horizon that covers us without a murmur?
Let old lands speak their speech,
Let tarnished canopies protect us.
Ibid., "In the Alps," St. 1

963. Shirley Jackson
(1920–1965)

1 School was recently over for the summer, and the feeling of liberty sat uneasily on most of them. . . .
"The Lottery"   *1948*

2 "Listening to the young folks, nothing's good enough
for *them*. Next thing you know, they'll be wanting to
go back to living in caves, nobody work any more, live
that way for a while."

Ibid.

3 I believe that all women, but especially housewives, tend to think in lists. . . . The idea of a series of items, following one another docilely, forms the only possible reasonable approach to life if you have to live it with a home and a husband and children, none of whom would dream of following one another docilely.

Life Among the Savages, Pt. II 1953

4 "Cocoa," she said. "Cocoa. Damn miserable puny stuff, fit for kittens and unwashed boys. Did *Shakespeare* drink cocoa?"

The Bird's Nest, Pt. I 1954

5 . . . I saw that Beth now, looking about her and drawing herself together, was endeavoring to *form* herself, as it were; let my reader who is puzzled by my awkward explanations close his eyes for no more than two minutes, and see if he does not find himself suddenly not a compact human being at all, but only a consciousness on a sea of sound and touch; it is only with the eyes open that a corporeal form returns, and assembles itself firmly around the hard core of sight.

Ibid., Pt. IV

6 Her manner of dress, of speech, of doing her hair, of spending her time, had not changed since it first became apparent to a far younger Morgen that in all her life to come no one was, in all probability, going to care in the slightest how she looked, or what she did, and the minor wrench of leaving humanity behind was more than compensated for by her complacent freedom from a thousand small irritations.

Ibid., Pt. V

7 . . . February, when the days of winter seem endless and no amount of wistful recollecting can bring back any air of summer. . . .

Raising Demons, Pt. II 1956

8 It has long been my belief that in times of great stress, such as a four-day vacation, the thin veneer of family unity wears off almost at once, and we are revealed in our true personalities. . . .

Ibid., Pt. IV

9 She looked out the window . . . savoring the extreme pleasure of being on a moving train with nothing to do for six hours but read and nap and go into the dining-

car, going farther and farther every minute from the children, from the kitchen floor, with even the hills being incredibly left behind, changing into fields and trees too far away from home to be daily.

"Pillar of Salt," *The Magic of Shirley Jackson*, Stanley Edgar Hyman, ed.
1966p

10 She walked quickly around her one-room apartment. . . . After more than four years in this one home she knew all its possibilities, how it could put on a sham appearance of warmth and welcome when she needed a place to hide in, how it stood over her in the night when she woke suddenly, how it could relax itself into a disagreeable unmade, badly-put-together state, mornings like this, anxious to drive her out and go back to sleep.

Ibid., "Elizabeth"

964. Gerda Lerner
(1920–   )

1 Black people cannot and will not become integrated into American society on any terms but those of self-determination and autonomy.

Black Women in White America,
Preface   *1972*

2 . . . black women . . . are trained from childhood to become workers, and expect to be financially self-supporting for most of their lives. They know they will have to work, whether they are married or single; work to them, unlike to white women, is not a liberating goal, but rather an imposed lifelong necessity.

Ibid.

965. Mary McGrory
(1920?–   )

1 But he [Richard M. Nixon] was like a kamikaze pilot who keeps apologizing for the attack.

Syndicated Newspaper Column
November 8, 1962

2 Somehow it sounded as though his [Richard M. Nixon's] zeal in providing a generation of peace rather than his efforts to cover up a generation of corruption had gotten him into trouble.

Ibid.   August 9, 1974

* * *

3 He [John F. Kennedy] came on, composed as a prince of the blood, chestnut thatch carefully brushed, facts straight, voice steady. "Look at him," breathed the proud Irishman next to me in the audience. "He's a thoroughbred."

Ibid.

966. Elaine Morgan
(1920–   )

1 The trouble with specialists is that they tend to think in grooves.

The Descent of Woman, Ch. 1   1972

2 We had taken the first step along the tortuous road that led to the sex war, sado-masochism, and ultimately to the whole contemporary snarl-up, to prostitution, prudery, Casanova, John Knox, Marie Stopes, white slavery, women's liberation, *Playboy* magazine, *crimes passionels*, censorship, strip clubs, alimony, pornography, and a dozen different brands of mania. This was the Fall. It had nothing to do with apples.

Ibid., Ch. 4

3 . . . everyone knows that you can't relieve an itch by stroking it gently.

Ibid., Ch. 5

4 Housewives and mothers seldom find it practicable to come out on strike. They have no union, anyway. But the rumblings of women's liberation are only one pointer to the fact that you already have a discontented work force. And if conditions continue to lag so far behind the industrial norm and the discomfort increases, you will find . . . that you will end up with an inferior product.

Ibid., Ch. 11

967. Eleanor Perry
(1920?–   )

1 "We've all known each other so long there's not even anyone to flirt with."
The Swimmer (screenplay)   *1967*

2 "That's your hang-up, Neddy-boy. You're afraid the sky will fall down if everybody doesn't love you. You'll lose the popularity contest, you won't be elected Head Boy—as if the whole world's a prep school!"
Ibid.

3 Rape has become a kind of favor done to the female—a fairly commonplace male fantasy.
Quoted in "Rebirth" by Kay Loveland and Estelle Changas, *The Hollywood Screenwriters*, Richard Corliss, ed.   *1972*

4 . . . so long as a woman is dependent on a man for her self-image or her self-esteem she will remain without any sense of her own worth—can never be a fully realized human being.
Ibid.

5 I believe that "the unexamined life is not worth living"—and what a glorious medium film is on which to conduct our examinations!
Ibid.

6 Given a skillful cinematographer and technical staff almost any creative person can direct a film.   Ibid.

968. Hazel Scott
(1920–   )

1 If you reach for something and find out it's the wrong thing, you change your program and move on.
Quoted in "Great (Hazel) Scott!" by Margo Jefferson, *Ms.* November, 1974

2 There's only one free person in this society, and he is white and male.   Ibid.

250

3 Who ever walked behind anyone to freedom? If we
  can't go hand in hand, I don't want to go.

Ibid.

4 There's a time when you have to explain to your children why they're born, and it's a marvelous thing if
  you know the reason by then.

Ibid.

969. Dinah Shore
(1920–   )

1 I earn and pay my own way as a great many women do
  today. Why should unmarried women be discriminated
  against—unmarried men are not.

Quoted in "Dinah," Los Angeles Times
April 16, 1974

2 I have never thought of participating in sports just for
  the sake of doing it for exercise or as a means to lose
  weight. And I've never taken up a sport just because it
  was a social fad. I really enjoy playing. It is a vital part
  of my life.

Ibid.

970. Harriet Van Horne
(1920–   )

1 Cooking is like love. It should be entered into with
  abandon or not at all.

Quoted in Vogue   October, 1956

971. Betty Friedan
(1921–   )

1 Over and over women heard in voices of tradition and
  Freudian sophistication that they could desire no
  greater destiny than to glory in their own femininity
  [and] to pity the neurotic, unfeminine, unhappy
  women who wanted to be poets or physicians or presidents.   The Feminine Mystique, Ch. 1   1963

2 It can be less painful for a woman not to hear the
  strange, dissatisfied voice stirring within her.   Ibid.

3 And strange new problems are being reported in the growing generations of children whose mothers were always there, driving them around, helping them with their homework—an inability to endure pain or discipline or pursue any self-sustained goal of any sort, a devastating boredom with life.

Ibid.

4 American women no longer know who they are.

Ibid., Ch. 3

5 How did Chinese women, after having their feet bound for many generations, finally discover they could run?

Ibid., Ch. 4

6 The most powerful influence on modern women, in terms of both functionalism and the feminine protest, was Margaret Mead. . . . She was, and still is, the symbol of the woman thinker in America.   Ibid., Ch. 6

7 Anthropologists today are less inclined to see in primitive civilization a laboratory for the observation of our own civilization, a scale model with all the irrelevancies blotted out; civilization is just not that irrelevant.

Ibid.

8 Female biology, women's "biological career-line," may be changeless . . . but the nature of the human relationship to biology *has* changed.   Ibid.

9 For, of course, the natural childbirth-breast-feeding movement Margaret Mead helped to inspire was not at all a return to primitive earth-mother maternity. It appealed to the independent, educated, spirited . . . woman . . . because it enabled her to experience childbirth not as a mindless female animal, an object manipulated by the obstetrician, but as a whole person, able to control her own body with her aware mind.

Ibid.

10 There is little or no intellectual challenge or discipline involved in merely learning to adjust.   Ibid., Ch. 7

11 A mystique does not compel its own acceptance.

Ibid., Ch. 8

12 How to put the libido back, restore the lost spontaneity, drive, love of life, the individuality, that sex in America seems to lack?   Ibid., Ch. 9

13 The glorification of the "woman's role," then, seems to be in proportion to society's reluctance to treat women as complete human beings; for the less real function that role has, the more it is decorated with meaningless details to conceal its emptiness.

Ibid., Ch. 10

14 Instead of fulfilling the promise of infinite orgastic bliss, sex in the America of the feminine mystique is becoming a strangely joyless national compulsion, if not a contemptuous mockery.

Ibid., Ch. 11

15 It is easier to live through someone else than to become complete yourself.

Ibid., Ch. 14

16 The problem that has no name—which is simply the fact that American women are kept from growing to their full human capacities—is taking a far greater toll on the physical and mental health of our country than any known disease.

Ibid.

17 It is better for a woman to compete impersonally in society, as men do, than to compete for dominance in her own home with her husband, compete with her neighbors for empty status, and so smother her son that he cannot compete at all.

Ibid., Ch. 18

18 That we have not made any respectable attempt to meet the special educational needs of women in the past is the clearest possible evidence of the fact that our educational objectives have been geared exclusively to the vocational patterns of men.

Ibid., Ch. 11

19 Women, because they are not generally the principal breadwinners, can be perhaps most useful as the trail blazers, working along the bypaths, doing the unusual job that men cannot afford to gamble on.

Ibid.

20 If divorce has increased one thousand percent, don't blame the woman's movement. Blame our obsolete sex roles on which our marriages were based.

Speech *January 20, 1974*

972. Zsa Zsa Gabor
(1921?–   )

1 Husbands are like fires. They go out when unattended.
Quoted in *Newsweek*   *March 28, 1960*

2 A man in love is incomplete until he has married. Then
he's finished.

Ibid.

973. Sybil Leek
(1921?–   )

1 As for the Devil, I never met him myself, but I am
gregarious enough to be polite to most people; so if I
meet a man with little horns on his head and a peculiar
taste in footwear, I'm not going to worry. You can't be
sure who the Devil is these days. He might be a TV or
movie producer in disguise.
Diary of a Witch, Ch. 1   *1968*

2 Perhaps telepathy will remain a mystery for many
more years but it has always been within the power of
a few people in every generation to transmit and receive thoughts. People in love often claim this power.
Maybe we are being forced to realize that love is in
itself a magical power and that awareness may be in-
strumental in preventing our own destruction.
Ibid., Ch. 6

3 We are about to move into the Aquarian age of clearer
thinking. Astrology and witchcraft both have a contribution to make to the new age, and it behooves the
practitioners of both to realize their responsibilities and
obligations to the science and the religion.
Ibid., Ch. 11

4 Reincarnation is nothing more than the law of evolution applied to the consciousness of the individual. As
in the material evolution of the birth, growth, and
death of man, so there is a beginning, growth and maturity in the consciousness. But there is not an end. The
spirit is our only link with the Godhead, the divine

force of life, and it is the indestructible part of ourselves.

Ibid., Ch. 12

5 We have to look at the broad spectrum of ESP, which can sometimes be a simple hunch, a flash of intuition, or an awareness outside the realm of the physical but not totally detached from it any more than the mind is detached from the organ of the brain.

ESP—The Magic Within You, Ch. 1   *1971*

6 We seem to be trapped by a civilization that has accelerated many physical aspects of evolution but has forgotten that other vital part of man—his mind and his psyche.

Ibid., Ch. 13

974. Eeva-Liisa Manner
(1921–   )

1 MAIJA. Artfulness is a kind of capital.
Show in May, Act I, Sc. 1   *1966*

2 PAAVO. Modesty makes women insincere.

Ibid.

3 LASSI. Women are awful—they know everything. Though they don't understand anything.

Ibid., Sc. 2

4 LASSI. Love makes *intelligent* beings depressed and flat. Only women, ostriches and monkeys are made happy by love. Oh yes, and parrots.

Ibid., Act II, Sc. 1

5 LASSI. The female is designed on the same principle as the starfish. Those creatures that the woman doesn't swallow she melts outside her body until the soft parts dissolve and only the shell remains.

Ibid.

6 LASSI. I love uncertain things . . . things that are certain bore me, make me depressed, like everlasting rain. And reliable and safe people are as boring as textbooks. Incalculable people are lovable, although they cause suffering too.

Ibid.

7 PAAVO. Illusions! Illusions. Illusion of innocent love. Illusion of the heart's goodness, illusion of the sacredness of the pure life. But your virtuousness is only love of comfort, bourgeois self-satisfaction. Give up what you hold so dear: your illusions, and you can return to reality and become your real self.

Ibid., Sc. 2

8 HELENA. If hope shows the depth of sorrow, then hopelessness must cure sorrow.

Ibid.

9 PAAVO. Great men are born in stable straw and they are put in a basket of reeds for the river to carry away. They are allowed to form their own souls—God looks after their bodies. They're not fed with warm milk, they must drink from the streams of the world, they do dirty work; the polisher of the mirror has dirty hands.

Ibid., Sc. 3

10 LASSI. Nothing is ever voluntary. Even when a person thinks he's doing something of his own free will, he's being compelled to do it. Only the dead are free, the chain is broken . . . but perhaps they miss their chains?

Ibid., Act III, Sc. 1

11 LASSI. Women! There isn't anything so bad that they don't soon start to enjoy it. Even if they lived in a barrel of shit they'd start making a home out of it, with everything nice and cozy.

Ibid.

12 The whole intelligence of a poem is in futility. . . .
"Untitled Poems," *The Other Voices,* Carol Cosman, ed.   1975

13 sleep builds stepping stones.   Ibid.

975. Del Martin
(1921–   )

1 At a time when women, the forgotten sex, are voicing their rage and demanding their personhood, it is fitting that we [lesbians] emerge from the shadows.

Lesbian/Woman, with Phyllis Lyon   1972

2 To understand the lesbian as a sexual being, one must understand woman as a sexual being.

Ibid.

3 It is only when she can denounce the idiocy of religious scriptures and legal strictures that bind her and can affirm her Lesbian nature as but a single facet of her whole personality that she can become fully human.

Ibid.

4 There is nothing mysterious or magical about lesbian lovemaking. . . . The mystery and the magic come from the person with whom you are making love.

Ibid.

5 Much polarity between men and women has centered around procreation. But the sex act itself is neither male nor female: it is a human being reaching out for the ultimate in communication with another human being.

Ibid.

6 Most human sexual behavior is *learned*. It is only in the lower animals that it is totally instinctive. The higher on the evolutionary scale you are, the less instinctive are your sexual relations. So our life experiences "teach" us our sexuality, which may turn out to be hetero, homo, or bi.

Ibid.

7 As leaders . . . we could not display fear. In the process we overcame our own fears.

Ibid.

976. Donna Reed
(1921–   )

1 If nuclear power plants are safe, let the commercial insurance industry insure them. Until these most expert judges of risk are willing to gamble with their money, I'm not willing to gamble with the health and safety of my family.

Quoted in the *Los Angeles Times*
March 12, 1974

977. Hannah Senesh
(1921–1944)

1 One needs something to believe in, something for
which one can have whole-hearted enthusiasm. One
needs to feel that one's life has meaning, that one is
needed in this world.

Hannah Senesh: Her Life and Diary
(1938)   *1966p*

2 I dream and plan as if there was nothing happening in
the world, as if there was no war, no destruction, as
if thousands upon thousands were not being killed
daily. . . .

Ibid. (November 2, 1940)

3 There are events without which one's life becomes unimportant, a worthless toy; and there are times when
one is commanded to do something, even at the price
of one's life.

Ibid. (December 25, 1943)

978. Alison Wyrley Birch
(1922–   )

1 There are sounds to seasons. There are sounds to
places, and there are sounds to every time in one's life.

Quoted in *The Christian Science
Monitor*   *January 23, 1974*

979. Helen Gurley Brown
(1922–   )

1 You may marry or you may not. In today's world that
is no longer the big question for women. Those who
glom on to men so that they can collapse with relief,
spend the rest of their days shining up their status symbol and figure they never have to reach, stretch, learn,
grow, face dragons or make a living again are the ones
to be pitied. They, in my opinion, are the unfulfilled
ones.

Sex and the Single Girl   *1963*

980. Judith Crist
(1922–   )

1 I am of the post-nickelodian pre-television generation,
the children of Loew's Paradise. . . . Movies were our
secret life. . . . There was somehow a perpetual edge
of guilt . . . from the conviction held (and instilled)
by parent and educator that time was better spent in
developing the mind and body anywhere but in a
moviehouse.

The Private Eye, the Cowboy and the
Very Naked Girl, Introduction   *1968*

2 Movies suddenly became "film" and "cinema" and "art
form" and terribly chic. And the impossible dream
came true overnight for those facile enough to latch on
to a good and going thing, and film criticism became
the means whereby a stream of young intellectuals
could go straight from the campus film society into the
professionals' screening room without managing to get
a glimpse of the real world in between.

Ibid.

3 The critics who love are the severe ones . . . we know
our relationship must be based on honesty.

Ibid.

4 In this lovely land of corrugated cartons and plastic
bags, we want our entertainment packaged as neatly as
the rest of our consumer goods: an attractive label on
the outside, a complete and accurate detailing of contents there or on the inside, no loose ends, no odd
parts, nothing left out.

Ibid., *"Hud:* Unpackaged Reality"
(June 2, 1963)

5 A moviegoer's version of not judging books by their
covers might well be an adage about not judging films
by their directors' statements of intent.

Ibid., "Two Men in a House"
(March 22, 1964)

6 In this era of affluence and of permissiveness, we have,
in all but cultural areas, bred a nation of overprivileged
youngsters, saturated with vitamins, television and plastic toys. But they are nurtured from infancy on a Dick-

and-Jane literary and artistic level; and the cultural drought, as far as entertainment is concerned, sets in when they are between six and eight.

Ibid., "Forgotten Audience: American
Children" (May 2, 1965)

7 Moviemaking, we are told, is a cooperative activity; hardy and rare and usually nonexistent is the individual who can take full credit for much more than a moment and super-perceptive and equally rare is the critic who can tell at a glance just where the credit lies. It's really no easier in the blame department.

Ibid., "Only in Hollywood—The
Oscar" (March 13, 1966)

8 Happiness is too many things these days for anyone to wish it on anyone lightly. So let's just wish each other a bileless New Year and leave it at that. . . .

Ibid., "1966 at Its Worst: The Dishonor
Roll" (January 1, 1967)

9 . . . the outcry against the current spate of sadism and violence in films is . . . more than justified by the indecencies that we are being subjected to on the big screen (and more and more on the little one at home), by the puddles of blood and piles of guts pouring forth from the quivering flesh that is being lashed and smashed, by the bouncing of breast and grinding of groin, by the brutalizing of men and desecration of women being fed to us by the hour for no possible social, moral or intellectual purpose beyond our erotic edification and sensual delight and, above all, the almighty box-office return.

Ibid., "Against the Groin"
(December, 1967)

981. Mavis Gallant
(1922–   )

1   Flor looked at his closed fist. "Why do people keep things?" she said.

"I don't know," said George. "I guess it proves you were somewhere."

Green Water, Green Sky, Ch. 1   *1959*

2 Success can only be measured in terms of distance traveled. . . .   *Ibid.*

3 I was always putting myself in my sister's place, adopting her credulousness, and even her memories, I saw, could be made mine. It was Isobel I imagined as the eternal heroine—never myself. I substituted her feelings for my own, and her face for any face described. Whatever the author's intentions, the heroine was my sister.

Its Image on the Mirror   1964

4 No people are ever as divided as those of the same blood. . . .

Ibid.

5 Until the time of my own marriage I had sworn I would settle for nothing less than a certain kind of love. However, I had become convinced, after listening to my mother and to others as well, that a union of that sort was too fantastic to exist; nor was it desirable. The reason for its undesirability was never plain. It was one of the definite statements of rejection young persons must learn to make; "Perfect love cannot last" is as good a beginning as any.

Ibid.

6 We admitted we loved her—we who dread the word. We would rather say we adore: it is so exaggerated it can't be true. Adore equals like, but love is compromising, eternal.

Ibid.

7 The Knights had been married nearly sixteen years. They considered themselves solidly united. Like many people no longer in love, they cemented their relationship with opinions, pet prejudices, secret meanings, a private vocabulary that enabled them to exchange amused glances over a dinner table and made them feel a shade superior to the world outside the house.

"Bernadette," *My Heart Is Broken*   1964

8 The world drew into itself, became smaller and smaller, was limited to her room, her table in the dining room, her own eyes in the mirror, her own hand curved around a glass. Dreams as thick as walls rose about her bed and sheltered her sleep. . . .

Ibid., "The Moabitess"

9 They were young and ambitious and frightened; and they were French, so that their learned behavior was all smoothness. There was no crevice where an emotion could hold.   Ibid., "The Cost of Living"

10   "What is the appeal about cats?" he said kindly.
"I've always wanted to know." . . .

    "They don't care if you like them. They haven't the
slightest notion of gratitude, and they never pretend.
They take what you have to offer, and away they go.
. . . It would be interesting to see what role the cat
fancier *is* trying on," said Walter. . . . "He says he
likes cats because they don't like anyone. I suppose he
is proving he is so tough he can exist without affection."

         Ibid., "An Unmarried Man's Summer"

11 "Don't cry whilst writing letters. The person receiving
the letter is apt to take it as a reproach. Undefined
misery is no use to anyone. Be clear, or, better still, be
silent. If you must tell the world about your personal
affairs, give examples. Don't just sob in the pillow hoping someone will overhear."

         A Fairly Good Time, Ch. 1   *1970*

12 She had the loaded handbag of someone who camps
out and seldom goes home, or who imagines life must
be full of emergencies.

         Ibid., Ch. 5

13 Swedish films had given her the impression that conversation in an unknown tongue consisted of nothing
except "Where is God?" and "Should one have children?" although, in reality, everyone in those foreign
countries was probably saying "How much does it
cost?" and "Pass the salt."

         Ibid.

14 [They] had been in a war they had not believed in and
that was not officially a war at all. They were not veterans and not entitled to pensions. Privilege, a token
income . . . were allowed for veterans of both world
wars, the survivors of Indo-China, the old soldiers of
the Resistance. But the combatants of Algeria seemed
like bad weather. They were not a useful memory.

         Ibid., Ch. 8

15 Good profession, good family, no money, foul temper—oh, the best of husbands.

         Ibid., Ch. 9

16 Nobody in movies ever runs out of cigarettes or has to
look for parking space.   *Ibid.,* Ch. 12

17 The worst punishment I can imagine must be solitary confinement with nothing for entertainment except news of the world.

Ibid.

18 She had gone into captivity believing in virtue and learned she could steal. Went in loving the poor, came out afraid of them; went in generous, came out grudging; went in with God, came out alone.

"The Pegnitz Junction," *The Pegnitz Junction* 1973

19 Now that he was rich he was not thought ignorant any more, but simply eccentric.

Ibid.

20 Everyone is lying; he will invent his own truth. Is it important if one-tenth of a lie is true? Is there a horror in a memory if it was only a dream?

Ibid., "Ernst in Civilian Clothes"

982. Judy Garland
(1922–1969)

1 . . . they [MGM] had us working days and nights on end. They'd give us pep-up pills to keep us on our feet long after we were exhausted. Then they'd take us to the studio hospital and knock us cold with sleeping pills—Mickey [Rooney] sprawled out on one bed and me on another. Then after four hours they'd wake us up and give us the pep-up pills again so we could work another seventy-two hours in a row. Half of the time we were hanging from the ceiling, but it became a way of life for us.

Quoted in *Judy Garland* by Anne Edwards, Ch. 11 *1975p*

2 Before every free conscience in America is subpoenaed, please speak up! Ibid., Ch. 19 (c.1947)

3 How strange when an illusion dies
It's as though you've lost a child. . . .

Ibid., "An Illusion"

4 We cast away priceless time in dreams,
Born of imagination, fed upon illusion, and put to death by reality. Ibid., "Imagination"

5 For 'twas not into my ear you whispered but into my
     heart.
   'Twas not my lips you kissed, but my soul.
                              Ibid., "My Love Is Lost"

983. Grace Hartigan
(1922–   )

1 . . . the face the world puts on to sell itself to the
   world.
                    Quoted by Cindy Nemser in *Art Talk*
                              (magazine)   *1975*

2 I'd like to think that there are some things that . . .
   can't be analyzed to the point where they're finished off,
   either.

                                             Ibid.

3 . . . I don't mind being miserable as long as I'm painting well.

                                             Ibid.

4 There's a time when what you're creating and the environment you're creating it in come together.

                                             Ibid.

984. Gladys Heldman
(1922–   )

1 It's a mental attitude you have about winning, about
   dying before you're willing to lose.
                    Quoted in "Queen of the Long-Way
                       Babies" by Dan Rosen, *Signature*
                                    August, 1974

2 Players are always in the foreground, and they should
   be . . . anything else would be like Sol Hurok thinking that *he* was the star when it is really the ballet.

                                             Ibid.

985. Eda J. Le Shan
(1922–   )

1 . . . most of us carry into marriage not only our childlike illusions, but we bring to it as well the demand that
it *has* to be wonderful, because it's *supposed* to be. Of
course the biggest illusion of all is that we are going to
do the job of parenthood so well: it will all be fun and
always deeply satisfying.
         How to Survive Parenthood, Ch. 2   *1965*

2 We are learning that there are no longer any simple
patterns or easy definitions. Each of us has to discover
who and what we are, and our own special qualities;
what makes us feel womanly. Passivity and weakness
do not describe the feminine woman; devotion to
kitchen or nursery serves us no better as a definition—
where and what is the indefinable something our feminist grandmothers were so eager to give up and we are
so anxious to recapture?
                                    Ibid., Ch. 8

3 Psychotherapy can be one of the greatest and most rewarding adventures, it can bring with it the deepest
feelings of personal worth, of purpose and richness in
living. It doesn't mean that one's life situation will
change dramatically or suddenly. . . . It does mean
that one can develop new capacities and strengths with
which to meet the natural vicissitudes of living; that
one may gain a sense of inner peace through greater
self-acceptance, through a more realistic perspective on
one's relationships and experiences.
                                    Ibid., Ch. 11

4 . . . in all our efforts to provide "advantages" we have
actually produced the busiest, most competitive, highly
pressured and over-organized generation of youngsters
in our history—and possibly the unhappiest. We seem
hell-bent on eliminating much of childhood.
                     The Conspiracy Against Childhood,
                                    Ch. 1   *1967*

5 The reason the young child learns [to talk] so well and
so fast is that *his* way of learning is his own best way.
When he is allowed this freedom to explore the world
of language, he pursues his own interest and curiosity.

. . . He comes at things from many directions and is therefore more likely to see the way they fit together and relate to one another. . . . He learns not to please others, but to please himself.

Ibid., Ch. 2

6 Babies are necessary to grown-ups. A new baby is like the beginning of all things—wonder, hope, a dream of possibilities. In a world that is cutting down its trees to build highways, losing its earth to concrete . . . babies are almost the only remaining link with nature, with the natural world of living things from which we spring.

Ibid.

7 Because Maria Montessori was herself a creative thinker, I cannot believe that she would be at all happy about what is being done in her name. The passionate fervor of today's Montessori proponents, their single-minded dependence on a narrow formulation and program despite all that has been learned about children and education since Dr. Montessori was alive, does not represent an objective or thoughtful pooling of all the resources at our disposal. . . .

Ibid., Ch. 3

8 If, when we provide "enrichment" programs, our aim is merely to put pressure on children for accelerated mental development, we may be adding to their feelings of unworthiness rather than relieving those they already have. . . . Instead of focusing our attention on developing readiness for academic achievement promulgating middle-class standards and behavior, we ought to be spending our time and our money on ways in which to help every child to feel that he is a person, that he is lovable and that he can contribute something of value to others.

Ibid., Ch. 4

9 We are not asking our children to do their own best but to be *the* best. Education is in danger of becoming a religion based on fear; its doctrine is to compete. The majority of our children are being led to believe that they are doomed to failure in a world which has room only for those at the top.

Ibid., Ch. 5

10 Excellence in life seems to me to be the way in which each human being makes the most of the adventure of living and becomes most truly and deeply himself, ful-

filling his own nature in the context of a good life with other people. . . . What he knows and what he feels have equal importance in his life. . . .

Ibid., Ch. 9

11 We have kept our children so busy with "useful" and "improving" activities that we are in danger of raising a generation of young people who are terrified of silence, of being alone with their own thoughts. . . .

Ibid., Ch. 11

986. Grace Paley
(1922–   )

1 He had had a habit throughout the twenty-seven years of making a narrow remark which, like a plumber's snake, could work its way through the ear down the throat, halfway to my heart. He would then disappear, leaving me choking with equipment.

Enormous Changes at the Last Minute   1960

2 They were busy as bees in a ladies' murmur about life and lives. They worked. They took vital facts from one another and looked as dedicated as a kibbutz.

Ibid.

3 . . . a very large family. Four brothers and three sisters, they wouldn't touch birth control with a basement beam. Orthodox. Constructive fucking. Builders, baby.

Ibid.

4 I have always required a man to be dependent on, even when it appeared that I had one already. I own two small boys whose dependence on me takes up my lumpen time and my bourgeois feelings.   Ibid.

5 I don't believe civilization can do a lot more than educate a person's senses. If it's truth and honor you want to refine, I think the Jews have some insight. Make no images, imitate no God. After all, in His field, the graphic arts, He is pre-eminent. Then let that One who made the tan deserts and the blue Van Allen belt and the green mountains of New England be in charge of Beauty, which He obviously understands, and let man, who was full of forgiveness at Jerusalem, and full of survival at Troy, let man be in charge of Good.

Ibid.

6 The man has the burden of the money. It's needed day after day. More and more of it. For ordinary things and for life. That's why holidays are a hard time for him. Another hard time is the weekend, when he's not making money or furthering himself.

Ibid.

7 Rosiness is not a worse windowpane than gloomy gray when viewing the world.

Ibid.

8 I was a fantastic student until ten, and then my mind began to wander.

Quoted in Grace Paley: "Art Is on the
Side of the Underdog" by Harriet
Shapiro, *Ms.*   *March, 1974*

9 There isn't a story written that isn't about blood and money. People and their relationship to each other is the blood, the family. And how they live, the money of it.

Ibid.

10 . . . I think art, literature, fiction, poetry, whatever it is, makes justice in the world. That's why it almost always has to be on the side of the underdog.

Ibid.

11 If you live an autonomous life you never really are repressed.

Ibid.

987. Vera Randal
(1922–   )

1 . . . I opened my eyes to the nightmare from which I knew, with a knowledge deeper and surer than words, I would not wake.

"Alice Blaine," *The Inner Room*   1964

2 Fury gathered until I was swollen with it.

Ibid.

3 Time, dough in a bowl, rose, doubling, trebling in bulk, and I was in the middle of the swelling, yeasty mass—lost.

Ibid.

4 ". . . If this is July, what, precisely, happened to June,
and a sizable slice of May?"

Ibid.

5 Christ, even a murderer was electrocuted only once.

Ibid.

6 "John is dead."
"Yes."
"I am also dead," I said numbly.
"You're not dead. You're very far from dead."
"I feel dead."
"That's different."
"Is it?" I said. "Is it really?"
"It is Really."

Ibid.

7 "I believe in people, which I suppose is a way of believing in God."

Ibid.

8 "There are many ways of crying."
"Yes." My tears were hidden behind my grinning
mask face. "Yes, there are." Ibid.

988. Alice Rossi
(1922–   )

1 The emancipation or liberation of women involves
more than political participation and the change of any
number of laws. Liberation is equally important in
areas other than politics; economics, reproduction,
household, sexual and cultural emancipation are relevant. *The Feminist Papers*, Preface   *1973*

2 A really radical break from the confinement of sex
roles might lie in women's search for mates from very
different social and intellectual circles, men who are
not vain, self-centered and ambitious but tenderly devoted to home and children and the living of life.
Ibid., Pt. I, "The Making of a
Cosmopolitan Humanist"

3 Scholars all too often move in a world as restricted as
that in which their subjects lived or from which they
escaped. Ibid.

4 As economic affluence increased with the growth of the new industrialism and expansion of trade, women's worth declined as producers and increased as consumers.

Ibid., Pt. II, Introduction

5 While social class rests on economic factors of income and power, social status rests on less tangible cultural factors of life styles.

Ibid.

6 Alcohol was a threat to women, for it released men from the moral control they had learned from a diet of preaching and scolding from ministers and mothers alike.

Ibid.

7 Students of women's lives have sometimes claimed that spinsterhood and childlessness are the price such women paid for the unusual career paths they pursued.

Ibid., "The Blackwell Clan"

8 The focus on heaven can be a lifetime pursuit, and there is no way to test whether the goal was worth the effort. . . .

Ibid.

9 It is curious that it may be the help of a housekeeper and a friend that facilitates a woman's life's work, while the closest analogy . . . one would find from the pen of a man is typically a tribute to his wife.

Ibid., "A Feminist Friendship"

10 Equal pay for equal work continues to be seen as applying to equal pay for men and women in the same occupation, while the larger point of continuing relevance in our day is that some occupations have depressed wages because women are the chief employees. The former is a pattern of sex discrimination, the latter of institutionalized sexism.

Ibid.

11 The single most impressive fact about the attempt by American women to obtain the right to vote is how long it took.

Ibid., "Along the Suffrage Trail"

12 Without the means to prevent, and to control the timing of conception, economic and political rights have limited meaning for women. If women cannot plan their pregnancies, they can plan little else in their lives. . . .

Ibid., "The Right to One's Body"

13 It has become more "reasonable" to argue that Adam was made from Eve than vice versa.
                    Ibid., "The 'Militant Madonna'"

14 The drum-beating martial mood of wartime is often followed by a pot-stirring and baby-rocking domestic ethos in its aftermath.
                    Ibid., Pt. IV, Introduction

15 For every war widow there may be several dozen wives who cope with the physical and emotional damage inflicted by war on their husbands and sons.
                    Ibid.

16 . . . sons forget what grandsons wish to remember. . . .
                    Ibid.

17 "Understanding" . . . is not a foundation for action if the terms in which a problem is "understood" tend toward acceptance of the status quo. . . .
                    Ibid.

18 Abridgement of any published book or essay is an assault, a cutting or pruning by one mind of the work of another.
                    Ibid., "Guineas and Locks"

19 Understanding through mastery and control versus understanding through empathetic projection and the absorption of the views of others . . . may be a comparison that frequently differentiates the sexes. . . .
                    Ibid., "Cultural Stretch"

989. Renee Winegarten
(1922–   )

1 Extremist movements . . . have played skillfully and successfully upon panic terrors and cultural decay and decadence.
                    "The Idea of Decadence," *Commentary*
                    September, 1974

2 The book of the faults and complexities of the present cannot be closed like that containing the difficulties and errors of the past. . . .   Ibid.

3 What lies behind the concept of decadence to render it so appealing to the imagination?   Ibid.

4 The mighty are fallen and we shall not look upon their like again.

Ibid.

5 We still tend to share the idea that civilization must be either growing and pressing ever onward and upward, or else disintegrating into nothingness, instead of going on, variously developing and changing in a multitude of different areas, in ways not always perceptible to the human eye.

Ibid.

6 If epochs can grow old and die, what is to prevent them from becoming subject to disease?

Ibid.

7 . . . the quest for origin and end, zenith and nadir, growth and decline, rise and fall, florescence and decadence. Where would writers be without these essential props for their narrative?

Ibid.

8 The sad, dim shades of twilight seemed so much more moving than the clarity of day. Ibid.

9 Old age cannot be cured. An epoch or a civilization cannot be prevented from breathing its last. A natural process that happens to all flesh and all human manifestations cannot be arrested. You can only wring your hands and utter a beautiful swan song. Ibid.

990. Shelley Winters
(1922–   )

1 It was so cold I almost got married.
Quoted in *The New York Times*
April 29, 1956

991. Diane Arbus
(1922–1971)

1 It's important to get out of your skin into somebody else's . . . that somebody else's tragedy is not the same as your own.

Diane Arbus   *1972p*

2 I really believe there are things nobody would see if I didn't photograph them.

Ibid.

3 Most people go through life dreading they'll have a traumatic experience. Freaks are born with their trauma. They've already passed it. They're aristocrats.

Ibid.

4 My favorite thing is to go where I've never been.

Ibid.

5 The world seemed to me to belong to the world. I could learn things but they never seemed to be my own experience.

Ibid.

992. Ursula Reilly Curtiss
(1923–   )

1 It was the old principle of getting back on the horse that had thrown you (although why, Kate had always wondered? Why not just take up some other sport?) but sometimes, like a number of laudable things, it was wearing.

The Wasp, Ch. 1   1963

2 After a second's astonishment, Kate let the lie stand. Like most lies it was much easier than the truth, and to contradict it might turn out to be a very wearying affair.

Ibid., Ch. 3

3 This was not love; it was exactly what Georgia had said: ownership. If you owned a race horse, you got the winner's stakes. If you owned a play, you got the royalties. If you owned a son. . . .

Ibid., Ch. 17

4 If you were healed of a dreadful wound, you did not want to keep the bandage.

Ibid., Ch. 18

993. Nadine Gordimer
(1923–   )

1 That was one of the things she held against the missionaries: how they stressed Christ's submission to humiliation, and so had conditioned the people of Africa to
humiliation by the white man.

> "Not for Publication," *Not for
> Publication and Other Stories*   1965

2 He was a Nyasa with a face so black that the blackness
was an inverted dazzle—you couldn't see what he was
thinking.

> Ibid., "The Pet"

3 It had proved impossible to anthropomorphize him into
a handsome, dignified, well-behaved bully-boy; and
somewhere along the unsuccessful process, he had lost
the instincts of a dog, into the bargain.

> Ibid.

4 I'm forty-nine but I could be twenty-five except for my
face and my legs.

> Ibid., "Good Climate, Friendly Inhabitants"

5 These [teenage] girls had dropped childhood, with its
bond of physical dependency on parents, behind them.
They had forgotten what they had been, and they did
not know that they would become what their parents
were. For the brief hiatus they occupied themselves
with preparations for a state of being very different—a
world that would never exist.

> Ibid., "Vital Statistics"

6 The two women gazed out of the slumped and sagging
bodies that had accumulated around them.

> Ibid.

7 Time is change; we measure its passage by how much
things alter.   *The Late Bourgeois World*   1966

8 Why am I idiotically timid before such people, while at
the same time so critical of their limitations?   Ibid.

9 Oh we bathed and perfumed and depilated white ladies,
in whose wombs the sanctity of the white race is en-

tombed! What concoction of musk and boiled petals can disguise the dirt done in the name of that sanctity?

Ibid.

10 "There's nothing moral about beauty."

Ibid.

11 It is in opposition (the disputed territory of the argument, the battle for self-definition that goes on beneath the words) . . . that intimacy takes place.

The Conservationist   1975

12 She filled her house with blacks, and white parsons who went around preaching Jesus was a revolutionary, and then when the police walked in she was surprised.

Ibid.

13 To keep anything the way you like it for yourself, you have to have the stomach to ignore—dead and hidden—whatever intrudes. . . .

Ibid.

14 Come to think of it all the earth is a graveyard, you never know when you're walking over heads—particularly this continent [Africa], cradle of man, prehistoric bones and the bits of shaped stone . . . that were weapons and utensils.

Ibid.

994. Carolina Maria de Jesus
(1923?–   )

1 Actually we are slaves to the cost of living.

*Child of the Dark: The Diary of
Carolina Maria de Jesus*
(July 15, 1955)   *1962*

2 I don't look for defects in children . . . neither in mine nor in others. I know that a child is not born with sense.

Ibid. (July 18, 1955)

3 The only thing that does not exist in the *favela** is friendship.

Ibid.

4 The book is man's best invention so far.

Ibid. (July 21, 1955)

* Barrio or ghetto.

5 I classify Sao Paulo this way: The Governor's Palace is the living room. The mayor's office is the dining room and the city is the garden. And the *favela* is the back yard where they throw the garbage.

Ibid. (May 15, 1958)

6 "You had faith, and now you don't have it any more?"

"No, my son, democracy is losing its followers. In our country everything is weakening. The money is weak. Democracy is weak and the politicians are very weak. Everything that is weak dies one day."

Ibid. (May 20, 1958)

7 She neglects children and collects men.

Ibid. (June 1, 1958)

8 A child is the root of the heart.

Ibid.

9 I read the masculine names of the defenders of the country, then I said to my mother: "Why don't you make me become a man?"

She replied: "If you walk under a rainbow, you'll become a man."

When a rainbow appeared I went running in its direction. But the rainbow was always a long way off. Just as the politicians are far from the people. . . . I returned and told my mother: "The rainbow ran away from me."

Ibid. (June 7, 1958)

10 Actually, the world is the way the whites want it. I'm not white, so I don't have anything to do with this disorganized world.

Ibid. (June 23, 1958)

11 I started thinking about the unfortunate children who, even being tiny, complain about their condition in the world. They say that Princess Margaret of England doesn't like being a Princess. Those are the breaks in life.

Ibid. (July 30, 1958)

995. Shirley Kaufman
(1923–   )

1 Through every night we hate,
preparing the next day's
war. . . .

"Mothers, Daughters,"
The Floor Keeps Turning   1970

996. Jean Kerr
(1923–   )

1 I'm tired of all this nonsense about beauty being only
skin-deep. That's deep enough. What do you want—an
adorable pancreas?

"Mirror, Mirror, on the Wall,"
The Snake Has All the Lines   1958

2 I feel about airplanes the way I feel about diets. It
seems to me that they are wonderful things for other
people to go on.   Ibid.

3 Marrying a man is like buying something you've been
admiring for a long time in a shop window. You may
love it when you get it home, but it doesn't always go
with everything else in the house.

Ibid., "The Ten Worst
Things About a Man"

4 TIFFANY. Practically everybody Daddy knows is divorced. It's not that they're worse than other people,
they're just richer.

Mary, Mary, Act I   1960

5 MARY. Well, being divorced is like being hit by a Mack
truck. If you live through it, you start looking very
carefully to the right and to the left.   Ibid.

6 BOB. I think success has no rules, but you can learn a
great deal from failure.   Ibid.

7 MARY. . . . if you were absolutely convinced that you
had no feeling in your hand, you'd be relieved to burn
your fingers.   Ibid., Act II

8 MARY. It was hard to communicate with you. You were always communicating with yourself. The line was busy.

Ibid.

9 SYDNEY. You don't seem to realize that a poor person who is unhappy is in a better position than a rich person who is unhappy. Because the poor person has hope. He thinks money would help.

Poor Richard, Act I   1963

10 SYDNEY. Even though a number of people have tried, no one has yet found a way to drink for a living.

Ibid.

11 SYDNEY. Our generation isn't looking for love. We're looking for desperation. We think it isn't real unless we have a fever of 103.

Ibid., Act III

12 RICHARD. See, I believe in words. I think when they're put together they should mean something. They have an exact meaning, a precise meaning. There is more precision in one good sonnet than there is in an Atlas missile.

Ibid.

13 JEFF. Man is the only animal that learns by being hypocritical. He pretends to be polite and then, eventually, he *becomes* polite.

Finishing Touches, Act I   1973

14 KATY. If there is a fifty-fifty chance of immortality, why not play it with the believers? . . . I think you should impose standards and disciplines on yourself so that you might just possibly slip into eternity with Thomas More instead of going to hell with Hitler.

Ibid., Act II

15 FELICIA. Hope is the feeling you have that the feeling you have isn't permanent.

Ibid., Act III

997. Denise Levertov
(1923–   )

1 two by two in the ark of
the ache of it.

"The Ache of Marriage,"
O Taste and See   1963

2 "Life after life after life goes by

without poetry,
without seemliness,
without love."
                    "The Mutes," *The Sorrow Dance*   *1966*

998. Inge Trachtenberg
(1923?–   )

1 . . . my tenth year is marked as the year in which
Adolf Hitler came to power in Germany. . . . Yet,
when that event took place, Father wasn't sure that it
was such a bad thing for Germany. Adolf Hitler had
promised bread and order; Father was in favor of
bread and order. . . . I, for one, had no premonition
of bad things to come.
                    So Slow the Dawning, Ch. 4   *1973*

2 Decent was more than moral, decent was also being a
good sport, a good friend, having a sense of humor,
being tough.
                    Ibid., Ch. 14

3 I did a lot of writing that winter. . . . Putting things
down lent them a sense of permanence, it seemed to
stem the feeling of rushing time which was suddenly so
compelling that I fancied hearing its sound.
                    Ibid., Ch. 16

999. Sarah Caldwell
(1924–   )

1 If you approach an opera as though it were something
that always went a certain way, that's what you get. I
approach an opera as though I didn't know it.
                    Quoted in "Sarah Caldwell: The
                    Flamboyant of the Opera" by Jane
                    Scovell Appleton, *Ms.*   *May, 1975*

2 The conductor and director must create the atmosphere, but a situation must exist where the singers can
think and use their own remarkable faculties. It's like
bringing up a gifted child.
                    Ibid.

3 We must continuously discipline ourselves to remember how it felt the first moment.

Ibid.

4 It [Tanglewood, summer home of the Boston Symphony Orchestra] was a place where gods strode the earth.

Quoted in "Music's Wonder Woman,"
Time   November 10, 1975

1000. Shirley Chisholm
(1924–   )

1 I was well on the way to forming my present attitude toward politics as it is practiced in the United States; it is a beautiful fraud that has been imposed on the people for years, whose practitioners exchange gilded promises for the most valuable thing their victims own, their votes. And who benefits most? The lawyers.

Unbought and Unbossed,
Pt. I, Ch. 4   1970

2 The seniority system keeps a handful of old men, many of them southern whites hostile to every progressive trend, in control of the Congress. These old men stand implacably across the paths that could lead us toward a better future. But worse than they, I think, are the majority of members of both Houses who continue to submit to the senility system. Apparently, they hope they, too, will grow to be old.

Ibid., Pt. II, Ch. 8

3 The difference between *de jure* and *de facto* segregation is the difference between open, forthright bigotry and the shamefaced kind that works through unwritten agreements between real estate dealers, school officials, and local politicians.

Ibid., Pt. IV, Ch. 14

4 I am a candidate for the Presidency of the United States. I make that statement proudly, in the full knowledge that, as a black person and as a female person, I do not have a chance of actually gaining that office in this election year.

Speech   June 4, 1972

5 We must get the message out that on these issues, child care, abortion and women in the labor force, white women must get in line behind us. The issue is survival.

Speech, Eastern Regional Conference
on Black Feminism   *November 30, 1973*

6 I ran because someone had to do it first. In this country everyone is supposed to be able to run for President, but that's never been really true. I ran *because* most people think the country isn't ready for a black candidate, not ready for a woman candidate. Someday. . . .

The Good Fight, Ch. 1   *1973*

7 Richard M. Nixon . . . has a deeper concern for his place in history than for the people he governs. And history will not fail to note that fact.

Ibid., Ch. 11

8 We Americans have a chance to become someday a nation in which all racial stocks and classes can exist in their own selfhoods, but meet on a basis of respect and equality and live together, socially, economically, and politically. We can become a dynamic equilibrium, a harmony of many different elements, in which the whole will be greater than all its parts and greater than any society the world has seen before. It can still happen.

Ibid., Ch. 14

1001. Carol Emshwiller
(1924?–   )

1 As a mother I have served longer than I expected.
"Autobiography," *Joy in Our Cause*   *1974*

2 For a long time I was powerless to resist: my father's opinions, marriage, and having three children, the lure of music.

Ibid.

3 Mother wants me to write something nice she can show to her friends.

Ibid.

1002. Janet Frame
(1924–   )

1 Every morning I woke in dread, waiting for the day
nurse to go on her rounds and announce from the list
of names in her hand whether or not I was for shock
treatment, the new and fashionable means of quieting
people and of making them realize that orders are to be
obeyed and floors are to be polished without anyone
protesting and faces are made to be fixed into smiles
and weeping is a crime.

Faces in the Water, Ch. 1   *1961*

2 For in spite of the snapdragons and the dusty millers
and the cherry blossoms, it was always winter.

Ibid., Ch. 2

3 Electricity, the peril the wind sings to in the wires on a
gray day.   Ibid.

4 . . . very often the law of extremity demands an attention to irrelevance. . . .   Ibid., Ch. 3

5 "For your own good" is a persuasive argument that
will eventually make man agree to his own destruction.

Ibid., Ch. 4

1003. Cloris Leachman
(1924–   )

1 Why can't we build orphanages next to homes for the
elderly? If someone's sitting in a rocker, it won't be
long before a kid will be in his lap.

Quoted in "I Love My Career and
I Love My Children . . ." by Jane
Wilkie, *Good Housekeeping*
October, 1973

1004. Phyllis Lyon
(1924–   )

Co-author with Del Martin. See 975: 1–7.

1005. Bess Myerson
(1924–   )

1 . . . the accomplice to the crime of corruption is frequently our own indifference.
> Quoted in "Impeachment?"
> by Claire Safran, *Redbook*
> *April, 1974*

2 It's always time for a change for the better, and for a good fight for the full human rights of every individual.
> Quoted in *AFTRA Magazine*
> *Summer, 1974*

1006. Alma Routsong
(1924–   )

1 Time enough later to teach her that it's better to be a real woman than an imitation man, and that when someone chooses a woman to go away with it's because a woman is what's preferred.
> *A Place for Us*   1969

2 [I] wonder if what makes men walk lordlike and speak so masterfully is having the love of women.   Ibid.

1007. Phyllis Schlafly
(1924–   )

1 The advance planning and sense stimuli employed to capture a $10 million cigarette or soap market are nothing compared to the brainwashing and propaganda blitzes used to ensure control of the largest cash market in the world: the Executive Branch of the United States Government.
> *A Choice Not an Echo,* Ch. 1   1964

2 The moral sickness of the Federal Government becomes more apparent every day. Public officials are caught in a giant web of payoffs, bribes, perversion, and conflicts of interest, so that few dare speak out against the establishment.
> *Safe—Not Sorry,* Ch. 1   1967

3 America is waiting for an Attorney General who will enforce the law—and a President with the courage to demand that he do so.

Ibid., Ch. 8

4 The urgent need today is to develop and support leaders on every level of government who are independent of the bossism of every political machine—the big-city machine, the liberal Democrat machine, and the Republican kingmaker machine.

Ibid., Ch. 9

5 The left wing forces—both obvious and hidden—which have been running our country for the last seven years understand and appreciate the importance of *political action*. Their long tentacles reach out in many fields: to "orchestrate" propaganda through the communications media, the indoctrinate youth in our schools and universities, to create a Socialist intellectual climate through tax-exempt foundations, and to bend business into line with Government contracts.

Ibid., Ch. 12

6 One of the favorite slogans of the liberals is "U for Unity must precede V for Victory." Those who play this game forget that U and V are both preceded by P for Principle.

Ibid., Ch. 13

7 The claim that American women are downtrodden and unfairly treated is the fraud of the century.

Quoted by Lisa Cronin Wohl in *Ms.*
March, 1974

1008. Sally Weinraub
(1924–   )

1 Architects believed less and less in doors these days, so that houses were becoming like beehives, arches leading into chambers and more arches. It was lucky that Americans were still puritan in their habits. You could be alone in the bathroom.

"Knifed with a Black Shadow,"
American Scene: New Voices,
Don Wolfe, ed.   *1963*

1009. Shana Alexander
(1925–   )

1 Tadpole into frog, sketch into statue, tribe into stage—evolution is fascinating to watch. To me it is most interesting when one can observe the evolution of a single man.

> "Evolution of a Rebel Priest" (April, 1966), *The Feminine Eye*   1970

2 Faithful horoscope-watching, practiced daily, provides just the sort of small but warm and infinitely reassuring fillip that gets matters off to a spirited start.

> Ibid., "A Delicious Appeal to Unreason" (May, 1966)

3 The sad truth is that excellence makes people nervous.

> Ibid., "Neglected Kids—the Bright Ones" (June, 1966)

4 A plane, if you're traveling alone, is also a good place to be melancholy. . . . A plane is a bad place for an all-out sleep, but a good place to begin rest and recovery from the trip to the faraway places you've been, a decompression chamber between Here and There. Though a plane is not the ideal place really to think, to reassess or reevaluate things, it is a great place to have the illusion of doing so, and often the illusion will suffice.

> Ibid., "Overcuddle and Megalull" (February, 1967)

5 Mankind still has monsters, of course. The trouble is that they are no longer mythological. Rather, they are the terrifying things man creates with his technology and then cannot control—things like Peenemünde; things like smog, that foul thousand-mile blob visible from any jet; things like the cataclysmic, coiling, deadly dragon that is Vietnam.

> Ibid., "More Monsters, Please!" (December, 1967)

6 Roughly speaking, the President of the United States knows what his job is. Constitution and custom spell it out, for him as well as for us. His wife has no such

luck. The First Lady has no rules; rather, each new woman must make her own.

> Ibid., "The Best First Lady"
> (December, 1968)

7 . . . when two people marry they become in the eyes of the law one person, and that one person is the husband!

> *State-by-State Guide to Women's*
> *Legal Rights*, Introduction   *1975*

8 But certainly I knew that what all women's magazines were giving women to read was largely illusion, fantasy, and too often cruel deception. . . . I wanted to feed them reality, and clothe them with armor against the exploitation of women's needs and dreams which I knew abounded in the closed, essentially fake world of ladies' magazines.

> Ibid.

9 The law changes and flows like water, and . . . the stream of women's rights law has become a sudden rushing torrent.

> Ibid.

10 The [quail] females are so dowdy, drab, dun-colored, and diligent in their pecking, so hopelessly plodding compared to the handsome high-stepping ring-neck males, that for an atavistic moment I wonder anew whether and how the human female will ever transcend the lower, more dependent, less rights-ful station to which her reproductive nature has until the last-minute invention of The Pill confined her.   Ibid.

1010. Dede Allen
(1925–   )

1 Editing [film] is really a creative art. Any editor needs to know certain techniques, but the real decisions are made in her or his head.

> Quoted in "The Power Behind the
> Screen" by Geraldine Febrikant, *Ms.*
> *February, 1974*

2 You know, when you're young and curious, people love to teach you.   Ibid.

1011. Svetlana Alliluyeva
(1925–   )

1 I think that before the marriage, it should be love. So if
I will love this country and this country will love me,
then the marriage will be settled.
Quoted in *Newsweek*   *May 8, 1967*

2 Moscow, breathing fire like a human volcano with its
smoldering lava of passion, ambition and politics, its
hurly-burly of meetings and entertainment. . . .
Moscow seethes and bubbles and gasps for air. It's always thirsting for something new, the newest events,
the latest sensation. Everyone wants to be the first to
know. It's the rhythm of life today.
Two Letters to a Friend,
Introduction (July 16, 1963)   *1967*

3 He [her father, Stalin] is gone, but his shadow still
stands over all of us. It still dictates to us and we, very
often, obey.   *Ibid., Ch. 2*

4 Russia is immense, you cannot please everyone.
"Brajesh Singh in Moscow,"
Only One Year   *1969*

5 . . . as a result of half a century of Soviet rule people
have been weaned from a belief in human kindness.
Ibid., "The Journey's End"

1012. Marilyn Bender
(1925–   )

1 Female clothing has been disappearing literally and
philosophically.
The Beautiful People, Ch. 1   *1967*

2 To whip up desire for something that people don't
really need, at least not in endless quantity, glamorous
idols are essential. If desire begets need, then envy begets desire. The stimulation of envy or a longing to imitate is the function of the idol. The fashion industry,
through its press agents and an eagerly cooperative,
self-serving press, had to manufacture new goddesses.
Ibid., Ch. 3

3 What caused this . . . renaissance of the dandy in an era of technology? Pessimists attributed it to male decline. As women became more aggressive, invaded masculine professions and usurped male prerogatives, men fell back on being peacocks, they reasoned. With clothes, men were reconstructing their diminished manhood.

Ibid., Ch. 10

4 Any survey of what businessmen are reading runs smack into the open secret that most businessmen aren't. Reading books, that is.

"The Business of Reading About Business," *Saturday Review of the Society*   *April, 1973*

5 Just as the court flunky tasted the king's food to screen it for poison, so today the corporate sovereign has his literary fare digested and presented in capsule form or laced into his speeches by his ghost writer.

Ibid.

1013. Joyce Brothers
(1925–   )

1 Marriage is not just spiritual communion and passionate embraces; marriage is also three-meals-a-day and remembering to carry out the trash.

"When Your Husband's Affection Cools," *Good Housekeeping May, 1972*

2 Anger repressed can poison a relationship as surely as the cruelest words.   Ibid.

1014. Kathryn Clarenbach
(1925?–   )

1 Liberation means having a voice in the significant decisions which affect one's own life and the wider society, . . . having access to whatever avenue or pathway one's commitment and bent may lead. It means the assumption of independent responsibility for the utilization of potential and opportunities.

Quoted in *NOW Accomplishments*   *1973*

2 The overemphasis on protecting girls from strain or injury and underemphasis on developing skills and experiencing teamwork fits neatly into the pattern of the
second sex. . . . Girls are the spectators and the
cheerleaders. . . . Perfect preparation for the adult
role of woman—to stand decoratively on the sidelines
of history and cheer on the men who make the decisions. . . .

Sex Role Stereotyping in the Schools 1973

3 Women who have had the regular experience of performing before others, of learning to win and lose, of
cooperating in team efforts, will be far less fearful of
running for office, better able to take public positions
on issues in the face of public opposition. By working
toward some balance in physical activity, we may begin
to achieve a more wholesome, democratic balance in
all phases of our lives.

Quoted in "Old School System Curbed
Sportswomen," *Los Angeles Times*
April 24, 1974

1015. Elizabeth Gould Davis
(1925–1974)

1 The deeper the archeologists dig, the further back go
the origins of man and society—and the less sure we
are that civilization has followed the steady upward
course so thoroughly believed in by the Victorians. It is
more likely that the greatest civilizations of the past
have yet to be discovered.

The First Sex, Prologue 1971

2 Maleness remains a recessive genetic trait like color-
blindness and hemophilia, with which it is linked. The
suspicion that maleness is abnormal and that the Y
chromosome is an accidental mutation boding no good
for the race is strongly supported by the recent discovery by geneticists that congenital killers and criminals
are possessed of not one but *two* Y chromosomes, bearing a double dose, as it were, of genetically undesirable
maleness.

Ibid., Pt. I, Ch. 1

3 It is . . . possible that the women of the old gynocra-
cies brought on their own downfall by selecting the

289

phallic wild men over the more civilized men of their own pacific and gentle world.

Ibid., Ch. 5

4 When man substituted God for the Great Goddess he at the same time substituted authoritarian for humanistic values.

Ibid., Ch. 7

5 In the Judeo-Christian creed the male body is the temple of God, while the female body is an object made for man's exploitation.

Ibid., Pt. II, Ch. 9

6 The status of Western women has steadily declined since the advent of Christianity—and is still declining. . . . The Semitic myth of male supremacy was first preached in Europe to a pagan people to whom it came as a radical and astonishing novelty.

Ibid., Pt. IV, Ch. 14

7 They [nineteenth-century women] were a special kind of property, not quite like houses or beasts of burden, yet not quite people. . . . Her place in the scheme of things, if she was fortunate, was that of a household pet.

Ibid., Ch. 20

8 It is men, not women, who have promoted the cult of brutal masculinity; and because men admire muscle and physical force, they assume that women do too.

Ibid., Ch. 21

9 The innately logical mind of woman, her unique sense of balance, orderliness, and reason, rebels at the terrible realization that justice has been an empty word, that she has been forced for nearly two millennia to worship false gods and to prostrate herself at their empty shrines.

Ibid.

10 If the human race is unhappy today, as all modern philosophers agree that it is, it is only because it is uncomfortable in the mirror image society man has made—the topsy-turvy world in which nature's supporting pillar is forced to serve as the cornice of the architrave, while the cornice struggles to support the building. The fact is that men need women more than women need men; and so, aware of this fact, man has sought to keep

woman dependent upon him economically as the only method open to him of making himself necessary to her.

Ibid., Ch. 22

1016. Flannery O'Connor
(1925–1964)

1 The old man would point to his grandson, Haze. He had a particular disrespect for him because his own face was repeated almost exactly in the child's and seemed to mock him.

Wise Blood, Ch. 1   *1949*

2 "I'm going to preach there was no Fall because there was nothing to fall from and no Redemption because there was no Fall and no Judgment because there wasn't the first two. Nothing matters but that Jesus was a liar."

Ibid., Ch. 6

3 She felt justified in getting anything at all back that she could, money or anything else, as if she had once owned the earth and been dispossessed of it. She couldn't look at anything steadily without wanting it, and what provoked her most was the thought that there might be something valuable hidden near her, something she couldn't see.

Ibid., Ch. 14

4 "I call myself The Misfit," he said, "because I can't make what all I done wrong fit what all I gone through in punishment."

"A Good Man Is Hard to Find,"
A Good Man Is Hard to Find   *1955*

5 "Lady, a man is divided into two parts, body and spirit. . . . A body and a spirit," he repeated. "The body, lady, is like a house it don't go anywhere; but the spirit, lady, is like a automobile: always on the move, always. . . ."

Ibid., "The Life You Save
May Be Your Own"

6 Mr. Head stood very still and felt the action of mercy touch him again but this time he knew that there were no words in the world that could name it. He under-

291

stood that it grew out of agony, which is not denied to any man and which is given in strange ways to children. He understood it was all a man could carry into death to give his Maker and he suddenly burned with shame that he had so little of it to take with him. He stood appalled, judging himself with the thoroughness of God, while the action of mercy covered his pride like a flame and consumed it.

> Ibid., "The Artificial Nigger"

7 Living had got to be such a habit with him that he couldn't conceive of any other condition.

> Ibid., "A Late Encounter with the Enemy"

8 He had schooled him in the evils that befall prophets; in those that come from the world, which are trifling, and those that come from the Lord and burn the prophet clean; for he himself had been burned clean and burned clean again. He had learned by fire.

> *The Violent Bear It Away,*
> Pt. I, Ch. 1   *1955*

9 Then the revelation came, silent, implacable, direct as a bullet. He did not look into the eyes of any fiery beast or see a burning bush.

> Ibid., Ch. 3

10 Once or twice I have been asked what the peacock is "good for"—a question which gets no answer from me because it deserves none.

> "Peacocks Are a Puzzle," *Mystery
> and Manners*   *1957*

11 "Knowing who you are is good for one generation only."

> "Everything That Rises Must
> Converge," *Everything That
> Rises Must Converge*   *1965p*

12 She was a good Christian woman with a large respect for religion, though she did not, of course, believe any of it was true.

> Ibid., "Greenleaf"

13 He would have hastened his end but suicide would not have been a victory. Death was coming to him legitimately, as a justification, as a gift from life. That was his greatest triumph.

> Ibid., "The Enduring Chill"

14 He had stuffed his own emptiness with good work like a glutton.

> Ibid., "The Lame Shall Enter First"

1017. Naomi Streshinsky
(1925–   )

1 The danger of a gift is an intriguing concept. Primitive man may have believed that the gift contained the spirit of the donor and therein lay its potential harm. The belief in the donor's spirit dissolved from modern man but the danger is still very much present.

> *Welfare Rights Organizations*, Ch. 2   1970

2 Political acceptability of social welfare can be translated to mean what the general public will permit to be granted, out of its tax money to poor people, just because they are in need and with no strings attached. Attitudes of hostility toward and derogation of the assisted poor puts serious obstacles in the way of future programs and are precisely the ones which contribute to the present bind.

> Ibid., Ch. 6

1018. Toni Carabillo
(1926–   )

1 But powerlessness is still each woman's most critical problem, whether or not she is a social activist. It is at the root of most of her psychological disorders.

> Address, "Power Is the Name of the
> Game," California NOW State
> Conference, San Diego
> *October 28, 1973*

2 The sudden acquisition of power by those who have never had it before can be intoxicating, and we run the risk of becoming absorbed in petty power games with our organization [NOW] that in the last analysis can only be self-defeating.

> Ibid.

3 For the one equality women all over the world have already achieved is the *Equality of Consequences*. No inventory of the major challenges and crises of our

times discloses any from whose effects women will be exempt by virtue of our sex.

> Address, "Sharing the Power, the Glory—and the Pain," NOW Western Regional Conference, Long Beach, California
>
> *November 24, 1974*

4 We know that poverty in this country is primarily the problem of *all* women—that most women are only a husband away from welfare.

> Ibid.

5 . . . we must learn that we can disagree with each other on issues, without becoming deadly enemies, and without totally devastating our opposition. We can in fact continue to acknowledge and admire the skills and dedication, the genuine accomplishments and contributions of those with whom we are otherwise in dissent.

> Ibid.

6 . . . we have learned from the experience of the first feminist movement that to stop short of the basic reordering of society, as it is reflected in sex role stereotypes, is too small a victory.

> Address, "Womanpower and the Media," National Association of Broadcasters *1974*

7 Rock music consistently degrades women and makes it clear her place in this man's world is limited to the kitchen and bedroom. Rock music has been rightly characterized, in our view, as a "frenzied celebration of masculine supremacy."

> Ibid.

8 . . . women are not a special interest group in the usual sense of the term. We are half the population. When the image of women presented in the media is offensive, it is offensive to women of all social classes, races, religions and ethnic origins.

> Ibid.

9 Not only the CIA, but the FBI, as well as many state and community police departments, have devoted vast resources to monitoring the activities of concerned citizens working in concert to make social changes within our system. The "flatfoot mentality" insists that any individual or organization that wants to change *anything*

in our present system is somehow subversive of "the American way," and should be under continuous surveillance—a task that appears to absorb most of our resources for fighting genuine crime.

"The 'Flatfoot Mentality,' " *Hollywood
NOW News   August, 1975*

1019. Elizabeth Douvan
(1926–   )

* * *

1 The dream of college apparently serves as a substitute for more direct preoccupation with marriage: girls who do not plan to go to college are more explicit in their desire to marry, and have a more developed sense of their own sex role.

"Motivational Factors in College
Entrance," *The American College,*
with Carol Kaye

2 College and travel are alternatives to a more open interest in sexuality.

Ibid.

1020. Rosalyn Drexler
(1926–   )

1 Working with women is a new adventure; it is exciting. We are pioneering, beginning again. There is a feeling of conspiracy, that we are going to forge ahead.

Quoted in *AFTRA Magazine
Summer, 1974*

2 "I'm just a dog. Look, no opposable thumb."
The Cosmopolitan Girl   1975

3 He visited the Museum of Modern Art, and was standing near the pool looking at his dark reflection when a curator of the museum noticed him. "My, my, what a fine work of art that is!" the curator said to himself. "I must have it installed immediately."   Ibid.

4 We reject the notion that the work that brings in more money is not more valuable. The ability to earn money, or the fact that one already has it, should carry more weight in a relationship.   Ibid.

1021. Marie Edwards
(1926?–   )

1 Books, magazines, counselors, therapists sell one message to unmarrieds: "Shape up, go where other singles are, entertain more, raise your sex quotient, get involved, get closer, be more open, more honest, more intimate, above all, find Mr. Right or Miss Wonderful and *get married.*" *The Challenge of Being Single,*
with Eleanor Hoover   *1975*

2 ". . . an intense, one-to-one involvement is as socially conditioned as a hamburger and malt. . . ."   Ibid.

1022. Elizabeth II
(1926–   )

1 My whole life, whether it be long or short, shall be devoted to your [the public's] service and the service of our great imperial family to which we all belong. But I shall not have strength to carry out this resolution alone unless you join in it with me.
Radio Broadcast   *April 21, 1947*

1023. Cissy Farenthold
(1926–   )

1 I am working for the time when unqualified blacks, browns and women join the unqualified men in running our government.
Quoted in the *Los Angeles Times*
September 18, 1974

1024. Wilma Scott Heide
(1926–   )

1 The only jobs for which no man is qualified are human incubator and wet nurse. Likewise, the only job for which no woman is or can be qualified is sperm donor.
Quoted in *NOW Official Biography*   *1971*

2 . . . we whose hands have rocked the cradle, are now using our heads to rock the boat. . . .

Ibid.

3 . . . we will no longer be led only by that half of the population whose socialization, through toys, games, values and expectations, sanctions violence as the final assertion of manhood, synonymous with nationhood.

Ibid.

4 The pedestal is immobilizing and subtly insulting whether or not some women yet realize it. We must move up from the pedestal.

Ibid.

5 The path to freedom for women *or* men does *not* lie *down* the bunny trail!

Ibid.

6 To date, we have taught men to be brave and women to care. Now we must enlarge our concepts of bravery and caring. Men must be *brave enough to care* sensitively, compassionately and contrary to the masculine mystique about the quality and equality of our society. Women must *care enough* about their families and all families to *bravely assert* their voices and intellects to every aspect of every institution, whatever the feminine mystique. Every social trait labelled masculine or feminine is in truth a human trait. It is our human right to develop and contribute our talents whatever our race, sex, religion, ancestry, age. Human rights are indivisible!

Ibid.

7 As your president [of NOW] . . . I am one of thousands of us privileged to experience the joy, the risks, the gratifications, bone weariness, tragedies and triumphs of activist feminism. There are women and men and children in our lives and whose lives we touch who may never know how profoundly we care about ourselves and them and the quality of the world we must share and make liveable for all. We are self-helpers with the courage of our commitment.

Quoted in *NOW Accomplishments*   1973

8 Now that we've organized [NOW] . . . all over the United States and initiated an international movement and actions, it must be apparent that feminism is no passing fad but indeed a profound, universal behavior revolution.   Quoted in "About Women,"

Los Angeles Times
May 12, 1974

1025. Carolyn Heilbrun
(1926–   )

1 Ideas move fast when their time comes.
Toward a Recognition of Androgyny   1973

2 Androgyny suggests a spirit of reconciliation between the sexes; it suggests, further, a full range of experience open to individuals who may as women be aggressive, as men, tender; it suggests a spectrum upon which human beings choose their places without regard to propriety or custom.

Ibid., Introduction

3 Most of us nowadays regard the Victorian age as part of the very remote past. . . . Yet in the matter of sexual polarization and the rejection of androgyny we still accept the convictions of Victorianism; we view everything, from our study of animal habits to our reading of literature, through the paternalistic eyes of the Victorian era.

Ibid.

4 What is important now is that we free ourselves from the prison of gender and, before it is too late, deliver the world from the almost exclusive control of the masculine impulse.

Ibid.

5 Great periods of civilization, however much they may have owed their beginnings to the aggressive dominance of the male principle, have always been marked by some sort of rise in the status of women. This in its turn is a manifestation of something more profound: the recognition of the importance of the "feminine" principle, not as other, but as necessary to wholeness.

Ibid., Pt. I

6 Today's shocks are tomorrow's conventions.

Ibid., Pt. II

7 Routine, disposable novels, able to provide relief or distraction but not in themselves valuable—like the smoked cigarette, the used whore, the quick drink—are exactly suited to the conventions of their consumers.

Ibid.

8 . . . ardent, intelligent, sweet, sensitive, cultivated, erudite. These are the adjectives of praise in an androgynous world. Those who consider them epithets of shame or folly ought not to be trusted with leadership, for they will be men hot for power and revenge, certain of right and wrong.

Ibid., Pt. III

9 Queens may rule either as monarchs or as nationalized angels in the house.

Ibid.

10 From the critics of the past I have learned the futility of concerning onself with the present.

Ibid., Afterword

11 The genuine solitaries of life fear intimacy more than loneliness. The married are those who have taken the terrible risk of intimacy and, having taken it, know life without intimacy to be impossible.

"Marriage Is the Message," Ms.
August, 1974

12 Only a marriage with partners strong enough to risk divorce is strong enough to avoid it. . . .

Ibid.

13 Marriage today must . . . be concerned not with the inviolable commitment of constancy and unending passion, but with the changing patterns of liberty and discovery.

Ibid.

1026. Aileen Clarke Hernandez
(1926–   )

1 My comments to the thousands of persons at the peace march [the 1971 Another Mother for Peace march in Los Angeles] were directed not just against the Vietnam War, but against *all* war, against the masculine mystique which glorifies violence as a solution to problems, and against the vast diverting of American energies and resources from socially needed programs into socially destructive wars.

Letter to Eve Norman, Quoted in
the NOW Newsletter
April 29, 1971

2 This movement . . . is the last stage of the drive for equality for women. We are determined that our daughters and granddaughters will live as free human beings, secure in their personhood, and dedicated to making this nation and the world a humane place in which to live.

> Address, National Conference of
> NOW, Los Angeles
> *September 3–6, 1971*

3 There are no such things as women's issues! All issues are women's issues. The difference that we bring to existing issues of our society, the issues of war and peace; the issues of poverty; the issues of child care; the issues of political power—the difference that we bring is that we are going to bring the full, loud, clear determined voice of women into deciding how those issues are going to be addressed.

> Ibid.

4 We need to get about the business of becoming persons. We need to get about the business of addressing the major issues of society as full-fledged human beings in a society that puts humanity at the head of its list, rather than masculinity at the head of its list.

> Ibid.

1027. Sue Kaufman
(1926–   )

1 Now Accounts is really a very good word. Accounts in its reportorial not calculative sense. Account, accounting—an account of what is going on. Better than journal or diary by far. *Diary* makes me think of those girls at camp. . . . *Journal* makes me think of all those college Lit courses. . . . Anyway, *Accounts* is good. Accounts is best. Yes, Accounts does very well indeed.

> "Friday, September 12,"
> *Diary of a Mad Housewife*   1967

2 I was afraid that if I opened my mouth, like Gerald McBoing-Boing, terrible inhuman sounds would come out—brakes screeching, metal clashing, tires skidding, trains roaring past in the night.

> Ibid., "Saturday, October 7"

3 People. Along with doormen, elevator men and head-waiters, the opinions of People matter greatly to Jonathan these days. And who are People? His great secret public—strangers, anybody he doesn't know.

Ibid., "Monday, October 30"

4 "Make yourself a nice hut tuddy, and while you sip it, read Proust. Proust is the only thing when you're sick." . . . I skipped the hut tuddy, but by God it worked. Saved me. Was the antibiotic which wouldn't "touch" the Thing I had. Marvelous crazy poet. Marvelous Proust.

Ibid., "Friday, November 17"

5 "I'm sure he'd be delighted to meet you at long last—the model husband for the cured analysand. . . . You must give him your views of what both working roles in a successful marriage should be—he'll be thrilled by the brilliant simplicity of it all. You know—the Forceful Dominant Male, the Submissive Woman? The Breadwinner who has every right to expect the Obedient Wife to carry out all his orders? He'll lap it up."

Ibid., "Thursday, December 7"

6 Ever since she had gotten out of hospital, her eye kept seeking out and fastening on the cruel, the ugly, the sordid—trying to turn every nasty little incident or detail into some sort of concrete proof of just how rotten the world had become.

Falling Bodies 1974

7 "In violent and chaotic times such as these, our only chance for survival lies in creating our own little islands of sanity and order, in making little havens of our homes."

Ibid.

8 Burt told her that he loved her, she told him that she loved him. She thought she didn't mean it. She thought she was being very advanced, very pre-liberated, shattering the damned double standard and lying while she did it, if that's what was required.

Ibid.

9 "I loved my mother. And she died a horrible death. In unspeakable agony."

"She was *not* in agony when she died. . . . And you didn't love her. You wanted to love her and tried

301

to love her, though God only knows why—but you *hated* her. With damned good reason. She was a castrating bitch, who cut your poor father's nuts off and finally drove him to drink himself to death. . . . It makes my blood run cold just imagining what that poor guy must've gone through, and what you must've gone through as a child. I've always felt it was proof of your terrific strength that you'd managed to come out of that relatively unscathed. But now she's finally gotten at you anyway. Finally did it by dying, the bitch—and screw that business about not speaking ill of the dead: she was a *bitch*."   Ibid.

1028. Gertrude Lemp Kerbis
(1926–   )

1 It was hell for women architects then. They didn't want us in school or in the profession. . . . One thing I've never understood about this prejudice is that it's so strange in view of the fact that the drive to build has always been in women.

> Quoted in *Women at Work*
> by Betty Medsger   *1975*

1029. Margaret Laurence
(1926–   )

1 Each day dies with sleep.

> *A Jest of God* (later known as
> *Rachel, Rachel*), Ch. 3   *1966*

2 Holidays are enticing only for the first week or so. After that, it is no longer such a novelty to rise late and have little to do.

> Ibid., Ch. 4

3 "Presentation is all—that's what I believe. Everybody knows a product has to be attractively packaged—it's the first rule of sales—isn't that so?"   Ibid., Ch. 7

4 "The prime purpose of a funeral director is not all this beautician deal which some members of the profession go in for so much. No. It's this—to take over. Reassure people."   Ibid.

5   "Death's unmentionable?"

"Not exactly unmentionable, but let's face it, most of us could get along without it."

"I don't see how."

Ibid.

6 How strange to have to keep on retreating to the only existing privacy, the only place one is permitted to be unquestionably alone, the lavatory.

Ibid., Ch. 9

7 I was always afraid that I might become a fool. Yet I could almost smile with some grotesque lightheadedness at that fool of a fear, that poor fear of fools, now that I really am one.

Ibid., Ch. 10

8 "You are out of danger," he said. I laughed, I guess, and said, "How can I be—I don't feel dead yet."

Ibid., Ch. 11

9 God's mercy on reluctant jesters. God's grace on fools. God's pity on God.

Ibid., Ch. 12

1030. Harper Lee
(1926–   )

1 A day was twenty-four hours long but seemed longer. There was no hurry, for there was nowhere to go, nothing to buy and no money to buy it with, nothing to see outside the boundaries of Maycomb County. But it was a time of vague optimism for some of the people: Maycomb County had recently been told that it had nothing to fear but fear itself.

To Kill a Mockingbird,
Pt. I, Ch. 1   *1960*

2 Until I feared I would lose it, I never loved to read. One does not love breathing.

Ibid., Ch. 2

3 "People in their right minds never take pride in talents," said Miss Maudie.

Ibid., Ch. 10

4 "The one thing that doesn't abide by majority rule is a person's conscience."

Ibid., Ch. 11

5 Never, never, never, on cross-examination ask a witness a question you don't already know the answer to, was a tenet I absorbed with my baby-food. Do it, and you'll often get an answer you don't want, an answer that might wreck your case. *Ibid.*, Ch. 17

6 "Our courts have their faults, as does any human institution, but in this country our courts are the great levelers, and in our courts all men are created equal. I'm no idealist to believe firmly in the integrity of our courts and in the jury system—that is no ideal to me, it is a living, working reality. Gentlemen, a court is no better than each man of you sitting before me on this jury. A court is only as sound as its jury, and a jury is only as sound as the men who make it up." *Ibid.*, Ch. 20

7 "As you grow older, you'll see white men cheat black men every day of your life, but let me tell you something and don't you forget it—whenever a white man does that to a black man, no matter who he is, how rich he is, or how fine a family he comes from, that white man is trash." *Ibid.*, Ch. 23

1031. Pat Loud
(1926–   )

1 A miserable marriage can wobble along for years until something comes along and pushes one of the people over the brink. It's usually another man or woman. For me, it was a whole production staff and camera crew.
Pat Loud: A Woman's Story, with Nora Johnson   *1974*

2 College for women was a refinement whose main purpose was to better prepare you for your ultimate destiny . . . to make you a more desirable product.
Ibid.

3 Life was diapers and little jars of puréed apricots and bottles and playpens and rectal thermometers, and all those small dirty faces and all those questions.
Ibid.

4 Housework isn't bad in itself—the trouble with it is that it's inhumanely lonely.   *Ibid.*

1032. Marilyn Monroe
(1926–1962)

1 I've been on a calendar, but never on time.
Quoted in Look   January 16, 1962

2 A career is born in public—talent in privacy.
Quoted in "Marilyn: The Woman Who
Died Too Soon" by Gloria Steinem,
The First Ms. Reader, Francine
Klagsbrun, ed.   1972p

3 I have too many fantasies to be a housewife. . . . I guess I *am* a fantasy.   **Ibid.**

4 I don't want to make money. I just want to be wonderful.   **Ibid.**

5 I hope at some future time to make a glowing report on the wonders that psychiatrists can do for you.   **Ibid.**

6 I am always running into peoples' unconscious.
Quoted in Marilyn by Norman Mailer   1973p

1033. Patricia Neal
(1926–   )

1 It [Hollywood] always sounds glamorous when you're young.
Quoted in Time   March 20, 1964

2 It's very important not to pamper or indulge them [brain-injured or handicapped children] or to treat them differently from the other children in the family. But this is very difficult . . . although . . . I have never ever spanked Theo [her son] for anything . . . now I regret having ever spanked any of them, for I've come to believe it doesn't do that much good—they turn out the same way anyhow.
Quoted in "Triumph Over Tragedy"
by Patricia Baum, Parents'
Magazine   November, 1975

3 Tennessee hillbillies don't conk out that easily.

Ibid.

1034. Charlotte Painter
(1926–   )

1 We are looking for some way to live in a world gone
mad. We have left America the beautiful. But not because we know a better place.

*Confession from the Malaga
Madhouse   1971*

2 If a thing is absolutely true, how can it not also be a
lie? An absolute must contain its opposite.

Ibid.

3 Not persuaded enough against violence to go to jail for
it. Not persuaded he can kill either. Not interested in
that Army, that War, sure enough of himself only to
know that he doesn't yet know the Way. . . .

Ibid.

4 The wars that always go on. You know, they don't
have to. If everybody played war instead of really,
really doing it.

Ibid.

5 The passion for destruction, glorious destruction. Must
we seek grace in violence, more than any other way?

Ibid.

6 I don't know where in this shrunken world to take you,
son, to let you grow to manhood.   Ibid.

7 To a lover of literature, life tends to will o' wisp on
either side of the poem, the story, the play.

Revelations: Diaries of Women,
with Mary Jane Moffat,
Afterword   *1974*

8 We need only discover within ourselves how and when
to call upon either of the functions we need—a task
that may, like the *via longissima* of the alchemists, take
more lives than one.   Ibid.

9 If we can distinguish between specialized art, as designed for an intellectual, educated group, and primitive art, as created through a group's unconscious symbols, then perhaps we can talk about some diaries as
primitive.

Ibid.

306

10 . . . perhaps we have not fully understood that anger is a secondary emotional cover for hurt. (Righteous indignation feels good; hurts do not.)

Ibid.

11 . . . as awareness increases, the need for personal secrecy almost proportionately decreases.

Ibid.

12 Habits do not like to be abandoned, and besides they have the virtue of being tools.

Ibid.

13 Psychic bisexuality is a de-conditioning process, which can eventually eliminate sexist limitations for both men and women.

Ibid.

1035. Cynthia Propper Seton
(1926–   )

1 To Angela her grandmother was old but had not grown older and was never younger. This is a usual way with grandmothers. She had the very shape of the old: vaguely conical, shortish, roundish; and was fortified by a carapace of corset under which it would have been shocking to surmise a live, warm, woman's body.

The Sea Change of Angela Lewes,
Ch. 1   *1971*

2 Well, banality is a terribly likely consequence of the underuse of a good mind. That is why in particular it is a female affliction.

Ibid., Ch. 9

3 "It sometimes looks to me," said Angela, "that a middle-class marriage is a careful mismatching of two innocents—and the game is called Making the Best of It, while in actual fact each one does a terrible thing to the spirit of the other. . . . And you wonder why they endure each other, why they stand for it? And the explanation is that they really answer each other's needs, unconscious needs, and are in fact often admirably suited to each other, and that, unbelievable as it might seem from the outside, they do really *love* each other."

Ibid., Ch. 12

4 Angela was spinning off, and Charlie was letting her. The shift in their marital relationship was remarkable

for the absence of tension, of conflict—a peaceful *de-*consummation devoutly to be wished in the generality of aging marriages. Angela was becoming her own person, her own woman, and was alternately exhilarated and complacent. . . .

Ibid., Ch. 18

5 To pursue yourself is an interesting and absorbing thing to do. Once you have caught the scent of a hidden being, your own hidden being, you won't readily be deflected from the tracking down of it.

Ibid., Ch. 25

6 "Holding hands is a very intimate thing to do," she found herself whispering. "Even to hold a child's hand. It's very touching."

Ibid.

7 She had trouble defining herself independently of her husband, tried to talk to him about it, but he said nonsense, he had no trouble defining her at all.

The Half-Sisters   1974

1036. Joan Sutherland
(1926–   )

1 I know I'm not exactly a bombshell, but one has to make the best of what one's got.

Quoted in "Joan Sutherland," *Divas:
Impressions of Six Opera Superstars*
by Winthrop Sargeant   1959

2 If I weren't reasonably placid, I don't think I could cope with this sort of life. To be a diva, you've got to be absolutely like a horse.

Ibid.

3 But I think Australians have a sort of independence, and I think that, rightly or wrongly, they tend to make their own decisions as to how a thing has gone. Pioneers are apt to be like that. I think that it's not a bad idea. You can listen to what everybody says, but the fact remains that you've got to get out there and do the thing yourself.

Ibid.

1037. Johnnie Tillmon
(1926–   )

1 I'm a woman. I'm a black woman. I'm a poor woman.
I'm a fat woman. I'm a middle-aged woman. And I'm
on welfare. In this country, if you're any one of those
things, you count less as a person. If you're *all* those
things, you just don't count, except as a statistic. I am a
statistic.

> "Welfare Is a Woman's Issue,"
> *The First Ms. Reader,*
> Francine Klagsbrun, ed.   *1972*

2 Welfare is like a traffic accident. It can happen to anybody, but especially it happens to women.

> Ibid.

3 Women aren't supposed to work. They're supposed to
be married.

> Ibid.

4 Wages are the measure of dignity that society puts on a
job.

> Ibid.

1038. Lynn Caine
(1927?–   )

1 After my husband died, I felt like one of those spiraled
shells washed up on the beach . . . no flesh, no life.
. . . We add ourselves to our men, we exist in their
reflection. And then? If they die?

> *Widow*   *1974*

2 Since every death diminishes us a little, we grieve—not
so much for the death as for ourselves.   Ibid.

3 "Widow" is a harsh and hurtful word. It comes from
the Sanskrit and it means "empty." I have been empty
too long.   Ibid.

4 One of the chores of grief involves going over and over
in one's mind the circumstances that led to the death,
the details of the death itself.   Ibid.

1039. Midge Decter
(1927–   )

1 Shifts in prejudice can work both ways.

The Liberated Woman and Other
Americans, Pt. I, Ch. 3   *1971*

2 Ideas are powerful things, requiring not a studious con-
templation but an action, even if it is only an inner
action. Their acquisition obligates each man in some
way to change his life, even if it is only his inner life.
They demand to be stood for. They dictate where a
man must concentrate his vision. They determine his
moral and intellectual priorities. They provide him with
allies and make him enemies. In short, ideas impose an
interest in their ultimate fate which goes far beyond the
realm of the merely reasonable.

Ibid., Pt. II, Ch. 2

3 . . . because I am a New Yorker, my experience is the
more truly, the more typically, American one. It is my
America that is moving in on them [Middle America].
God is about to bless them with an opportunity, and
may He also save them from it, but there is no turning
back now.

Ibid., Pt. III, Ch. 6

4 The hatred of the youth culture for adult society is not
a disinterested judgment but a terror-ridden refusal to
be hooked into the, if you will, ecological chain of
breathing, growing, and dying. It is the demand, in
other words, to remain children.

The New Chastity and Other
Arguments Against Women's
Liberation, Ch. 1   *1972*

5 Women's Liberation calls it enslavement but the real
truth about the sexual revolution is that it has made of
sex an almost chaotically limitless and therefore un-
manageable realm in the life of women.

Ibid., Ch. 2

6 The fundamental impulse of the movement is neither
masturbatory nor concretely lesbian—although it of
course offers warm houseroom to both these possibilities; it is an impulse to maidenhood—to that condition

in which a woman might pretend to a false fear or loathing of the penis in order to escape from any responsibility for the pleasure and well-being of the man who possesses it. *Ibid.*

7 Consciousness-raising groups are of a piece with a whole cultural pattern that has been growing up. This pattern begins with the term "rapping"—which is a process in which people in groups pretend that they are not simply self-absorbed because they are talking to each other.

Speech, Women's National Book Association, Quoted in "On Consciousness-Raising," *Crazy Salad* by Nora Ephron   1973

8 It might sound a paradoxical thing to say—for surely never has a generation of children occupied more sheer hours of parental time—but the truth is that we neglected you. We allowed you a charade of trivial freedoms in order to avoid making those impositions on you that are in the end both the training ground and proving ground for true independence. We pronounced you strong when you were still weak in order to avoid the struggles with you that would have fed your true strength. We proclaimed you sound when you were foolish in order to avoid taking part in the long, slow, slogging effort that is the only route to genuine maturity of mind and feeling. Thus, it was no small anomaly of your growing up that while you were the most indulged generation, you were also in many ways the most abandoned to your own meager devices by those into whose safe-keeping you had been given.

Liberal Parents/Radical Children, Ch. 1   1975

9 All they wished for her was that she should turn herself into a little replica of them.

Ibid., Ch. 3

1040. Anne Edwards
(1927–   )

1 What a difficult swallowing of ego and pride she [Judy Garland] must have suffered with each pill—what a frightening loss of self.   *Judy Garland*   1975

311

2 That was, of course, the problem—she *begged*, not demanded. She wanted a happy world and everyone in it happy, but she was at a loss as to how to accomplish this.

Ibid.

1041. Althea Gibson
(1927–   )

1 I always wanted to be somebody. I guess that's why I kept running away from home when I was a kid even though I took some terrible whippings for it.

*I Always Wanted to Be
Somebody*, Ch. 1   1958

2 I was excited. I was confident, too. I don't mean that I wasn't nervous, because I was. But I was nervous and confident at the same time, nervous about going out there in front of all those people, with so much at stake, and confident that I was going to go out there and win.

Ibid., Ch. 8

3 I don't want to be put on a pedestal. I just want to be reasonably successful and live a normal life with all the conveniences to make it so. I think I've already got the main thing I've always wanted, which is to be somebody, to have identity. I'm Althea Gibson, the tennis champion. I hope it makes me happy.

Ibid., Ch. 9

1042. Ruth Prawer Jhabvala
(1927–   )

1 ". . . what she wants is a live guru—someone to inspire her . . . snatch her up and out of herself—simultaneously destroy and create her."

Travelers   1973

2 These diseases that people get in India, they're not physical, they're purely psychic. We only get them because we try to resist India—because we shut ourselves up in our little Western egos and don't want to give ourselves. But once we learn to yield, then they must fall away.

Ibid.

3 "Take me, make what you will of me, I have joy in my submission."

Ibid.

4 "It is only," he says, "when you have given up all enjoyment that it is no longer enjoyment, it is only then that you can have these things back again."

Ibid.

5 "India . . . is not a place that one can pick up and put down again as if nothing had happened. In a way it's not so much a country as an experience, and whether it turns out to be a good or a bad one depends, I suppose, on oneself."

Ibid.

1043. Beverly Jones
(1927–   )

1 Automation and unions have led to a continuously shortened day for men but the work day of housewives with children has remained constant.

"The Dynamics of Marriage and
Motherhood," The Florida Paper
on Women's Liberation   1970

2 Now, as always, the most automated appliance in a household is the mother.

Ibid.

3 If enforced wakefulness is the handmaiden and necessary precursor to serious brainwashing, a mother—after her first child—is ready for her final demise.

Ibid.

4 Romance, like the rabbit at the dog track, is the illusive, fake, and never-attained reward which for the benefit and amusement of our masters keeps us running and thinking in safe circles.

Ibid.

5 We who have been raised on pap must develop a passion for honest appraisal.

Ibid.

1044. Coretta Scott King
(1927–)

1 There is a spirit and a need and a man at the beginning of every great human advance. Each of these must be right for that particular moment of history, or nothing happens.

> *My Life with Martin Luther King, Jr.,*
> Ch. 6   *1969*

2 My husband often told the children that if a man had nothing that was worth dying for, then he was not fit to live.

> Ibid., Press Conference (April, 1968)

3 We are concerned not only about the Negro poor, but the poor all over America and all over the world. Every man deserves a right to a job or an income so that he can pursue liberty, life, and happiness. Our great nation, as he often said, has the resources, but his question was: Do we have the will?

> Ibid., Speech, Memphis City Hall
> (April 8, 1968)

4 The more visible signs of protest are gone, but I think there is a realization that the tactics of the late sixties are not sufficient to meet the challenges of the seventies.

> Speech, Quoted in the *Los Angeles Times*   *May 14, 1974*

1045. Leontyne Price
(1927–)

1 I think that recording is in a way much more personal than stage performance. In a theater the audience sees and hears you. So the costumes and the general *mise en scène* help you do the job, because they can see. In recording, you have to see and hear for them with the voice—which makes it much more personal.

> Quoted in "Leontyne Price," *Divas:*
> *Impressions of Six Opera Superstars*
> by Winthrop Sargeant   *1959*

2 I feel that you have to rest the voice and avoid pressure for considerable periods. You have to reflect, too. I've been singing less and less everywhere. You cannot keep up that kind of pressure for considerable periods. I'm asked to be booked more and more, but look, I'd like to find out who I am. If I do have some success, I'd like to try to enjoy it, for heaven's sake! What is the point of having it otherwise? Everybody else gets excited, but *you're* the one who's always tired. That's not life. That's not living.

Ibid.

3 All token blacks have the same experience. I have been pointed at as a solution to things that have not *begun* to be solved, because pointing at us token blacks eases the conscience of millions, and I think this is dreadfully wrong.

Ibid.

1046. Lillian Ross
(1927–)

1 Good will was stamped on the faces of all, but there was no indication as to whom or what it was directed toward. As they entered, the guests exchanged quick glances, as though they were assuring each other and themselves that they were there.

Picture, Ch. 1   1952

2 His name was not engraved on a brass plate on his door; it was typed on a white card placed in a slot, from which it could easily be removed.

Ibid., Ch. 3

1047. Una Stannard
(1927–)

1 Woman's mask of beauty is the face of the child, a revelation of the tragic sexual immaturity of both sexes in our culture.

"The Mask of Beauty," *Woman in Sexist Society*, Vivian Gornick and Barbara Moran, eds.   1971

1048. Maya Angelou
(1928–   )

1 All of childhood's unanswered questions must finally be
passed back to [one's hometown] and answered there.
Heroes and bogey men, values and dislikes, are first
encountered and labeled in that early environment. In
later years they change faces, places and maybe races,
tactics, intensities and goals, but beneath those penetra-
ble masks they wear forever the stocking-capped faces
of childhood.

I Know Why the Caged Bird Sings,
Ch. 4   *1969*

2 She said that I must always be intolerant of ignorance
but understanding of illiteracy. That some people, unable to go to school, were more educated and even more
intelligent than college professors. She encouraged me
to listen carefully to what country people called mother
wit. That in those homely sayings was couched the collective wisdom of generations.

Ibid., Ch. 15

3 Children's talent to endure stems from their ignorance
of alternatives.   Ibid., Ch. 17

4 The quality of strength lined with tenderness is an un-
beatable combination, as are intelligence and necessity
when unblunted by formal education.   Ibid., Ch. 29

5 At fifteen life had taught me undeniably that surrender,
in its place, was as honorable as resistance, especially if
one had no choice.   Ibid., Ch. 31

6 The fact that the adult American Negro female
emerges a formidable character is often met with
amazement, distaste and even belligerance. It is seldom
accepted as an inevitable outcome of the struggle won
by survivors, and deserves respect if not enthusiastic
acceptance.   Ibid., Ch. 34

7 I believe most plain girls are virtuous because of the
scarcity of opportunity to be otherwise. They shield
themselves with an aura of unavailableness (for which
after a time they begin to take credit) largely as a defense tactic.   Ibid., Ch. 35

8 My life has been one great big joke,
  A dance that's walked
  A song that's spoke,
  I laugh so hard I almost choke
  When I think about myself.
> "When I Think About Myself,"
> *Just Give Me a Cool Drink of Water*
> *'fore I Diiie* 1971

9 For Africa to me . . . is more than a glamorous fact.
  It is a historical truth. No man can know where he is
  going unless he knows exactly where he has been and
  exactly how he arrived at his present place.
> Quoted in *The New York Times*
> April 16, 1972

10 One would say of my life—born loser—had to be:
   from a broken family, raped at eight, unwed mother at
   sixteen. . . . It's a fact but not the truth. In the black
   community, however bad it looks, there's a lot of love
   and so much humor.
> Quoted by Jane Julianelli in
> *Harper's Bazaar* November, 1972

11 I speak to the black experience, but I am always talking about the human condition—about what we can
   endure, dream, fail at, and still survive.
> Quoted in *Current Bigraphies* 1974

12 A textured guilt was my familiar, my bed mate to
   whom I had turned my back. My daily companion
   whose hand I would not hold. The Christian teaching
   dinned into my ears. . . .
> *Gather Together in My Name,* Preface 1974

13 "I probably couldn't learn to cook creole food, anyway. It's too complicated."
   "Sheeit. Ain't nothing but onions, green peppers and
   garlic. Put that in everything and you got creole food."
> Ibid., Ch. 3

14 "You a cherry, ain't you?"
   "Yes." Lying would get me nothing.
   "Well, that's a thirty-second business. When you turn
   the first trick, you'll be a 'ho. A stone 'ho. I mean for
   life. . . . I'm a damn good one. I'm a mud kicker. In
   the streets I make more money by accident than most
   bitches make on purpose."
> Ibid., Ch. 27

15 Separate from my boundaries, I had not known before
that he had and would have a life beyond being my
son, my pretty baby, my cute doll, my charge. In the
plowed farmyard near Bakersfield, I began to understand the uniqueness of the person. He was three and I
was nineteen, and never again would I think of him as a
beautiful appendage of myself.

Ibid., Ch. 29

1049. Shirley Temple Black
(1928–   )

1 Nonsense, all of it. Sunnybrook Farm is now a parking
lot; the petticoats are in the garbage can, where they
belong in this modern world; and I *detest* censorship.
Quoted in McCall's   January, 1967

2 Won't the new "Suggested for Mature Audience" protect our youngsters from such films? I don't believe so.
I know many forty-five-year-old men with the mentali-
ties of six-year-olds, and my feeling is that they should
not see such pictures, either.
Ibid.

3 Our whole way of life today is dedicated to the *removal
of risk*. Cradle to grave we are supported, insulated,
and isolated from the risks of life—and if we fall, our
government stands ready with Bandaids of every size.
Speech, Kiwanis International
Convention, Texas (June, 1967),
Quoted in The Sinking of The Lollipop
by Rodney G. Minott   1968

1050. Mary Daly
(1928–   )

1 The becoming of androgynous human persons implies a
radical change in the fabric of human consciousness
and in styles of human behavior.
Beyond God the Father, Ch. 1   1973

2 . . . tokenism does not change stereotypes of social
systems but works to preserve them, since it dulls the
revolutionary impulse.
Ibid.

3 Courage to be is the key to the revelatory power of the feminist revolution.

Ibid.

4 It is the creative potential itself in human beings that is the image of God.

Ibid.

5 . . . "God's plan" is often a front for men's plans and a cover for inadequacy, ignorance and evil.

Ibid.

6 I have already suggested that if God is male, then male is God. The divine patriarch castrates women as long as he is allowed to live on in the human imagination.

Ibid.

7 People attempt to overcome the threat of non-being by denying the self. The outcome of this is ironic: that which is dreaded triumphs, for we are caught in the self-contradictory bind of shrinking our being to avoid nonbeing.

Ibid.

8 It is not good enough to talk about evil abstractly while lending implicit support to traditional images that legitimate specific social evils.

Ibid., Ch. 2

9 Why indeed must "God" be a noun? Why not a verb— the most active and dynamic of all.　　　　Ibid.

10 The image of Mary as Virgin, moreover, has an (unintended) aspect of pointing to independence for women. This aspect of the symbol is of course generally unnoticed by theologians.　　　　Ibid., Ch. 3

11 Sexist society maintains its grasp over the psyche by keeping it divided against itself.　　　　Ibid., Ch. 4

12 . . . we will look upon the earth and her sister planets as being *with* us, not *for* us. One does not rape a sister.

Ibid., Ch. 6

13 I had explained that a woman's asking for equality in the church would be comparable to a black person's demanding equality in the Ku Klux Klan.

"New Autobiographical Preface"
(1968), *The Church and the
Second Sex*　　1975

14 The liberation of language is rooted in the liberation of ourselves.

Ibid.

1051. Muriel Fox
(1928–   )

1 While you don't need a formal written contract before you get married, I think it's important for both partners to spell out what they expect from each other. . . . There are always plenty of surprises—and lots of give and take—once you're married.

Quoted in "Wait Late to Marry"
by Barbara Jordan Moore,
New Woman   October, 1971

2 I realize that what happened to my mother was very wrong. She got pigeonholed in the wrong job. That job was housewife. She hated it and was a tragically inefficient housekeeper. There was no valid reason why she should have got stuck in that job when she could have filled many others with distinction.

Ibid.

3 Women and men have to fight together to change society—and both will benefit. We [her husband and herself] are strongly pro-marriage. I think it is a grave mistake for young girls to think that it has to be a career versus marriage, equality versus love. Partnership, not dependence, is the real romance in marriage.

Ibid.

4 Total commitment to family and total commitment to career is possible, but fatiguing.

Ibid.

1052. Thea Musgrave
(1928–   )

1 Music is a human art, not a sexual one. Sex is no more important than eye color.

Quoted in "A Matter of Art, Not Sex,"
Time   November 10, 1975

1058. Beah Richards
(1928?–   )

1 Having grown up in a racist culture where two and two
are not five, I have found life to be incredibly theatrical
and theatre to be profoundly lifeless.
*A Black Woman Speaks and
Other Poems,* Preface   *1974*

2 . . . nature is neither reasonable nor just. Nature is
exact.   Ibid.

3 Heaven and earth!
How is it that bodies join
but never meet?
Ibid., "It's Time for Love," St. 2

4 Lord,
there is no death,
no numb, no glacial sorrow
like the love of loveless love,
a tender grunting, sweating horror of obscenity.
Ibid., "Love Is Cause It Has to Be," St. 6

5 If I cannot with my blind eyes see
that to betray or deny my brother
is but to diminish me
then you may pity me. . . .
Ibid., "The Liberal," St. 11

1054. Anne Sexton
(1928–1974)

1 love your self's self where it lives.
"The Double Image," *To Bedlam
and Partway Back*   *1960*

2 . . . I gather
guilt like a young intern
his symptoms, his certain evidence.   Ibid.

3   You, Dr. Martin, walk
from breakfast to madness.
Ibid., "You, Dr. Martin," St. 1

4   I am queen of all my sins
forgotten. Am I still lost?

Ibid., Last St.

5 Today life opened inside me like an egg. . . .

"Live," *Live or Die*   *1966*

6 lovers sprouting in the yard
like celery stalks. . . .

Ibid.

7 I say *Live, Live* because of the sun,
the dream, the excitable gift.

Ibid.

8 The trouble with being a woman,
  Skeezis,
is being a little girl
  in the first place.

"Hurry Up Please It's Time,"
The Death Notebooks   *1974*

9 What is death, I ask: What is life, you ask.   Ibid.

10 Even without wars, life is dangerous.   Ibid.

11 I would have taken care of daisies, giving them an aspi-
rin every hour and cutting their stems properly, but
with roses I'm reckless. When they arrive in their long
white box, they're already in the death house.

"A Small Journal" (November
6, 1971) *The Poet's Story,*
Howard Moss, ed.   *1974*

12 I took the radio, my vigil keeper, and played it for my
waking, sleeping ever since. In memoriam. It goes everywhere with me like a dog on a leash.

Ibid. (November 8, 1971)

13 Generally speaking, mental hospitals are lonely places,
they are full of televisions and medications.

Ibid.

14 The sea is mother-death and she is a mighty female, the
one who wins, the one who sucks us all up.

Ibid. (November 19, 1971)

15 It doesn't matter who my father was; it matters who I
remember he was.

Ibid. (January 1, 1972, 12:30 A.M.)

16 God owns heaven
but He craves the earth.

> "The Earth," St. 2, *The Awful*
> *Rowing Toward God*   1975p

17 The eyes, opening and shutting like cameras
and never forgetting, recording by thousands. . . .

> Ibid., St. 3

18 The tongue, the Chinese say,
is like a sharp knife:
it kills
without drawing blood.

> Ibid., "The Dead Heart," St. 3

1055. Muriel Siebert
(1928?–   )

1 I know a twenty-eight-year-old woman, a recent graduate of Harvard Business School. She asked me the
other day if I wasn't afraid of what people will say if I
associate with the women's movement. What she
doesn't understand is that it's because of the movement
and people like me that it's now not as difficult for her
to make it.

> Quoted in *Women at Work*
> by Betty Medsger   1975

1056. Agnes Varda
(1928–   )

1 If you ask me, is it difficult to be a woman director? I'd
say that it's difficult to be a director, period! It's difficult to be free; it's difficult not to be drowned in the
system. It's difficult for women, and it's difficult for
men, the same way.

> Quoted in "An Interview with
> Agnes Varda" by Barbara Confino,
> *Saturday Review*   *August 12, 1972*

2 The image of woman is crucial, and in the . . .
movies that image is always switching between the nun
and the whore, the mama and the bitch. We have put
up with that for years, and it has to be changed. It is
the image that is important, not so much who is making the film.

> Ibid.

3 Humor is such a strong weapon, such a strong answer.
Women have to make jokes about themselves, laugh
about themselves, because they have nothing to lose.

Ibid.

1057. Anne Frank
(1929–1945)

1 I soothe my conscience now with the thought that it is
better for hard words to be on paper than that Mummy
should carry them in her heart.

The Diary of a Young Girl
(January 2, 1944)   1952p

2 Mummy herself has told us that she looked upon us
more as her friends than her daughters. Now that is all
very fine, but still, a friend can't take a mother's place.
I need my mother as an example which I can follow, I
want to be able to respect her.

Ibid. (January 15, 1944)

3 I think what is happening to me is so wonderful, and
not only what can be seen on my body, but all that is
taking place inside. I never discuss myself or any of
these things with anybody; that is why I have to talk to
myself about them.

Ibid.

4 We all live with the objective of being happy; our lives
are all different and yet the same.

Ibid. (July 6, 1944)

5 Laziness may *appear* attractive, but work *gives* satisfaction.

Ibid.

6 Parents can only give good advice or put them on the
right paths, but the final forming of a person's character lies in their own hands. . . .

Ibid. (July 15, 1944)

7 I'm awfully scared that everyone who knows me as I
always am will discover that I have another side, a
finer and better side. I'm afraid they'll laugh at me,
think I'm ridiculous and sentimental, not take me seriously. . . .

Ibid. (August 1, 1944)

1058. Linda Goodman
(1929?–   )

1 It seems to be quite a leap from the . . . lost continent of Atlantis to the jet-propelled twentieth century. But how far is it really? Perhaps only a dream or two.

Linda Goodman's Sun Signs,
Afterword   *1968*

2 Alone among the sciences, astrology has spanned the centuries and made the journey intact. We shouldn't be surprised that it remains with us, unchanged by time—because astrology is truth—and truth is eternal.

Ibid.

3 Astrological language is a golden cord that binds us to a dim past while it prepares us for an exciting future of planetary explorations.

Ibid.

1059. Shirley Ann Grau
(1929–   )

1 I know that I shall hurt as much as I have been hurt. I shall destroy as much as I have lost. It's a way to live, you know. It's a way to keep your heart ticking under the sheltering arches of your ribs. And that's enough for now.

"Abigail," *The Keepers of the House*   *1964*

2 She thought of all the distance between the two parts of her, the white and the black. And it seemed to her that those two halves would pull away and separate and leave her there in the open, popped out like a kernel from its husk.

Ibid., "Margaret"

3 Why does it take so much trouble to keep your stomach full and quiet?

Ibid.

4 And isn't it funny, she thought, that it takes two generations to kill off a man? . . . First him, and then his memory. . . .   Ibid.

5 There's only one night like that—ever—where you're filled with wonder and excitement for no other reason but the earth is beautiful and mysterious and your body is young and strong. . . . We hadn't really been friends before. It just sort of happened that we found ourselves together. It wasn't anything personal. It would have been the same with any man. . . . It happens like that and it's not the less precious. It's the thing you value and not the man. It happened that way with me.

Ibid.

6 Me? What am I? Nothing. The legs on which dinner comes to the table, the arms by which cocktails enter the living room, the hands that drive cars. I am the eyes that see nothing, the ears that don't hear. I'm invisible too. They look and don't see me. When they move, I have to guess their direction and get myself out of the way. If they were to walk into me—all six feet of black skin and white bone—they'd never again be able to pretend that I wasn't there. And I'd be looking for another job.

"Stanley," *The Condor Passes*   1971

7 He had to humor his body occasionally so that the rest of the time it obeyed his will.

Ibid., "The Old Man"

8 Why, she thought, do I always get angry at my mother? For not leaving me a memory, for being so vague and gentle and so busy with her job of procreating that she hardly noticed her children once they left her womb. . . .

Ibid., "Anna"

9 Took as much skill to get rid of a girl as to get one. He was learning how to do both.

Ibid., "Robert"

10 Her Father was waiting. When she saw him, she felt the usual shift in her feelings. A lift, a jump, a tug. Pleasure, but not totally. Love, but not completely. Dependence. Fear, familiarity, identification. That's part of me there, walking along. Tree from which I sprang. His spasm produced me. Shake of his body and here I am. . . .   Ibid., "Margaret"

11 To hell with love, Margaret thought. It's an ache in my stomach, it's a terrible feeling in my head, it's a skin-

crawling fear that I've done something wrong. I've forgotten the password. And the frog isn't going to change into Prince Charming, the secret door isn't going to open. And the world is going to end any minute.

Ibid.

12 "You forget places you've been and you forget women you've had, but you don't forget fighting."

"Homecoming," The Wind Shifting West   1973

13 Before, I used to like it [the highway], especially the sounds: the tires whistling and singing on the wet, and hissing on the dry. The soft growling sound—kind of like a sigh—when some trucker tested his air brakes. The way horns echo way off in the distance. The thin little screech of car brakes, too, almost like a laugh. And something else—a steady even whisper. Day and night, no difference. It ran like electric wires singing. Or maybe kind of like breathing. . . . But I didn't like the highway any more. . . . Like Joe would say, the highway brought everything to us, and took it away too.

Ibid., "The Last Gas Station"

14 It hurts to worry this much, she thought. It really hurts like a cut, or a broken bone. It hurts more than my broken arm when I fell off the climbing bars in the third grade. A lot more than that. It hurts so much that it can't hurt any more.   Ibid., "Sea Change"

15 Later on things did stop and time ended, and she perched on a single spot, weightless and empty in herself. Quite detached from her body, her mind stole out, prowling like a cat in the shadows, searching. And it found that there was nothing on any side of her, that she hung like a point, like a star in the empty sky.

Ibid.

16 "Haven't you ever noticed how highways always get beautiful near the state capital?"

Ibid., "The Way Back"

17 Trees come out of acorns, no matter how unlikely that seems. An acorn is just a tree's way back into the ground. For another try. Another trip through. One life or another. And what came out of sex now. Love maybe. But that wasn't as sure as a tree. Or maybe a tree was as unsure as Love. One capsule life or another.

Ibid.

18 Women's lib is one of those great amorphous things. I don't think that you can characterize it as a single movement. It's really rather strange. . . . [But] you can't legislate equality. Until the basic feelings of people are changed, the facts won't change.

Quoted in "Profile . . . Shirley Ann
Grau" by Louis Gallo, *New Orleans*
February, 1974

19 Women use children as excuses not to do anything.

Ibid.

20 A lot more people can write than do. I think writers are only *born* in a small sense. You're born with a feeling for words and writers deliberately set out to develop this innate feeling. If you are born with or acquire this feeling for words, then you can become a writer.

Ibid.

21 One of my current pet theories is that the writer is a kind of evangelist, more subtle than Billy Graham, of course, but of the same stuff.

Ibid.

22 Nothing in life has bells ringing or choruses singing. I've long ago stopped looking for glamour and drama. Life isn't like that. As a matter of fact, it's the search for instant gratification that is so harmful to young writers. . . . The realization that something is good material for a story is no big bang. No need to dignify it with an explosion. Instant bangs never happen. No writer I know talks about it in those terms. Nonwriters tend to think of it that way, but writing is day to day grubby hard work. It's isolated and time consuming.

Ibid.

1060. Matina Horner
(1929?–   )

1 Unusual excellence in women was clearly associated with them with the loss of femininity, social rejection, personal or societal destruction or some combination of the above.

Women and Success: The Anatomy
of Achievement   1964

1061. Jill Johnston
(1929–)

1 I have a case of the most exquisite paranoia. It's a wonderful feeling. For a female lesbian bastard writer mental case I'm doing awfully well.

Lesbian Nation: The Feminist
Solution   1973

2 It's necessary in order to attract attention, to dazzle at all costs, to be disapproved of by serious people and quoted by the foolish.

Ibid.

3 I had the correct instinct to fuck things up but no political philosophy to clarify a course of action.

Ibid.

4 I never said I was a dyke even to a dyke because there wasn't a dyke in the land who thought she should be a dyke or even thought she was a dyke so how could we talk about it.

Ibid.

5 Bisexuality is not so much a copout as a fearful compromise.   Ibid.

6 . . . we as womenfolk can't as i see it be all that smug and satisfied about where we're at anyhow until the ascending female principle is better established at large.

Gullible's Travels   1974

7 . . . i want these women in office who're in touch with their feelings and who know perfectly well when they're bullshitting and who don't have to displace their concealed feelings by dropping bombs on people who live thousands of miles away. . . .   Ibid.

1062. Ursula K. Le Guin
(1929–)

1 When action grows unprofitable, gather information; when information grows unprofitable, sleep.

The Left Hand of Darkness,
Ch. 3   1969

2 Legends of prediction are common throughout the whole Household of Man. Gods speak, spirits speak, computers speak. Oracular ambiguity or statistical probability provides loopholes, and discrepancies are expunged by Faith.

Ibid., Ch. 4

3 A man wants his virility regarded, a woman wants her femininity appreciated, however indirect and subtle the indications of regard and appreciation. On [the planet] Winter they will not exist. One is respected and judged only as a human being. It is an appalling experience.

Ibid., Ch. 7

4 . . . primitiveness and civilization are degrees of the same thing. If civilization has an opposite, it is war. Of those two things, you have either one, or the other. Not both.

Ibid., Ch. 8

5 To oppose something is to maintain it.

Ibid., Ch. 11

6 It is a terrible thing, this kindness that human beings do not lose. Terrible because when we are finally naked in the dark and cold, it is all we have. We who are so rich, so full of strength, wind up with that small change. We have nothing else to give.

Ibid., Ch. 13

7 What is more arrogant than honesty?

Ibid., Ch. 15

8 It is good to have an end to journey towards; but it is the journey that matters, in the end.

Ibid.

9 I certainly wasn't happy. Happiness has to do with reason, and only reason earns it. What I was given was the thing you can't earn, and can't keep, and often don't even recognize at the time; I mean joy.

Ibid., Ch. 18

10 He could also, now he was listening, hear doors, typewriters, voices, toilets flushing, in offices all up and down the hall and above him and underneath him. The real trick was to learn how not to hear them. The only solid partitions left were inside the head.

The Lathe of Heaven, Ch. 2   1971

11 "What the brain does by itself is infinitely more fascinating and complex than any response it can make to chemical stimulation. . . ." *Ibid.*, Ch. 3

12 He was not interested in detached knowledge, science for science's sake: there was no use learning anything if it was of no use. Relevance was his touchstone.

Ibid., Ch. 5

13 A person is defined solely by the extent of his influence over other people, by the sphere of his interrelationships; and morality is an utterly meaningless term unless defined as the good one does to others, the fulfilling of one's function in the sociopolitical whole.

Ibid.

14 He had grown up in a country run by politicians who sent the pilots to man the bombers to kill the babies to make the world safe for children to grow up in.

Ibid., Ch. 6

15 A person who believes, as she did, that things fit: that there is a whole of which one is a part, and that in being a part one is whole: such a person has no desire whatever, at any time, to play God. Only those who have denied their being yearn to play at it.

Ibid., Ch. 7

16 The quality of the will to power is, precisely, growth. Achievement is its cancellation. To be, the will to power must increase with each fulfillment, making the fulfillment only a step to a further one. The vaster the power gained the vaster the appetite for more.

Ibid., Ch. 9

17 He knew that in so far as one denies what is, one is possessed by what is not, the compulsions, the fantasies, the terrors that flock to fill the void.

Ibid., Ch. 10

18 Love doesn't just sit there, like a stone, it has to be made, like dread; re-made all the time, made new.

Ibid.

19 Outside the locked room is the landscape of time, in which the spirit may, with luck and courage, construct the fragile, makeshift, improbable roads and cities of fidelity: a landscape inhabitable by human beings.

The Dispossessed   1975

1063. Melina Mercouri
(1929–   )

1 When you are born and they tell you "what a pity that you are so clever, so intelligent, so beautiful but you are not a man," you are ashamed of your condition as a woman. I wanted to act like a man because the man was the master.

Quoted in "Greece: Survival of
the Shrewdest" by Susan
Margolis, Ms.   October, 1973

1064. Jeanne Moreau
(1929–   )

1 I have always liked things that are difficult, I have always had the urge to open forbidden doors, with a curiosity and an obstinacy that verge on masochism.

Quoted in "Jeanne Moreau," The
Egotists by Oriana Fallaci   1963

2 Success is like a liberation or the first phase of a love story. . . .

Ibid.

3 I don't think success is harmful, as so many people say. Rather, I believe it indispensable to talent, if for nothing else than to increase the talent.   Ibid.

4 For me it's not possible to forget, and I don't understand people who, when the love is ended, can bury the other person in hatred or oblivion. For me, a man I have loved becomes a kind of brother.   Ibid.

1065. Jacqueline Kennedy Onassis
(1929–   )

1 Can anyone understand how it is to have lived in the White House, and then, suddenly, to be living alone as the President's widow?

Quoted by Billy Baldwin in
McCall's   December, 1974

1066. Adrienne Rich
(1929–   )

1   Facts could be kept separate
    by a convention; that was what
made childhood possible. Now knowledge finds me out;
  in all its risible untidiness. . . .
> "From Morning-Glory to Petersburg"
> (1954), *Snapshots of a
> Daughter-in-Law*   *1963*

2 We who were loved will never
  unlive that crippling fever.
> Ibid., "After a Sentence in 'Malte
> Laurids Brigge' " (1958)

3 A thinking woman sleeps with monsters.
> Ibid., "Snapshots of a Daughter-in-
> Law," Pt. III, St. 1 (1958–1960)

4 Bemused by gallantry, we hear
  our mediocrity over-praised,
  indolence read as abnegation,
  slattern thought styled intuition,
  every lapse forgiven, our crime
  only to cast too bold a shadow
  or smash the mould straight off.
> Ibid., Pt. IX, St. 2

5 Nothing changes. The bones of the mammoths are still
  in the earth.
> Ibid., "End of an Era," St. 4 (1961)

6 Only to have a grief
  equal to all these tears!
> Ibid., "Peeling Onions," St. 1 (1961)

7 I'd call it love if love
  didn't take so many years
  but lust too is a jewel
  a sweet flower. . . .   "Two Songs," Pt. I (1964),
> *Necessities of Life*   *1966*

8 The future reconnoiters in dirty boots
  along the cranberry-dark horizon.
> Ibid., "Autumn Sequence," Pt. III,
> St. 4 (1964)

9 The mind's passion is all for singling out.
Obscurity has another tale to tell.
Ibid., "Focus," St. 7 (1965)

10 Desire. Desire. The nebula
opens in space, unseen
your heart utters its great beats
in solitude. . . .
"The Demon Lover," *Leaflets*　1969

11 Posterity trembles like a leaf
and we go on making heirs and heirlooms.
Ibid.

12 Only where there is language is there world.　Ibid.

13 5. . . . A language is a map of our failures.
"The Burning of Paper Instead
of Children" (1958),
The Will to Change　1971

14 Humans lived here once; it became sacred only when
they went away.
Ibid., "Shooting Script Part I," Pt. IV,
St. 9 (November, 1969–February, 1970)

15 　　　　I am an instrument in the shape
of a woman trying to translate pulsations
into images　　for the relief of the body
and the reconstruction of the mind.
Ibid., "Planetarium," St. 14 (1968)

16 The victory carried like a corpse
from town to town
begins to crawl in the casket.
Ibid., "Letters: March 1969: 1" (1969)

17 the moment of change is the only poem. . . .
Ibid., "Images for Godard,"
Pt. V, St. 7 (1970)

18 Finality broods upon the things that pass. . . .
"A Walk by the Charles" (1950s),
Poems: Selected and New, 1950–1974
1975

19 The friend I can trust is the one who will let me have
my death.
The rest are actors who want me to stay and further
the plot.　　　　Ibid., Untitled (1960s)

20 . . . Love, our subject:
we've trained it like ivy to our walls
baked it like bread in our ovens
worn it like lead on our ankles

Ibid., Untitled (1970s)

1067. Beverly Sills
(1929–   )

1 I don't want to be an exhibitionistic coloratura who merely sings notes. I'm interested in the *character*.
Quoted in "Beverly Sills," *Divas: Impressions of Six Opera Superstars* by Winthrop Sargeant   *1959*

2 In a way, retarded children are satisfying. Everything is a triumph. Even getting Bucky to manage to get a spoon to his mouth was a triumph. God compensates.
Ibid.

3 I would willingly give up my whole career if I could have just one normal child. . . .
Ibid.

4 A happy woman is one who has no cares at all; a cheerful woman is one who has cares but doesn't let them get her down.
Interview, "60 Minutes," CBS-TV   *1975*

5 There is something in me—I just can't stand to admit defeat.
Ibid.

6 My singing is very therapeutic. For three hours I have no troubles—I know how it's all going to come out.
Ibid.

1068. Alisa Wells
(1929–   )

1 I understood not a word he spoke that first night, and little in the endless ones following; but his words, gestures, challenges were speaking to something, someone deep within me.
Quoted in *The Woman's Eye* by Anne Tucker   *1973*

2 Now the real beginnings of the "freedom" which we have discussed for many years—and a heady freedom it is, coming after so many years of reaching outward for it—to finally discover all I had to do was reach inward, and it was there waiting all the time for me!   Ibid.

1069. Maria Castellani
(fl. 1930s)

1 Fascism recognizes women as a part of the life force of the country, laying down a division of duties between the two sexes, without putting obstacles in the way of those women who by their intellectual gifts reach the highest positions.

Italian Women, Past and Present   *1937*

1070. Elisabeth Craigin
(fl. 1930s)

1 A so-called Lesbian alliance can be of the most rarefied purity, and those who do not believe it are merely judging in ignorance of the facts.

Either Is Love   *1937*

1071. Lydia Gottschewski
(fl. 1930s)

1 It is a curious fact that pacifism . . . is a mark of an age weak in faith, whereas the people of religious times have honored war as God's rod of chastisement. . . . Only the age of enlightenment has wished to decide the great questions of world history at the table of diplomats.

Women in the New State   *1934*

1072. Jane Screven Heyward
(fl. 1930s–1939)

* * *

1 More brightly must my spirit shine
Since grace of Beauty is not mine.

"The Spirit's Grace"

2 The dear old ladies whose cheeks are pink
In spite of the years of winter's chill,
Are like the Autumn leaves, I think,
A little crumpled, but lovely still.

"Autumn Leaves"

1073. Esther Lape
(fl. 1930s)

1 We have no illusions about the flexibility of the Nobel
Committee. Its statements reflect a rigidity *extraordinaire*.

Letter to A. David Gurewitsch
(December 30, 1964), Quoted in
Eleanor: The Years Alone
by Joseph P. Lash   *1972*

1074. Frances Newton
(fl. 1930s)

1 There, in that manufactured park with its ghoulish artificiality, with its interminable monuments to bad taste,
wealth and social position, we were planning to place
the body of a beautiful and dignified old man who had
lived generously and loved beauty.

Light, Like the Sun   *1937*

2 I can stand what I know. It's what I don't know that
frightens me.

Ibid.

1075. Alice M. Shepard
(fl. 1930s)

* * *

1 They shall not pass, tho' battleline
May bend, and foe with foe combine,
Tho' death rain on them from the sky
Till every fighting man shall die,
France shall not yield to German Rhine.

"They Shall Not Pass"

1076. Mabel Elsworth Todd
(fl. 1930s)

1 In the expiratory phase lies renewal of vigor through some hidden form of muscular release. . . .
The Balancing of Forces in the
Human Body   1929

2 Emotion constantly finds expression in bodily position. . . .   Ibid.

1077. Bertye Young Williams
(fl. 1930s–1951)

*   *   *

1 He who follows Beauty
Breaks his foolish heart.   **"Song Against Beauty"**

1078. Nguyen Thi Binh
(1930–   )

1 I was tortured [in the 1950s] by the Vietnamese, with the French directing, just as now it is with the Americans directing.

Quoted in "Madame Binh" by Becca
Wilson, *New York Review of Books*
June 25, 1975

2 We were moving from one place to another, always moving . . . we lived underground often, never coming into the air except at night. 1957 through 1959: those were the black years. By 1960 the people could not bear it any longer. They demanded the right to fight and protect themselves.   Ibid.

3 We tell our children that the bombs cannot kill everyone, that they must not be afraid. . . . We know our sacrifice is necessary. If the bombs do not fall on you, they fall on friends. We accept fate. We are calm. It is useless to be a pessimist. Some day we will win a beautiful life, if not for ourselves, then for our children.

Ibid.

1079. Julie Anne Bovasso
(1930–   )

1 BEBE. I want to know you. And I want you to know me and understand me. What good is love without understanding? How can we love each other if we don't know each other and understand each other? How can we understand each other if we don't know each other? And how can we know each other if we don't love each other?

Schubert's Last Serenade   1972

1080. Lee Grant
(1930?–   )

1 The more stringent the conditions are, the more the actor uses them—like hurdlers, or emotional stuntmen.
"Selling Out to Hollywood, or Home,"
The New York Times   *August 12, 1973*

2 This is a period of great *angst*. The impermanence and flimsiness of houses built on faults, subject to landslides, add to a former apartment dweller's sense of insecurity. The stage-set quality of the streets, the green and blue spotlights illuminating every sallow palm in front of Hollywood court apartments, the 40-foot neon cross overlooking the freeway.

Ibid.

3 One's art adjusts to economic necessity if your metabolism does.

Ibid.

4 As more of us [actresses] are moving into producing and directing, the level of creativity among women has become very high, and therefore our relationships have changed—have themselves become more creative.
"Art Catches Up to Life," *Ms.*
November, 1975

5 . . . art always seems to be catching up to life.

Ibid.

339

1081. Lorraine Hansberry
(1930–1965)

1 WALTER. Baby, don't *nothing* happen for you in this world 'less you pay *somebody* off!

> *A Raisin in the Sun*, Act I, Sc. 1
> *1958*

2 BENEATHA. Why do you give money at church for the missionary work?

MAMA. Well, that's to help save people.

BENEATHA. You mean save them from *heathenism* . . . I'm afraid they need more salvation from the British and the French.

> Ibid., Sc. 2

3 LINDNER. And at the moment the overwhelming majority of our people out there feel that people get along better, take more of a common interest in the life of the community, when they share a common background. I want you to believe me when I tell you that race prejudice simply doesn't enter into it.

> Ibid., Act II, Sc. 3

4 ASAGAI. Ah, I like the look of packing crates! A household in preparation for a journey! . . . Something full of the flow of life. . . . Movement, progress. . . .

> Ibid., Act III

5 BENEATHA. While I was sleeping in my bed in there, things were happening in this world that directly concerned me—and nobody asked me, consulted me—they just went out and did things—and changed my life.

> Ibid.

6 BENEATHA. Don't you see there isn't any real progress, Asagai, there is only one large circle that we march in, around and around, each of us with our own little picture—in front of us—our own little mirage that we think is the future.

> Ibid.

1082. Maureen Howard
(1930–   )

1 I started that book but something happened, my brother's children, my mother's gall bladder, something happened so I never finished.

Bridgeport Bus   1966

2 When I go home my mother and I play a cannibal game; we eat each other over the years, tender morsel by morsel, until there is nothing left but dry bone and wig.

Ibid.

3 . . . the ivy remembered another season, though I suppose it was the future that I really admired in them, because I had none.

Ibid.

4 I have a world now, about the size of a circle of light thrown by a desk lamp, that is mine and safe from my mother and the zipper company and my brother's children.

Ibid.

5 . . . they spoke to me. That happens now and again, even when you become a sophisticated reader with all kinds of critical impedimenta: you read something that is so direct, so pertinent to exactly where you are—the way you feel and your precise frame of mind.

Ibid.

6 . . . my mother is soothed at last by her television, watching lives much more professional than ours.

Ibid.

7 She was a survivor, frail, helpless, but a survivor: the past was one prop, the bottle another.

"Three Cheers for Mr. Spears,"
Before My Time   1974

8 "The process of losing my faith was so gradual," said Mr. Spears, "I didn't seem to notice it. I've thought since that it was a counterpart of attaining my physical growth, which I never noticed either. One day it was complete—my height and my loss of faith—and it was easy, painless. I wish that I had suffered."   Ibid.

341

1083. Dolores Huerta
(1930–   )

1 How do I stop eleven million people from buying the grape?

Quoted in "Stopping Traffic: One
Woman's Cause" by Barbara L. Baer,
The Progressive   *September, 1975*

2 . . . if you haven't forgiven yourself something, how can you forgive others?   Ibid.

3 Walk the street with us into history. Get off the sidewalk. Stop being vegetables. Work for justice. *Viva* the boycott!   Ibid.

1084. Carol Kaye
(1930?–   )

Co-author with Elizabeth Douvan. See 1019: 1–2.

1085. Abbey Lincoln
(1930–   )

1 The fact that white people readily and proudly call themselves "white," glorify all that is white, and whitewash all that is glorified, becomes unnatural and bigoted in its intent only when these same whites deny persons of African heritage who are Black the natural and inalienable right to readily—proudly—call themselves "black," glorify all that is black, and blackwash all that is glorified.

"Who Will Revere the Black Woman?,"
Negro Digest   *September, 1966*

2 Black womanhood is outraged and humiliated. Black womanhood cries for dignity and restitution and salvation. Black womanhood wants and needs protection, and keeping and holding. Who will assuage her indignation? Who will keep her precious and pure? Who will glorify and proclaim her beautiful image? To whom will she cry rape?   Ibid.

1086. Gay Gaer Luce
(1930–)

1 Swept along in the concepts of their business-oriented culture, many people berate themselves if they are not as consistent and productive as machines.
Body Time, Preface   *1971*

2 Even as small children we are trained not to listen to our bodies or trust our sensations.
"Trust Your Body Rhythms,"
Psychology Today   *April, 1975*

3 Our harmony is maintained by nature, since we are not closed systems, but are part of the turning earth, the sun, moon and cosmos beyond. In contradiction with our inner clockwork, our urban culture bids us to forget our sources of health and harmony and live by artificial clocks.
Ibid.

4 . . . people are beginning to resist the rhythm of the machine and suspect that the path of inner harmony and health demands an inward attention.   Ibid.

1087. Loretta Lynn
(1930?–)

1 A woman's two cents worth is worth two cents in the music business.
Quoted in "Sexism Seen But Not Heard" by Tracy Hotchner,
Los Angeles Times   *May 26, 1974*

1088. Ann McGovern
(1930–)

1 Dumb. Dumb. Tiny drum beats. Dumb. Dumb. Her sister's favorite word. She called her dumb more than she called her Jane.
"Wonder Is Not Precisely Knowing,"
American Scene: New Voices,
Don Wolfe, ed.   *1963*

2 She shared much with her sister—the absence of a father, the presence of a shadowy unhappy mother. They
had one bike and one sled between them, and had
learned long ago that these possessions were not worth
the fights.

Ibid.

3 In those days, people did not think it was important for
girls to read. Some people thought too much reading
gave girls brain fever.

The Secret Soldier   1975

1089. Dory Previn
(1930–   )

1 men wander
women weep
women worry
while men are asleep

"Men Wander"   1971

2 I said
your words
till my throat
closed up
and I had
no voice
and I had
no choice
but to do your song
I was you baby
I was you too long   "I Was You"   1971

3 Would you care to stay till sunrise
it's completely your decision
it's just the night cuts through me like a knife
would you care to stay awhile and save my life?
"The Lady with the Braid"   1971

4 What most of us want is to be heard, to communicate—which gets back to the origins of music, which
are in the ballads of the wandering minstrel.

Quoted in "Sexism Seen But Not
Heard" by Tracy Hotchner,
Los Angeles Times   May 26, 1974

5 The infiltration of women writers into film will bring
new life to it because "the male idea" is in a state of
terminal perfection. . . . Films by and about women
will now answer the questions raised by male films and
then there will be a cycle when men will answer back.
Ibid.

1090. Dorothy Semenow
(1930–   )

1 I share with the client how I arrive at my responses. In
so doing, I demonstrate that analytic methods are
knowable and imply that the client too can master
them. This demystifies my utterances and punctures the
myth often held over from childhood by the client (and
by many of the rest of us too) that *big people,* originally *her parents* and now *the analyst,* can read her
mind and heart with their powerful x-ray vision and
thus know her sins *and* her destiny.
Address, "Principles of Feminist
Psychoanalysis," Cedars-Sinai
Hospital, Los Angeles   May, 1975

2 As early as possible in our analytic journey we try to
sketch what kind of treasures the client wants to build
into her life. True, she often comes to analysis caught
up and spilling over with what is wrong. But buried in
the suffering of those wrongs is some notion of stunted
rights. We uncover those rights lost in the client's yes-
terdays and add to them her hopes for her tomorrow.
Ibid.

1091. June L. Tapp
(1930–   )

1 If I had to describe something as divine it would be
what happens between people when they really get it
together. There is a kind of spark that makes it all
worthwhile. When you feel that spark, you get a good
deep feeling in your gut.
Quoted in "By Law Possessed"
by Carol Tavris, Psychology Today
May, 1975

2 . . . I cannot accept the idea of law as merely repressive or punitive. It can be expressive and conducive to the development of social values.

Quoted in "The Notion of Conspiracy Is Not Tasty to Americans" by Gordon Bermant, *Psychology Today* May, 1975

3 Now about the totalitarian liberal. . . . What I found . . . were groups who in principle or on paper were committed to religious values that looked liberal, but who held these views with a ferocity that would not, could not, allow for a truly democratic interpretation of the rights of others. Their liberality was more apparent than real.

Ibid.

4 The liberal view, it seems to me, encourages a diversity of views and open confrontation among them. The belief is that conflict or "dissensus," if properly harnessed, leads eventually to the most stable form of consensus. What is important in all this is the *process* by which the changes occur. The due process of law as we use it, I believe, rests squarely on the liberal idea of conflict and resolution.

Ibid.

5 Public participation—as in the jury trial—is the cornerstone in the administration of justice and vital to our system of law.

Ibid.

1092. Hilma Wolitzer
(1930–   )

1 There is something terrific about not knowing your father because it opens up possibilities. . . .

"Waiting for Daddy," *Esquire* July, 1971

2 Their kitchen was full of piecework and vague hope.

Ibid.

3 I was drawn into the back seat of his father's green Pontiac and the pattern of those seat covers stays in my head forever.

Ibid.

4 It seemed strange that I could do all those things with him, discover all those sensations and odors and that new voice that came from the dark pit of my throat (*Don't—oh, yes, oh God*) and that my mother and grandmother didn't know.   Ibid.

1093. Patricia Carbine
(1931–   )

1 We're seeing women organize together . . . with the realization that collective or organized action is much more important than individual change.

> Quoted in *AFTRA Magazine*
> *Summer, 1974*

1094. Sally Gearhart
(1931–   )

1 I look forward with great anticipation to the death of the church. The sooner it dies, the sooner we can be about the business of living the gospel.

> "The Lesbian and God-the-Father
> or All the Church Needs Is a
> Good Lay—on Its Side"   *1972*

1095. Shirley Hazzard
(1931–   )

1 How long women take to leave a room, Tancredi thought. They can't simply get up and walk out—all this shambling and turning back on their tracks, chattering and embracing. . . .

> *The Evening of the Holiday*, Ch. 1   *1965*

2 When we are young, she thought, we worship romantic love for the wrong reasons . . . and, because of that, subsequently repudiate it. Only later, and for quite other reasons, we discover its true importance. And by then it has become tiring even to observe.

> Ibid., Ch. 2

3 One would always want to think of oneself as being on the side of love, ready to recognize it and wish it

well—but, when confronted with it in others, one so often resented it, questioned its true nature, secretly dismissed the particular instance as folly or promiscuity. Was it merely jealousy, or a reluctance to admit so noble and enviable a sentiment in anyone but oneself?

Ibid., Ch. 9

4 "Sometimes, surely, truth is closer to imagination—or to intelligence, to love—than to fact? To be accurate is not to be right."

Ibid., Ch. 11

5 "Perhaps if we lived with less physical beauty we would develop our true natures more."

Ibid., Ch. 13

6 "Do you ever notice," asked Luisa, "how easy it is to forgive a person any number of faults for one endearing characteristic, for a certain style, or some commitment to life—while someone with many good qualities is insupportable for a single defect if it happens to be a boring one?"

Ibid.

7 When someone dies a long-expected death, the waiting goes on for a while—the waiting for what has already taken place but cannot yet be properly comprehended or decently acted upon.

Ibid., Ch. 15

8 Mr. Bekkus frequently misused the word "hopefully." He also made a point of saying locate instead of find, utilize instead of use, and never lost an opportunity to indicate or communicate; and would slip in a "basically" when he felt unsure of his ground.

"Nothing in Excess," People in
Glass Houses   1967

9 Algie was collecting contradictions in terms: to a nucleus of "military intelligence" and "competent authorities" he had added such discoveries as the soul of efficiency, easy virtue, enlightened self-interest, Bankers Trust, and Christian Scientist.

Ibid.

10 Pylos' first official act was to name his new department. The interim titles that had been used—"Economic Relief of Under Privileged Territories" and "Mission for Under-Developed Lands"—were well

348

enough in their way, but they combined a note of condescension with initials which, when contracted, proved somewhat unfortunate.

Ibid., "The Story of Miss Sadie Graine"

11 Nothing, Izmet thought, makes a more fanatical official than a Latin. Organization is alien to their natures, but once they get the taste for it they take to it like drink.

Ibid., "Official Life"

12 When I was a child . . . I would think it must be marvellous to issue those proclamations of experience—"It was at least ten years ago" or "I hadn't seen him for twenty years." But chronological prestige is tenacious: once attained, it can't be shed; it increases moment by moment, day by day, pressing its honours on you until you are lavishly, overly endowed with them. Until you literally sink under them.

The Bay of Noon, Ch. 1   1970

13 Had I been accompanied, I might have laughed out loud . . . but solitude, which is held to be a cause of eccentricity, in fact imposes excessive normality, at least in public. . . .

Ibid.

14 . . . children . . . seldom have a proper sense of their own tragedy, discounting and keeping hidden the true horrors of their short lives, humbly imagining real calamity to be some prestigious drama of the grown-up world.   Ibid.

15 Words would have been as presumptuous as an embrace: yet the inadequacy of silence was painful.

Ibid., Ch. 6

16 Like many men who are compulsively cruel to their womenfolk, he also shed tears at the cinema, and showed a disproportionate concern for insects.

Ibid., Ch. 7

17 "People resort to violence," she said. . . . "not to relieve their feelings, but their thoughts. The demand for comprehension becomes too great, one would rather strike somebody than have to go on wondering about them."   Ibid., Ch. 8

18 The ultimate impression they made was of innocence—the novelty of passions not yet turned to slogans, of

349

gifts not deployed for gain, of goodwill not turned to self-importance.

Ibid., Ch. 9

19 He himself had strengthened this impression by the defences . . . he had constructed; had become their victim, like those heavily fortified towns that invite their own downfall by suggesting that there is something within to be assaulted.

Ibid., Ch. 13

20 Although I wished I hadn't come, it did not occur to me to go back. In matters of importance there is no such thing as "best avoided"—avoidance is only a vacuum that something else must fill. Everything is the inevitable.

Ibid., Ch. 15

1096. Margaret O'Shaughnessy Heckler
(1931–   )

1 When you undermine faith in a system, your child may not necessarily see the difference between the politician who is no longer respected and the policeman, the teacher, the parent.

Quoted in "Impeachment?" by
Claire Safran, Redbook   April, 1974

2 Once you start to separate public service from the enormous influence of the fat cats of society, you rob the vested interests of their most powerful weapons.

Ibid.

1097. Kristin Hunter
(1931–   )

1   "How does a person become an outlaw, DuBois?" Elgar inquired mildly. . . .

  "One is born to the calling," DuBois answered. "Many are called, but few choose. You see, society decides which of its segments are going to be outside its borders. Society says, 'These are the legitimate channels to my rewards. They are closed to you forever.' So then the outlawed segments must seek rewards through illegitimate channels. In other words, once my Great White Father declared me illegitimate, I had to be a bastard."

"Is Uncle Sam your Great White Father?"

"Exactly. The white society is my father and, in a figurative sense, every Negro's father. Our mother being Africa."

The Landlord   1966

2 "A landlord is supposed to be brutal, stingy, insulting, and arrogant. Like the police, like the magistrates, like all the authority-figures of white society. That's what we're used to. That's what we understand. We're accustomed to our enemies, we know how to deal with them. A landlord who tries to be a friend only confuses us."

Ibid.

3 Phosdicker was as honest as the day was long. He was an old-fashioned, dedicated civil servant; a fine, upright, honorable old man, Elgar thought. God help us all. A monster.

Ibid.

4 Borden [the psychiatrist], his one stable reference point in reality. The way sailors needed the North Star to guide them through black seas, Elgar needed Borden to help him find his way out of the gathering chaos.

Ibid.

5 "First it is necessary to stand on your own two feet. But the minute a man finds himself in that position, the next thing he should do is reach out his arms."

Ibid.

6 The most amazing thing about little children, Elgar decided . . . was their fantastic adaptability.

Ibid.

7 "Love can't last around poverty. Neither can a woman's looks."

Ibid.

8 "But generally speaking I've always been too confused about who I was to decide who I was better than."

Ibid.

9 Life was both simpler and more complicated than he had imagined. One did not, after all, change one's skin or one's society. One was given both, along with one's

identity, at birth. And all things ossified as one grew older. But within the rigid framework were loopholes of possibility, spaces in which small miracles might occur.

Ibid.

1098. Adrienne Kennedy
(1931–   )

1 SARAH. As for myself I long to become even a more pallid Negro than I am now; pallid like Negroes on the covers of American Negro magazines; soulless, educated and irrelevant. I want to possess no moral value, particularly value as to my being. I want not to be. I ask nothing except anonymity.

Funnyhouse of a Negro   1964

2 SARAH. For, like all educated Negroes—out of life and death essential—I find it necessary to maintain a stark fortress versus recognition of myself. My white friends like myself will be shrewd, intellectual and anxious for death. Anyone's death.

Ibid.

3 SARAH. I find there are no places only my *funnyhouse*.

Ibid.

4 SARAH. . . . for relationships was one of my last religions.

Ibid.

5 SARAH. I wanted to live in Genesis in the midst of golden savannas, nim and white frankopenny trees and white stallions roaming under a blue sky. I wanted to walk with a white dove. I wanted to be a Christian.

Ibid.

1099. Toni Morrison
(1931–   )

1 "Which you want? A whipping and no turnips or turnips and no whipping?"

The Bluest Eye   1961

2 . . . she lived out her days exploring her own thoughts and emotions, giving them full reign, feeling no obliga-

tion to please anybody unless their pleasure pleased her. . . .

Sula　1974

3 And like any artist with no art form, she became dangerous.

Ibid.

4 "I don't know everything, I just do everything."

Ibid.

5 "I know what every colored woman in this country is doing."
"What's that?"
"Dying."

Ibid.

6 "I sure did live in this world."
"Really? What have you got to show for it?"
"Show? To who? Girl, I got my mind. And what goes on in it. Which is to say, I got me."
"Lonely, ain't it?"
"Yes. But my lonely is *mine*. Now your lonely is somebody else.'s Made by somebody else and handed to you. Ain't that something? A secondhand lonely."

Ibid.

1100. Alice Munro
(1931–   )

1 Lovers. Not a soft word, as people thought, but cruel and tearing.

"Something I've Been Meaning to Tell
You," Something I've Been Meaning
to Tell You　1974

2 If they had been married, people would have said they were very happy.

Ibid.

3 But I never cleaned thoroughly enough, my reorganization proved to be haphazard, the disgraces came unfailingly to light, and it was clear how we failed, how disastrously we fell short of that ideal of order and cleanliness, household decency which I as much as anybody else believed in.

Ibid., "Winter World"

1101. Cynthia Ozick
(1931–   )

1 He had once demonstrated that, since God had made the world, and since there was no God, the world in all logic could not exist.

> *Trust*, Pt. I, Ch. 1   *1966*

2 It is true that money attracts; but much money repels.

> Ibid., Ch. 7

3 "He knows nothing about Literature—most great writers don't: all they know is life."

> Ibid., Pt. III, Ch. 1

4 "Superfluity, excess of custom, and superstition would climb like a choking vine on the Fence of the Law if skepticism did not continually hack them away to make freedom for purity."

> "The Pagan Rabbi" (1966), *The Pagan Rabbi and Other Stories 1971*

5 ". . . Paradise is only for those who have already been there."

> Ibid., "Envy; or, Yiddish in America" (1969)

6 It was the old recurrent groan of life. It was the sound of nature turning on its hinge. Everyone had a story to tell him. What resentments, what hatreds, what bitterness, how little good will!

> Ibid., "The Doctor's Wife" (1971)

7 Moral: In saying what is obvious, never choose cunning. Yelling works better.

> "We Are the Crazy Lady and Other Feisty Feminist Fables," *The First Ms. Reader*, Francine Klagsbrun, ed.   *1972*

8 Language makes culture, and we make a rotten culture when we abuse words.

> Ibid.

9 I'm not afraid of facts, I welcome facts *but a congeries of facts is not equivalent to an idea*. This is the essential fallacy of the so-called "scientific" mind. People who mistake facts for ideas are incomplete thinkers; they are gossips.

> Ibid.

10 Wondrous hole! Magical hole! Dazzlingly influential hole! Noble and effulgent hole! From this hole everything follows logically: first the baby, then the placenta, then, for years and years and years until death, a way of life. It is all logic, and she who lives by the hole will live also by its logic. It is, appropriately, logic with a hole in it.

Ibid., "The Hole/Birth Catalog"

11 The engineering is secondary to the vision.

Ibid.

12 If the fish had stuck to its gills there would have been no movement up to the land.

Ibid.

13 Judaism has no dying god, no embalming of dead bodies, above all no slightest version of death-instinct—"Choose life."

Ibid.

14 The usefulness of madmen is famous: they demonstrate society's logic flagrantly carried out down to its last scrimshaw scrap.

Ibid.

1102. Amanda Row
(1931–   )

1 Jocelyn's childhood stood on the bookcase: *Pollyanna, The Bobbsey Twins, Now We Are Six, Black Beauty,* and *The Little Minister* beside *Heidi.*

Where No Sea Runs   1963

1103. Jane Rule
(1931–   )

1 I didn't want to be a boy, ever, but I was outraged that his height and intelligence were graces for him and gaucheries for me.

Lesbian Images, Introduction   1975

2 I had never been as resigned to ready-made ideas as I was to ready-made clothes, perhaps because, although I couldn't sew, I could think.

Ibid.

3 Cleaving is an activity which should be left to snails for cleaning ponds and aquariums.

Ibid.

4 Morality, like language, is an invented structure for conserving and communicating order. And morality is learned, like language, by mimicking and remembering.
Ibid., "Myth and Morality, Sources of Law and Prejudice"

1104. Barbara Walters
(1931–)

1 . . . I happen to disagree with the well-entrenched theory that the art of conversation is merely the art of being a good listener. Such advice invites people to be cynical with one another and full of fake; when a conversation becomes a monologue, poked along with tiny cattle-prod questions, it isn't a conversation any more.
How to Talk with Practically Anybody About Practically Anything 1970

2 Celebrities used to be found in clusters, like oysters—and with much the same defensive mechanisms.

Ibid., Ch. 1

3 Don't confuse being stimulating with being blunt. . . .
Ibid., Ch. 2

4 If we could harness the destructive energy of disagreements over politics, we wouldn't need the bomb.
Ibid., Ch. 3

5 Parents of young children should realize that few people, and maybe no one, will find their children as enchanting as they do.

Ibid., Ch. 4

6 Most old people . . . are disheartened to be living in the ailing house of their bodies, to be limited physically and economically, to feel an encumbrance to others—guests who didn't have the good manners to leave when the party was over. Ibid.

7 It's a fact that it is much more comfortable to be in the position of the person who has been offended than to be the unfortunate cause of it. Ibid., Ch. 6

8 A great many people think that polysyllables are a sign of intelligence. . . .

Ibid., Ch. 8

9 The origin of a modern party is anthropological: humans meet and share food to lower hostility between them and indicate friendship.

Ibid., Ch. 9

10 Success can make you go one of two ways. It can make you a prima donna, or it can smooth the edges, take away the insecurities, let the nice things come out.

Quoted in "Barbara Walters—Star of the Morning," Newsweek   May 6, 1974

1105. Olga Connolly
(1932–   )

1 Society feels that sport must be justified, and we have gotten away from the Greek concept of mind and body. That is a failure of the physical education process.

Quoted in "Women in Sports: The Movement Is Real," Los Angeles Times   April 23, 1974

2 Women must be accepted as human beings, and it can't be done until women are physically strong enough to stand on their own feet.

Ibid.

1106. Eva Figes
(1932–   )

1 When modern woman discovered the orgasm it was (combined with modern birth control) perhaps the biggest single nail in the coffin of male dominance.

Quoted in The Descent of Woman by Elaine Morgan   1972

2 Either one goes on gradually liberating the divorce laws, until marriage stands exposed as a hollow sham in which no one would wish to engage, or one takes a short cut and abolishes marriage altogether. . . .

Patriarchal Attitudes   1972

3 Providing for one's family as a good husband and father is a water-tight excuse for making money hand

over fist. Greed may be a sin, exploitation of other people might, on the face of it, look rather nasty, but who can blame a man for "doing the best" for his children?

"A View of My Own," Nova
January, 1973

4 The law of individualism and private enterprise is that God helps those who help themselves; what is more, He is actually on their side, since it is a sin not to make use of the talents God gave you. So poverty definitely implies not only laziness but a fall from grace: God disapproves of paupers.

Ibid.

5 . . . unless society recognises that its responsibility extends far beyond the provision of free schooling, the money spent on state education is largely wasted. School becomes just another way of institutionalising the poor.

Ibid.

1107. Penelope Gilliatt
(1932–)

1 The reason why her face was unlined was perhaps that no expression ever passed through it, the owner having developed a reputation for herself as a sort of Delphic presence simply by a habit of nonparticipation that had begun as a defence against the efforts of a boisterous English nanny to boot her into vivacity.

A State of Change, Pt. I, Ch. 3   1967

2   "Why is it that beautiful women never seem to have any curiosity?"

"Is it because they know they're classical? With classical things the Lord finished the job. Ordinary ugly people know they're deficient and they go on looking for the pieces."

Ibid., Pt. II, Ch. 8

3 ALEX. I can't see why having an affair with someone on and off is any worse than being married for a course or two at mealtimes.

"Monday," Sunday Bloody Sunday   1971

4 MRS. GREVILLE. Darling, you keep throwing in your hand because you haven't got the whole thing. There *is* no whole thing. One has to make it work.

Ibid.

5 ALEX. I've had this business that anything is better than nothing. There are times when nothing has to be better than anything.

Ibid., "Saturday"

6 I do wish people wouldn't call English people eccentric!

Quoted in "Rebirth?" by James Childs,
The Hollywood Screenwriters,
Richard Corliss, ed.   1972

7 Critics are probably more prone to clichés than fiction writers who pluck things out of the air.

Ibid.

8 The odd thing is, whatever you've been stingy about is something you never use anyway. It's like life itself . . . spend it—spend it because you have it.

Ibid.

9 Gossip columnists at it again. What a lousy job, thriving on invented rows.

Ibid.

10 It would be difficult for a woman to be, I should think, the production head of a studio or a manager without being called a bull-dyke.

Ibid.

11 Woman's past place in film history has been more significant in countries that aren't as prick-proud as England, America, Japan. . . .

Ibid.

1108. Hannah Green
(1932–   )

1 "On my surface . . . there must be no sign showing, no seam—a perfect surface."

I Never Promised You a Rose Garden,
Ch. 1   1964

2 A child's independence is too big a risk for the shaky balance of some parents.   Ibid., Ch. 5

3 She had opened her mind to the words the way an eye used to darkness, veiled with its lashes, opens cautiously to the light, and, finding it even a little blinding,

closes itself too late. The light had come, and come invincibly, even after the eye had renounced it. It was too late to unsee.

Ibid., Ch. 8

4 "Look here," Furii said. "I never promised you a rose garden. I never promised you perfect justice. . . ."

Ibid., Ch. 13

5 When she was this great soaring creature it seemed as if it was the earth ones who were damned and wrong, not she, who was so complete in beauty and anger. It seemed to her that they slept and were blind.

Ibid., Ch. 16

6 "I had known all those years and years how sick I was, and nobody else would admit it."

"You were asked to mistrust even the reality to which you were closest and which you could discern as clearly as daylight. Small wonder that mental patients have so low a tolerance for lies."

Ibid., Ch. 17

7 "If I can teach you something, it may mean that I can count at least somewhere."

Ibid.

8 Later, they began to explore the secret idea that Deborah shared with all the ill—that she had infinitely more power than the ordinary person and was at the same time also his inferior.

Ibid.

9 Outside the doors of study . . . an angel waits.

Ibid., Ch. 20

10 "And if I fight, then for *what*?"

"For nothing easy or sweet, and I told you that last year and the year before that. For your own challenge, for your own mistakes and the punishment for them, for your own definition of love and of sanity—a good strong self with which to begin to live." Ibid., Ch. 21

11 "Besides, I like an anger that is not fearful and guilty and can come out in a good and vigorous England."

Ibid.

12 Now that she held this tremulous but growing conviction that she was alive, she began to be in love with the new world.

Ibid., Ch. 23

13 The girl . . . was a gentle, generous veteran of mechanical psychiatry in a dozen other hospitals. Her
memory had been ravaged, but her sickness was still
intact.

Ibid., Ch. 27

14 "The senses are not discreet!"

Ibid., Ch. 28

1109. Jacquelyne Jackson
(1932–)

1 Those black males who try to hold women down are
expressing in sexist terms the same kinds of expressions
in racist terms which they would deny. . . .

Speech, First National Conference on
Black Women   March, 1974

1110. Edna O'Brien
(1932–)

1 "Any news?" she said suddenly. When she said this I
always felt obliged to entertain her, even if I had to tell
lies.

The Country Girls, Ch. 3   1960

2   "Are you fast?" Baba asked bluntly.
  "What's fast?" I interrupted. The word puzzled me.
  "It's a woman who has a baby quicker than another
woman," Baba said quickly, impatiently.

Ibid., Ch. 9

3 He had what I call a very religious smile. An inner
smile that came on and off, governed as it were by his
private joy in what he heard or saw. . . .

The Love Object   1963

4 I did not sleep. I never do when I am over-happy, over-
unhappy, or in bed with a strange man.

Ibid.

5 When something has been perfect . . . there is a tendency to try hard to repeat it.   Ibid.

6 Bad moments, like good ones, tend to be grouped together. . . .   Ibid.

7 It is impossible to insist that bad news delivered in a certain manner and at a certain time will have a less awful effect.

Ibid.

8 There is something about holding on to things that I find therapeutic.

Ibid.

9 "I am committing suicide through lack of intelligence, and through not knowing, not learning to know, how to live."

Ibid.

10 . . . it is a shocking fact that although absence does not make love less it cools down our physical need for the ones we love.

Ibid.

11 I would mend and with vengeance.

Ibid.

12 That was the first time it occurred to me that all my life I had feared imprisonment, the nun's cell, the hospital bed, the places where one faced the self without distraction, without the crutches of other people. . . .

Ibid.

13 . . . a nothing is a dreadful thing to hold on to.

Ibid.

14 Later she came in the house and sat in front of the telephone, staring at it, waiting for it to come to life, hoping, beseeching, lifting it from time to time to make sure it was not out of order, then, relieved at its regular purr, she would drop it suddenly in case he should be dialing at that very moment, which he wasn't.

August Is a Wicked Month, Ch. 3   1965

15 . . . she longed for him as she stood in the street and thought the wickedest thing he had done was to come like that and give her false hope, and renew her life for an evening when she had resigned herself to being almost dead.

Ibid.

16 "After the rich, the most obnoxious people in the world are those who serve the rich."   Ibid., Ch. 8

17 Kindness. The most unkindest thing of all.

Ibid., Ch. 11

18 There are times when the thing we are seeing changes before our very eyes, and if it is a landscape we praise nature, and if it is a spectre, we shudder or cross ourselves, but if it is a loved one that defects, we excuse ourselves and say we have to be somewhere, and are already late for our next appointment.

"A Scandalous Woman," *A Scandalous Woman* 1974

19 Do you know what I hate about myself, I have never done a brave thing, I have never risked death.

Ibid., "Over"

20 . . . at heart she was quite willful and rebellious. . . . She had developed these traits of niceness and agreeableness simply to get away from people—to keep them from pestering her.

Ibid., "Honeymoon"

21 She thought of the bigness and wonder of destiny, meeting him in a packed train had been a fluke, and this now was a fluke, and things would either convene to shut that door, or open it a little, or open and close it alternately, and they would be together, or not be together as life the gaffer thought fit.

Ibid., "A Journey"

22 But it is not good to repudiate the dead because they do not leave you alone, they are like dogs that bark intermittently at night.

Ibid., "Love-Child"

1111. Sylvia Plath
(1932–1963)

1 . . . they all wanted to adopt me in some way, and, for the price of their care and influence, have me resemble them.

The Bell Jar 1963p

2 I pushed myself into a flight I knew I couldn't stop by skill or any belated access of will.

Ibid.

3 "What does a woman see in a woman that she can't see in a man?" Doctor Nolan paused. Then she said, "Tenderness."

Ibid.

4 . . . I guess I feel about a hot bath the way those religious people feel about holy water. . . . The longer I lay there in the clear hot water the purer I felt, and when I stepped out at last and wrapped myself in one of the big, soft, white, hotel bath-towels I felt pure and sweet as a new baby.

Ibid., Ch. 2

5 "Do you know what a poem is, Esther?"
"No, what?" I would say.
"A piece of dust."
Then just as he was smiling and starting to look proud, I would say, "So are the cadavers you cut up. So are the people you think you're curing. They're dust as dust as dust. I reckon a good poem lasts a whole lot longer than a hundred of those people put together."

Ibid., Ch. 5

6 I never wanted to get married. The last thing I wanted was infinite security, and to be the place an arrow shoots off from. I wanted change and excitement and to shoot off in all directions myself, like the colored arrows from a Fourth of July rocket.

Ibid., Ch. 7

7 "If neurotic is wanting two mutually exclusive things at one and the same time, then I'm neurotic as hell. I'll be flying back and forth between one mutually exclusive thing and another for the rest of my days."

Ibid., Ch. 8

8 . . . I had followed the green, luminous course of the second hand and the minute hand and the hour hand of the bedside clock through their circles and semicircles, every night for seven nights, without missing a second, or a minute, or an hour.

Ibid., Ch. 11

9 They understood things of the spirit in Japan. They disemboweled themselves when anything went wrong. . . . It must take a lot of courage to die like that.

Ibid.

10 I stored the fact . . . in the corner of my mind the way a squirrel stores a nut.   *Ibid.,* Ch. 15

11 I lay, rapt and naked, on Irwin's ruffled blanket, waiting for the miraculous change to make itself felt. But all I felt was a sharp, startlingly bad pain.   *Ibid.,* Ch. 19

12 Sunday—the doctor's paradise! Doctors at country clubs, doctors at the seaside, doctors with mistresses, doctors with wives, doctors in church, doctors in yachts, doctors everywhere resolutely being people, not doctors.

Ibid.

13 I took a deep breath and listened to the old brag of my heart. I am, I am, I am.
Ibid., Ch. 20

14 A living doll, everywhere you look.
It can sew, it can cook,
It can talk, talk, talk.

It works, there is nothing wrong with it.
You have a hole, it's a poultice.
You have an eye, it's an image.
My boy, it's your last resort.
Will you marry it, marry it, marry it.
"The Applicant," Ariel   1966p

15 Out of the ash
I rise with my red hair
and I eat men like air.
Ibid., "Lady Lazarus"

16 Viciousness in the kitchen!
Ibid., "Lesbos"

17 And your first gift is making stone out of everything.
I wake to a mausoleum; you are here,
Ticking your fingers on the marble table, looking for
    cigarettes,
Spiteful as a woman, but not so nervous,
And dying to say something answerable.
Ibid., "The Rival"

18 How long can I be a wall around my green property?
How long can my hands
Be a bandage to his hurt, and my words
Bright birds in the sky, consoling? consoling?
It is a terrible thing
To be so open: it is as if my heart
Put on a face and walked into the world. . . .
"A Poem for Three Voices"   1968p

19   What would the dark
Do without fevers to eat?
What would the light
Do without eyes to knife. . . .
"The Jailor," Encounter   1969p

20 Widow. The word consumes itself. . . .
        "Widow," *Crossing the Water*   *1971p*

                    * * *

21 I am no drudge
   Though for years I have eaten dust
   and dried plates with my dense hair.
                        "The Babysitters"

22 Spiderlike, I spin mirrors,
   Loyal to my own image,
   Uttering nothing but blood.
                      "Childless Woman"

23 Is there no way out of the mind?   "Apprehensions"

1112. Harriet Rosenstein
                (1932?–   )

1 . . . violent outrage and equally violent despair seem
  inevitable responses to our era. All the horrors committed in the name of national honor or the sanctity of the
  family or individual integrity have caught up with us.
          "Reconsidering Sylvia Plath," *The
          First Ms. Reader*, Francine
          Klagsbrun, ed.   *1972*

2 . . . the novel . . . traditionally, at least, has depended on the pretense of objectivity to lend it the status of truth: a little world seen full and clear.
                                Ibid.

3 Destiny is something men select; women achieve it only
  by default or stupendous suffering.
                  Quoted in *Ms.*   *July, 1974*

4 Fiction, it seems, even living fiction, excuses just about
  anything.   Ibid.

1113. Alix Kates Shulman
                (1932–   )

1 Why was everything nice he did for me a bribe or a
  favor, while my kindnesses to him were my duty?
                      *Memoirs of an Ex-Prom
                      Queen*, Ch. 1   *1972*

2 If, as the girls always said, it's never too early to think about whom to marry, then it could certainly not be too early to think about who to be. Being somebody had to come first, because, of course, somebody could get a much better husband than nobody.

Ibid., Ch. 2

3 In Columbia [University] waters I had to swim carefully to avoid being caught in the net laid for nonconforming traffickers in capitalism.

Ibid., Ch. 6

1114. Elizabeth Taylor
(1932–   )

1 When people say: she's got everything, I've only one answer: I haven't had tomorrow.

Elizabeth Taylor   1965

2 My God, I was on a merry-go-round for so long. Now I've stopped spinning. I'm not afraid of myself. I'm no longer afraid of what I will do. I have absolute faith in our future. Richard [Burton] has given me all this.

Ibid.

3 I want to be known as an actress. I'm not royalty.

Interview in *The New York Times*
(1964), Quoted in *Elizabeth*
by Dick Sheppard   1974

1115. Megan Terry
(1932–   )

1 CHESTER. My God, the human baby! A few weeks after birth, any other animal can fend for itself. But *you*! A basket case till you're twenty-one.

The Magic Realist   1968

2 CHESTER. Fourteen mewling brats and not a business brain in a bucketful.

Ibid.

3 CHESTER. Tighten the belt. Tough it out, fellow Americans, tough it out!

Ibid.

1116. Robin Worthington
(1932–   )

1 Mental health, like dandruff, crops up when you least expect it.

Thinking About Marriage   1971

2 The battle to keep up appearances unnecessarily, the mask—whatever name you give creeping perfectionism—robs us of our energies.

Ibid.

1117. Maureen Duffy
(1933–   )

1 We all have to rise in the end, not just one or two who were smart enough, had will enough for their own salvation, but all the halt, the maimed and the blind of us which is most of us.

The Microcosm   1966

2 All reduction of people to objects, all imposition of labels and patterns to which they must conform, all segregation can lead only to destruction.

Rites   1969

3 The pain of love is the pain of being alive. It's a perpetual wound.

Wounds   1969

4 Love is the only effective counter to death.

Ibid.

5 You will be wondering, putative reader, why I have reported all this. The answer is quite simple: it interests me, and you, forgive me, don't. I am not trying to tell you anything; I am at my childlike, priestlike task of creation.

Love Child   1971

6 I think basically I just think I want everyone and don't really want anybody.

Ibid.

1118. Cynthia Fuchs Epstein
(1933–)

1 During World War II, for instance, when the young men were off at war, dating did not consume the time of the college co-ed and she redirected her energies to study. . . . Work became an alternative even for those who did marry. Once engaged in an occupation, many had so firm a foothold they were loath to give it up.

Woman's Place   1970

1119. Pozzi Escot
(1933–)

1 In our [Peruvian] schools we teach Bach, Beethoven and Brahms but nothing that has been composed in the past 70 years.

Quoted in "A Matter of Art, Not Sex,"
Time   November 10, 1975

1120. Barbara C. Gelpi
(1933–)

1 . . . the masculine and feminine principles are not simply arbitrary manila folders for filing certain qualities; they are transcendent functions, spiritual realities which must be taken into account in the psychological makeup of every human being.

"The Androgyne," *Women and
Analysis*, Jean Strouse, ed.   1974

2 Consciousness, as we tend to conceive of it, brings humanity into being—and that is good—but has certain negative consequences as well. Though it is man's triumph, it is divisive, separating him from the natural rhythms of life by virtue of the fact that he can observe those rhythms, looking forward and backward. He becomes then subject to the peculiarly human fear of death and the human affliction of boredom. He becomes also aware of his separateness, his individuality—and that is an achievement—but at the same time

becomes competitive, suffering all the endless human misery which competition involves.

Ibid.

3 If women could help society to throw off the heavy yoke of the Fathers they might eventually move humanity forward. . . .

Ibid.

4 With myths, dreams, visions, poems, stories, conversations we must imagine a race in which both mind and soul are of equal importance and may be equally fulfilled for both sexes.

Ibid.

1121. Ruth Bader Ginsberg
(1933–   )

1 In commercial law, the person duped was too often a woman. In a section on land tenure, one 1968 textbook explains that "land, like women, was meant to be possessed."

Quoted in "Portia Faces Life—The
Trials of Law School" by Susan
Edmiston, Ms.   April, 1974

2 The emphasis must be not on the right to abortion but on the right to privacy and reproductive control.

Ibid.

1122. Yoko Ono
(1933–   )

1 I wonder why men can get serious at all. They have this delicate long thing hanging outside their bodies, which goes up and down by its own will. . . . If I were a man I would always be laughing at myself.

"On Film No. 4," (1967),
Grapefruit   1970

* * *

2 Don't be too clever or we'll scratch your goodies out . . . or we'll blow your sillies off.

"Catman"

3 I'm a sphinx
Stamped on the Hilton poster
Hoping to see the desert. . . .
"A Thousand Times Yes"

4 The no that was hanging over the buildings
Faded like the moon at dawn.
Ibid.

5 I have a woman inside my soul.
"I Have a Woman Inside My Soul"

6 Keep your intentions in a clear bottle
and leave it on the shelf when you rap.
"Peter the Dealer"

7 On a windy day let's go flying
There may be no trees to rest on
There may be no clouds to ride
But we'll have our wings and the wind will be with us
That's enough for me, that's enough for me.
"Song for John"

8 The bed is shining like an old scripture
That's never been opened before.
"Winter Song"

9 What a bastard the world is.
"What a Bastard the World Is"

1123. Suzy Parker
(1933–   )

1 I thank God for high cheekbones every time I look in
the mirror in the morning.
Quoted in *This Fabulous Century:
1950–1960*   1970

1124. Jill Robinson
(1933?–   )

1 Somewhere there was a gentle man with a cock that
wore a jaunty grin and stayed long enough for you to
get to know him.
Bed/Time/Story, Pt. I   1974

2 The fame fraud is so complete that all the Hollywood kids think everyone else has money. It is the suburban delusion. But then, suburbia was invented by Hollywood.

Ibid.

3 I could hear the lovely, tiny swallowing gulps—you cover all ages in the sex-play cycle, from nursing infant to death in one terrifying swoop of the sexual plot.

Ibid.

4 We have to get where we are going. In New York the getting is the thing.

Ibid., Pt. II

5 And grownups have to act as if they know. That's how they show they love you, by knowing more stuff; it makes you feel secure.

Ibid.

6 The transcontinental jet flight is a condensed metaphor of the escapist's Geographical Change. One starts out with the gorgeous hope that the self one abhors can be left behind. Three thousand miles is a powerful distance; such speed, such height should get you away before that self can catch up.

Ibid.

7 "Ambition is destruction, only competence matters. . . ."

Ibid.

8 "Everyone's parent is only a fantasy finally, neither as magical as, forgive me, you are, nor as prosaic. It is the image one has created in the head that one is fighting. Not the real parent at all."

Ibid.

9 "It's a big risk—to stop drinking, going straight. Who knows? What you've got in mind could be very boring."

Ibid.

1125. Miriam Schneir
(1933–   )

1 The decline of feminism after the First World War is attributable at least in part to the eventual concentra-

tion of the women's movements on the single narrow issue of suffrage—which was won. Other factors which have been cited are the postwar economic depression; the growing influence of anti-feminist Freudianism; and the development in Germany and the Soviet Union of authoritarian governments which tended to foster male supremacist values.

Feminism: The Essential Historical
Writings, Introduction   1972

2 . . . centuries of slavery do not provide a fertile soil for intellectual development or expression.

Ibid.

1126. Susan Sontag
(1933–   )

1 Ambition if it feeds at all, does so on the ambition of others.

The Benefactor, Ch. 1   1963

2 I was not looking for my dreams to interpret my life, but rather for my life to interpret my dreams.

Ibid., Ch. 4

3 The love of the famous, like all strong passions, is quite abstract. Its intensity can be measured mathematically, and it is independent of persons.

Ibid., Ch. 9

4 Persons who merely have-a-life customarily move in a dense fluid. That's how they're able to conduct their lives at all. Their living depends on not seeing. But when this fluid evaporates, an uncensored, fetid, appalling underlife is disclosed. Lost continents are brought to view, bearing the ruins of doomed cities, the sparsely fleshed skeletons of ancient creatures immobilized in their death throes, a landscape of unparalleled savagery. One can redeem skeletons and abandoned cities as human. But not a lost, dehumanized nature.

Death Kit   1967

5 How does an inexpressive face age? More slowly, one would suppose.   Ibid.

6 Wiser and wiser. The scrim was raised. The gauzy light became, suddenly, knife-sharp. Almost gouged out his

heart. Wiser. And suffering, for the first time. But not truly wise, wise enough to transcend suffering; and never likely to be.

Ibid.

1127. Rosalie Sorrels
(1933–   )

1 Foreigners extol the American "energy," attributing to it both our unparalleled economic prosperity and the splendid vivacity of our arts and entertainments. But surely this is energy bad at its source and for which we pay too high a price, a hypernatural and humanly disproportionate dynamism that flays everyone's nerves raw.

"What's Happening in America"
(1966), Styles of Radical Will
1969

2 This is a doomed country, it seems to me; I only pray that, when America founders, it doesn't drag the rest of the planet down, too. But one should notice that, during its long elephantine agony, America is also producing its subtlest minority generation of the decent and sensitive, young people who are alienated *as* Americans.

Ibid.

3 Though no longer a confession, art is more than ever a deliverance, an exercise in asceticism. Through it, the artist becomes purified—of himself and, eventually, of his art.

Ibid., "The Aesthetics of Silence" (1967)

4 The characteristic aim of modern art, to be *unacceptable* to its audience, inversely states the unacceptability to the artist of the very presence of an audience— audience in the modern sense, an assembly of voyeuristic spectators. Ibid.

5 Experiences aren't pornographic; only images and representations—structures of the imagination—are.

Ibid., "The Pornographic
Imagination" (1967)

6 Human sexuality is, quite apart from Christian repressions, a highly questionable phenomenon, and belongs,

at least potentially, among the extreme rather than the ordinary experiences of humanity. Tamed as it may be, sexuality remains one of the demonic forces in human consciousness—pushing us at intervals close to taboo and dangerous desires, which range from the impulse to commit sudden arbitrary violence upon another person to the voluptuous yearning for the extinction of one's consciousness, for death itself. Even on the level of simply physical sensation and mood, making love surely resembles having an epileptic fit at least as much, if not more, than it does eating a meal or conversing with someone.

Ibid.

7 Let her discover all the things that she can do.
Sooner or later she's gonna discover
She can do without you.
"She Can Do Without You"   1974

8 There's no more rooms to retire to,
I've got to move, there's no place to stay.
I've nothing that's mine but my shadow,
If you need one, I'll give that away.
"Travelin' Lady"   1974

9 What can I say, but that it's not easy?
I cannot lift the stones out of your way,
And I can't cry your bitter tears for you.
I would if I could, what can I say?
"Apple of My Eye"   1974

10 I like to sing for my friends; I don't want to sing in fucking stadiums. I like to be able to see who I'm singing to, look them right in the eye and talk to them. . . . I can't get into that thing where you keep swelling up bigger and bigger, publicity, super-hype, higher prices, more equipment. . . . If you come around with a seven-piece band, three roadies, a manager and groupies . . . you lose your mobility and miss all the *good* times.

Quoted in "Rosalie Sorrels" by Amie
Hill, Rolling Stone
January 28, 1975

1128. Helen Vendler
(1933–   )

1 It is a crushing burden . . . to reinterpret in a personal, and personally acceptable, way every conventional liturgical and religious act; to make devotion always singular, never simply communal . . . to particularize, not to merge; to individuate, not to accede.

The Poetry of George Herbert,
Introduction   *1975*

1129. Nina Voronel
(1933–   )

1 In Russia today, anything new is dangerous.

Quoted in "Russia: No Exit for These
Four Women" by Ruth Gruber, *Ms.*
April, 1974

2 . . . I believe devoutly in the Word. The Word can save all, destroy all, stop the inevitable, and express the inexpressible.

Ibid.

3 The echoes of pogroms sob in my verses
Making contact with history.

Ibid., "I Am a Jew"

1130. Freda Adler
(1934–   )

1 The phenomenon of female criminality is but one wave in this rising tide of female assertiveness—a wave which has not yet crested and may even be seeking its level uncomfortably close to the high-water mark set by male violence.

Sisters in Crime, Prologue   *1975*

2 The type of fig leaf which each culture employs to cover its social taboos offers a two-fold description of its morality. It reveals that certain unacknowledged behavior exists and it suggests the form that such behavior takes.

Ibid., Ch. 3

3 Euphemisms, like fashions, have their day and pass, perhaps to return at another time. Like the guests at a masquerade ball, they enjoy social approval only so long as they retain the capacity for deception.

Ibid.

4 But there is another side to chivalry. If it dispenses leniency, it may with equal justification invoke control.

Ibid., Ch. 4

5 Of all the tyrannies which have usurped power over humanity, few have been able to enslave the mind and body as imperiously as drug addiction.

Ibid., Ch. 5

6 Man is not only an animal with a body and a being with a brain but also a social creature who is so ineluctably interconnected with his social group that he is hardly comprehensible outside it. . . .

Ibid.

7 Stripped of ethical rationalizations and philosophical pretensions, a crime is anything that a group in power chooses to prohibit.

Ibid., Ch. 7

8 That man is a creature who needs order yet yearns for change is the creative contradiction at the heart of the laws which structure his conformity and define his deviancy.

Ibid., Ch. 8

9 Woman throughout the ages has been mistress to the law, as man has been its master. . . . The controversy between rule of law and rule of men was never relevant to women—because, along with juveniles, imbeciles, and other classes of legal nonpersons, they had no access to law except through men.

Ibid., Ch. 9

10 It is little wonder that rape is one of the least-reported crimes. Perhaps it is the only crime in which the victim becomes the accused and, in reality, it is she who must prove her good reputation, her mental soundness, and her impeccable propriety.

Ibid.

11 The Rubicons which women must cross, the sex barriers which they must breach, are ultimately those that exist in their own minds. . . . Like a distant planet, it [equality] has moved within their ken but will forever elude their grasp. It will remain for another generation of women. . . .

Ibid., Epilogue

1131. Brigitte Bardot
(1934–)

1 I leave before being left. I decide.
Quoted in *Newsweek*   *March 5, 1973*

1132. Arlene Croce
(1934?–)

* * *

1 At least some of the men who write sex books admit
that they really don't understand female sexuality.
Freud was one. Masters is another—that was why he
got Johnson.

Quoted in *Commentary*

1133. Diane Di Prima
(1934–)

1 When the radio told me there was dancing in the
   streets,
I knew we had engineered another coup;
Bought off another army.
"Goodbye Nkrumah," St. 1,
Intrepid #VI   *1966*

2 We buy the arms and the armed men, we have placed
   them
on all the thrones of South America
we are burning the jungles, the beasts will rise up
   against us
Ibid., St. 4

3 Had you lived longer than your twenty-six years
You, too, wd have come up against it like a wall—
That the Beauty you saw was bought
At too great a price
Even in those days. . . .
"Ode to Keats," St. 1, *The East Side
Scene,* Allen De Loach, ed.   *1968*

378

1134. Oriana Fallaci
(1934?–   )

1 Listening to someone talk isn't at all like listening to
their words played over on a machine. What you hear
when you have a face before you is never what you
hear when you have before you a winding tape.

The Egotists, Foreword   1963

2 If I were to give human semblance to the America of
today, this hated and often misunderstood country, I
would choose Norman Mailer to be the model. . . .
One tries to catch America—Mailer's stare—and one
doesn't know which eye to choose, which eye to re-
spond to. As a result one cannot reach a moral decision
about him. But the practical dilemma remains: Should
one be his friend or his enemy? Most people consider
him an enemy; to be his friend is anything but easy.

Ibid., "Norman Mailer"

3 He [Nguyen Cao Ky] is the most famous man in
South Vietnam and also the most hated. Reactionaries
hate him because he is the most hostile enemy of the
reactionaries; liberals hate him because he is the most
hostile enemy of the liberals; Americans hate him because he is the most hostile enemy of the Americans.

Ibid., "Nguyen Cao Ky"

4 We are all going to become Swedish, and we do not
understand these Americans who, like adolescents, always speak of sex, and who, like adolescents, all of a
sudden have discovered that sex is good not only for
procreating children.

Ibid., "Hugh Hefner"

5 Glory is a heavy burden, a murdering poison, and to
bear it is an art. And to have that art is rare.

Ibid., "Federico Fellini"

6 Every time she passed a mirror she was unable to resist
the temptation of looking at the one thing that interested her most in the world—herself. And every time
she was a bit disappointed—almost as if the girl facing
her was some other person.

Penelope at War, Ch. 1   1966

7 But, with the optimism of those beings who will not give up even in the face of obvious defeat and who blindly raise their heads again after defeat thinking that it might have been worse and all is not lost, Giovanna did not want to understand—far less withdraw in good order.

Ibid., Ch. 5

8 I'm going to show you the real New York—witty, smart, and international—like any metropolis. Tell me this—where in Europe can you find old Hungary, old Russia, old France, old Italy? In Europe you're trying to copy America, you're almost American. But here you'll find Europeans who immigrated a hundred years ago—and we haven't spoiled them. Oh, Gio! You must see why I love New York. Because the whole world's in New York. . . .

Ibid., Ch. 8

9 "You know that everyone else is at home—with his beer, his wife, his children, those children dressed like elves, in yellow, red, that well-dressed wife looking at the TV, that cool beer, that family, that is safe because they listen to the transistor radio, because they believe in business and civil religion, because they conform in a country where conformity means salvation. . . . Lastly, you understand why the rule of God and of America is the rule of selection, why it's a man-made law, why spiritual values are earthly values, why America is God equals America equals Business equals America equals God. And there's no alternative: you have to be on the side of God equals America equals Business equals America equals God, or else you're alone. Alone and damned like me, understand?"

Ibid., Ch. 10

10 "America's a hard school, I know, but hard schools make excellent graduates."

Ibid., Ch. 16

11 "I think when men die they do what the trees do in winter when they go dry, but then spring comes and they're reborn. So life must be something else."

Nothing, and So Be It, Ch. 1   1972

12 But here's what I learned in this war, in this country, in this city: to love the miracle of having been born.

Ibid., Ch. 3

13. Have you ever thought that war is a madhouse and that everyone in the war is a patient? Tell me, how can a normal man get up in the morning knowing that in an hour or a minute he may no longer be there? How can he walk through heaps of decomposing corpses and then sit down at the table and calmly eat a roll? How can he defy nightmare-like risks and then be ashamed of panicking for a moment?

Ibid., Ch. 6

1135. Marilyn Horne
(1934–   )

1 Ninety percent of what's wrong with singers today is that they don't breathe right.
Quoted in "Marilyn Horne," Divas:
Impressions of Six Opera Superstars
by Winthrop Sargeant   1959

2 You have to know exactly what you want out of your career. If you want to be a star, you don't bother with other things.

Ibid.

3 The thing to do [for insomnia] is to get an opera score and read that. That will bore you to death.

Ibid.

1136. Louise Kapp Howe
(1934–   )

1 Despite the focus in the media on the affluent and the poor, the average man is neither. Despite the concentration in TV commercials on the blond, blue-eyed WASP, the real American prototype is of Italian or Irish or Polish or Greek or Lithuanian or German or Hungarian or Russian or any of the still amazing number of national origins represented in this country—a "white ethnic," sociologists somberly call him.
The White Majority, Introduction   1970

2 . . . if the error of the sixties was that the people of the white majority were never given a concrete personal reason for social advance, the clear and present danger of the seventies is that they won't be warned in

time against the threat of social repression being waged in their name.

Ibid., Afterword

3 We all know what the American family is supposed to look like. We can't help it. The picture has been imprinted on our brains since we were tiny, through children's books, schools, radio, television, movies, newspapers, the lectures if not the examples of many of our parents, the speeches if not the examples of many of our politicians. . . . Now, the striking point about our model family is not simply the compete-compete, consume-consume style of life it urges us to follow. . . . The striking point, in the face of all the propaganda, is how few Americans actually live this way.

The Future of the Family,
Introduction   1972

4. . . the assumption of a male-breadwinner society . . . ends up determining the lives of everyone within a family, whether a male breadwinner is present or not, whether one is living by the rules in suburbia or trying to break them on a commune.

Ibid.

5 While politicians carry on about the sanctity of the American family, we learn . . . that in the scale of national priorities our children and families really come last. After freeways. After pork subsidies. After the billions spent on munitions in the name of national defense. It is now time . . . to reverse the usual procedure. It is time to *change the economy* to meet the needs of American families.

Ibid.

1137. Diane Johnson
(1934–   )

1 Waiting to be murdered has given me you might say something to live for.

The Shadow Knows   1974

2 We are surrounded by the enraged.

Ibid.

1138. Audre Lorde
(1934–   )

1 Since Naturally Black is Naturally Beautiful
I must be proud
And, naturally,
Black and
Beautiful
Who always was a trifle
Yellow
And plain though proud
Before.
>   "Naturally," St. 1, *Cables to Rage*   1970

2 There are so many roots to the
    tree of anger
that sometimes the branches
    shatter
before they bear.
>   "From a Land Where Other People
>   Live," *From a Land Where
>   Other People Live*   1975

3 . . . which me will survive all these liberations.
>   Ibid.

1139. Shirley MacLaine
(1934–   )

1 The pain of leaving those you grow to love is only the
prelude to understanding yourself and others.
>   *Don't Fall Off the Mountain*   1975

2 I asked, "Why, because a tree's arm got sick, did they
have to cut down the whole body?" And they told me
the tree doctor had said it was the right thing to do.
>   Ibid., Ch. 1

3 For if the talent or individuality is there, it should be
expressed. If it doesn't find its way out into the air, it
can turn inward and gnaw like the fox at the Spartan
boy's belly.
>   Ibid., Ch. 4

4 In Japan, courtesy had an esthetic value far greater than good manners in the West. A negative truth is frequently subordinate to the virtue of courtesy. Courtesy, therefore, is more of a virtue than honesty.

Ibid., Ch. 5

5 The more I traveled the more I realized that fear makes strangers of people who should be friends.

Ibid., Ch. 13

6 It was a circus without a tent; without brass bands and popcorn. The animals leaped with what looked like unfounded joy to me but to them was simply the way they always felt. . . . Africa seemed the harmonious voice of creation. Everything alive was inextricably intertwined until death. And even death was part of the life harmony.

Ibid., Ch. 13

7 India is a paradox, passionate, pulsating, even humorous in her poverty. And in her villages the subhuman drama plays itself out against a backdrop of such beauty that it seems grotesque mockery.

Ibid., Ch. 14

8 Freedom, with her front windows open and unlocked, with breezes and challenges blowing in. I wished that she [MacLaine's daughter, Sasha] would know herself through freedom. I wished that underneath she would understand that there is no such thing as being safe—that there are no safe havens for anyone who wants to know the TRUTH, *whatever* it is, about himself or others.

Ibid., Ch. 19

9 If you attach yourself to one person, you ultimately end up having an unhealthy relationship.

Quoted in "The Odyssey of Shirley MacLaine" by Arthur Bell, *Viva October, 1974*

10 The notion of good and evil being fought outside the confines of our responsibility is anathema to me. Good and evil is in us. Good and evil is what we decide it should be. I have more faith in human beings than that. We can figure out what we're doing. We don't have to shove it off on God and the fucking devil.

Ibid.

11 Hollywood always had a streak of the totalitarian in just about everything it did.

You Can Get There from Here, Ch. 2   1975

12 . . . the more I became involved in "big time" politics the more I realized how vicious the in-fighting could get in the desire to "make things better."

Ibid., Ch. 11

13 I hoped that the trip would be the best of all journeys: a journey into ourselves.

Ibid., Ch. 15

14 I stood in one nursery, watching the children, and I realized that an exaggerated sense of competition was being educated out of China's New Society through its children. . . . It made me wonder if the sense of competition was innate in human nature at all, and because the children seemed so happy and secure I wondered whether mothers and fathers were necessary to children in the same way we believed when their environment was healthy and happy otherwise.

Ibid., Ch. 18

15 China was proud now—of herself and of her potential. She had pulled herself to dignity and unity and that spirit literally pervaded the communes, the backbone of China. The Chinese countryside was where the revolution was won and the countryside was the secret of China's future.

Ibid., Ch. 20

16 In some ways, America had grown up to be a masterpiece of self-concern.

Ibid., Epilogue

17 Perhaps Western values, for the past five hundred years, had been a human distortion, perhaps competition was simply not compatible with harmony, not conducive to human happiness, perhaps the competitive urge came only from the exaggerated emphasis on the individual. Maybe the individual was simply not as important as the group.

Ibid.

18 I realized that if what we call human nature can be changed, then absolutely *anything* is possible. And from that moment, my life changed.

Ibid.

19 I was not a soldier or a philosopher or a politician; I could cure no disease, solve no economic problems, or lead any revolution. But, I could dance, I could sing. I could make people laugh. I could make people cry.

Ibid.

1140. Kate Millett
(1934–   )

1 . . . it is the threadbare tactic of justifying social and temperamental differences by biological ones.

Sexual Politics   1969

2 The care of children, even from the period when their cognitive powers first emerge, is infinitely better left to the best-trained practitioners of both sexes who have chosen it as a vocation, rather than to harried and all too frequently unhappy persons with little time or taste for the work of educating minds however young or beloved. . . . The family, as that term is presently understood, must go.

Ibid.

3 Many women do not recognize themselves as discriminated against; no better proof could be found of the totality of their conditioning.

Ibid.

4 Sexual congress in a Mailer novel is always a matter of strenuous endeavor, rather like mountain climbing—a matter of straining after achievement.

Ibid.

5 Perhaps nothing is so depressing an index of the inhumanity of the male supremacist mentality as the fact that the more genial human traits are assigned to the underclass: affection, response to sympathy, kindness, cheerfulness.

Ibid.

6 . . . I see the function of true Erotica (writing which is pro-, not antisexual) as one not only permissible but worthy of encouragement and social approval, as its laudable and legitimate function is to increase sexual appetite just as culinary prose encourages other appetites.

Ibid.

7 For our highly repressive and Puritan tradition has almost hopelessly confused sexuality with sadism, cruelty, and that which is in general inhumane and antisocial. This is a deplorable state of affairs.

Ibid.

8 . . . the female is rendered innocuous by her socialization. Before assault she is almost universally defenseless both by her physical and emotional training.

Ibid.

9 Isn't privacy about keeping taboos in their place?
Speech, Women's Writer's
Conference, Los Angeles
March 22, 1975

10 Aren't women prudes if they don't and prostitutes if they do?
Ibid.

1141. Patricia Simon
(1934–)

1 An old French farm built on levels up and down a hillside near Grasse—overlooking, in the middle distance, the quiet cluster of the town and, in the further distance, hills, and beyond them other hills, and other hills, in a gentle, fertile, dreamlike landscape that continued forever—the Alpes-Maritimes.
"The Making of a Masterpiece,"
McCall's October, 1970

2 Flowers and sunlight, air and silence—*"luxe, calme et volupté."*
Ibid.

1142. Gloria Steinem
(1934–)

1 The first problem for all of us, men and women, is not to learn, but to unlearn.
"A New Egalitarian Life Style,"
The New York Times
August 26, 1971

2 It's clear that most American children suffer too much mother and too little father.
Ibid.

3 We [women] are not more moral, we are only less corrupted by power.

Ibid.

4 . . . no man can call himself liberal, or radical, or even a conservative advocate of fair play, if his work depends in any way on the unpaid or underpaid labor of women at home, or in the office.

Ibid.

5 We are human beings first, with minor differences from men that apply largely to the act of reproduction. We share the dreams, capabilities, and weaknesses of all human beings, but our occasional pregnancies and other visible differences have been used—even more pervasively, if less brutally, than radical differences have been used—to mark us for an elaborate division of labor that may once have been practical but has since become cruel and false. The division is continued for clear reason, consciously or not: the economic and social profit of men as a group.

"Sisterhood," *The First Ms. Reader,*
Francine Klagsbrun, ed.   *1972*

6 God knows (*she* knows) that women try.

Ibid.

7 As for logic, it's in the eye of the logician.   Ibid.

8 The status quo protects itself by punishing all challengers.   Ibid.

9 I have met brave women who are exploring the outer edge of human possibility, with no history to guide them, and with a courage to make themselves vulnerable that I find moving beyond words.   Ibid.

10 She [Marilyn Monroe] was an actress, a person on whom no one's fate depended, and yet her energy and terrible openness to life had made some connection with strangers.

Ibid., "Marilyn: The Woman Who
Died Too Soon"

11 The long history of antiobscenity laws makes it very clear that such laws are most often invoked against political and life-style dissidents.

"Gazette News: Obscene?," *Ms.*
October, 1973

12 The definition of woman's work is shitwork.

Quoted in "Freelancer with No Time
to Write" by John Brady, *Writer's
Digest*   February, 1974

13 . . . intelligence at the service of poor instinct is really
dangerous. . . .   Ibid.

14 Ten years from now, as I see it, either the movements
for change will be totally annihilated, dispirited or
ground down—or they will really have entered the
main stream and created major changes. It has come to
the point of maximum push.

Quoted in "Impeachment?" by Claire
Safran, *Redbook*   April, 1974

15 . . . the new women in politics seem to be saying that
we already know how to lose, thank you very much.
Now we want to learn how to win.

"Victory with Honor," *Ms.*   April, 1974

16 A government's responsibility to its young citizens does
not magically begin at the age of six. It makes more
sense to extend the free universal school system down-
ward—with the necessary reforms and community control that child care should have from the start.

Ibid.

1143. Susan Brownmiller
(1935–   )

1 Man's discovery that his genitalia could serve as a
weapon to generate fear must rank as one of the most
important discoveries of prehistoric times, along with
the use of fire and the first crude stone axe. From prehistoric times to the present, I believe, rape has played
a critical function. It is nothing more or less than a
conscious process of intimidation by which all men
keep all women in a state of fear.

*Against Our Will: Men, Women,
and Rape*   1975

2 "Hero" is the surprising word that men employ when
they speak of Jack the Ripper.   Ibid.

3 . . . the incidence of actual rape combined with the
looming spectre of the black man as rapist, to which

the black man in the name of his manhood now contributes, must be understood as a control mechanism against the freedom, mobility and aspirations of all women, white and black. The crossroads of racism and sexism had to be a violent meeting place. There is no use pretending it doesn't exist.

Ibid.

4 It has been argued that, when killing is viewed as not only permissible but heroic behavior sanctioned by one's government or cause, the fine distinction between taking a human life and other forms of impermissible violence gets lost, and rape becomes an unfortunate but inevitable by-product of the necessary game called war.

Ibid.

5 Fighting back. On a multiplicity of levels, that is the activity we must engage in. . . .

Ibid.

6 My purpose in this book has been to give rape its history. Now we must deny it a future.

Ibid.

1144. Joan Didion
(1935–   )

1 New York is full of people on this kind of leave of absence, of people with a feeling for the tangential adventure, the risk adventure, the interlude that's not likely to end in any double-ring ceremony.

"New York: The Great Reprieve,"
Mademoiselle   February, 1961

2 Was there ever in anyone's life span a point free in time, devoid of memory, a night when choice was any more than the sum of all the choices gone before?

Run River, Ch. 4   1963

3 "I think nobody owns land until their dead are in it. . . ."

Ibid., Ch. 8

4 She knew clocks weren't supposed to stop, don't be silly. She knew they needed a clock. But she could not work with it going every second. When it was going every second that way she could not seem to take her

390

eyes off it, and because it made no noise she found herself making the noise for it in her mind.

Ibid., Ch. 18

5 . . . the day that I did not make Phi Beta Kappa nonetheless marked the end of something, and innocence may well be the word for it. I lost the conviction that lights would always turn green for me . . . lost a certain touching faith in the totem power of good manners, clean hair, and proven competence on the Stanford-Binet scale. To such doubtful amulets had my self-respect been pinned, and I faced myself that day with the nonplussed apprehension of someone who has come across a vampire and has no crucifix at hand.

"On Self-Respect" (1961), *Slouching Towards Bethlehem* 1968

6 As an adjective, the very word "Hollywood" has long been pejorative and suggestive of something referred to as "the System." . . . The System not only strangles talent but poisons the soul, a fact supported by rich webs of lore.

Ibid., "I Can't Get That Monster Out of My Mind" (1964)

7 Because when we start deceiving ourselves into thinking not that we want something or need something, not that it is a pragmatic necessity for us to have it, but that it is a *moral imperative* that we have it, then is when we join the fashionable madmen, and then is when the thin whine of hysteria is heard in the land, and then is when we are in bad trouble. And I suspect we are already there.

Ibid., "On Morality" (1965)

8 There has always been that divergence between our official and our unofficial heroes. It is impossible to think of Howard Hughes without seeing the apparently bottomless gulf between what we say we want and what we do want, between what we officially admire and secretly desire, between, in the largest sense, the people we marry and the people we love.

Ibid., "7000 Romaine, Los Angeles 38" (1967)

9 In the absence of a natural disaster we are left again to our own uneasy devices.

"A Problem of Making Connections," *Life* December 5, 1969

10 Acquaintances read the New York *Times* and try to tell me the news of the world. I listen to call-in shows.

Ibid.

11 "I am what I am. To look for 'reasons' is beside the point."

Play It As It Lays   1970

12 Whether or not Carter could afford the rent, whether it was a month like this one when he was making a lot of money or a month when the lawyers were talking about bankruptcy, the boy came twice a week to vacuum the pool and the man came four days a week to work on the roses and the water in the pool was 85 degrees.

Ibid., Ch. 4

13 Each believed the other a murderer of time, a destroyer of life itself,

Ibid.

14 . . . they would exchange the addresses of new astrologers and the tag lines of old jokes.

Ibid., Ch. 10

15 The way he looked was the problem. He looked exactly the same. He looked untouched, and she did not.

Ibid.

16 "Hear that scraping, Maria?" the doctor said. "That should be the sound of music to you. . . ."

Ibid., Ch. 25

17 She had to have a telephone. There was no one to whom she wanted to talk but she had to have a telephone.

Ibid., Ch. 35

18   "I'm sorry."
   "I know you're sorry. I'm sorry."
   "We could try," one or the other would say after a while.
   "We've already tried," the other would say.

Ibid., Ch. 37

19 Maria could never keep up her end of the dialogue with hairdressers.

Ibid., Ch. 45

20 She had watched them in supermarkets and she knew the signs. At 7:00 on a Saturday evening they would be standing in the checkout line reading the horoscope in *Harper's Bazaar* and in their carts would be a single lamb chop and maybe two cans of cat food and the Sunday morning paper, the early edition with the comics wrapped outside.

Ibid., Ch. 46

21 . . . she had deliberately not counted the months but she must have been counting them unawares, must have been keeping a relentless count somewhere, because this was the day, the day the baby would have been born.

Ibid., Ch. 54

22 She did not much like him but she liked his not knowing her.

Ibid., Ch. 60

23 To hear someone's voice she looked in the telephone book and dialed a few prayers. . . .

Ibid., Ch. 64

24 By the end of a week she was thinking constantly about where her body stopped and the air began, about the exact point in space and time that was the difference between *Maria* and *other*.

Ibid., Ch. 65

25 I am not much engaged by the problems of what you might call our day but I am burdened by the particular. . . . *Ibid.*, Ch. 68

26 Some nights he said that he was tired, and some nights she said that she wanted to read, and other nights no one said anything. *Ibid.*, Ch. 69

27 My father advised me that life itself was a crap game: it was one of the two lessons I learned as a child. The other was that overturning a rock was apt to reveal a rattlesnake. As lessons go those two seem to hold up, but not to apply. *Ibid.*, Ch. 74

28 I know something about dread myself, and appreciate the elaborate systems with which some people manage to fill the void, appreciate all the opiates of the people.
Quoted in *Ms.* *January, 1973*

1145. Lois Gould
(1935?–)

1 Danny Mack got past the nurses at two-fifteen by impersonating a doctor. All he did was clip four ballpoint pens on his vest pocket and march in looking preoccupied.

Such Good Friends 1970

2 "Hogamous, Higamous, men are polygamous, Higamous, Hogamous, women monogamous."

Ibid.

3 . . . you can't . . . sneak around trying to correct the conjugal imbalance sheet: doing unto others what I did last night. The sheer symmetry of it scares people; how can they tell the victims from the perpetrators? In the dark they are all to blame.

Ibid.

4 Life is the only sentence which doesn't end with a period.

Ibid.

5 ". . . the city *requires* a funeral. . . . All the ordinances are designed with your friendly funeral directors in mind—not to mention the cemeteries and coffin makers and gravestone cutters."

Ibid.

6 *Things* have squatter's rights; why else do we call them *belongings?*

Ibid.

7 What it is, I guess, is that I don't really miss *him;* I miss something that must have been *us.* Because we *were* something, in spite of each other, weren't we?

Ibid.

8 Amos Lowen taught his daughters carefully that poor was a curse word, and that if money couldn't buy happiness—a point he never conceded—there were still plenty of other selections.

Necessary Objects 1972

9 She hated the powdered oil smell they put on the baby. Rubbing away all his natural sourness and anointing

him with foreign substances that were all ironically labeled *Baby*. So that he would never recognize his own body in the dark, the way she could recognize hers now. Small victory, discovering your acrid identity after eighteen years. Buried alive under thousands of layers of powdered oil.

Ibid.

10 "We are selling elegance. The idea of elegance. Throwaway chic, we are the last *word* in throwaway chic. . . . We have an image. I have. Either we can afford to be subtle, either we live *up* to the image, or we're just another tacky dress shop. I mean, if we've got it, I say we don't *have* to flaunt it."

Ibid.

11 Making love as if it were something one could make, as if it were making do or making believe. Hating her own hands, hating the thin desperate clinging body that responded by heart to echoes of old movements, like a mechanical toy. . . . Its working was an unbearable affront; it accused her. It made her admit the truth. I don't care if it still works, I hate it—*I don't want it any more.*

Ibid.

12 One of the new computers in the billing department had gone berserk, possibly from the strain of replacing five elderly bookkeepers, and a hundred thousand dollars' worth of credit had been erroneously issued to delinquent charge-account customers before anyone caught it.

Ibid.

13 "Why the hell don't women ever make a scene? Men are *always* making scenes, yelling in the halls. Why can't *you* yell in the halls?"
"Because," she sighed, "women don't get away with yelling in the halls. They call you a hysterical bitch if you yell in the halls."
"Also," Sophy noted wryly, "they fire you. It's *their* halls." *Final Analysis* 1974

14 She burst into tears. Just like a woman. Tears of rage: the ultimate toy weapon. *Ibid.*

15 "Women always run away," she said. "That's why women never get to run anything else. They can't stand the heat, so they get *back* in the kitchen." *Ibid.*

16 Make up. Meaning invent. Make up something more acceptable, because that face you have on right there will not do.

Ibid.

17 The only reason I hated him was that I had needed him so much. That's when I found out about need. It goes much better with hate than with love.

Ibid.

1146. Jane Howard
(1935–   )

1 An encounter group is a gathering, for a few hours or a few days, of twelve or eighteen personable, responsible, certifiably normal and temporarily smelly people. Their destination is intimacy, trust and awareness of why they behave as they do in groups; their vehicle is candor.

"Whatever Possessed Me,"
Please Touch   1970

2 The genealogy of the human potential movement is as hard to trace as a foundling baby's. Foundlings have no known ancestors, but the movement is alleged to have preposterously many.

Ibid., "Notes Toward History"

3 The re-entry from encounter groups to reality, and the business of keeping alive the elusive benefits of sensitivity training, are problems that preoccupy every student of the human potential movement.

Ibid., "Back Home"

4 Group philosophy—wise group philosophy, anyway—does not prescribe that you run to inform your old landlord that everyone secretly thinks he's effeminate, or your boss that you have always thought he was a stupid tyrant. The aim is first to know, in your head and below it, what you think and feel, and then to reflect on newly unearthed alternatives to your accustomed ways of being. Once it is unlocked, the door between your feelings and the cosmos need not be kept yawning open. It can be left ajar.

Ibid.

5 Parents, however old they and we may grow to be, serve among other things to shield us from a sense of

our doom. As long as they are around, we can avoid the fact of our mortality; we can still be innocent children.

A different Woman   1973

6 New links must be forged as old ones rust.

Ibid., Ch. 1

7 I wish women in the gay liberation movement Godspeed, although I take issue with their premise that all men, without exception, are intruding vandals bent only on the oppression of womankind. I submit that some of them can be welcome guests.

Ibid, Ch. 9

8 Wholesomeness is exotic to me. I pretended to like the era of strobe lights and deafening acid rock in discotheques but a lot of that sixties frenzy really just made me nervous. More and more I am drawn toward stillness.

Ibid., Ch. 34

1147. Anne Richardson Roiphe
(1935–   )

1 But how to burn it out—to purify one's mind of worms and grubs and frights of strangers, and a fear of the black Walpurgisnacht, when all the demons will run loose over the suburban lawns saying "You must now be slaves. Take your turn. It's only fair. The master must grovel in the dirt." I mean to say that despite my concern for civil liberties, for equality, for justice in Mississippi—I am blond, and blond is still beautiful, and if I have one life to lead it will be as a white, and I am a mass of internal contradictions, all of which cause me to finally attempt some rite which will bring salvation, save me from a system I despise but still carry within me like any other of my vital organs.

"Out of Week One," *Up the Sandbox!*   1970

2   "What the world needs," he said, "is not a Joan of Arc, the kind of woman who allows herself to be burned on the cross. That's just a bourgeois invention meant to frighten little girls into staying home. What we require is a real female military social leader."

"But that"—I smiled at him—"is just impossible. Women are tied to husband and children. Women are constructed to be penetrated; a sword or a gun in their hands is a joke or a mistake. They are open holes in which things are poured. Occasionally, it's true, a woman can become a volcano, but that's about it."

> *Ibid.*, "Out of Week Two"

3 What I'm doing in this car flying down these screaming highways is getting my tail to Juarez so I can legally rid myself of the crummy son-of-a-bitch who promised me a tomorrow like a yummy fruitcake and delivered instead wilted lettuce, rotted cucumber, a garbage of a life.

> *Long Division*   1972

4 She tried to be respectable because respectability kept away the chaos that sometimes overwhelmed her, causing her to call out in her sleep, screaming wild sounds, a warning to the future, a mourning for the past.

> *Ibid.*

1148. Judith Rossner
(1935–   )

1 A nightmare is terrifying because it can never be undone. . . . While in the beautiful well-ordered lie of our everyday lives there was almost nothing we could not do.

> *Nine Months in the Life of an Old Maid*, Pt. I   1969

2 "Being a witch is like royalty," I said calmly. "You have to inherit it from someone."

> *Ibid.*

3 As Lily had lost me years before from not caring, you lost me that day from caring but not nearly enough.

> *Ibid.*

4 Identity is a bag and a gag. Yet it exists for me with all the force of a fatal disease. Obviously I am here, a mind and a body. To say there's no proof my body exists would be arty and specious and if my mind is more ephemeral, less provable, the solution of being a writer with solid (touchable, tearable, burnable) books is as close as anyone has come to a perfect answer. The obvious reason that every asshole in the world wants to write.

> *Ibid.*, Pt. II

5 It is easier to betray than to remain loyal. It takes far less courage to kill yourself than it takes to make yourself wake up one more time. It's harder to stay where you are than to get out. (For everyone but you, that is.)

Ibid.

6 Love is the direct opposite of hate. By *definition* it's something you can't feel for more than a few minutes at a time, so what's all this bullshit about loving somebody for the rest of your life?

Ibid.

7 So often I heard people paying blind obeisance to change—as though it had some virtue of its own. Change or we will die. Change or we will stagnate. Evergreens don't stagnate. The perennials that year after year die down for winter then come up the following summer neither die nor stagnate, and if they change at all it is usually for the worse.

Ibid.

8 "I've been accused of selling out so often that it's made me realize what extraordinary resources people saw in me in the first place. It's why I can afford to sell out my ideas; I know something new'll spring up to replace the ones I'm unloading."

Ibid.

9 What was she to say now to her father, who thought change was the only serious mistake that could be made in a life?

Any Minute I Can Split   1972

10 "That's the New York thing, isn't it. People who seem absolutely crazy going around telling you how crazy they used to be before they had therapy."

Ibid.

11 "Self-government is a form of self-control, self-limitation. It goes against our whole grain. We're [Americans] supposed to go after what we want, not question whether we really need it."   Ibid.

12 "But I've been miserable ever since I came back. From Puerto Rico, that's where I had it [the abortion], it was like a vacation. It's almost like—it's not supposed to be that easy. It's too big a sin to get off that lightly."

Looking for Mr. Goodbar   1975

13 He always said she was smart, but their conversations were a mined field in which at any moment she might make the wrong verbal move and find her ignorance exploding in her face.

Ibid.

14 Sometimes she thought that the TV wasn't so much an escape as a filter through which he saw and heard everything but was kept from being affected by it too much.

Ibid.

15 A lie was something that hadn't happened but might just as well have.

Ibid.

16 "The point is," Evelyn said, "we're taught that we have to be perfect. Like objects in a museum, not people. People don't have to be perfect, only objects do."

Ibid.

1149. Françoise Sagan
(1935–   )

1 It is healthier to see the good points of others than to analyze our own bad ones.

A Certain Smile, Pt. I, Ch. 5   *1956*

2 We had the same gait, the same habits and lived in the same rhythm; our bodies suited each other, and all was well. I had no right to regret his failure to make the tremendous effort required of love, the effort to know and shatter the solitude of another.

Ibid., Pt. II, Ch. 2

3 "Look here, why don't you love me? I should feel so much more peaceful. Why not put up that pane of glass called passion between us? It may distort things at times, but it's wonderfully convenient." But no, we were two of a kind, allies and accomplices. In terms of grammar, I could not become the object, or he the subject. He had neither the capacity nor the desire to define our roles in any such way.

Ibid.

1150. Audrey Thomas
(1935–)

1 How could I tell her that she was wrong about things
when essentially she was right? Life was cruel, people
hurt and betrayed one another, grew old and died
alone.

Songs My Mother Taught Me   1973

2 . . . cats everywhere asleep on the shelves like motor-
ized bookends.

Ibid.

1151. Judith Viorst
(1935?–)

1 The honeymoon is over
And we find that dining by candlelight makes us
squint,
And that all the time
I was letting him borrow my comb and hang up his wet
raincoat in my closet,
I was really waiting
To stop letting him.

"The Honeymoon Is Over," *It's Hard
to Be Hip Over Thirty and Other
Tragedies of Married Life*   1968

2 With four walk-in closets to walk in,
Three bushes, two shrubs, and one tree,
The suburbs are good for the children,
But no place for grown-ups to be.

Ibid., "The Suburbs Are Good for
the Children"

3 But it's hard to be hip over thirty
When everyone else is nineteen,
When the last dance we learned was the Lindy,
And the last we heard, girls who looked like Barbara
Streisand
Were trying to do something about it.

Ibid., "It's Hard to Be Hip Over Thirty"

4 Love is much nicer to be in than an automobile accident, a tight girdle, a higher tax bracket or a holding
pattern over Philadelphia.
"What IS This Thing Called Love?,"
Redbook   *February, 1975*

5 Brevity may be the soul of wit, but not when someone's
saying, "I love you."

Ibid.

1152. Sandy Boucher
(1936–   )

1 My father's voice says, Watch out for little men. They
are more aggressive, meaner, nastier, trickier, more
combative. A big man is secure in his strength, so he
doesn't push it. A little man is always proving something. The same goes for little dogs versus big dogs.
"Mountain Radio," *Assaults and*
Rituals   *1975*

2 Thus we were equally, though differently, sophisticated,
and our game was the same: not to *care*—to arrive at
each other without being there.

Ibid.

3 The reality it took me ten hard years to discover is that
a dyke is a flaming threat to some of the most cherished institutions of this society, and it is for this reason
that Lenora was viewed with hatred and treated with
cruelty.

Ibid.

1153. Natalya Gorbanevskaya
(1936–   )

1 Opening the window, I open myself.
Untitled Poem, *Poems, the Trial,*
Prison   *1972*

2 I am awaiting the birth of my child quite calmly, and
neither my pregnancy nor the birth will prevent me
from doing what I wish—which includes participating
in every protest against any act of tyranny.
Red Square at Noon   *1972*

1154. Sandra Hochman
(1936–   )

1 What I wanted
Was to be myself again.

> "The Inheritance," *Love Letters
> from Asia*   1967

1155. Xaviera Hollander
(1936?–   )

1 *Mundus vult decipi decipiatur ergo.* The world wants
to be cheated, so cheat.

> *The Happy Hooker,* with Robin Moore
> and Yvonne Dunleavy, Ch. 1   1972

2 For me the madam life has become a big ego trip. I
enjoy the independence and what's more, for me prostitution is not just a way to make a living, but a real
calling, which I enjoy.

> Ibid., Ch. 10

3 There is only one other profession that outranks bankers as dedicated clients, and that is the stockbroker.
. . . When the stocks go up, the cocks go up!

> Ibid., Ch. 11

4 Actually, if my business was legitimate, I would deduct
a substantial percentage for depreciation of my body.

> Ibid., Ch. 14

5 . . . if my business could be made legal . . . I and
women like me could make a big contribution to what
Mayor Lindsay calls "Fun City," and the city and state
could derive the money in taxes and licensing fees that
I pay off to crooked cops and political figures.

> Ibid.

1156. Barbara Jordan
(1936–   )

1 I never intended to become a run-of-the-mill person.

> Quoted in *Newsweek*   *November 4, 1974*

2 Politicians don't talk about "wielding power." That's so crass. The only thing I can hope is that I will continue to be able to influence the Congress by . . . persuasion. . . . Nothing heavy-handed. Just openness and good relations.

Quoted in "Barbara Jordan" by
Charles L. Sanders, Ebony
February, 1975

3 . . . if I have anything special that makes me "influential" I simply don't know how to define it. If I knew the ingredients I would bottle them, package them and sell them, because I want everyone to be able to work together in a spirit of cooperation and compromise and accommodation without, you know, any caving in or anyone being woefully violated personally or in terms of his principles.

Ibid.

4 If you're going to play the game properly you'd better know every rule.

Ibid.

1157. June Jordan
(1936–   )

1 There was no loneliness in the living room. So it was a good part, and maybe the best part, of the house.

New Life, New Room   1975

2 "But what's more important. Building a bridge or taking care of a baby?"

Ibid.

1158. Dacia Maraini
(1936–   )

1 He talked and talked because he didn't know what to say.

The Holiday, Ch. 1   1962

2 "Our strength is like the sea," Pompei announced, lifting his chin up proudly. "Nothing can divert it. Elastic and mobile, strong. That's the main thing. Strong with an immense strength."

Ibid., Ch. 8

3 the disgust with myself, weak and weary
   throughout my intestines
   I couldn't stop it nor vomit it. . . .

                          "His Foot on the Sand,"
           Crudelta all 'Aria Aperia   1966

4 the nausea of being the thing I was
   leapt from my throat like sobbing. . . .   Ibid.

                      *   *   *

5 A woman who writes poetry and knows
   she is woman, has no choice but to hang on tight
   to contents because the sophistication
   of forms is something that belongs to power
   and the power that woman has is always an
   un-power, a scorching inheritance never entirely hers.

   Her voice may be hard and earthen
   but it is the voice of a lioness that has been
   reared too long a sensible sheep. . . .
                          "Woman's Poetry," *Donne Mie*

1159. Rochelle Owens
(1936–   )

1 CY. And I have no hate for anybody, but wanting to
   love the animals the way I do. *They*, mean folks, hate
   my face.   *Futz,* Sc. 1   1961

2 CY. I don't want no sow with two feet but with four!
   Them repeats true things with their grunts not like you
   human-daughter.   Ibid.

3 CY. I wasn't near people. They came to me and looked
   under my trousers all the way up to their dirty hearts.
   They minded my *own* life.   Ibid., Sc. 2

4 KATKA. Depression is often a sign of worthy pleasure.
                                           Ibid., Sc. 5

5 ALICE. Hypocrites, what hypocrites! Jerusalem is always a pretext for getting to Constantinople!
                          Istanbul, Sc. 2   1965

6 BECLCH. Your lesson to your son is a hangnail to us—
   we don't need it.
                          Beclch, Act I, Sc. 1   1966

7 BECLCH. No, sweet Jose . . . a cock fight is not cruel . . . for me . . . us to see . . . it's simply an evil reality . . . that's all. . . .

Ibid., Sc. 2

8 BECLCH. Persecution is a fact of the condition of being a monarch!

Ibid., Act II, Sc. 2

9 MARX. Labor! Sucking Capital! Captial! The exploiting class! The milking class—the ruling class!

The Karl Marx Play   1971

10 MARX. . . . the bourgeoisie, the fat enemy will get their reactionary asses *schtupped* up with horseshit and whipped cream! A new era will dawn.

Ibid.

11 MARX. Little rolls with butter is good! Viennese torte is good! And a revolution is good!

Ibid.

12 MARX. Beware the eternal, unredeemed Jew, the everlasting bargainers! They are hot for buying and selling, they would kill my beautiful revolution!

Ibid.

13 MARX. Machinery sweeps away every moral and material restriction, in its blind unrestrainable passion, its werewolf hunger.

Ibid.

14 MARX. Economics is not only a cause. But the *only* cause for all human rancor. All human exploitation.

Ibid.

1160. Marge Piercy
(1936–   )

1 Reflecting the values of the larger capitalistic society, there is no prestige whatsoever attached to actually working. Workers are invisible.

"The Grand Coolie Damn,"
Sisterhood Is Powerful,
Robin Morgan, ed.   1970

2 In an elitist world, it's always "women and children last."

Ibid.

3 One trouble: to be a professional anything in the United States is to think of oneself as an expert and one's ideas as semi-sacred, and to treat others in a certain way—professionally.

Ibid.

4 The ruling class isn't dissatisfied: they are healthy, well-fed, live in beauty, enjoy their own importance: fun-loving cannibals.

Ibid.

5 There are lies that glow so brightly we consent
to give a finger and then an arm
to let them burn.

Ibid., "Song of the Fucked Duck" (1969)

6 The will to be totally rational
is the will to be made out of glass and steel:
and to use others as if they were glass and steel.

Ibid.

7 The manipulator liberates only
the mad bulldozers of the ego to level the ground.

Ibid.

8 "You're not pretty, Miriam-mine, so you better be smart. But not too smart."

Small Changes 1973

9 "All women hustle. Women watch faces, voices, gestures, moods. The person who has to survive through cunning."

Ibid.

10 "You and I both have livers, large and small intestines, kidneys, spines, blood vessels, nerves, spleens, stomachs, hearts and, I had thought, brains in common. What conclusions do you draw from anatomy? That I am about to take you to the cleaners?"

Ibid.

1161. Gail Sheehy
(1936?–   )

1 For there is no more defiant denial of one man's ability to possess one woman exclusively than the prostitute who refuses to be redeemed.

Hustling, Ch. 1   1971

2 Into this anonymous pit they climb—a fumbling, frightened, pathetic man and a cold, contemptuous, violated
woman—prepared to exchange for twenty dollars no
more than ten minutes of animal sex, untouched by a
stroke of their common humanity.

Ibid., Ch. 3

3 It is a silly question to ask a prostitute why she does
it. . . . These are the highest-paid "professional"
women in America.

Ibid., Ch. 4

4 The prostitutes continue to take all the arrests, the police to suffer frustration, the lawyers to mine gold, the
operators to laugh, the landowners to insist they have
no responsibility, the mayor to issue press releases. The
nature of the beast is, in a word, greed.   *Ibid., Ch. 5*

5 . . . the upper East Side of Manhattan. This is the
province of Let's Pretend located in the state of An-
omie.   *Ibid.*

6 The difference between the call girl and the courtesan
. . . comes down to one word. Discipline.

Ibid., Ch. 9

7 The best way to attract money, she had discovered, was
to give the appearance of having it.   *Ibid.*

1162. Lily Tomlin
(1936–   )

1 If you have a psychotic fixation and you go to the doctor and you want these two fingers amputated, he will
not cut them off. But he *will* remove your genitals. I
have more trouble getting a prescription for Valium
than I do having my uterus lowered and made into a
penis.

Quoted by David Felton in
Rolling Stone   *October 24, 1974*

2 Thanks to medical technology, major breakthroughs in
psychiatric care, I'm no longer a woman obsessed with
an unnatural craving. Just another normal . . . very
socially acceptable . . . alcoholic.

Ibid., "Rubber Freak"*

* Character created by Lily Tomlin.

3 If you can't be direct, why be?

Ibid., "Mary Jean"*

4 Once poor, always waitin'. Rich is just a way of wantin' bigger.

Ibid., "Wanda V."*

5 Lady . . . lady, I do not make up things. That is lies. Lies is not true. But the truth could be made up if you know how. And that's the truth.   Ibid., "Edith Ann"*

1163. Sidney Abbott
(1937–   )

1 Lesbianism is far more than a sexual preference: it is a political stance.

Sappho Was a Right-On Woman,
with Barbara J. Love   1972

2 . . . a woman who wants a woman usually wants a woman.

Ibid.

3 There is no political gain in silence and submission.

Ibid.

4 Multiple relationships made it possible to comprehend people, not acquire them or own them.   Ibid.

1164. Margaret Lowe Benston
(1937–   )

1 In sheer quantity, household labor, including child care, constitutes a huge amount of socially necessary production. Nevertheless, in a society based on commodity production, it is not usually considered as "real work" since it is outside of trade and the marketplace. . . . In a society in which money determines value, women are a group who work outside the money economy.

"The Political Economy
of Women's Lib," Monthly Review
September, 1969

* Characters created by Lily Tomlin.

2 Industrialization is, in itself, a great force for human good; exploitation and dehumanization go with capitalism and not necessarily with industrialization.

Ibid.

3 Once women are freed from private production in the home, it will probably be very difficult to maintain for any long period of time a rigid definition of jobs by sex.

Ibid.

4 . . . possible alternatives—cooperatives, the kibbutz, etc. . . . show that psychic needs for community and warmth can in fact be better satisfied if other structures are substituted for the nuclear family.

Ibid.

1165. Sallie Bingham
(1937–   )

1 The clock would never let him forget the amount of time he was wasting. . . .

"Winter Term," *Mademoiselle*   *July, 1958*

2 . . . he wondered again, how much of her desire was passion and how much grasping: girls used sex to get a hold on you, he knew—it was so easy for them to pretend to be excited.

Ibid.

1166. Toni Cade
(1937?–   )

1 Personally, Freud's "anatomy is destiny" has always horrified me. *Kirche, Kusse, Kuche, Kinde* made me sick. Career woman versus wife-mother has always struck me as a false dichotomy. The-pill'll-make-you-gals-run-wild a lot of male chauvinist anxiety. Dump-the-pill a truncated statement. I think most women have pondered, those who have the heart to ponder at all, the oppressive nature of pregnancy, the tyranny of the child burden, the stupidity of male-female divisions, the obscene nature of employment discrimination. And day-care and nurseries being what they are, paid maternity leaves being rare, the whole memory of wham bam thank you ma'am and the Big Getaway a horrible

nightmare, poverty so ugly, the family unit being the last word in socializing institutions to prepare us all for the ultimate rip-off and perpetuate the status quo, and abortion fatalities being what they are—of course the pill.

"The Pill," *Onyx*   *August, 1969*

2 We are involved in a struggle for liberation: liberation from the exploitive and dehumanizing system of racism, from the manipulative control of a corporate society; liberation from the constrictive norms of "mainstream" culture, from the synthetic myths that encourage us to fashion ourselves rashly from without (reaction) rather than from within (creation).

The Black Woman, Preface   *1970*

3 The genocidal bloodbath of centuries and centuries of witch hunts sheds some light on the hysterical attitude white men have regarding their women.

Ibid., Lecture, "The Scattered Sopranoes," Livingston College Black Women's Seminar (December, 1969)

4 Revolution begins with the self, in the self. The individual, the basic revolutionary unit, must be purged of poison and lies that assault the ego and threaten the heart, that hazard the next larger unit—the couple or pair, that jeopardize the still larger unit—the family or cell, that put the entire movement in peril.

Ibid.

5 Not all speed is movement. . . . Ain't no such animal as an instant guerilla.

Ibid.

1167. Marian Wright Edelman
(1937–   )

1 Just because a child's parents are poor or uneducated is no reason to deprive the child of basic human rights to health care, education, proper nutrition. Clearly we ignore the needs of black children, poor children, and handicapped children in the country.

Quoted in "Society's Pushed-Out Children" by Margie Casady, *Psychology Today*   *June, 1975*

2 Some school officials have forgotten the reason they are there. Expediency and efficiency in administration have somehow become more important than educating children.

Ibid.

3 Parents have become so convinced that educators know what is best for children that they forget that they themselves are really the experts.

Ibid.

4 I've been struck by the upside-down priorities of the juvenile-justice system. We are willing to spend the least amount of money to keep a kid at home, more to put him in a foster home, and the most to institutionalize him.

Ibid.

1168. Jane Fonda
(1937–)

1 I don't care about the Oscar. I make movies to support the causes I believe in, not for any honors. I couldn't care less whether I win an Oscar or not.

Quoted in Jane: An Intimate Biography
of Jane Fonda by Thomas Kiernan,
Prologue   1973

2 I didn't like what I saw the acting profession do to people who went into the theater. All the young actresses I've met are obsessed with the theater. They think and talk only about one thing. Nothing else matters to them. It's terribly unhealthy to sacrifice everything—family, children—for a goal. I hope I never get that way. I don't believe in concentrating your life in terms of one profession, no matter what it is.

Ibid., Pt. II, Ch. 8 (c.1958)

3 Before I went into analysis, I told everyone lies—but when you spend all that money, you tell the truth. I learned that I had grown up in an atmosphere where nobody told the truth. Everyone was so concerned with appearances that life was just one big lie. Now all I want to do is live a life of truth. Analysis has also taught me that you should know who to love and who to hate and who to just plain like, and it's important to know the difference.

Ibid., Ch. 13 (c.1962)

4 You can do one of two things: just shut up, which is something I don't find easy, or learn an awful lot very fast, which is what I tried to do.

Ibid., Pt. IV, Ch. 22

5 Prostitutes are the inevitable product of a society that places ultimate importance on money, possessions and competition.

Ibid., Ch. 24 (c.1970)

6 All I can say is that through the people I've met, the experiences I've had, the reading I've done, I realize the American system must be changed. I see an alternative to the usual way of living and relating to people. And this alternative is a total change of our structures and institutions—through Socialism. Of course I am a Socialist. But without a theory, without an ideology.

Ibid., Ch. 26 (c.1971)

1169. Kathleen Fraser
(1937–   )

1 He is all of him urge.

Untitled Poem, *What I Want*   *1974*

2 I think you have many shelves
but never put love there.

Ibid., Untitled Poem

3 "Personal things is all I care about."

Ibid., Untitled Poem

1170. Gail Godwin
(1937–   )

1 "The only reason people forget is because they want to. If we were all clear, with no aberrations, we could remember everything, before we were born, even."

The Perfectionists, Ch. 1   1970

2 Anchored by the heavy bright heat, she closed her eyes and ears and let it press her down. *Let* the sun bake her senseless in the hottest part of the day. Let it broil her brain free of all complexities. Let it burn her back into the same earth which held the bones of ancient peasants and the decayed petals of bygone flowers. She

did not wish to compete, or to understand or to partici-
pate anymore. . . . She felt tight in the head, like
something was growing—a flower someone planted in a
pot too small.

Ibid., Ch. 2

3 "You sort of glitter rather than glow. Small talk comes
easy to you. You dress well. You are all crisp, sharp
edges. You look like one of those young career women
on the go."

Ibid., Ch. 8

4 "With a husband you have to keep up appearances. I
don't care who says not. They have their aura, we have
ours. They are eternally different auras."

Ibid., Ch. 12

5 . . . life is a disease. . . .

The Odd Woman   1974

6 . . . trying to organize the loneliness and the weather
and the long night into something of abiding shape and
beauty.

Ibid.

7 . . . though all came to horrible ends, they kept track
of themselves so beautifully along the way.

Ibid.

8 "Good teaching is one-fourth preparation and three-
fourths theatre. . . ."

Ibid.

9 I turn into an anachronism every time I come home,
she thought angrily. I start measuring myself by standards thirty, fifty, a hundred years old.

Ibid.

1171. Bessie Head
(1937–   )

1 But in a society like this, which man cared to be owned
and possessed when there were so many women freely
available? And even all the excessive love-making was
purposeless, aimless, just like tipping everything into an
awful cesspit where no one really cared to take a second look.

When Rain Clouds Gather, Ch. 8   1968

2 He wanted a flower garden of yellow daisies because they were the only flower which resembled the face of his wife and the sun of his love.

Maru, Pt. I   *1971*

3 And if the white man thought that Asians were a low, filthy nation, Asians could still smile with relief—at least, they were not Africans. And if the white man thought that Africans were a low, filthy nation, Africans in southern Africa could still smile—at least, they were not bushmen. They all have their monsters.

Ibid.

4 Love is mutually feeding each other, not one living on another like a ghoul.   *A Question of Power*   *1973*

1172. Barbara J. Love
(1937–   )

Co-author with Sidney Abbot. See 1163: 1–4.

1173. Liane Norman
(1937–   )

1 If conscience is regarded as imperative, then compliance with its dictates commends a society not to forgive, but to celebrate, its conscientious citizens.

"Selective Conscientious Objection,"
The Center Magazine   *May/June, 1972*

2 To kill implies that the claims of some men to life are better than others. . . .   *Ibid.*

3 While the State may respectfully require obedience on many matters, it cannot violate the moral nature of a man, convert him into a serviceable criminal, and expect his loyalty and devotion.   *Ibid.*

4 . . . if the Indochina war proves anything at all, it is the susceptibility of government to self-deluded error.

Ibid.

5 Whenever government's interests become by definition more substantial than the humanity of its citizens, the drift toward government by divine right gathers momentum.   *Ibid.*

1174. Eleanor Holmes Norton
(1937–   )

1 Racial oppression of black people in America has done
what neither class oppression nor sexual oppression,
with all their perniciousness, has ever done: destroyed
an entire people and their culture.

> "For Sadie and Maude,"
> *Sisterhood Is Powerful,*
> Robin Morgan, ed.   *1970*

2 There is no reason to repeat bad history.

> Ibid.

3 On the road to equality there is no better place for
blacks to detour around American values than in forgo-
ing its example in the treatment of its women and the
organization of its family life.   Ibid.

4 With children no longer the universally accepted reason for marriage, marriages are going to have to exist
on their own merits.   Ibid.

5 There are not many males, black or white, who wish to
get involved with a woman who's committed to her
own development.

> Quoted in "The Black Family and
> Feminism" by C. Ware, *The First Ms.
> Reader,* Francine Klagsbrun, ed.
> *1972*

1175. Jill Ruckelshaus
(1937?–   )

1 Women's rights in essence is really a movement for
freedom, a movement for equality, for the dignity of all
women, for those who work outside the home and
those who dedicate themselves with more altruism than
any profession I know to being wives and mothers,
cooks and chauffeurs, decorators and child psychologists and loving human beings.

> Quoted in "Jill Ruckelshaus: Lady of
> Liberty" by Frederic A. Birmingham,
> *Saturday Evening Post*   *March 3, 1973*

2 I have no hostility towards men. Some of my best friends are men. I married a man, and my father was a man.

Ibid.

3 What the emergence of woman as a politicial force means is that we are quite ready now to take on responsibilities as equals, not protected partners.

Ibid.

4 The best way to win an argument is to begin by being right. . . .

Ibid.

5 The family is the building block for whatever solidarity there is in society.

Ibid.

6 It occurred to me when I was thirteen and wearing white gloves and Mary Janes and going to dancing school, that no one should have to dance backward all their lives.

Speech   *1973*

7 The Equal Rights Amendment is designed to establish in our Constitution the clear moral value judgment that all Americans, women and men, stand equal under the law. . . . It will give woman's role in the home new status, recognizing that the homemaker's role in a marriage has economic value. . . . Critics say ERA will open the draft to women. At the moment, the United States has an oversubscribed volunteer army, many of whom are women. ERA means that women who serve will get equal benefits.

Quoted in "Forum," *Ladies' Home
Journal   August, 1975*

1176. Diane B. Schulder
(1937–   )

1 Law is a reflection and a source of prejudice. It both enforces and suggests forms of bias.

"Does the Law Oppress Women?,"
Sisterhood Is Powerful,
Robin Morgan, ed.   *1970*

2 Legislation and case law still exist in some parts of the United States permitting the "passion shooting" by a husband of a wife; the reverse, of course, is known as homicide.

Ibid.

3 . . . prejudice (the mythology of class oppression) is enshrined in laws. Laws lead to enforcement of practices. Practices reinforce and lead to prejudice. The cycle continues. . . .

Ibid.

1177. Diane Wakoski
(1937–   )

1   thinking how cage life drove an animal into mazes of
    himself,
his cage mates chosen for him his life circumscribed
    and focused
on eating, his play watched by it-doesn't-matter-whom,
    just
watched, always watched.

The Birds of Paradise Being Very
Plain Birds," St. 5, The East Side
Scene, Allen De Loach, ed.   1968

2   It happens all the time, I told her,
some of us have bad vision, are crippled, have defects,
    and
our reality is a different one, not the
correct and ascertainable one,
and sometimes it makes us dotty and lonely
but also it makes us poets.

Ibid., St. 9

3 My face
that my friends tell me is so full of character;
my face
I have hated for so many years;
my face
I have made an angry contract to live with
though no one could love it.

"I Have Had to Learn to Live with
My Face," St. 2, The Motorcycle
Betrayal Poems   1971

4 I wonder how we learn to live
   with our faces?
   They must hide so much pain,
   so many deep trenches of blood,
   so much that would terrorize and drive others away, if
      they
   could see it. The struggle to control it
   articulates the face

Ibid., St. 12

1178. Renata Adler
(1938–   )

1 I . . . doubt that film can ever argue effectively
   against its own material: that a genuine antiwar film,
   say, can be made on the basis of even the ugliest battle
   scenes. . . . No matter what filmmakers intend, film
   always argues yes. People have been modeling their
   lives after films for years, but the medium is somehow
   unsuited to moral lessons, cautionary tales or polemics
   of any kind. If you want to make a pacifist film, you
   must make an exemplary film about peaceful men.

"The Movies Make Heroes of Them
All" (January 7, 1968),
A Year in the Dark   1969

2 Everyone dances, and sings and draws and acts, or
   knows to a degree what these involve. It is precisely
   because so few people make films that they belong
   more or less equally to everyone—are put arbitrarily
   before people for equal comment, within limitations of
   taste and experience, like a passing day.

Ibid., "Time, Old Movies, and
Exhausting Life" (August 4, 1968)

3 Though films become more daring sexually, they are
   probably less sexy than they ever were. There haven't
   been any convincing love scenes or romances in the
   movies in a while. (Nobody even seems to neck in
   theaters any more.) . . . When the mechanics and
   sadism quotients go up, the movie love interest goes
   dead, and the film just lies there, giving a certain
   amount of offense.

Ibid., "Temper, Misogyny, and
Couples in Theaters" (October 13, 1968)

419

4 The writer has a grudge against society, which he documents with accounts of unsatisfying sex, unrealized ambition, unmitigated loneliness, and a sense of local and global distress. The square, overpopulation, the bourgeois, the bomb and the cocktail party are variously identified as sources of the grudge. There follows a little obscenity here, a dash of philosophy there, considerable whining overall, and a modern satirical novel is born.

"Salt into Old Scars" (June 22, 1963),
Toward a Radical Middle 1971

5 When a society becomes so benevolent that there can be no legitimate confusion between personal insufficiencies and social grievances, the armed rebel has simply lost his cause to the good citizen, and his arms to the sick man of violence, in exile or in crime.

Ibid., "Sartre, Saint Genet, and the
Bureaucrat" (November 9, 1963)

6 If anything has characterized the [peace] movement, from its beginning and in all its parts, it has been a spirit of decentralization, local autonomy, personal choice, and freedom from dogma.

Ibid., "Early Radicalism: The Price
of Peace Is Confusion"
(December 1, 1965)

7 . . . nothing defines the quality of life in a community more clearly than people who regard themselves, or whom the consensus chooses to regard, as mentally unwell.

Ibid., "The Thursday Group" (April 15, 1967)

1179. Ti-Grace Atkinson
(1938?–   )

1 Love is the victim's response to the rapist.

Quoted in "Rebellion" by Irma Kurtz,
Sunday Times Magazine (London)
September 14, 1969

1180. Rona Barrett
(1938–   )

1 It's ironic, but until you can free those final monsters within the jungle of yourself, your life, your soul is up for grabs.

Miss Rona: An Autobiography,
Prologue   *1974*

2 . . . the *healthy*, the *strong* individual, is the one who asks for help when he needs it. Whether he's got an abscess on his knee or in his soul.

Ibid., Ch. 15

1181. Vivian Gornick
(1938–   )

1 Behind the "passive" exterior of many women there lies a growing anger over lost energies and confused lives, an anger so sharp in its fury but so diffuse in its focus that one can only describe it as the price society must pay for creating a patriarchal system in the first place, and for now refusing to let it go. And make no mistake, it is not letting go.

"Why Women Fear Success,"
The First Ms. Reader,
Francine Klagsbrun, ed.   *1972*

2 She takes daily walks on the land that was once the bottom of the sea, marking and classifying, sifting through her thoughts the meaning of the jagged edges of discontent that have begun to make inroads anew inside her.

"Stillness at the Center," *Ms.*   *October, 1973*

3 There is a desperate lack of variety to the poverty here [Egypt], a kind of stupor of simplicity, an aimlessness that covers the people in a thick expressionless haze. . . .

In Search of Ali-Mahmoud   *1973*

4 If the word for London is decency and the word for New York is violence, then, beyond doubt, the word for Cairo is tenderness. Tenderness is what pervades the air here.   Ibid., Pt. I

5 I lived once in the American desert. The solitude opens up. It becomes an enormous surrounding comfort. But the solitude in the city is a confusing and painful thing.
Ibid., Pt. II

6 Suddenly, I see that the diffused love, which is the deepest lesson of the East, has within it the seeds of nonpossessive love. And with a surprised weariness I remember my own country. For God knows, those clutched, nonseparating marriages of the West don't indicate *love*.
Ibid., Pt. IV

1182. Barbara Howar
(1938?–)

1 . . . the cocktail party remains a vital Washington institution, the official intelligence system.
Laughing All the Way, Ch. 5   1973

2 In our long history of shooting politicians . . . I have come to feel that Washington politicians look upon these events as little more than temporary setbacks in the continuing process of government.   Ibid., Ch. 12

3 Eventually most television stations around the country achieved their minority quota by hiring "twofers," which is a trade expression meaning a "black, female, on-air personality," two television unthinkables, at one salary—a salary, I might add, that generally falls short of the "equal pay for equal work" cliché.
Ibid., Ch. 15

4 Kissinger likes intrigue rather than confrontation. . . . [He] believes all power begins in the White House. It is his firm belief that he and the President know what is best; the rest of us are to be patient and they will announce our destiny.   Ibid., Ch. 16

5 Those complicated people that make Washington the mysterious jungle it is, those famous men and women who to the rest of the world are glamorous and powerful, even ruthless, public figures, have in them a specialness that is inconsistent with the city's official image—a combination of worldly involvement and personal commitment that makes Washington genuine despite its reach for power.   Ibid., Ch. 21

1183. Jane Kramer
(1938?–   )

1 Prophecy today is hardly the romantic business that it used to be. The old tools of the trade, like the sword, the hair shirt, and the long fast in the wilderness, have given way to more contemporary, mundane instruments of doom—the book, the picket and the petition the sit-in . . . at City Hall.

> "The Ranks and Rungs of Mrs. Jacobs' Ladder," *Off Washington Square*   1963

2 Dawia maintained that the Europeans were . . . favored by Allah because Allah liked automobiles and was hoping that the Europeans would bring their cars to Heaven with them. Omar, however, said no, that Allah loved the Europeans because the Europeans always got to their appointments on time.

> *Honor to the Bride*, Pt. I   1973

3 "It is a burden to have daughters," Dawia said, sighing. "My husband looks at Jmaa now and he says, 'What can I expect from her? More of the same problems I have suffered with the first two.' "

"He has a point," Musa remarked. "Having daughters is not profitable."

> Ibid., Pt. II

1184. Mary Jane Moffat
(1938?–   )

1 Why do women keep diaries? . . . The form has been an important outlet for women partly because it is an analogue to their lives: emotional, fragmentary, interrupted, modest, not to be taken seriously, private, restricted, daily, trivial, formless, concerned with self, as endless as their tasks.

> *Revelations: Diaries of Women*, with Charlotte Painter, Foreword   1974

1185. Joyce Carol Oates
(1938–   )

1 "Personal relationships start off so cleanly but then become too involved."

"Norman and the Killer," *Upon the
Sweeping Flood and Other Stories*   1965

2 "Nothing can be right and balanced again until justice is won—the injured party has to have justice. Do you understand that? Nothing can be right, for years, for lifetimes, until that first crime is punished. Or else we'd all be animals."

Ibid.

3 Anger always excited and pleased them; it was sacred.
A Garden of Earthly Delights,
Pt. I, Ch. 1   1967

4 The only trouble was that here an odor of harsh antiseptic was everywhere, floating everywhere . . . it seemed to be eating its way into your lungs to get you clean even if it killed you.

Ibid., Ch. 8

5 She felt like a plant of some kind, like a flower on a stalk that only looked slender but was really tough, tough as steel, like the flowers in fields that could be blown down flat by the wind but yet rose again slowly coming back to life.

Ibid., Pt. II, Ch. 6

6 Whoever was stupid was beneath worry or thought; you did not have to figure them out. This eliminated hundreds of people. In this life you had time only for a certain amount of thinking, and there was no need to waste any of it on people who were not threatening.

Ibid., Pt. III, Ch. 7

7 Swan smiled. He did not know what his smile meant: just the reaction of witnessing rituals, ceremonies that have been repeated many times.

Ibid., Ch. 9

8 This is a work of history in fictional form—that is, in personal perspective, which is the only kind of history that exists.   *Them*, Author's Note   1969

9 Shakily he thought of the future: that night, and the next day, and the real future. The future was important, not the present. These minutes spent around the supper table, these ten or fifteen minutes he had to get through, were not important except as they were part of a process leading to the future, a future that would be a good surprise, he felt sure.

Ibid., Pt. I, Ch. 9

10 She ransacked her mind but there was nothing in it.

Ibid., Ch. 15

11 "I admit that I have no fixed income like your friend, and I have no desire for it," he said to Faye. "I like adventure. I don't dare prophesy where my liking for adventure will lead."

Ibid., Pt. II, Ch. 2

12 ". . . women don't understand these things. They only understand money when they can see it. They're very crude essentially. They don't understand where money comes from or what it means or how a man can be worth money though he hasn't any at the moment. But a man understands all that."   *Ibid.*

13 She would have a baby with her husband, to make up for the absence of love, to locate love, to fix herself in a certain place, but she would not really love him.

Ibid., Pt. III, Ch. 1

14 . . . it is a fever, this racing, this constant thought.
"What Is the Connection Between Men and Women?," *Mademoiselle February, 1970*

15 Old women snore violently. They are like bodies into which bizarre animals have crept at night; the animals are vicious, bawdy, noisy. How they snore! There is no shame to their snoring. Old women turn into old men.

Ibid.

16 In love there are two things: bodies and words.

Ibid.

17 In the catatonic state small wars are waged in the body, acted out, memorized, rehearsed, unleashed, begun again, repeated.   *Ibid.*

18 Her mind churns so that she can't hear, she can't think.

Ibid.

19 He hated her for the selfishness of her death and for her having eclipsed him forever, obliterated him as if she had smashed an insect under her shoe.

"The Wheel of Love," (1967), *The Wheel of Love and Other Stories* 1970

20 "Loneliness is dangerous. It's bad for you to be alone, to be lonely, because if aloneness does not lead to God, it leads to the devil. It leads to the self."

Ibid., "Shame" (1968)

21 Night comes to the desert all at once, as if someone turned off a light.

Ibid., "Interior Monologue" (1969)

22 When a marriage ends, who is left to understand it?

Ibid., "Unmailed, Unwritten Letters" (1969)

23 Minutes pass in silence, mysteriously. It is those few minutes that pass after we make love that are most mysterious to me, uncanny.

Ibid.

24 . . . the necessity for patience had aged her magically; she was content in her age.

Ibid., "Bodies" (1970)

25 The ringing of a telephone is always louder in an empty house.

Ibid., "I Was in Love" (1970)

26 Before falling in love, I was defined. Now I am undefined, weeds are growing between my ribs.

Ibid.

27 "We're off! Another week come and gone! Month in, month out! Even, odd—black, white—life, death—father, son. The cycles continue!"

Ibid., "Wild Saturday" (1970)

28 Premeditated crime: the longer the meditating, the dreaming, the more triumphant the execution!

Do with Me What You Will, Pt. I, Ch. 1 1970

29 "I don't think that California is a healthy place. . . . Things disintegrate there."

Ibid., Ch. 8

30 The plaque at the front of the courtroom, high on the wall, was permanent and yet its words were new each time Jack read them, read them half against his will, his eyes moving restlessly forward and up to them while testimony droned on: *Conscience Speaks the Truth.*

Ibid., Pt. II, Ch. 6

31 The worst cynicism: a belief in luck.

Ibid., Ch. 15

32 . . . he believed in the justice of his using any legal methods he could improvise to force the other side into compromise or into dismissals of charges, or to lead a jury into the verdict he wanted. Why not? He was a defense lawyer, not a judge or a juror or a policeman or a legislator or a theoretician or an anarchist or a murderer.

Ibid.

33 . . . like all virtuous people he imagines he must speak the truth. . . .

Ibid.

34 Light love draws us up into the galaxy . . . but heavy love drags us down into the mud of self and the great mud of wars. . . . Down in the mud we fight one another, compete from birth till death; in the galaxy we are free of that tragic struggle.

Ibid., Ch. 10

35 You're such a virgin, a sweet perpetual virgin. You're so perfect that you turn other people hard as ice. . . .

Ibid., Ch. 15

36 Nothing is accidental in the universe—this is one of my Laws of Physics—except the entire universe itself, which is Pure Accident, pure divinity.

Ibid., "The Summing Up: Meredith Dawe"

37 What relationship had a dagger to the human hand, that it must be invented, imagined out of the shape of the hand?—where did the sharpness come from, was it from the soul and its unstoppable imaginings?—because the hand in itself was so defenseless, so vulnerable in its flesh.

Ibid., "Elena"

427

1186. Diane Ravitch
(1938–   )

1 The ladder was there, "from the gutter to the university," and for those stalwart enough to ascend it, the schools were a boon and a path out of poverty.

The Great School Wars   *1974*

1187. Maria Isabel Barreno
(1939–   )

1 . . . all friendship between women has a uterine air about it, the air of a slow, bloody, cruel, incomplete exchange, of an original situation being repeated all over again.

New Portuguese Letters, with Maria
Fatima Velho da Costa and Maria
Teresa Horta   *1972*

2 The time of discipline began. Each of us the pupil of whichever one of us could best teach what each of us needed to learn.

Ibid.

3 . . . we are still the property of men, the spoils today of warriors who pretend to be our comrades in the struggle, but who merely seek to mount us. . . .

Ibid.

4 One lives and endures one's life with others, within matrices, but it is only alone, truly alone that one bursts apart, springs forth.   Ibid.

5 Let no one tell me that silence gives consent, because whoever is silent dissents.   Ibid.

1188. Judy Chicago
(1939–   )

1 We have made a space to house our spirit, to give form to our dreams. . . .

"Let Sisterhood Be Powerful,"
Womanspace   *February/March, 1973*

2 . . . I suddenly knew that I was alone forever, that I could lose the people I loved any time, any moment, and that the only thing I had in this life was myself.

> *Through the Flower: My Struggle as a Woman Artist*, Ch. 1   1975

3 I did not understand that wanting doesn't always lead to action.

> Ibid., Ch. 4

4 The acceptance of women as authority figures or as role models is an important step in female education. . . . It is this process of identification, respect, and then self-respect that promotes growth.

> Ibid., Ch. 5

5 We were wedded together on the basis of mutual work and goals.

> Ibid., Ch. 9

1189. Judy Collins
(1939–)

1 I look in the mirror through the eyes of the child that was me.

> "Secret Gardens of the Heart"   1972

2 Secret gardens of the heart where the old stay young forever. . . .

> Ibid.

1190. Yaël Dayan
(1939–)

1 Within me I would be the mistress; outside, if necessary, a slave. I would knit my world together, make contact with the outside world, write the right kind of letters, and be as I thought appropriate to different people.

> *New Face in the Mirror*   1959

2 High society is, of course, mainly habit. . . .   Ibid.

3 My father, I remembered, had no fears at all. In that he differed greatly from me. But he could not be called a courageous man because he had no fears to overcome.

> Ibid.

4 He picked up some earth and poured it into the boy's palm. "Grasp it, feel it, taste it. There is your God. If you want to pray, boy, pray to the sky to bring rain to our land and not virtue to your souls."

Envy the Frightened, Ch. 4   *1960*

5 It is very difficult to analyze the deed, to know how much of it was a result of youthful stupidity, what part the physical attraction of the mountain and snow played in it, what part looking for danger. Or perhaps it was an unconscious will to encounter fear, an element within him stronger than himself.   *Ibid.*, Ch. 16

6 It wasn't a battle really, as it wasn't a war. Nor was it a game, not when you heard the poisonous shrieking of the bullets—confused, scattered, searching above your heads—there was no feeling of deep revenge or hatred. It was almost as quiet as a day's work, only moments seemed eternal and seconds endless. . . . Not a war, or a battle, but a fight.   *Ibid.*, Ch. 18

7   "Do you think he is a brave man?" . . .
   "Either too much of a coward to face it—or the bravest, facing it in solitude, not sharing the fear. Perhaps we'll never find out."

Death Had Two Sons, Ch. 1   *1967*

8 She was friendless and yet a friend to others and the same intensity with which she ignored the future marked her passionate attitude to the past.

Ibid., Ch. 8

9 How long it takes us to gather the component parts of our memory—the problems, self-appraisals, the self-analysis, our little daily dilemmas, petty quests for comfort. And how quickly they all can disappear.

Israel Journal: June, 1967   *1967*

10 People in politics are not very kind to each other.

Quoted in the *Los Angeles Times*
March 7, 1974

1191. Shelagh Delaney
(1939–   )

1 HELEN. The only consolation I can find in your immediate presence is your ultimate absence.

A Taste of Honey, Act. I, Sc. 1   *1959*

2 BOY. Women never have young minds. They are born three thousand years old.

Ibid., Sc. 2

3 JO. In this country [England] there are only two seasons, winter and winter.

Ibid.

4 HELEN. Why don't you learn from my mistakes? It takes half your life to learn from your own.

Ibid.

5 JO. We don't ask for life, we have it thrust upon us.

Ibid., Act II, Sc. 2

6 GEOF. You need somebody to love you while you're looking for someone to love.

Ibid.

7 I am here and I am safe and I am sick of it.

"Sweetly Sings the Donkey," *Sweetly Sings the Donkey* 1963

8 "He was very ugly but people can't help the faces they're born with."

Ibid.

9 According to her, only a revolution will ever bring true democracy to this country and the sooner revolution comes (she said) the better and even though hundreds of innocents will be slaughtered they will die in a good cause and men must be willing to sacrifice themselves. But that depends I suppose on which men you're thinking of. . . .

Ibid.

10 He didn't play with his food anymore till it got cold; instead, down it went like fuel into a furnace keeping the ovens hot, and the energy at boiling point, as Tom hurtled through his life catching up with himself at last.

Ibid., "Tom Riley"

11 We teach you the pleasure of physical exercise—the team-spirit of games, too, for when you leave school finally you will find that life is a game, sometimes serious, sometimes fun, but a game that must be played with true team-spirit—there is no room for the outsider in life.

Ibid., "The Teacher"

12 "There aren't enough secrets to go round anymore. Some spies are having to invent secrets in order to earn a living. . . . I can't help wondering what will happen when redundant spies join the ranks of the unemployed."

Ibid., "My Uncle, the Spy"

13 . . . Poles seem to be as much condemned to a diet of caviar, vodka and the Polka as the English are to rare old port and pheasant.

Ibid., "Vodka and Small Pieces of Gold"

1192. Colette Dowling
(1939?–   )

1 . . . the fifties . . . was a time of fevered fantasies—dreams of freedom and adulthood.

"A Woman Sounds Off on Those
Sexy Magazines," *Redbook*
April, 1974

2 I tell you, the great divide is still with us, the awful split, the Us and Them. Like a rubber band tautened to the snapping point, the polarization of the sexes continues, because we lack the courage to face our likenesses and admit to our real need.   Ibid.

1193. Margaret Drabble
(1939–   )

1 It appalled him, the complacency with which such friends would describe the advantages of living in a mixed area. As though they licensed seedy old ladies and black men to walk their streets, teaching their children of poverty and despair, as their pet hamsters and guinea pigs taught them of sex and death.

The Needle's Eye, Pt. I   *1972*

2 . . . affluence was, quite simply, a question of texture. . . . The threadbare carpets of infancy, the coconut matting, the ill-laid linoleum, the utility furniture, the curious upholstery . . . had all spoken of a life too near the bones of subsistence, too little padded, too severely worn.   Ibid.

3 Rose . . . had the sense that there was something unpleasant that she had promised herself that she would
do. While she gave the children their breakfast and
drank a cup of tea, she tried to work out what it could
be—unearthing accidentally, as she did so, a whole
heaped cupboard-full of nasty obligations, such as shoe-
buying and glazier-visiting, and of nagging guilts, about
people she should have rung back and hadn't, people
she should have written to and hadn't, birthday presents
unbought and promises unfulfilled.

Ibid.

4 . . . she used to pray . . . and she still prayed, occasionally, not incessantly as she had done through childhood, but every now and then a natural or man-made
calamity would push her imperiously to her knees, a
massacre, an earthquake, a drowning, and she would
implore justice, mercy, intercession, explanation, not
praying any more for herself, as she had once so fu-
tilely done . . . wondering even as she knelt whether
there were any use in such genuflections, and yet
pushed down as certainly as if a hand had descended
on her head to thrust her from above, crushing her hair
and weighing on her skull.

Ibid., Pt. II

5 How easy it was to underestimate what had been endured.

Ibid.

6 . . . if I'd known twenty years ago. . . . A pity,
really, that one couldn't have had that particular thrill
then—the thrill of knowing. It wasn't worth much now.
"A Success Story," _Spare Rib_
Magazine 1972

7 People like admiration more than anything. Whatever
can one do about it?

Ibid.

8 We seek a utopia in the past, a possible if not ideal
society. We seek golden worlds from which we are ban-
ished, they recede infinitely, for there never was a
golden world, there was never anything but toil and
subsistence, cruelty and dullness.

The Realms of Gold 1975

9 "Much have I travelled in the realms of gold."

Ibid.

10 "To hear him talk of tradition and the individual talent was to enter into a world where old labels had meanings."

Ibid.

11 She taught herself, over the years, to see his death as a healing of some kind, the end of a long illness, a sacrifice. Taken from them for their better health.

Ibid.

12 . . . the human mind can bear planty of reality but not too much unintermittent gloom.

Ibid.

13 As a geologist, he took a long view of time: even longer than Frances Wingate, archaeologist, and very much longer than Karel Schmidt, historian.   Ibid.

1194. Roxanne Dunbar
(1939–   )

1 Man, in conquering nature, conquered the female, who had worked with nature, not against it, to produce food and to reproduce the human race.

"Feminine Liberation as the Basis for Social Revolution," *Sisterhood Is Powerful*, Robin Morgan, ed.   *1970*

2 We live under an international caste system, at the top of which is the Western white male ruling class, and at the very bottom of which is the female of the nonwhite colonized world.   Ibid.

3 In reality, the family has fallen apart. Nearly half of all marriages end in divorce, and the family unit is a decadent, energy-absorbing, destructive, wasteful institution for everyone except the ruling class for which the institution was created.   Ibid.

1195. Terry Garthwaite
(1939–   )

1 from bessie to bebe to billie to boz
there's a lot more power than the wizard of oz

"Rock and Roller"   *1975*

1196. Joan Goulianos
(1939–   )

1 . . . these . . . women . . . wrote in a world which
was controlled by men, a world in which women's revelations, if they were anything but conventional, might
not be welcomed, might not be recognized, and they
wrote nevertheless.

By a Woman Writt, Introduction
(February, 1972)   *1973*

2 But, overall, it was men who were the critics, the publishers, the professors, the sources of support. It was
men who had the power to praise women's works, to
bring them to public attention, or to ridicule them, to
doom them . . . to obscurity.

Ibid.

1197. Germaine Greer
(1939–   )

1 The consequences of militancy do not disappear when
the need for militancy is over. Freedom is fragile and
must be protected. To sacrifice it, even as a temporary
measure, is to betray it.

The Female Eunuch,
Introduction   *1971*

2 If marriage and family depend upon the castration of
women let them change or disappear.

Ibid., "The Psychological Sell"

3 What is the arms race and the cold war but the continuation of male competitiveness and aggression into the
inhuman sphere of computer-run institutions? If
women are to cease producing cannon fodder for the
final holocaust they must rescue men from the perversi-
ties of their own polarization.

Ibid.

4 Womanpower means the self-determination of women,
and that means that all the baggage of paternalistic society will have to be thrown overboard.

Ibid., "Womanpower"

5 Every time a man unburdens his heart to a stranger he reaffirms the love that unites humanity.

Ibid., "The Ideal"

6 The only causes of regret are laziness, outbursts of temper, hurting others, prejudice, jealousy and envy.

Ibid.

7 Our life-style contains more *Thanatos* than *Eros*, for egotism, exploitation, deception, obsession and addiction have more place in us than eroticism, joy, generosity and spontaneity.

Ibid.

8 As soon as we find ourselves working at being indispensable, rigging up a pattern of vulnerability in our loved ones, we ought to know that our love has taken the socially sanctioned form of egotism.

Ibid., "Egotism"

9 Love, love, love—all the wretched cant of it, masking egotism, lust, masochism, fantasy under a mythology of sentimental postures.

Ibid., "Obsession"

10 Shared but secret behavior will cement any group into a conspiracy. . . . Changing partners is such a thoroughly unspontaneous activity, so divorced from the vagaries of genuine sexual desire—no more than a variant on the square dance. In such a transaction sex is the sufferer: passion becomes lechery.

Ibid., "Family"

11 There is no such thing as security. There never has been.

Ibid., "Security"

12 Although security is not in the nature of things, we invent strategies for outwitting fortune, and call them after their guiding deity—insurance, assurance, social security.

Ibid.

13 Security is when everything is settled, when nothing can happen to you; security is the denial of life. Human beings are better equipped to cope with disaster and hardship than they are with unvarying security, but as long as security is the highest value in a community they can have little opportunity to decide this for themselves.

Ibid.

14 Loneliness is never more cruel than when it is felt in close propinquity with someone who has ceased to communicate.

> Ibid.

15 Women have very little idea of how much men hate them.

> Ibid., "Loathing and Disgust"

1198. Maria Teresa Horta
(1939–   )

Co-author with Maria Isabel Barreno and Maria Fatima Velho da Costa. See 1187: 1–5.

1199. Barbara Kolb
(1939–   )

1 . . . composing a piece of music is very feminine. It is sensitive, emotional, contemplative. By comparison, doing housework is positively masculine.

> Quoted in "A Matter of Art, Not Sex,"
> *Time*   November 10, 1975

1200. Letty Cottin Pogrebin
(1939–   )

1 . . . lifestyles and sex roles are passed from parents to children as inexorably as blue eyes or small feet.

> "Down with Sexist Upbringing,"
> *The First Ms. Reader*, Francine
> Klagsbrun, ed.   *1972*

2 In school books, the Dick and Jane syndrome reinforced our emerging attitudes. The arithmetic books posed appropriate conundrums: "Ann has three pies . . . Dan has three rockets. . . ." We read the nuances between the lines: Ann keeps her eye on the oven; Dan sets his sights on the moon.   Ibid.

3 Boys don't make passes at female smart-asses.   Ibid.

4 . . . children's liberation is the next item on our civil rights shopping list.   Ibid.

1201. Joan Rivers
(1939–   )

1 The psychic scars caused by believing that you are ugly leave a permanent mark on your personality.

Quoted in "An Ugly Duckling Complex" by Lydia Lane, *Los Angeles Times*   May 10, 1974

2 There is not one female comic who was beautiful as a little girl.

Ibid.

3 Diets, like clothes, should be tailored to you.

Ibid.

1202. Susan Sherman
(1939–   )

1 Analysis. Cross-reference analysis. The age of analysis. Psychological, philosophical, poetic analysis. Not the event, but the picturing of the event.

"The Fourth Wall," St. 2, *El Corno Emplumado*   1966

1203. Joan Silver
(1939?–   )

1 Standing erect, like overgrown bookends on either side of Mr. MacAfee's desk, were two Air Force officers.

Limbo, Ch. 1, with Linda Gottlieb   1972

2 Just as war bound together the men under fire, Mary Kaye thought, it united the women left behind back home.

Ibid., Ch. 5

3 The mother of an eighteen-year-old boy who had had to secure his mother's consent for enlisting in the Army, she now cried at the slightest provocation. "How could I tell him not to go?" she once asked Fay Clausen, the tears brimming in her eyes. "He always

loved guns—from the time he was just a little boy he would play with toy guns, BB guns—you know, pretended he was in the marines and things. I once got him that big illustrated history of the Second World War—it cost seventeen dollars—from American Heritage, and he read it over and over again."

Ibid., Ch. 8

4 Red Fortner felt an unaccustomed clutch in his throat. Those savages over there! We ought to bomb the hell out of them, blast them from the face of the earth! He wished some of his dove colleagues at the office could hear this girl, so young, so pretty, so brave, without even a father for her child! They'd change their tune all right.

Ibid., Ch. 22

1204. Naomi Weisstein
(1939–   )

1 . . . there isn't the tiniest shred of evidence that . . . fantasies of servitude and childish dependence have anything to do with woman's true potential. . . .

Address, " 'Kinder, Kuche, Kirche' as Scientific Law: Psychology Constructs the Female," American Studies Association, California *October 26, 1968*

2 To summarize: the first reason for psychology's failure to understand what people are and how they act is that clinicians and psychiatrists, who are generally the theoreticians on these matters, have essentially made up myths without any evidence to support these myths; the second reason for psychology's failure is that personality theory has looked for inner traits when it should have been looking at social context.

Ibid.

3 . . . in order to understand why people do what they do, and certainly in order to change what people do, psychologists must turn away from the theory of the causal nature of the inner dynamic and look at the social context within which individuals live. Ibid.

4 Until psychologists realize that it is they who are limiting discovery of human potential . . . by their as-

sumption that people move in a context-free ether, with only their innate dispositions and their individual traits determining what they will do, then psychology will have nothing of substance to offer in this task.

Ibid.

5 Psychology has nothing to say about what women are really like, what they need and what they want, for the simple reason that psychology does not know. Yet psychologists will hold forth endlessly on the true nature of woman, with dismaying enthusiasm and disquieting certitude.

"Woman as Nigger," *Psychology Today*   *October, 1969*

6 The problem with insight, sensitivity and intuition is that they tend to confirm our biases. At one time people were convinced of their ability to identify witches. All it required was sensitivity to the workings of the devil. Clinical experience is not the same thing as empirical evidence.

Ibid.

7 . . . a typical minority-group sterotype—woman as nigger—if she knows her place (home), she is really a quite lovable, loving creature, happy and childlike.

Ibid.

8 Except for their genitals, I don't know what immutable differences exist between men and women. Perhaps there are some other unchangeable differences; probably there are a number of irrelevant differences. But it is clear that until social expectations for men and women are equal, until we provide equal respect for both sexes, answers to this question will simply reflect our prejudices.

Ibid.

9 Why have they been telling us women lately that we have no sense of humor—when we are always laughing? . . . And when we're not laughing, we're smiling.

Introduction to *All She Needs* by Ellen Levine   *1973*

10 Humor as a weapon in the social arsenal constructed to maintain caste, class, race, and sex inequalities is a very common thing.

Ibid.

1205. Louise Bernikow
(1940–   )

1 Pep is what happened in American history before *vi-gah,* but it only applied to females. Pep was cheerfulness. It mysteriously resided in the Ipana smile.
> "Confessions of an Ex-Cheerleader,"
> *Ms.*   October, 1973

2 Everytime I say "sure" when I mean "no," every time I smile brightly when I'm exploding with rage, every time I imagine my man's achievement is my own, I know the cheerleader never really died. I feel her shaking her ass inside me and I hear her breathless, girlish voice mutter "T-E-A-M, Yea, Team."
> Ibid.

3 The question arises as to whether it is possible *not* to live in the world of men and still to live in the world. The answer arises nearly as quickly that this can only happen if men are not thought of as "the world."
> *The World Split Open*, Introduction   1974

1206. Isabel do Carmo
(1940–   )

1 The movement [in Spain] must be accompanied by force. . . . There must be an armed insurrection.
> Quoted in *Time*   October 30, 1975

2 There can be no halfway solutions, no half measures. That won't work. We must have either pure socialism or we will go back to fascism.   Ibid.

3 In our party, being a woman is no problem. After all, it is a revolutionary party.   Ibid.

1207. Phyllis Chesler
(1940–   )

1 At this moment in history only women can (if they will) support the entry or re-entry of women into the human race.   *Women and Madness*   1972

2 There is a double standard of mental health—one for men, another for women—existing among most clinicians. . . . For a woman to be healthy, she must "adjust" to and accept the behavioral norms for her sex—passivity, acquiescence, self-sacrifice, and lack of ambition—even though these kinds of "loser" behaviors are generally regarded as socially undesirable (i.e., nonmasculine).

                                                                    Ibid.

3 While [women] live longer than ever before, and longer than men, there is less and less use for them in the only place they have been given—within the family. Many newly useless women are emerging more publicly and visibly into insanity and institutions.

                                                                    Ibid.

4 In addition, asylum life resembles traditional family treatment of the female adolescent in its official imposition of celibacy and its institutional responses to sexuality and aggression—fear, scorn, and punishment.

                                                                    Ibid.

1208. Frances Fitzgerald
(1940–   )

1 By intervening in the Vietnamese struggle the United States was attempting to fit its global strategies into a world of hillocks and hamlets, to reduce its majestic concerns for the containment of Communism and the security of the Free World to a dimension where governments rose and fell as a result of arguments between two colonels' wives.

             Fire in the Lake, Pt. I, Ch. 1   *1972*

2 Americans see history as a straight line and themselves standing at the cutting edge of it as representatives for all mankind. They believe in the future as if it were a religion; they believe that there is nothing they cannot accomplish, that solutions wait somewhere for all problems, like brides.   Ibid.

3 In a sense, the design of the Confucian world resembled that of a Japanese garden where every rock, opaque and indifferent in itself, takes on significance from its relation to the surrounding objects.   Ibid.

4 For most Americans, Southeast Asia came to look like the most complicated place in the world. And naturally enough, for the American official effort to fit the new evidence into the old official assumptions was something like the effort of the seventeenth-century astronomers to fit their observations of the planets into the Ptolemaic theory of the universe.

Ibid., Ch. 2

5 The Americans began by underestimating the Vietnamese guerrillas, but in the end they made them larger than life. During the invasion of Cambodia in 1970, American officials spoke of plans to capture the enemy's command headquarters for the south as if there existed a reverse Pentagon in the jungle. . . Paradoxically, the exaggeration diminished them, for in the dimension of mythology all things are fabulous and unaccountable. By turning their enemy into a mirror image of themselves, the Americans obscured the nature of the Vietnamese accomplishment.

Ibid., Ch. 4

6 Quite consciously, Ho Chi Minh forswore the grand patriarchal tradition of the Confucian emperors. Consciously he created an "image" of himself as "Uncle Ho"—the gentle, bachelor relative who has only disinterested affection for the children who are *not* his own sons. As a warrior and a politician he acted ruthlessly upon occasion, but in public and as head of state he took pains to promote that family feeling which Vietnamese have often had for their leaders, and which he felt was the proper relationship between the people and their government.

Ibid.

7 . . . [Lyndon B.] Johnson condemned his officials who worked on Vietnam to the excruciating mental task of holding reality and the official version of reality together as they moved farther and farther apart.

Ibid., Pt. II, Ch. 13

8 . . . the Americans were once again embarked upon a heroic and (for themselves) almost painless conquest of an inferior race. . . . [They] were white men in Asia, and they could not conceive that they might fail in their enterprise, could not conceive that they could be morally wrong.

Ibid.

9 . . . the American government did not want to face the consequences of peace. It was, after all, one thing to wish for an end to the war and quite another to confront the issues upon which the war had begun. President Johnson had wanted to end the war; so, too, had President Kennedy. But to end the war and not to lose it: the distinction was crucial, and particularly crucial after all the American lives that had been spent and all the political rhetoric expended.

Ibid., Pt. III, Ch. 17

10 Personally, socially, politically, the disorder of the cities is a highly unstable condition—a vacuum that craves the oxygen of organized society. The Americans might force the Vietnamese to accept the disorder for years, but behind the dam of American troops and American money the pressure is building towards one of those sudden historical shifts when "individualism" and its attendant corruption gives way to the discipline of the revolutionary community.

Ibid.

1209. Judy Grahn
(1940–   )

1 a woman is talking to death. . . .
   "A Woman Is Talking to Death" *1974*

2 . . . I looked into the mirror
and nobody was there to testify.

Ibid.

1210. Joan Haggerty
(1940–   )

1 It was the novelty of the attraction that captivated her as much as the woman herself.

   Daughters of the Moon *1971*

2 Afterwards, you know, afterwards, I often feel like being fucked by a man too. . . . You *tune* me, d'you see, and then I want a man to counter me, but we together, we just keep traveling to strung out space. We can't comfort each other.

Ibid.

1211. Molly Haskell
(1940–   )

1 One of the definitions of the loss of innocence is perhaps the fragmenting of that united self—a split that is
different, and emblematic, not only for each sex, but
also for each era.

From Reverence to Rape   1973

2 . . . the propaganda arm of the American Dream machine, Hollywood. . . .

Ibid.

3 If there has been a falling off in feminine eroticism on
the screen, it is from the *loss* of humor, or that aspect
of humor that gives distance and perspective, rather
than from an excess of it.

Ibid.

4 But one of the attributes of love, like art, is to bring
harmony and order out of chaos, to introduce meaning
and affect where before there was none, to give
rhythmic variations, highs and lows to a landscape that
was previously flat.

Ibid.

5 . . . Chaplin and Keaton developed wit and ingenuity
the way other men develop muscles.

Ibid.

6 The mammary fixation is the most infantile—and most
American—of the sex fetishes. . . .

Ibid.

7 Our sexual emancipators and evangelists sometimes
miss half of the truth: that if puritanism is the source of
our greatest hypocrisies and most crippling illusions it
is, as the primal anxiety whose therapy is civilization
itself, the source of much, perhaps most, of our
achievement.   Ibid.

8 There have been very few heroines in literature who
defined their lives morally rather than romantically and
likewise but a handful in film. . . .   Ibid.

9 Politics remains the most heavily—and jealously—
masculine area. . . .   Ibid.

445

10 The idea that acting is quintessentially "feminine" carries with it a barely perceptible sneer, a suggestion that it is not the noblest or most dignified of professions. Acting is role-playing, role-playing is lying, and lying is a woman's game.

Ibid.

11 . . . her [Marilyn Monroe's] suicide, as suicides do, casts a retrospective light on her life. Her "ending" gives her a beginning and middle, turns her into a work of art with a message and a meaning.

Ibid.

12 We have ample evidence of the fakery that went into creating the stars' facades, of the misery that went on behind these, and of the tyranny of studio despots who insisted on the image at the expense of the human being underneath. All of which inevitably raises the question whether it is possible to be both a star and a human being. If it isn't, how many would have traded stardom for pale humanity?

Ibid.

1212. Arlie Hochschild
(1940–   )

1 It has become a sad commonplace to associate being old with being alone. We call isolation a punishment for the prisoner, but perhaps a majority of American old people are in some degree isolated or soon will be.

"Communal Living in Old Age," *The Future of the Family,* Louise Kapp Howe, ed.   *1972*

2 . . . the decline of the extended family creates the need for a new social shelter, another pool of friendships, another bond with society apart from family.

Ibid.

1213. Juliet Mitchell
(1940–   )

1 Socialism should properly mean not the abolition of the family, but the diversification of the socially acknowledged relationships which are today forcibly and rigidly

compressed. This would mean a plural . . . range of institutions which matched the free invention and variety of men and women.

"Women—The Longest Revolution,"
New Left Review
November/December, 1966

2 Circumstantial accounts of the future are idealistic and, worse, static.

Ibid.

3 A fixed image of the future is in the worst sense ahistorical. . . .

Ibid.

4 Anatomy may, at its point of hypothetical normality, give us two opposite but equal sexes (with the atrophied sex organs of the other present in each), but Freudian psychoanalytic theory does not.

"On Freud and the Distinction
Between the Sexes," *Women and
Analysis,* Jean Strouse, ed.   1974

5 It seems to me that in Freud's psychoanalytical schema, here, as elsewhere, we have at least the beginnings of an analysis of the way in which a patriarchal society bequeaths its structures to each of us . . . and which, unless patriarchy is demolished, we will pass on willy-nilly to our children and our children's children. Individual experimentation with communes and so forth can do no more than register protest. . . . Present or absent, "the father" always has his place.

Ibid.

1214. Valerie Solanis
(1940–)

1 Life in this society being, at best, an utter bore and no aspect of society being at all relevant to women, there remains to civic-minded, responsible, thrill-seeking females only to overthrow the government, eliminate the money system, institute complete automation and destroy the male sex.

SCUM Manifesto*   *1967–1968*

2 Dropping out gives control to those few who don't drop out; dropping out is exactly what the establishment

* SCUM is an acronym for Society for Cutting Up Men.

leaders want; it plays into the hands of the enemy; it strengthens the system instead of undermining it, since it is based entirely on non-participation, passivity, apathy and non-involvement. . . .

Ibid.

3 To be sure he's a "Man," the male must see to it that the female be clearly a "Woman," the opposite of a "Man," that is, the female must act like a faggot.

Ibid.

1215. Maria Fatima Velho da Costa
(1940?–   )

Co-author with Maria Isabel Barreno and Maria Teresa Horta. See 1187: 1–5.

1216. Joan Baez
(1941–   )

1 Only you and I can help the sun rise each coming morning.
If we don't, it may drench itself out in sorrow.
"Farewell Angelina"   1965

2 Jesus, gold and silver—you have no boots on, and you have no helmet or gun—no briefcase.
Powerful Jesus gold and silver with young, hundred-year-old eyes.
You look around and you know you must have failed somewhere.

Ibid.

3 . . . hypothetical questions get hypothetical answers.
Daybreak   1966

4 . . . you don't get to choose how you're going to die. Or when. You can only decide how you're going to live. Now.

Ibid.

5 War was going on long before anybody dreamed up Communism. It's just the latest justification for self-righteousness.

Ibid.

6 There's a consensus out that it's OK to kill when your government decides who to kill. If you kill inside the country you get in trouble. If you kill outside the country, right time, right season, latest enemy, you get a medal.

Ibid.

7 If it's natural to kill why do men have to go into training to learn how?

Ibid.

8 That's all nonviolence is—organized love.

Ibid.

9 "Don't you believe in self-defense?"
"No, that's how the Mafia got started."

Ibid.

10 The point of nonviolence is to build a floor, a strong new floor, beneath which we can no longer sink. A platform which stands a few feet above napalm, torture, exploitation, poison gas, A and H bombs, the works. Give man a decent place to stand.

Ibid.

11 By the middle of the twentieth century men had reached a peak of insanity. They grouped together in primitive nation-states, each nation-state condoning organized murder as the way to deal with international differences. . . .

Ibid.

12 Instead of getting hard ourselves and trying to compete, women should try and give their best qualities to men—bring them softness, teach them how to cry.

Quoted in "Sexism Seen But Not
Heard" by Tracy Hotchner,
Los Angeles Times · *May 26, 1974*

13 And if you're offering me diamonds and rust
I've already paid.

"Diamonds and Rust"   *1975*

14 Unguarded fantasies flying too far
Memories tumbling like sweets from a jar. . . .

"Winds of the Old Days"   *1975*

1217. Bridget Rose Dugdale
(1941–   )

1 For how long you sentence me is of no relevance; I regard it with the contempt it deserves. I am guilty and proudly so if guilty has come to describe one who takes up arms to defend the people of Ireland against the English tyrant.

> Quoted in "Englishwoman Trips on
> Revolutionary Road" by Tom Lambert,
> *Los Angeles Times*   June 26, 1974

1218. Nora Ephron
(1941–   )

1 We have lived through the era when happiness was a warm puppy, and the era when happiness was a dry martini, and now we have come to the era when happiness is "knowing what your uterus looks like."

> "Vaginal Politics" (December, 1972),
> *Crazy Salad*   1975

2 . . . I cannot understand any woman's wanting to be the first woman to do anything. . . . It is a devastating burden and I could not take it, could not be a pioneer, a Symbol of Something Greater.

> Ibid., "Bernice Gera, First Lady
> Umpire" (January, 1973)

3 Consciousness-raising is at the very least supposed to bring about an intimacy, but what it seems instead to bring about are the trappings of intimacy, the illusion of intimacy, a semblance of intimacy.

> Ibid., "On Consciousness-Raising"
> (March, 1973)

4 I am not sure that even with a leader, encounter therapy works; without a leader, it is dangerous.

> Ibid.

5 I am uncomfortable flirting, it requires a great deal of energy and ego, and I manage to do it only a couple of times a year, and not with interview subjects.

> Ibid., "A Star Is Born" (October, 1973)

6 She [Rose Mary Woods] has often said that she was very much impressed by him [Nixon] before she even knew him, because he kept such neat expense accounts.
>   Ibid., "Rose Mary Woods—The Lady or the Tiger?" (March, 1974)

1219. Linda Gottlieb
(1941?–)

Co-author with Joan Silver. See 1203: 1–4.

1220. Barbara Grizzuti Harrison
(1941–)

1 Profoundly ignorant, we were obliged to invent.
>   "Talking Dirty," *Ms.*   October, 1973

2 Fantasies are more than substitutes for unpleasant reality; they are also dress rehearsals, plans. All acts performed in the world begin in the imagination.
>   Ibid.

3 To offer the complexities of life as an excuse for not addressing oneself to the simpler, more manageable (trivial) aspects of daily existence is a perversity often indulged in by artists, husbands, intellectuals—and critics of the Women's Movement.
>   *Unlearning the Lie: Sexism in School*, Introduction   1973

4 True revolutionaries are like God—they create the world in their own image. Our awesome responsibility to ourselves, to our children, and to the future is to create ourselves in the image of goodness, because the future depends on the nobility of our imaginings.
>   Ibid., Ch. 9

5 Women's propensity to share confidences is universal. We confirm our reality by sharing.
>   "Secrets Women Tell Each Other," *McCall's*   August, 1975

6 I refuse to believe that trading recipes is silly. Tuna-fish casserole is at least as real as corporate stock.
>   Ibid.

7 . . . to have a crisis, and act upon it, is one thing. To dwell in perpetual crisis is another.

Ibid.

8 Kindness and intelligence don't always deliver us from the pitfalls and traps: there are always failures of love, of will, of imagination. There is no way to take the danger out of human relationships.

Ibid.

1221. Marie Herbert
(1941–)

1 The Eskimos described everyone other than themselves as Kasdlunas. They called themselves the Inuit—which simply means "the people." For centuries, since they never saw anyone else, they believed they were the only human beings in the world.

The Snow People, Ch. 5   1973

2 Unlike children in other countries, the Eskimos played no games of war. They played with imaginary rifles and harpoons, but these were never directed against people but against the formidable beasts that haunted the vast wastes of their land.

Ibid.

1222. Shirbey Johnson
(1941–)

1 . . . women are carrying a new attitude. They've cast aside the old stereotypes. They don't believe you have to be ugly or have big muscles to play sports.

Quoted in "Women in Sports: The
Movement Is Real," Los Angeles
Times   April 23, 1974

2 As coaches and facilities are slowly upgraded, as girls get interested at earlier ages, they become integrated into the sports system more naturally.

Ibid.

1223. Carole King
(1941–   )

1 When my soul was in the lost-and-found
   You came along to claim it.
   　　　　　　　　"A Natural Woman"　　1967

2 You've got to get up every morning with a smile on
   　　your face
   And show the world all the love in your heart
   Then people gonna treat you better
   You're gonna find, yes you will
   That you're beautiful as you feel.
   　　　　　　　　　　　　"Beautiful"　　1971

3 Doesn't anybody stay in one place any more?
   　　　　　　　　"So Far Away"　　1971

4 My life has been a tapestry of rich and royal hue.
   An everlasting vision of the everchanging view.
   　　　　　　　　　　　"Tapestry"　　1971

5 Winter, spring, summer or fall
   All you have to do is call
   And I'll be there,
   You've got a friend.
   　　　　　　"You've Got a Friend"　　1971

1224. Robin Morgan
(1941–   )

1 . . . it isn't until you begin to fight in your own cause
   that you (a) become really committed to winning, and
   (b) become a genuine ally of other people struggling
   for their freedom.

   　　　　　　　Sisterhood Is Powerful,
   　　　　　　　Introduction　　1970

2 . . . although every organized patriarchal religion
   works overtime to contribute its own brand of myso-
   gyny to the myth of woman-hate, woman-fear, and
   woman-evil, the Roman Catholic Church also carries
   the immense power of very directly affecting women's
   lives everywhere by its stand against birth control and

abortion, and by its use of skillful and wealthy lobbies to prevent legislative change. It is an obscenity—an all-male hierarchy, celibate or not, that presumes to rule on the lives and bodies of millions of women.

> *Ibid.*

3 There's something contagious about demanding freedom.

> *Ibid.*

4 Anthropologists continue to turn up examples which prove that competitive, aggressive, war-like cultures are those in which sexual stereotypes are most polarized, while those social structures allowing for an overlap of roles and functions between men and women (in tasks, childrearing, decision-making, etc.) tend to be collectivist, cooperative and peaceful.

> *Ibid.*

5   poetry can be quite dangerous propaganda,
especially since all worthwhile propaganda
ought to move its readers like a poem.
Graffiti do that; so do some songs,
and rarely, poems on a page.

> *Ibid.*, "Letter to a Sister Underground"

6   the Conquerors.
They're always watching,
invisibly electroded in our brains,
to be certain we implode our rage against each other
and not explode it against them.

> *Ibid.*

7 Don't accept rides from strange men,
and remember that all men are strange as hell.

> *Ibid.*

8 And I will speak less and less to you
And more and more in crazy gibberish you cannot understand:
witches' incantations, poetry, old women's mutterings. . . .

> "Monster," *Monster*   1972

9 Some have named this space where we are rooted
a place of death.
We fix them with our callous eyes
and call it, rather, a terrain of resurrection.

> *Ibid.*, "Easter Island, I: Embarcation"

10 Meanwhile, for now, this must suffice:
that murder and resurrection are the levers of change,
that creation and complexity are one,
that miracle is contradiction.

Ibid., "II: Arrival"

11 All the secretaries hunch at their IBM's,
snickering at keys.
What they know could bring down the government.

"On the Watergate Women," St. 7   *1974*

12 This quality of grief
could bring down
mankind.

Ibid., St. 20

1225. Gail Parent
(1941?–   )

1 Do you want to live in a world where a man lies about calories?

"The Facts," *Sheila Levine Is Dead
and Living in New York*   *1972*

2 Don't we realize we're a business, we single girls are? There are magazines for us, special departments in stores for us. Every building that goes up in Manhattan has more than fifty percent efficiency apartments . . . for the one million girls who have very little use for them.

Ibid., "On Jobs and Apartments"

3 *Fact:* Girls who are having a good sex thing stay in New York. The rest want to spend their summer vacations in Europe.   Ibid., "Europe"

4 What happened to the good old days of homemade ice cream and Trojans? . . . When did it become the woman's chore.   Ibid., "The Second Year"

5 . . . volleyball is a Jewish sport. It's fun, and nobody can get hurt.   Ibid., "Fire Island"

6 Thank you, Agatha, for the lovely bracelet, but I still haven't changed my mind. I have no desire to touch you in places that I already own. Sincerely, Sheila Levine."   Ibid., "Enough Already"

7 Do you realize the planning that goes into a death? Probably even more than goes into a marriage. This, after all, really is for eternity.

Ibid.

8 Actually, I have only two things to worry about now: afterlife and reincarnation.

Ibid., "The End"

1226. Judith Rascoe
(1941–   )

1 "There are more important rights than the so-called right to know. That is not the right that is being violated nowadays. People have the right to know *something*. They have the right to know that something is being done. That is more important than the right to know. They have the right to know how long they will have to wait until something is done. That is more important than the right to know. I know you would rather know that I am doing something than know what I am doing."

"Evening's Down Under,"
Yours and Mine   1973

2 . . . the grandmother opens the envelope with the letter-opener that Helen's first husband gave her and finds a colored photograph of Helen's second husband and his new wife, Myrna, surrounded by Myrna's children from her first marriage: "Season's Greetings from the Hannibals!"

Ibid., "Yours and Mine"

1227. Helen Reddy
(1941–   )

1 I am Woman, hear me roar
In numbers too big to ignore,
And I know too much
To go back and pretend.

"I Am Woman"   1972

2 But I'm still an embryo
With a long, long way to go.

Ibid.

3 Yes, I am wise, but it's wisdom born of pain
  Yes, I've paid the price, but look how much I've gained
  I am strong, I am invincible, I am Woman.

  Ibid.

4 Women temper men. We have a good influence on
  them.

  Interview on ABC-TV   *March 1, 1974*

5 Glamour to me is being spotlessly clean and courteous
  at all times.

  Quoted in the *Los Angeles Times*
  April 23, 1974

6 Gentleness is not a quality exclusive to women.

  Ibid.

7 The most exciting thing about women's liberation is
  that this century will be able to take advantage of talent
  and potential genius that have been wasted because of
  taboos.

  Ibid.

1228. Buffy Sainte-Marie
(1941–   )

1 We'll make a space in the lives that we planned
  And here I'll stay until it's time for you to go.
              "Until It's Time for You to Go"   *1965*

2 And yet where in your history books is the tale
  of the genocide basic to this country's birth?
  of the preachers who lied?
  how the Bill of Rights failed.
                "My Country 'Tis of Thy People
                You're Dying"   *1966*

3 You have to sniff out joy, keep your nose to the joy-
  trail.

  Quoted by Susan Braudy in *Ms.*
  March, 1975

4 Music has been my playmate, my lover, and my crying
  towel. It gets me off like nothing else.

  Ibid.

5 The white man wants everyone who isn't white to think
  white.   *Ibid.*

6 . . . red, I mean, *white* tape. , . . .

Ibid.

7 Here the melting pot stands open—if you're willing to get bleached first.

Ibid.

1229. Susan Fromberg Schaeffer
(1941–   )

1 The sky is reduced,
A narrow blue ribbon banding the lake.
Someone is wrapping things up.

"Post Mortem," St. 1, *The Witch
and the Weather Report*   1972

2 What can be wrong
That some days I hug this house
Around me like a shawl, and feel
Each window like a tatter in its skin,
Or worse, bright eyes I must not look through?

Ibid., "Housewife" St. 1

3 The assistants, relying on the proverbial competition among pre-meds, had assumed there would be no help among the gladiators, no risks taken which might raise the curve. It seemed to Elizabeth that higher mathematics were useless to them in real life; the students did not care how high the curve spiraled, provided they were on top, climbing the beanstalk, collecting the golden eggs, the medical acceptances, the gallstones in jars.

Falling, Ch. 1   1973

4 In her drugged state, she felt only a euphoria, as if all the pain of her life had become a vast salty water, buoying up, where she floated on the great blue waves of a vast, melodramatic sea.

Ibid.

5 "Time is only a force; it is neither good nor evil, only necessary."

Ibid., Ch. 6

1230. Judy Wenning
(1941?–   )

1 Women are freer to express their competitiveness now. Women's competitiveness in the past has been limited to competing for men, but those days are over. It's no longer a totally negative thing.

> Quoted in "Women in Sports: The Movement Is Real," *Los Angeles Times*   *April 23, 1974*

1231. Ama Ata Aidoo
(1942–   )

1   "Sissie, men are like that."
  "They are selfish."
  "No, it's just that women allow them to behave the way they do instead of seizing some freedom themselves."

> *No Sweetness Here*   1970

2 People are worms, and even the God who created them is immensely bored with their antics.

> Ibid.

3 . . . tears . . . one of the most potent weapons in woman's bitchy and inexhaustible arsenal.

> Ibid.

4 Eternal death has worked like a warrior rat, with a diabolical sense of duty, to gnaw at my bottom.

> "The Message," *Fragment from a Lost Diary and Other Stories,* Naomi Katz and Nancy Milton, eds.   *1973*

5 It's a sad moment, really, when parents first become a bit frightened of their children.

> Ibid.

6 "She's a natural for the part of the Great Earth Mother. But I rather resent being viewed in such an agricultural light."

> Ibid.

7 The fact is that women . . . have inherited, through bitter centuries, a ruthless sense of self-preservation. . . . That cool, subtle determination to find her security and hang on to it, that all's-fair attitude—not in love, which she discounted, but in war, for it *was* war, the gaining or losing of a kingdom. . . . As it was, victory, conquest, success, call it what you will, was the only virtue. And, of course, the really absurd thing was that nobody would have been more appalled . . . if you had called her a feminist.

> Ibid.

1232. Alta
(1942–   )

1 [Of] course, if you think only terrible people go to prison, that solves that problem.

> Untitled Poem   *1972*

2 if you come in me
a child is likely to
come back out.
my name is alta.
i am a woman.

> Untitled Poem   *1969–1973*

3 I want to say the words that take you
back there. . . .
there, where
you would like to be again.

> Untitled Poem   *1969–1973*

1233. Eve Babitz
(1942?–   )

1 Culturally, Los Angeles has always been a humid jungle alive with seething L.A. projects that I guess people from other places can't see. It takes a certain kind of innocence to like L.A., anyway. . . . When people are not happy, they fight against L.A. and say it's a "wasteland," and other helpful descriptions.

> "Daughters of the Wasteland,"
> *Eve's Hollywood*   *1974*

2 When they reach the age of *fifteen* and their beauty arrives, it's very exciting—like coming into an inheritance. . . . *Ibid.*, "The Sheik"

3 Packaging is all heaven is. *Ibid.*, "Rosewood Casket"

4 It's the frames which make some things important and some things forgotten. It's all only frames from which the content rises. *Ibid.*

5 We made the smell of Banana in Chemistry once, and I nearly cried because it actually smelled like Bananas and was so simple and so fake.

Ibid., "The Answer"

6 But by the time I'd grown up, I naturally supposed that I'd grown up.

Ibid., "The Academy"

1234. Charlotte Bingham
(1942–   )

1 I was thinking in bed the other night I must have been out with nearly three hundred men, and I still haven't found a Superman. I don't know what a Superman is, but I know there must be one somewhere.
Coronet Among the Weeds, Ch. 1   1963

2 I think it must have been quite fun when women were rather mysterious and men didn't know all about them. Look at the end product of women being free. I mean, go on, look at it. It's a poor old career girl sitting in her digs wondering whether she ought to ring up her boyfriend or not.

Ibid.

3 Beatniks were too conventional anyway. I mean they thought they were getting away from it, which is pretty corny. You never do. You just change one thing for another.

Ibid., Ch. 5

4 An isolated outbreak of virginity like Lucinda's is a rash on the face of society. It arouses only pity from the married, and embarrassment from the single.
Lucinda, Ch. 1   1966

5 "And the only way to avoid playing the game is never to belong to a club, class, set, or trade union. As soon as you do, you're accepting someone else's rules, and as soon as you do that, you start looking down on the other chap with different rules."

Ibid., Ch. 3

6 "I'm glad you understand, Mr. Flint, I'm the last person in the world who would wish to ruin my life by inheriting a fortune. There are quite enough evils in it, without complicating the issues with money."

Ibid., Ch. 8

1235. Susan Castro
(1942–   )

1 All children are musicians; all children are artists. Everything they do at this age [two and a-half to five] is new. Play is work for them that constantly extends their limits—it is a most vital creative function. If we can make it rich, the best that is human will flourish within the child.

Quoted in "A New Era in Day Care"
by Mildred Hamilton, San Francisco
Chronicle   December 19, 1971

2 I am opposed to the custodial idea of day care. That is a mistake. Enrichment is what we are after.

Ibid.

3 The merits of good child care for all who need it or want it are many. The health and well-being of our society depends on it. Those unconvinced are people who have no need of high quality public programs, and who choose not to see the children and parents who suffer from lack of them.

"The Impediments to Public Day Care
Programs in San Francisco"   1974

4 At all levels of government, the question is one of priorities and money. The contradiction between what consumers (the bulk of whom are low-income) pay out in taxes and what they receive in goods and services is simply sharper the closer it is to home.

Ibid.

5 Some of us would like to ignore the institutions and the money problems. I do not see how that is possible. The provision of child care on even a moderate scale requires the use of institutional money, public money. I have no trouble with using public money. Child care and other services [are] exactly what it should be used for.

Address, University of California
Conference on Child Care, Berkeley
April, 1975

1236. Carol Glassman
(1942?–)

1 For its recipients, the welfare system carried with it most of the hazards of "housewife and mother," and a few of the rewards. Domination by a husband was replaced with control over every aspect of a woman's life by the welfare agency. Strangers could knock at any hour to pass judgment on her performance as mother, housekeeper, and cook—as well as her fidelity to the welfare board. The welfare board, like a jealous husband, doesn't want to see any men around who might threaten its place as provider and authority.

"Women and the Welfare System,"
Sisterhood Is Powerful,
Robin Morgan, ed.   1970

2 Throughout the welfare department one finds the combined view that poverty is due to individual *fault* and that *something is wrong with women who don't have men.*

Ibid.

3 It is the woman who is ultimately held responsible for pregnancy. While not being allowed to have control over her body, she is nevertheless held responsible for its products.

Ibid.

1237. Marilyn Hacker
(1942–   )

1 The child of wonder, deep in his
   gut, knows how long forever is,
   and, like a haunted anarchist,
   hears a repeated order hissed
   not to exist.

"Chanson de L'Enfant Prodigue,"
Presentation Piece   *1974*

2 I am in exile in my own land.

Ibid., "Exiles," St. 1

3 Between us on our wide bed we cuddle an incubus
   whom we have filled with voyages. We wake
   more apart than before, with open hands.

Ibid., "The Navigators, I," St. 1

4   "Have you done
   flaunting your cunt and your pen in her face
   when she's not looking? high above your bed,
   like a lamppost with eyes, stern as a pay toilet,
   she stands, waiting to be told off
   and tolled out."

Ibid., "For Elektra," St. 2

5 I wish I had a lover instead of letters
   from strangers. The arrival of the mail
   is the only time that someone hands
   me movement. Nothing real is going to happen
   yet, except this dessicated ritual.

Ibid., "Waiting," St. 5

1238. Flora Purim
(1942–   )

1 Clear days, feel so good and free
   So light as a feather can be. . . .

"Light as a Feather"   *1973*

1239. Sally Quinn
(1942?–   )

1 Washington is . . . a company town. Most of the interesting people in Washington either work for the government or write about it.

We're Going to Make You a Star   1975

2 . . . there has been such a mythology built up around the supposed glamour of television life that it's hard for the average person to imagine turning down anything on TV.

Ibid.

1240. Marjorie Rosen
(1942–   )

1 Does art reflect life? In movies, yes. Because more than any other art form, films have been a mirror held up to society's porous face.

Popcorn Venus, Preface   1973

2 Movies have always been a form of popular culture that altered the way women looked at the world and reflected how men intended to keep it.

Ibid.

3 Which is strongest—the reality out of which the illusion is created, the celluloid illusion itself, or the need for illusion? Do we hold the mirror up and dive in? And if we do, what are the consequences? And what are the responsibilities of the illusion makers?

Ibid., Pt. I, Ch. 2

4 Women were the sacrificial lambs of the Depression, but amid the collective pain of the nation's empty bellies, they scarcely felt the knife.

Ibid., Pt. III, Ch. 8

5 It's unfortunate that Hollywood could not visualize a woman of mental acumen unless she was fixing up a mess her man/boss had made, covering a scoop to prove herself to a man, or deftly forging a life of dishonesty.

Ibid.

6 Hollywood expediently ignored reality.

Ibid.

7 If proof were needed of the power of woman's film image on women in life, the number of platinum heads tells the story.

Ibid., Ch. 9

8 Studios, purporting to ease the anguish of Depression reality, transformed movies into the politics of fantasy, the great black-and-white opiate of the masses.

Ibid.

9 On December 7, 1941, the Japanese bombed hell out of Pearl Harbor. Johnny got his gun. America mobilized. And social roles shifted with a speed that would have sent Wonder Woman into paroxysms of power pride.

Ibid., Pt. IV, Ch. 12

10 The forties, since dubbed the era of "women's pictures." . . . Women, neither as bored, listless, nor depressed as they had been a decade earlier, were not as malleable either; hence, where the screen had not long before created a reality for them, now the females created their own. The Hollywood product mirrored—and altered—it.

Ibid.

11 Women's films [in the fifties] became "how-to's" on catching and keeping a man. Veneer. Appearance. Sex Appeal. Hollywood descended into mammary madness.

Ibid., Pt. V, Ch. 17

12 Still, we chiefly remember the fifties, not for the horror of civil defense drills or witchhunts, but for kitschy fads like hoola hoops and poodle cuts and crinolines. For Lucy and Miltie and Howdy and Kukla. . . . One of the few constants during the decade was the direction women were heading: backward.

Ibid.

13 Sex, drugs, rapping, a passion for total independence to "do their thing" forced renunciation of traditional values—the popular artifice of clothing, purchasing power, education, employment. Looking "natural," they created costumes out of odds and ends and nodded off in the name of peace and love. They were flower children.

Ibid., Pt. VI, Ch. 21

14 Once upon a time sex was romance. . . . Today, however, to be clinical is to be in.

Ibid., Ch. 22

15 It is ironic that sixties' and seventies' women have seized on a more productive lifestyle than ever before, but the [film] industry has turned its back on reflecting it in any constructive or analytical way.

Ibid.

1241. Susan C. Ross
(1942–   )

1 The court will even make up or accept a spurious purpose for the law in order to justify differential treatment.

The Rights of Women, Ch. 1   1973

2 No one can ever be sure how courts will interpret any new law or amendment.

Ibid.

3 The brutal fact is that convicted women . . . have not yet won the right to equal treatment in the criminal and juvenile justice system.

Ibid., Ch. 5

4 . . . alimony is one way of compensating women for those financial disabilities aggravated, or caused, by marriage: unequal educational opportunities; unequal employment opportunities; and an unequal division of family responsibilities, with no compensation for the spouse who works in the home. . . . Thus, women should not be cowed into believing that to ask for alimony is to be unliberated, or that their husbands provide alimony out of the largesse of their noble hearts.

Ibid., Ch. 7

5 For many persons, law appears to be black magic—an obscure domain that can be fathomed only by the professional initiated into its mysteries.

Ibid., Ch. 10

6 The concept of *enforcing* a right gives meaning to the concept of the right itself.

Ibid.

7 Law then is not a preordained set of doctrines, applied rigidly and unswervingly in every situation. Rather, law is molded from the arguments and decisions of thousands of persons. It is very much a human process, a game of trying to convince others . . . that your view of what the law requires is correct.

Ibid.

1242. Sally E. Shaywitz
(1942–)

1 . . . just as breast milk cannot be duplicated, neither can a mother.

"Catch 22 for Mothers," *The New York Times Magazine*   *March 4, 1973*

2 It is misleading and unfair to imply that an intelligent woman must "rise above" her maternal instincts and return to work when many intelligent, sensitive women have found that the reverse is better for them.

Ibid.

3 To be somebody, a woman does not have to be more like a man, but has to be more of a woman.   *Ibid.*

1243. Barbra Streisand
(1942–)

1 Success to me is having ten honeydew melons and eating only the top half of each one.

Quoted in *Life*   *September 20, 1963*

1244. Charlotte Bonny Cohen
(1943–)

1 For the Chinese Communists, ideology is always ahead of practice.

"Chung-kuo Fu Nu (Women of China)," *Sisterhood Is Powerful,* Robin Morgan, ed.   *1970*

2 There is a great difference between the top and the bottom of the Chinese power pyramid.   *Ibid.*

3 The commune was a sudden attempt to overcome past failures. For women this meant resolving the contradiction between the desire to work and the necessity of being a housewife.

Ibid.

4 China is not our model. . . . But Mao and the Chinese Communists do show us that society is changed by changing people's daily lives. Working side by side with men partially liberates women. Freedom—however you want it—comes from new ways of living together.

Ibid.

1245. Nikki Giovanni
(1943–   )

1 Why, LBJ has made it
quite clear to me
He doesn't give a
Good goddamn what I think
(else why would he continue to *masterbate* in public?)
"A Historical Footnote to Consider
Only When All Else Fails," St. 2,
*Black Feeling/Black Talk/Black
Judgement*   1970

2 A nigger can die
We ain't got to prove we can die
We got to prove we can kill
Ibid., "The True Import of Present
Dialogue, Black vs. Negro"

3 But we can't be Black
And not be crazy.
Ibid., "A Short Essay of Affirmation
Explaining Why," St. 7

4   But on the other hand the whole point
of points is pointless when its boiled all the way down
to the least common denominator. But I was never one
to deal with fractions when there are so many wholes
that cannot be dissected—at least these poor hands
lack both skill and tool and perhaps this poor heart
lacks even the inclination to try because emotion is

of itself a wasteful thing because it lacks the power
to fulfill itself.

> Ibid., "Letter to a Bourgeois Friend
> Whom Once I Loved (And Maybe
> Still Do If Love Is Valid)"

5 Mistakes are a fact of life
It is the response to error that counts

> Ibid., "Of Liberation," St. 16

6 There is a new game I must tell you of
It's called Catch The Leader Lying
(And knowing your sense of the absurd
you will enjoy this)

> Ibid., "Poem for Black Boys," St. 5

7 And you will understand all too soon
That you, my children of battle, are your heroes
You must invent your own games and teach us old
ones
how to play

> Ibid., St. 8

8 His headstone said
FREE AT LAST, FREE AT LAST
But death is a slave's freedom
We seek the freedom of free men
And the construction of a world
Where Martin Luther King could have lived
and preached non-violence

> Ibid., "The Funeral of
> Martin Luther King, Jr."

9 In the name of peace
They waged the wars
ain't they got no shame

> Ibid., "The Great Pax Whitie," St. 3

10 and nothing is worse
than a
dream deferred

> Ibid., "From a Logical Point of
> View," St. 1

11 You could say we've lost our innocence. That's a little
worse than losing the nickel to put in Sunday school,
though not quite as bad as losing the dime for ice cream
afterward.

> *Spin a Soft Black Song,*
> Introduction   *1971*

12 You can have Jesus but give me the world. I'll take it
even though it's losing twenty-five percent of its energy
every one hundred years or something ridiculous.

James Baldwin—Nikki Giovanni:
A Dialogue   1973

13 I think one of the nicest things that we created as a
generation was just the fact that we could say, Hey, I
don't like white people.

Ibid.

14 Everybody's dead.

Ibid.

15 You have to decide who you are going to smile at. Job
or no job. Future or no future. 'Cause all those reasons
you give me for your actions don't make sense if I can't
enjoy you. I think men are very different from women.
But I think men build their standards on false ratio-
nales. The question is: What makes a man? The question is: Can you be a man wherever you are and whatever the circumstances?

Ibid.

1246. Susan Griffin
(1943–   )

1 In no state can a man be accused of raping his wife.
How can any man steal what already belongs to him?
Quoted in *Ramparts*   September, 1971

2 "do you know why
we di-
vorced? . . .
We would go to the movies
your father and I."
I nodded at her.
"And I'd come out
being Carol Lombard,
only he refused
to be Humphrey Bogart."
"Grenadine," *Dear Sky*   1973

3 I've been inside institutions,
my family,
kindergarten,

grammar school, high
school, college and then
marriage, waiting
to be
grown up, graduated, & divorced,
but before I
turned around,
here I am
back in as the
jailor, a
mother and a
teacher.   Ibid., "Letter to the Outside"

4 sleep leads to dreaming
   waking to imagination and to
   imagine what we
   could be, o,
   what we could be.   Ibid., "To Gather Ourselves"

                        *   *   *

5 because tiredness at least
   you
   have always been
   faithful.   "Tiredness Cycle"

1247. Erica Jong
(1943?–   )

1 I am thinking of the onion again, . . . Not self-
   righteous
   like the proletarian potato, nor a siren like the apple.
   No
   show-off like the banana. But a modest, self-effacing
   vegetable, questioning, introspective, peeling itself
   away,
   or merely radiating halos like lake ripples.
                              "Fruits and Vegetables,"
                        Fruits and Vegetables   1971

2 Everyone has talent. What is rare is the courage to follow the talent to the dark place where it leads.
                        "The Artist as Housewife: The
                           Housewife as Artist," *The First
                              Ms. Reader,* Francine
                              Klagsbrun, ed.   1972

3 If sex and creativity are often seen by dictators as subversive activities, it's because they lead to the knowledge that you own your own body (and with it your
own voice), and that's the most revolutionary insight of
all.

Ibid.

4 Perhaps all artists were, in a sense, housewives: tenders
of the earth household.

Ibid.

5 I can live without it all—
love with its blood pump,
sex with its messy hungers,
men with their peacock strutting,
their silly sexual baggage,
their wet tongues in my ear
and their words like little sugar suckers
with sour centers.

"Becoming a Nun," About Women,
Stephen Berg and S. J. Marks, eds.
1973

6 . . . he never regarded himself as crazy. The world
was.

Fear of Flying 1973

7 Q: Why does a Jew always answer a question with a
question?
A: And why should a Jew not answer a question with a
question?

Ibid., Ch. 1

8 Growing up female in America. What a liability! You
grew up with your ears full of cosmetic ads, love
songs, advice columns, whoreoscopes, Hollywood gossip, and moral dilemmas on the level of TV soap op-
eras. What litanies the advertisers of the good life
chanted at you! What curious catechisms!

Ibid.

9 Solitude is un-American.

Ibid.

10 Phallocentric, someone once said of Freud. He thought
the sun revolved around the penis. And the daughter,
too.

Ibid., Ch. 2

11 Throughout all of history, books were written with
sperm, not menstrual blood.

Ibid.

12 Europe is dusty plush,
  First-class carriages
  with first-class dust.
Ibid., "The 8:29 to Frankfurt," Ch. 4

13 Men have always detested women's gossip because they
  suspect the truth: their measurements are being taken
  and compared.
Ibid., Ch. 6

14 Gossip is the opiate of the oppressed.
Ibid.

15 There is nothing fiercer than a failed artist. The energy
  remains, but, having no outlet, it implodes in a great
  black fart of rage which smokes up all the inner windows of the soul.
Ibid., Ch. 9

16 Coupling doesn't always have to do with sex. . . .
  Two people holding each other up like flying buttresses.
  Two people depending on each other and babying each
  other and defending each other against the world outside. Sometimes it was worth all the disadvantages of
  marriage just to have that: one friend in an indifferent
  world.
Ibid., Ch. 10

17 The idea of the future is our greatest entertainment,
  amusement, and time-killer. Take it away and there is
  only the past—and a windshield spattered with dead
  bugs.
Ibid., Ch. 11

18 The cure for starvation in India *and* the cure for overpopulation—both in one big swallow! Ibid., Ch. 17

19 It was easy enough to kill yourself in a fit of despair. It
  was easy enough to play the martyr. It was harder to
  do nothing. To endure your life. To wait. Ibid.

20 Surviving meant being born over and over.
Ibid., Ch. 19

21 Each month
  the blood sheets down
  like good red rain.

  I am the gardener.
  Nothing grows without me.
"Gardener," *Half-Lives*   1973

22 It is a sad paradox that when male authors impersonate women, they are said to be dealing with "cosmic, major concerns"—but when we impersonate *ourselves* we are said to be writing "women's fiction" or "women's po-etry."

> "Colette: The Difficulty of Loving,"
> *Ms.*   *April, 1974*

1248. Janis Joplin
(1943–1970)

1 They ain't never gonna love you any better, babe
And they're nee-eever gonna love you ri-ight
So you better dig it right now, right now.

> "Kozmic Blues"   *1969*

2 Don't compromise yourself. You are all you've got.

> Quoted in *Reader's Digest*
> *April, 1973p*

* * *

3 You got to get it while you can. . . .

> "Get It While You Can"

4 Oh Lord won't you buy me a night on the town?

> "Oh Lord Won't You Buy Me a
> Mercedes-Benz"

1249. Sally Kempton
(1943?–   )

1 I became a feminist as an alternative to becoming a masochist.

> "Cutting Loose," *Esquire*   *July, 1970*

2 All children are potential victims, dependent upon the world's good will.   Ibid.

3 Men have laid down the rules and definitions by which the world is run, and one of the objects of their defini-tions is woman.   Ibid.

4 Men define intelligence, men define usefulness, men tell us what is beautiful, men even tell us what is womanly.   Ibid.

5 Constance Chatterley was a male invention; Lawrence invented her, I used to think, specifically to make me feel guilty because I didn't have the right kind of orgasms.

Ibid.

6 Self-love depressed becomes self-loathing.

Ibid.

7 And yet wherever there exists the display of power there is politics, and in women's relations with men there is a continual transfer of power, there is, continually, politics.

Ibid.

8 Women are natural guerrillas. Scheming, we nestle into the enemy's bed, avoiding open warfare, watching the options, playing the odds.

Ibid.

9 . . . women are the true maintenance class. Society is built upon their acquiescence, and upon their small and necessary labors.

Ibid.

10 When men imagine a female uprising they imagine a world in which women rule men as men have ruled women: their guilt, which is the guilt of every ruling class, will allow them to see no middle ground.

Ibid.

11 To discover that something has been wrong is not necessarily to make it right.

Ibid.

12 It is hard to fight an enemy who has outposts in your head.

Ibid.

1250. Billie Jean King
(1943–   )

1 I've always wanted to equalize things for us. . . . Women can be great athletes. And I think we'll find in the next decade that women athletes will finally get the attention they deserve.

Interview   *September, 1973*

2 I'm not sure if it's the environment in which you live or if it's innate, because I've always played better under pressure, even when I was a youngster.

Quoted by Marlene Jensen in
The Sportswoman
November/December 1973

3 I think self-awareness is probably the most important thing towards being a champion.

Ibid.

1251. Susan Lydon
(1943?–   )

1 The Victorians had needed to repress sexuality for the success of Western industrialized society; in particular, the total repression of woman's sexuality was crucial to ensure her subjugation. So the Victorian, . . . supported by Freud, passed on to us the heritage of the double standard.

"The Politics of Orgasm,"
Ramparts   *December, 1968*

2 Our society treats sex as a sport, with its record-breakers, its judges, its rules and its spectators.

Ibid.

1252. Joni Mitchell
(1943–   )

1 Moons and Junes and Ferris wheels
The dizzy dancing way you feel
As every fairy tale comes real
I've looked at love that way

"Both Sides, Now"   *1969*

2 I've looked at life from both sides now
From up and down, and still somehow
It's life's illusions I recall
I really don't know life at all

Ibid.

3 Woke up, it was a Chelsea morning, and the first thing that I knew
There was milk and toast and honey and a bowl of oranges, too

477

And the sun poured in like butterscotch and stuck to
all my senses

Oh, won't you stay
We'll put on the day
And we'll talk in present tenses
"Chelsea Morning"   1969

4 if you're feeling contempt
well then you tell it
if you're tired of the silent night
Jesus, well then you yell it
"Judgement of the Moon and Stars"
1972

5 Mama thinks she spoilt me
Papa knows somehow he set me free
Mama thinks she spoilt me rotten
She blames herself
But Papa he blesses me
"Let the Wind Carry Me"   1972

6 Golden in time
Cities under sand
Power, ideals and beauty
Fading in everyone's hands.
"The Hissing of Summer Lawns"
1975

7 Critics of all express
Judges in black and white
Saying it's wrong
Saying it's right
Compelled by standards
Of some ideals we fight

Ibid.

8 Sweet bird you are
Brighter than a falling star
All these vain promises on beauty jars
Somewhere in your wings on time
You might be laughing. . . .
"Sweet Bird"   1975

9 We are stardust, we are golden.
"Woodstock"   1975

1253. Gail Thain Parker
(1943–   )

1 . . . Quaker meetings [were] the first enclaves in American society in which women were encouraged to speak out in public . . . [with] the faith . . . that each individual, regardless of sex, had to act according to his inner lights. . . .

The Oven Birds, Introduction, Pt. I
1972

2 Literature was a great factor in the socialization of women, and without novels (and poems) which portrayed women on an heroic scale, whole generations of nascent feminists might be stunted in their development. *Ibid.*

3 Sentimentalism restructured the Calvinist model of salvation, making the capacity to feel, and above all to weep, in itself evidence of redemption. *Ibid.*

4 In the process of getting ahead in the world, of becoming smart and up-to-date, they have lost the ability to really feel. *Ibid., Pt. II*

5 What this country needs is a *good* impeachment. In itself impeachment is not evil or divisive, unless it is done cheaply. If it is done admirably and it tears the country apart, then the country is so fragile that anything could tear it apart.

Quoted in "Impeachment?"
by Claire Safran, *Redbook*
April, 1974

1254. Susan Shnall
(1943–   )

1 The professed purpose of the United States military is to maintain the peace, but its methods toward this goal are destructive and have resulted in the promotion of suffering and death of foreign peoples, as well as of its own. "Women in the Military,"
Sisterhood Is Powerful,
Robin Morgan, ed. *1970*

2 Because I wore a peace symbol, I had to have an extra interview to determine my suitability as a member of the military.

Ibid.

1255. Viva
(1943–   )

1 I think that he exercised a lot of restraint, limiting his kicks to the wall and a painting. I only wish that the heads of governments had the same instincts.

The Baby   1975

2 Like marriage, nursing was turning out to be one of those painful addictions; damned if you do, damned if you don't.

Ibid.

3 If Mother had let us go to bed whenever we wanted, not forced us to go to church, allowed us to masturbate, go to bars at night, see any movie we wanted, eat whenever we felt like it, sleep with her and Daddy, then I'm sure we'd now be exactly the way she had hoped us to be.

Ibid.

1256. Ingrid Bengis
(1944?–   )

1 No amount of evidence is ever sufficient to compensate for the deviousness with which human beings manage to conceal themselves. . . .

"Monroe According to Mailer," *Ms.*
October, 1973

2 Imagination has always had powers of resurrection that no science can match.

Ibid.

3 The form that our bodies take, particularly with women, dictates more often than we wish it would the form that a portion of our lives will take.   Ibid.

4 Psychic starvation is a desperate business: one does not wait around for Baked Alaska.   Ibid.

5 The real trap of fame is its irresistibility.

Ibid.

6 Once I had abandoned the search for everyone else's truth, I quickly discovered that the job of defining my own truth was far more complex than I had anticipated.

Combat in the Erogenous zone,
Introduction   1973

7 The real questions are the ones that obtrude upon your consciousness whether you like it or not, the ones that make your mind start vibrating like a jackhammer, the ones that you "come to terms with" only to discover that they are still there. The real questions refuse to be placated. They barge into your life at the times when it seems most important for them to stay away. They are the questions asked most frequently and answered most inadequately, the ones that reveal their true natures slowly, reluctantly, most often against your will.

Ibid., "Man-Hating"

8 One of these days I'm going to put bandaids across my mouth so that smiling will become less of a reflex in uncomfortable situations.

Ibid.

9 For me words still possess their primitive, mystical, incantatory healing powers. I am inclined to use them as part of an attempt to make my own reality more real for others, as part of an effort to transcend emotional damage. For me, words are a form of action, capable of influencing change. Their articulation represents a complete, lived experience.

Ibid.

10 Let me off this idiot merry-go-round. My psyche is not an ideological playground. My inner feelings, at their most genuine, are not ruled by social decree.

Ibid., "Love"

11 When all of the remedies and all of the rhetorical armor have been dropped, the absence of love in our lives is what makes them seem raw and unfinished.

Ibid.

12 What about the fact that everything ever constructed by civilization seems to be a dam against disintegration.

Ibid.

1257. Rita Mae Brown
(1944–   )

1 One doesn't get liberated by hiding. One doesn't possess integrity by passing for "white."

> Untitled Essay   *March, 1970*

2 To love without role, without power plays, is revolution.

> *Ibid.*

3 I do not want to be separate from any woman . . . [but] until heterosexuals will treat lesbians as full human beings and fight the enormity of male supremacy with us, I have no option but to be separate from them, just as they have no option but to be separate from men until men begin to change their own sexism.

> Untitled Essay   *May, 1970*

4 I move in the shadow of the great guillotine
That rhythmically does its work
On heads remaining unbowed.

> "The Self Affirms Herself" (1966)
> *The Hand That Cradles the Rock*
> *1971*

5 I've come through a land
You'll never know.

> Ibid., "The Bourgeois Question" (1967)

6 An army of lovers shall not fail.

> Ibid., "Sappho's Reply" (1970)

1258. Angela Davis
(1944–   )

1 Domestic labor was the only meaningful labor for the slave community.

> "Reflections on the Black Woman's
> Role in the Community of Slaves,"
> *The Black Scholar*   *December, 1971*

2 In order to function as slave, the black woman had to be annulled as woman, that is, as woman in her histori-

cal stance of wardship under the entire male hierarchy. The sheer force of things rendered her equal to her man.

Ibid.

3 Expending indispensable labor for the enrichment of her [the black woman's] oppressor, she could attain a practical awareness of the oppressor's utter dependence on her—for the master needs the slave far more than the slave needs the master.

Ibid.

4 The master subjected her to the most elemental form of terrorism distinctly suited to the female: rape.

Ibid.

5 In fact, the intense levels of resistance historically maintained by black people—and thus the historical function of the Black Liberation Struggle as harbinger of change throughout society—are due in part to the greater *objective* equality between the black man and woman.

Ibid.

6 We, the black women of today, must accept the full weight of a legacy wrought in blood by our mothers in chains. As heirs to a tradition of perseverance and heroic resistance, we must hasten to take our place wherever our people are forging toward freedom.

Ibid.

7 . . . the brother . . . had painted a night sky on the ceiling of his cell, because it had been years since he had seen the moon and stars.

An Autobiography   1974

8 When the iron door was opened, sounds peculiar to jails and prisons poured into my ears—the screams, the metallic clanging, officers' keys clinking.

Ibid.

9 Trapped in this wasteland inhabited by the sick, the drugged and their indifferent keepers. . . .

Ibid.

10 But before my thoughts led me further in the direction of self-pity, I brought them to a halt, reminding myself that this was precisely what solitary confinement was supposed to evoke.

Ibid.

11 Jails and prisons are designed to break human beings, to convert the population into specimens in a zoo—obedient to our keepers, but dangerous to each other.

Ibid.

12 I was bewildered and awed by the way in which the vast majority of the jail population had neatly organized itself into generations of families: mothers/wives, fathers/husbands, sons and daughters, even aunts, uncles, grandmothers and grandfathers.

Ibid.

13 Many of them—both the butches and the femmes—had obviously decided to take up homosexuality during their jail terms in order to make that time a little more exciting, in order to forget the squalor and degradation around them.

Ibid.

14 Many people are unaware of the fact that jail and prison are two entirely different institutions. People in prison have already been convicted. Jails are primarily for pretrial confinement, holding places until prisoners are either convicted or found innocent. More than half of the jail population have never been convicted of anything, yet they languish in those cells.

Ibid.

15 Racism, in the first place, is a weapon used by the wealthy to increase the profits they bring in by paying Black workers less for their work.

Ibid.

1259. Claudia Dreifus
(1944–   )

1 We spent a winter learning the feminist basics from the textbook of each other's lives. . . .

Woman's Fate, Introduction   *1973*

2 . . . girls enforce the cultural code that men invent.

Ibid., "The Adolescent Experience"

1260. Marcia Gillespie
(1944–   )

1 We have been looking at it [feminism] warily. Black women need economic equality but it doesn't apply for

me to call a black man a male chauvinist pig. Our anger is not at our men. I don't think they have been the enemy.

Quoted in "About Women," *Los
Angeles Times*   May 12, 1974

1261. Julia Phillips
(1944?–   )

1 Here's how I define the role of producer: the producer is there long before the shooting starts, and way after the shooting stops.

Quoted in *American Film Magazine*
December, 1975

2 As a director you become the focal point, and if you look tired your crew will feel tired. But I'm not worried about stamina. I've found that women . . . generate more energy than anyone else on a [film] set. And as a producer, I've had to build up twice as much creative energy because half of it was drained just getting a picture off the ground.

Ibid.

3 It [filmmaking] has to be in your blood because three times a day you ask yourself why are you doing this. Especially when you've done it before and you know up front it's going to be pure torture. But if you love the screenplay, and the director and cast amplify it, then it's magic—and the rewards are fantastic.   Ibid.

1262. Arlene Raven
(1944–   )

1 In my view, the content of feminist art, and its deepest meaning, is consciousness: a woman's full awareness of herself as an entity, including her sensations, her emotions, and her thoughts—mind in its broadest sense.

"Woman's Art: The Development of
a Theoretical Perspective," *Womanspace*   *February/March, 1973*

2 . . . if art is about consciousness grounded in reality, good art is about high consciousness—a real world view about the real world.   Ibid.

3 Historical consciousness is in no way separate from self-consciousness. The way in which we think of ourselves has everything to do with how our world sees us and how we can see ourselves successfully acknowledged by that world. **Ibid.**

4 The artist who shows us his/her world without this essential sense of optimism is without hope and without power: We can empathize with that art, but it cannot inspire in us the high level of human aspiration that we need to enrich ourselves, to grow, and to change.

Ibid.

5 Animals which are traditionally referred to as female include the cow, sow, bitch and cat—all derogatory words in our language when they are applied to human beings. English does not use gender extensively, but its linguistic sexism is intact because sexism is intact.

Ibid.

1263. Alice Walker
(1944–   )

1 The sight of a Black nun strikes their sentimentality; and, as I am unalterably rooted in native ground they consider me a work of primitive art, housed in a magical color; the incarnation of civilized, anti-heathenism, and the fruit of a triumphing idea.

"The Diary of an African Nun,"
Freedomways   Summer, 1968

2 How teach a barren world to dance? It is a contradiction that divides the world. **Ibid.**

3 She wants to live for once. But doesn't know quite what that means. Wonders if she has ever done it. If she ever will.

"Roselily," *In Love and Trouble: Stories of Black Women*   1973

4 I wait, beautiful and perfect in every limb, cooking supper as if my life depended on it. Lying unresisting on his bed like a drowned body washed to shore. But he is not happy. For he knows now that I intend to do nothing but say yes until he is completely exhausted.

Ibid., "Really, *Doesn't* Crime Pay?"

5 A slight, pretty flower that grows on any ground, and flowers pledge no allegiance to banners of any man.

> Ibid., "The Child Who Favored Daughter"

6 They stumbled blindly through their lives: creatures so abused and mutilated in body, so dimmed and confused by pain, that they considered themselves unworthy even of hope . . . exquisite butterflies trapped in an evil honey, toiling away their lives in an era, a century, that did not acknowledge them, except as "the *mule* of the world."

> "In Search of Our Mother's Gardens,"
> *Ms.* May, 1974

7 In search of my mother's garden I found my own.

> Ibid.

1264. Victoria Billings
(1945–   )

1 Sexual liberation, as a slogan, turns out to be another kind of bondage. For a woman it offers orgasm as her ultimate and major fulfillment; it's better than mother-hood.

> "What Is Individuality?," *The Womansbook* 1974

2 Whether he admits it or not, a man has been brought up to look at money as a sign of his virility, a symbol of his power, a bigger phallic symbol than a Porsche.

> Ibid., "Getting It Together"

3 The best thing that could happen to motherhood already has. Fewer women are going into it.

> Ibid., "Meeting Your Personal Needs"

4 Physicians tend to take women's complaints less seriously so you're more apt to pay for a sympathetic smile than a diagnosis. You're also more apt to be tranquilized instead of being treated.

> Ibid.

5 Constant togetherness is fine—but only for Siamese twins.

> Ibid., "A Love to Believe In"

6 Rape is a culturally fostered means of suppressing women. Legally we say we deplore it, but mythically we romanticize and perpetuate it, and privately we excuse and overlook it. . . .

> Ibid., "Sex: We Need Another Revolution"

1265. Annie Dillard
(1945–   )

1 We wake, if we ever wake at all, to mystery, rumors of
death, beauty, violence.
Pilgrim at Tinker Creek, Ch. 1   *1974*

2 Every live thing is a survivor on a kind of extended
emergency bivouac.
Ibid.

3 Cruelty is a mystery, and the waste of pain.
Ibid.

4 I am an explorer, then, and I am also a stalker, or the
instrument of the hunt itself.
Ibid.

5 The world's spiritual geniuses seem to discover universally that the mind's muddy river, this ceaseless flow of
trivia and trash, cannot be dammed, and that trying to
dam it is a waste of effort that might lead to madness.
Ibid., Ch. 2

6 The secret of seeing is to sail on solar wind. Hone and
spread your spirit till you yourself are a sail, whetted,
translucent, broadside to the merest puff.
Ibid.

7 It is ironic that the one thing that all religions recognize as separating us from our creator—our very self-
consciousness—is also the one thing that divides us
from our fellow creatures. It was a bitter birthday present from evolution. . . .
Ibid., Ch. 6

8 No; we have been as usual asking the wrong question.
It does not matter a hoot what the mockingbird on the
chimney is singing. . . . The real and proper question
is: Why is it beautiful?   Ibid., Ch. 7

9 Somewhere, and I can't find where, I read about an
Eskimo hunter who asked the local missionary priest,
"If I did not know about God and sin, would I go to
hell?" "No," said the priest, "not if you did not know."
"Then why," asked the Eskimo earnestly, "did you tell
me?"   Ibid.

10 I don't know what it is about fecundity that so appalls. I suppose it is the teeming evidence that birth and growth, which we value, are ubiquitous and blind, that life itself is so astonishingly cheap, that nature is as careless as it is bountiful, and that with extravagance goes a crushing waste that will one day include our own cheap lives. . . .

Ibid., Ch. 10

11 The world has signed a pact with the devil; it had to. . . . The terms are clear: if you want to live, you have to die; you cannot have mountains and creeks without space, and space is a beauty married to a blind man. The blind man is Freedom, or Time, and he does not go anywhere without his great dog Death. The world came into being with the signing of the contract.

Ibid.

12 I am a frayed and nibbled survivor in a fallen world and I am getting along. I am aging and eaten and have done my share of eating too.

Ibid., Ch. 13

13 The universe was not made in jest but in solemn incomprehensible earnest. By a power that is unfathomably secret, and holy, and fleet. There is nothing to be done about it, but ignore it, or see. And then you walk fearlessly, eating what you must, growing wherever you can. . . .

Ibid., Ch. 15

1266. Shulamith Firestone
(1945–   )

1 Perhaps it is true that a presentation of only the female side of things . . . is limited. But . . . is it any more limited than the prevailing male view of things, which—when not taken as absolute truth—is at least seen as "serious," relevant and important.

The Dialectic of Sex   1970

2 A man is allowed to blaspheme the world because it belongs to him to damn.

Ibid.

3 I submit that women's history has been hushed up for the same reason that black history has been hushed

up . . . and that is that a feminist movement poses a direct threat to the establishment. From the beginning it exposed the hypocrisy of the male power structure.

Ibid., Ch. 2

4 I conclude that, contrary to what most historians would have us believe, women's rights were never won. The Women's Rights Movement did not fold because it accomplished its objectives, but because it was defeated. *Seeming* freedoms appear to have been won.

Ibid.

5 The bar is the male kingdom. For centuries it was the bastion of male privilege, the gathering place for men away from their women, a place where men could go to freely indulge in The Bull Session . . . a serious political function: the release of the guilty anxiety of the oppressor class.

"The Bar as Microcosm,"
Voices from Women's Liberation,
Leslie B. Tanner, ed.　*1970*

1267. Ruth Iskin
(1945–　　)

1 In the dealer-critic system, galleries exist primarily for sale purposes and it is the critic's role to promote the art product by establishing its value and providing a justification for its importance.

"A Space of Our Own, Its Meaning
and Implications," *Womanspace*
February/March, 1973

2 The star system: the focus on the artist and his/her entire career, which was a by-product of the sale orientation developed in the dealer-critic system, replaced the older emphasis on individual paintings and schools of painters, which prevailed in the academy.

Ibid.

1268. Kathy Kahn
(1945–)

1 There is still a natural tendency for the people of one class to look down on people who they think are lower class—as if they are less than human.

> Quoted in "Kathy Kahn: Voice of
> Poor White Women" by Meridee
> Merzer, *Viva*   *April, 1974*

2 In places like the textile mills, where superhuman production rates are set, the people have to take speed (amphetamines) in order to keep up production. . . . Virtually every factory in this country is run on speed, grass, or some other kind of upper.

> Ibid.

3 I do not believe in being paid for organizing . . . because a revolution is a revolution. And nobody— *nobody*—gets paid for making a revolution.   Ibid.

1269. Paula Nelson
(1945–)

1 Women's battle for financial equality has barely been joined, much less won. Society still traditionally assigns to woman the role of money-handler rather than money-maker, and our assigned specialty is far more likely to be home economics than financial economics.

> *The Joy of Money*, Ch. 1   *1975*

2 The making of money simply is not a sex-linked skill. Women can and are turning it all around. We are discovering for ourselves the challenge—and the joy—of money.   Ibid.

3 A good rule to follow here is that a credit card—and I speak from sad experience—should never be used unless you already have the money in the bank or can clearly identify where the money will come from, and when. . . . A credit card is a money tool, *not* a supplement to money. The failure to make this distinction has "supplemented" many a poor soul right into bankruptcy.   Ibid., Ch. 4

4 . . . launching your own business is like writing your own personal declaration of independence from the corporate beehive, where you sell bits of your life in forty-hour (or longer) chunks in return for a paycheck. . . . Going into business for yourself, becoming an entrepreneur, is the modern-day equivalent of pioneering on the old frontier.

Ibid., Ch. 6

5 Americans want action for their money. They are fascinated by its self-reproducing qualities if it's put to work. . . . Gold-hoarding goes against the American grain; it fits in better with European pessimism than with America's traditional optimism.

Ibid., Ch. 15

1270. Karin Sheldon
(1945–   )

1 Environment, in all its forms and relations, sustains us. We depend upon it. I truly believe that the fundamental principles of ecology govern our lives, wherever we live, and that we must wake up to this fact or be lost.

Quoted in "Found Women: Defusing the Atomic Establishment" by Anna Mayo, *Ms.*   *October, 1973*

1271. Anne Tucker
(1945–   )

1 Society's double behavioral standard for women and for men is, in fact, a more effective deterrent than economic discrimination because it is more insidious, less tangible. Economic disadvantages involve ascertainable amounts, but the very nature of societal value judgments makes them harder to define, their effects harder to relate.

The Woman's Eye, Introduction   *1973*

2 All art requires courage.

Ibid.

3 Exploration, whether of jungles or minds, is considered unfeminine.   *Ibid.*

4 For centuries men have defined themselves in terms of other men, but women have been defined by and in terms of men. . . . The ubiquitous nature of masculine images of Woman has contributed significantly to the struggles of woman artists because that which is publicly acceptable art does not conform with their own needs and experiences, and their own art does not conform with popular standards.

Ibid.

1272. Candice Bergen
(1946–   )

1 Hollywood is like Picasso's bathroom.
Quoted by Sheila Graham in the
New York Post   *February 14, 1967*

2 THE MAN. You've been renovated, my sweet, like an urban renewal project!
The Freezer   *1968*

3 THE MAN. Can't they realize that mankind was founded on two basic principles? *Religion and Death?* The one motivates the other. *Both* motivate the man!
Ibid.

4 THE MAN. Man has always been under death's dictatorship, always questioned it, always challenged it.
Ibid.

1273. Jacqueline Bisset
(1946–   )

1 Character contributes to beauty. It fortifies a woman as her youth fades. A mode of conduct, a standard of courage, discipline, fortitude and integrity can do a great deal to make a woman beautiful.
Quoted by Lydia Lane in the
Los Angeles Times   *May 16, 1974*

1274. Carter Heyward
(1946–)

1 I'm a priest, not a priestess. . . . "Priestess" implies
mumbo jumbo and all sorts of pagan goings-on. Those
who oppose us would love to call us priestesses. They
can call us all the names in the world—it's better than
being invisible.

> Quoted in "Who's Afraid of
> Women Priests?" by Malcolm Boyd,
> *Ms.*   *December, 1974*

2 It's obvious throughout secular and church history that
significant legislation follows only after dramatic action.

> Ibid.

1275. Mary McCaslin
(1946?–)

1 Bury me out on the lone prairie
Near the mountains I could never see

The speakers, they all gasp to clear their lungs for their
luncheon speeches
This year's new campaign is save the canyons and the
beaches   "The Dealers"   *1975*

1276. Honor Moore
(1946–)

1 I have thought the cancer was in my control.
If I decide she will recover, it will go away. . . .
> *Mourning Pictures* (verse play)   *1974*

2 A ring or two.
Her turquoise beads
The green-striped chair
What will she leave me
Except alone, alone by myself?
No one to have the final word.
> Ibid., "What Will She Leave Me?"

1277. Laura Nyro
(1946–   )

1 And when I die
and when I'm gone
there'll be one child born
and a world to carry on. . . . .
"And When I Die"   *1966*

2 I was born from love
and my poor mother worked the mines
I was raised on the good book Jesus
till I read between the lines. . . .
"Stoney End"   *1966*

3 Nothing cures like time and love. . . .
"Time and Love"   *1966*

4 I've got a lot of patience, baby
And that's a lot of patience to lose.
"When I Was a Freeport"   *1971*

5 money   money   money
do you feel like a pawn
in your own world?
you found the system
and you lost the pearl. . . .
"Money"   *1975*

1278. Judee Sill
(1946?–   )

1 The great storm raged and the power kept growin',
Dragons rose from the land below
And even now I wonder where I'm goin'
Ever since a long time ago,
I've tried to let my feelin's show.
"The Phoenix"   *1969*

1279. Barbara Smith
(1946–   )

1 Then there was the magazine called LIFE
which promised more about the Deaths.

> "Poems for My Sister (One) Birmingham
> Sunday, 1963," *Southern Voices*
> *August/September, 1974*

1280. Bernadette Devlin
(1947–   )

1 To gain that which is worth having, it may be necessary to lose everything else.

> *The Price of My Soul,* Preface   *1969*

1281. Melanie
(1947–   )

1 don't hold the sprout against the seed
don't hold this need against me. . . .

> "Gather on a Hill of Wildflowers"
> *1975*

1282. Sally Priesand
(1947–   )

1 Clergy are father figures to many women, and sometimes they are threatened by another woman accom-
plishing what they see as strictly male goals. But I can
see them replacing that feeling with a sense of pride
that women can have that role.

> Quoted in *Women at Work*
> by Betty Medsger   *1975*

1283. Victoria Bond
(1949–   )

1 The conductor traditionally has been anything but a
mother figure. The conductor is much more like a gen-

eral than a mother or teacher. It's a kind of enforced leadership, the kind of leadership more likely to be expected of men than women. A woman conductor, because of those traditions, must rely completely on being able to transmit authority purely on the grounds of her musical ability.

Quoted in *Women at Work*
by Betty Medsger   1975

1284. Gayl Jones
(1949–   )

1 "My great-grandmama told my grandmama the part she lived through that my grandmama didn't live through and my grandmama told my mama what they both lived through and my mama told me what they all lived through and we were supposed to pass it down like that from generation to generation so we'd never forget."

Corregidora   1975

2 It was as if the words were helping her, as if the words repeated again and again could be a substitute for memory, were somehow more than the memory.

Ibid.

1285. Alicia Bay Laurel
(1949–   )

1 When we depend less on industrially produced consumer goods, we can live in quiet places. Our bodies become vigorous; we discover the serenity of living with the rhythms of the earth. We cease oppressing one another.

Living on the Earth   1971

2 Let's all go out into the sunshine, take off our clothes, dance and sing and make love and get enlightened.

Quoted in *Contemporary Authors*
1974

1286. Holly Near
(1949–   )

1 First he'll want to talk about it
   Then he'll want to fight
   Then he'll want to make love to me all night
   My man's been laid off, got trouble, got trouble. . . .
                                  "Laid Off"   1973

2 Get off me baby, get off and leave me alone
   I'm lonely when you're gone but I'm lonelier when
     you're home. . . .   "Get Off Me Baby"   1973

3 Well if you think traveling three is a drag
   Pack up loner
   I've got my own bag full of dreams for this little child
     of wonder
   And you can only stay if you start to understand. . . .
                                  "Started Out Fine"   1973

1287. Theodora Van Runkle
(1949?–   )

1 Death is very sophisticated. It's like a Noel Coward
   comedy. You light a cigarette and wait for it in the
   library.

                          Quoted in "People You Should Know"
                          by Mary Reinholz, *Viva*   *April, 1974*

2 Just at a time when women are becoming free and
   buoyant, and developing sexually and in a feeling way,
   they're dressing to look like huge, tottering objects, like
   courtesans during the Renaissance period.   Ibid.

1288. Gigliola Pierobon
(1950?–   )

1 It is horrible to listen to men in black togas [in court]
   having discussions about your morals, your cystitis,
   your feelings, your womb, the way you straddled your
   legs.   "Gazette News: Abortion in
                          Italy," *Ms.*   *October, 1973*

1289. Arianna Stassinopoulos
(1950–   )

1 Whether we regard the Women's Liberation movement
as a serious threat, a passing convulsion, or a fashionable idiocy, it is a movement that mounts an attack on
practically everything that women value today and in-
troduces the language and sentiments of political confrontation into the area of personal relationships. . . .
*"The Emancipated Woman," The
Female Woman   1973*

2 It would be futile to attempt to fit women into a masculine pattern of attitudes, skills and abilities and disas-
trous to force them to suppress their specifically female
characteristics and abilities by keeping up the pretense
that there are no differences between the sexes.
Ibid., "The Natural Woman"

3 Emancipation means equal status for different roles.
. . . Liberation . . . is a demand for the abolition of
wife and mother, the dissolution of the family. . . .
Ibid., "The Family Woman"

4 Our current obsession with creativity is the result of
our continued striving for immortality in an era when
most people no longer believe in an after-life.
Ibid., "The Working Woman"

5 Not only is it harder to be a man, it is also harder to
become one.
Ibid., "The Male Man"

6 Liberation is an evershifting horizon, a total ideology
that can never fulfill its promises. . . . It has the therapeutic quality of providing emotionally charged rituals
of solidarity in hatred—it is the amphetamine of its believers.
*Ibid., "The Liberated Woman? . . .
and Her Liberators"*

1290. Barbara Holland
(1951–)

1 Speech that is but percussion under melody
 is bones to music. I do not understand
 a word you say, and yet you tell me in your rhythms
 your harmonies, and richness of their structure.

"Translation," St. 1
The East Side Scene
Allen De Loach, ed.   196

1291. Janis Ian
(1951–)

1   How do you do
     would you like
     to be friends?
 No I just want a bed for the night
 Someone to tell me they care.
 You can fake it, that's all right
 In the morning I won't be here.

"The Come On"   197

1292. Phoebe Snow
(1951–)

1 Sometimes this face looks so funny
 That I hide it behind a book
 Sometimes this face has so much class
 That I have to sneak a second look.

"Either or Both"   1973

2 It must be Sunday
 Everybody's telling the truth. . . .

"It Must Be Sunday"   1973

1293. Denise M. Boudrot
(1952–)

1 I don't ride to beat the boys, just to win.

Quoted in Women at Work
by Betty Medsger   1975

Contemporary / No Date

1294. Isidora Aguirre

1 CAROLINA. Besides, when I say "nothing," what I mean is: everything.

Express for Santiago 1960

2 CARLOS. Remember: don't start conversations with strangers on a trip. No way of getting rid of them later!

Ibid.

3 CAROLINA. It's awful to be the wife of a lawyer.

Ibid.

1295. Dora Alonso

1 The shadow, the color of the man, and the kind of living, all are the same; black in one hundred tones, either so light as to be cinnamon flesh or as dark as black coffee, it carries the sign of subjection.

"Time Gone By," *Fragment from a Lost Diary and Other Stories,* Naomi Katz and Nancy Milton, eds. 1973

2 Life goes on, buried in pain for those who wait; swollen with haughtiness and arrogance for those who fear.

Ibid.

3 There's no higher right than might, and I am mighty.

Ibid.

4 Her body broke down like the collapse of forked poles which could no longer bear the weight of an entire life dedicated to obedience, without a single pillar of rebellion to hold up the structure.

Ibid.

1296. Geneviève Antoine-Dariaux

1 [Habit]
is the chloroform of love.
is the cement that unites married couples.
is getting stuck in the mud of daily routine.
is the fog that masks the most beautiful scenery.
is the end of everything.

"The Men in Your Life"   1968

2 A stranger loses half his charm the day he is no longer a stranger.

Ibid.

3 She began to think about her friends' happy tranquillity, of their affection, of their two non-problem children: the boy wasn't on drugs; the girl wasn't a nymphomaniac; they weren't even quarrelsome. The kind of children nobody had any more.

The Fall Collection, Ch. 1   1973

4 Make ready-to-wear clothing like everybody else? Of course, after all, there is not much difference between the two. The creation is the same. It becomes haute couture if it's made to order with three fittings, or boutique if it's made in advance in standard sizes.

Ibid.

5 Elegance has become so rare today that a well-cut black jersey cape makes heads turn. It isn't chic to be chic any more!

Ibid., Ch. 3

6 The general rule should be respected without favoritism in business and there is no reason why the best workers should earn ten centimes more than the less good ones. Workers shouldn't depend on one boss' good will any more than they should be the victims of the ill will of the bad one.

Ibid., Ch. 7

1297. Frances M. Beal

1 The advertising media in this country continuously informs the American male of his need for indispensable signs of his virility. . . .

> "Double Jeopardy: To Be Black and Female" (1969), *Sisterhood Is Powerful*, Robin Morgan, ed.
> *1970*

2 Let me state here and now that the black woman in America can justly be described as a "slave of a slave."

> Ibid.

3 Men may be cruelly exploited and subjected to all sorts of dehumanizing tactics on the part of the ruling class, but they have someone who is below them—at least they're not women.

> Ibid.

4 Any white women's group that does not have an anti-imperialist and antiracist ideology has absolutely nothing in common with the black woman's struggle. Ibid.

5 To die for the revolution is a one-shot deal; to live for the revolution means taking on the more difficult commitment of changing our day-to-day life patterns.

> Ibid.

1298. Christine Billson

1 I am admired because I do things well. I cook, sew, knit, talk, work and make love very well. So I am a valuable item. Without me he would suffer. With him I am alone. I am as solitary as eternity and sometimes as stupid as clotted cream. Ha ha ha! Don't think! Act as if all the bills are paid.

> *You Can Touch Me*   1961

1299. Rosellen Brown

1 "Do you think there could be something like victims without crimes?"

> "A Letter to Ismael in the Grave," *Street Games*   1974

2 "I wish you were alive, I wish, I wish, so I could hate you and get on with it."

Ibid.

3 I know how he dreams me. I know because I dream his dreams.

Ibid., "How to Win"

4 . . . I remember sort of half dreaming as if I had dozed for a few unlikely minutes down by the bay and some sea animal had crawled up, slimy, from below the pilings, had bit me painfully between the legs, and had retreated to its secret life, invisible under the water, covered with blood like something wounded. For an initiation, I assume it was about average.

Ibid., "Street Games"

1300. Phila Henrietta Case

1 Oh! why does the wind blow upon me so wild?
Is it because I'm nobody's child?

"Nobody's Child"   1954

1301. Loma Chandler

1 Sometimes asylums are just what they should be—a resting place for people who get lost in life.

"They're Expecting Us," Reader's
Digest   October, 1973

2 A smile appeared upon her face as if she'd taken it directly from her handbag and pinned it there.

Ibid.

1302. Mildred Clingerman

1 Nobody really looks at a bartender. . . . Even the bar philosophers (the dreariest customers of all) prefer to study their own faces in the back-bar mirror. And however they accept their reflected images, whether shudderingly or with secret love, it is to this aloof image that they impart their whisky-wisdom, not to the bartender.

Stair Trick   1952

2 She faced him as if he were Judgment and she standing up pleading for mankind.

Ibid.

1303. Beatrice Conrad

1 Their lives had intertwined into a comfortable dependency, like the gnarled wisteria on their front porch, still twisted around the frail support which long ago it had outgrown.

"The Night of the Falling Star,"
American Scene: New Voices,
Don Wolfe, ed. *1963*

2 We are poor helpless creatures on an undistinguished planet in an obscure corner of a small and fading universe.

Ibid.

1304. Jeane Dixon

1 The rare and beautiful experiences of divine revelation are moments of special gifts. Each of us, however, lives each day with special gifts which are a part of our very being, and life is a process of discovering and developing these God-given gifts within each one of us.

My Life and Prophecies, with Rene
Noorbergen, Ch. 4 *1969*

1305. Helen Dudar

1 Contrary to the folklore of abortion as lifelong trauma, it is not necessarily a profoundly scarring one either.

"Abortion for the Asking," *Saturday*
Review of the Society *April, 1973*

2 In this era of radicalized and politicized clergy, it is no longer even surprising when a woman shows up at [an abortion] clinic with the blessing of her priest.

Ibid.

1306. Alice Embree

1 Shortly after the turn of the century, America marshalled her resources, contracted painfully, and gave birth to the New Technology. The father was a Corporation, and the New Technology grew up in the Corporate image.

"Media Images I: Madison Avenue
Brainwashing—The Facts,"
Sisterhood Is Powerful,
Robin Morgan, ed.   *1970*

2 Humans must breathe, but corporations must make money.

Ibid.

3 Women are the neglected orphans of the technological age.

Ibid.

4 The message of the media is the commercial.

Ibid.

5 America's technology has turned in upon itself; its corporate form makes it the servant of profits, not the servant of human needs.

Ibid.

1307. Joan Fleming

1 "It's the money," Molly said clumsily, "if you've once had no money, and I mean no money at all, it means something always ever afterwards."

The Chill and the Kill, Ch. 7   *1964*

2 "Folk love being told things about themselves they already know."

Ibid.

3 His despondent mood led to unusual frankness when he told Molly that, when he grew up, a murder at the end of a party was the regular thing but you didn't expect it of gentry; it made you lose heart, really it did.

Ibid.

1308. Mary Anne Guitar

1 We have to stop being so teacher-centered, and become student-centered. It's not what you think they need, but what they think they need. That's the functional approach.

"College Marriage Courses—Fun or Fraud?," *Mademoiselle*
February, 1961

1309. Eleanor Hoover

Co-author with Marie Edwards. See 1021: 1–2.

1310. Helen Hudson

1 A white casket with silver handles, she thought. Not a soft bed with a pink quilt but four sides and a lid that closes. To be shipped like a shoe in a box from this world to the next.

"Sunday Morning," *American Scene:
New Voices,* Don Wolfe, ed.   *1963*

2 As he worked, putting the mask of sleep over the faces of death, he felt a vague excitement, as though he were, indeed, reviving her, as though the eyes he had closed so carefully might open again and see him, without reproach: a kindly man who knew his trade and did it well.

Ibid.

1311. Mary Hyde

1 The art of managing men has to be learned from birth. . . . It depends to some extent on one's distribution of curves, a developed instinct, and a large degree of sheer feline cunning.

How to Manage Men   *1955*

1312. Susan Jacoby

1 Political détente notwithstanding, the Soviet Union is still a nation with a deeply ingrained suspicion of foreign influence.

Inside Soviet Schools   *1974*

2 A Russian child on a collective farm faces educational inequities as grave as those confronting a black American child in a city slum.

Ibid.

3 Educational opportunity for all citizens is as much an article of social faith in the Soviet Union as it is in the United States. Everyone believes in education: Party leaders, intellectuals, factory workers, farm laborers. The Soviets have much more faith than Americans in the ability of public institutions to transform their lives; schools—not Marxist-Leninist theory—are seen by parents as the key to a better future for their children.

Ibid.

4 . . . all foreigners regard other societies through the prisms of their own value systems.

Ibid.

5 I have always regarded the development of the individual as the only legitimate goal of education. . . .

Ibid.

6 Soviet schools are extraordinarily good at squeezing the fight out of the individuals they process.

Ibid.

1313. Lena Jeger

1 . . . no legislation can compel anybody to give the unmarried mother what she usually most needs—friendship, understanding and companionship in what is almost inevitably a lonely and deeply traumatic experience.

Illegitimate Children and Their
Parents, Foreword   *1951*

2 The child is different, not because he is illegitimate, but because he is fatherless and he is going to miss a father in the same way that any child who loses his father early, through death or separation, misses him.

Ibid.

3 . . . we feel that there is often too little concern with the unmarried father. In our social records he is an elusive figure, often anonymous, alternately reviled, beloved or blackmailed. . . . Often he needs as much help as the mother to regain a mental and emotional equilibrium and so to make subsequently a good husband to somebody, if not to the mother of his first child.

Ibid.

1314. Rosabeth Moss Kanter

1 The [commune] movement is part of a reawakening of belief in the possibilities for utopia that existed in the nineteenth century and exist again today, a belief that by creating the right social institution, human satisfaction and growth can be achieved.

"Getting It All Together: Communes Past, Present, Future," *The Future of the Family,* Louise Kapp Howe, ed.   *1972*

1315. Marjorie Karmel

1 It is a great pity that a man should stand back, helpless and inadequate, *de trop*, while his wife alone knows the profound experience of the birth of the child they have created together.

Thank You, Dr. Lamaze, Ch. 3   *1959*

2 Who ever said that doctors are truthful or even intelligent? You're getting a lot if they know their profession. Don't ask any more from them. They're only human after all—which is to say, you can't expect much."

Ibid., Ch. 7

3 "One-way first-name calling always means inequality—witness servants, children and dogs."

Ibid.

1316. Helen Lawrenson

1 They are a curious mixture of Spanish tradition, American imitation, and insular limitation. This explains why they never catch on to themselves.

"Latins Are Lousy Lovers,"
Esquire   October, 1939

2 Any definition of sophistication must include the word "worldliness"; and how can people be worldly who seem to have no inkling of what's going on in the world?   "A Farewell to Yesterday," *Latins Are Still Lousy Lovers*   1968

3 Most of today's film actresses are typical of a mass-production age: living dolls who look as if they came off an assembly line and whose uniformity of appearance is frequently a triumph of modern science, thanks to which they can be equipped with identical noses, breasts, teeth, eyelashes, and hair.

Ibid., "Where Did It Go?"

4 A skirt is no obstacle to extemporaneous sex, but it is physically impossible to make love to a girl while she is wearing trousers.

Ibid., "Androgyne, You're a Funny Valentine"

1317. Enriqueta Longauex y Vasquez

1 A woman who has no way of expressing herself and of realizing herself as a full human has nothing else to turn to but the owning of material things.

"The Mexican-American Woman,"
Sisterhood Is Powerful,
Robin Morgan, ed.   1970

2 The Anglo woman is always there with her superiority complex. The Chicana woman will be looked upon as having to prove herself even in the smallest task.

Ibid.

3 When a family is involved in a human rights movement, as is the Mexican-American family, there is little room for a woman's liberation movement alone.   Ibid.

1318. Norma Meacock

1 . . . in all my life I have never found reasoning satisfactory as a means of progress.
Thinking Girl   1968

2 If the texture of our daily life gets any thinner, it'll disappear up its own arsehole.

Ibid.

3 Being human, we should bear all we can.   Ibid.

1319. Susanna Millar

1 The term "play" has long been a linguistic wastepaper basket for behaviour which looks voluntary, but seems to have no obvious biological or social use.
The Psychology of Play, Foreword   1968

2 If animals play, this is because play is useful in the struggle for survival; because play practises and so perfects the skills needed in adult life.   Ibid., Ch. 1

3 For the healthy, a monotonous environment eventually produces discomfort, irritation and attempts to vary it.
Ibid., Ch. 4

4 The social life of a child starts when he is born.
Ibid., Ch. 7

5 It is the business of psychologists to be puzzled by every action, but if the questions are formulated so that they require answers in terms of special motives, they soon become unsatisfactory.   Ibid., Ch. 10

1320. Jane O'Reilly

1 . . . the click! of recognition, that parenthesis of truth around a little thing that completes the puzzle of reality in women's minds—the moment that brings a gleam to our eyes and means the revolution has begun.
"The Housewife's Moment of Truth,"
The First Ms. Reader, Francine
Klagsbrun, ed.   1972

2 Parables are unnecessary for recognizing the blatant absurdity of everyday life. Reality is lesson enough.

Ibid.

3 . . . housewives, the natural people to turn to when there is something unpleasant, inconvenient or inconclusive to be done.

Ibid.

4 Men will always opt for things that get finished and stay that way—putting up screens, but not planning menus.

Ibid.

1321. Anna Maria Ortese

1 It was the easiest and at the same time the most sinister thing possible that was happening to me: when one thing recalls another, and so on, till your present vanishes, and everything before you is purely past, the echo of a life that was more real than this one.

"The Lights of Genoa," Italian
Writing Today, Raleigh Trevelyan,
ed. 1967

2 History is something that, like the rest of Italy, it [Genoa] no longer has: but what it has is the present.

Ibid.

3 I was searching for a piece of luggage that seemed to have been mislaid, as my own life had for some time seemed slightly mislaid. . . .

Ibid.

4 I felt desolate at the thought of the inevitable rudeness or raucousness that, in Rome or to some extent anywhere else, greets anyone who is lost and stops someone to ask the way.　　　　　Ibid.

5 People were alone, and at the same time never alone, at least not in the terrible way you are in Milan and in Rome, where, if you aren't socially eminent or rich or important, others simply don't notice you, and if you're ill you could be thrown out with the rubbish. . . .

Ibid.

6 . . . in order to feel anything you need strength. . . .

Ibid.

1322. Carol Polowy

1 Educational institutions mirror the stereotypes of the larger society. The fact that education has become known as a "woman's field" stems at least in part from the identification of child-care and child-rearing as woman's work. Men frequently view teaching as a stepping stone to educational administration while women look to careers as classroom teachers.

> Address, "Sex Discrimination: The
> Legal Obligations of Educational
> Institutions," *Vital Speeches*
> *February 1, 1975*

2 When textbooks are examined in terms of their presentation and reinforcement of a social order, women and minority groups are dissatisfied with the lack of reality in the presentation.

> Ibid.

1323. Aurelia Potor

1 Middle-aged rabbits don't have a paunch, do have their own teeth and haven't lost their romantic appeal.

> Quoted in *The New York Times*
> *September 22, 1956*

1324. Muriel Resnik

1 JOHN. . . . that's nothing but a tax dodge! . . . This is what the Internal Revenue Service expects. It's all part of the game. They play their part, we have to play ours. It's our duty as American citizens!

> *Any Wednesday*, Act I, Sc. 1   *1963*

2 ELLEN. . . . it's so horrible to be—oh God—thirty. . . . Today is a turning point in my life, the beginning of the end. It's pushing forty—and menopause out there waiting to spring—and before you can even turn around you're a senior citizen.   Ibid.

3 JOHN. But she doesn't *know* I'm hurting her, so I'm not. Is that a happy woman? Is she? You see? We're

not hurting her, we're not taking anything away from her. In point of fact, having you in my life makes me happy, a happy husband for Dorothy! Far from hurting her, pet, we're *helping* her.

ELLEN. We are?

JOHN. Of course! If I didn't have you, Dorothy would be *miserable*!

Ibid., Act II, Sc. 1

4 JOHN. I happen to feel that suburbia is as much of a blight as billboards on country roads.

Ibid., Sc. 2

5 JOHN. I'll tell you about babies. Whenever I see one, I want to give it a cigar and discuss the Common Market.

Ibid.

1325. Virginie des Rieux

1 "Gentlemen, in life, there is one thing that fascinates everybody, and that's rear ends. Talk about backsides and only backsides, and you will have friends everywhere always."

La Satyre, Ch. 1   1967

* * *

2 Marriage is a lottery in which men stake their liberty and women their happiness.   Epigram

1326. Gabriela Roepke

1 AMANDA. I just can't seem to go on—without a good morning in a big baritone voice.

A White Butterfly   1960

2 SMITH. You lose an umbrella. You can also lose time.

Ibid.

3 SMITH. . . . the reflection in my shaving mirror tells me things nobody else ever would.   Ibid.

4 OLD LADY. The best thing others can do for us is to tell us lies.   Ibid.

1327. Betty Rollin

1 . . . biological *possibility* and desire are not the same as biological *need*. Women have child-bearing equipment. For them to choose not to use the equipment is no more blocking what is instinctive than it is for a man who, muscles or no, chooses not to be a weight-lifter.

"Motherhood: Who Needs It?," *Look*
May 16, 1971

2 How can birth-control programs really be effective as long as the concept of glorious motherhood remains unchanged? (Even poor old Planned Parenthood has to euphemize—why not Planned Unparenthood?)

Ibid.

3 Motherhood affords an instant identity. First, through wifehood, you are somebody's wife; then you are somebody's mother. Both give not only identity and activity, but status and stardom of a kind.

Ibid.

1328. Sonya Rudikoff

1 . . . the idea has gained currency that women have often been handicapped not only by a fear of failure—not unknown to men either—but by a fear of success as well.

"Women and Success," *Commentary*
October, 1974

2 Although there are countless alumni of the school of hard knocks, there has not yet been a move to accredit that institution.

Ibid.

3 History provides abundant examples of . . . women whose greatest gift was in redeeming, inspiring, liberating, and nurturing the gifts of others.

Ibid.

4 The embattled gates to equal rights have indeed opened up for modern women, but I sometimes think to myself: "That is not what I meant by freedom—it is only 'social progress.'"

Ibid.

5 There are surely lives which display very few of t
signs of success until very late, or after life is ov
There are lives of great significance which go unreco
nized by peers for a very long time, there are tho
who achieve nothing for themselves but leave a lega
for others who come after, there are lives sacrificed f
causes.

Ibi

6 Should we, perhaps, see the development of the cor
mune movement in another light, as a less expensi
form of summer camp for a growing population—pos
adolescent, post-industrial, post-Christian and unen
ployed? Article in *Commentary* 197

1329. Merle Shain

1 We tend to think of the rational as a higher order, br
it is the emotional that marks our lives. One ofte
learns more from ten days of agony than from ten year
of contentment. . . .

*Some Men are More Perfect Tha.
Others*, Pt. I, Ch. 1 197.

2 Most women would rather have someone whisper thei
name at optimum moments than rocket with contrac
tions to the moon. . . . Ibid., Ch.

3 So mistresses tend to get a steady diet of whippe
cream, but no meat and potatoes, and wives often ge
the reverse, when both would like a bit of each.

Ibid., Pt. II, Ch. 4

1330. Mary Jane Sherfey

1 There is a great difference between satisfaction and sa
tiation.

"A Theory on Female Sexuality,"
*Journal of the American Psycho-
analytical Association* 1966

2 The nature of female sexuality as here presented makes
it clear that . . . woman's inordinate orgasmic capacity did not evolve for monogamous, sedentary cultures.

Ibid.

3 The strength of the drive determines the force required to suppress it.

Ibid.

4 There is no such thing as a vaginal orgasm distinct from a clitoral orgasm. The nature of the orgasm is the same regardless of the erotogenic zone stimulated to produce it.

Ibid.

1331. Margaret Sloan

1 We feel that there can't be liberation for less than half a race. We want *all* black people in this country to be free.

Manifesto, National Black Feminist
Organization   *1975*

2 It has been hard for black women to emerge from the myriad of distorted images that have portrayed us as grinning Beulahs, castrating Sapphires, and pancake-box Jemimahs.

Ibid.

1332. Evelyn E. Smith

1 It turned out that all the scientists had been doing the same thing, making a lot of hoopla about inventing stuff—atom bombs, jet planes, television—when actually they did it all with witchcraft. Seems all the magicians had gone underground since the Age of Enlightenment and had been passing off their feats as science—except for a few unreconstructed gypsies.

The Martian and the Magician   *1952*

2 Enemies whispered that he had bewitched the voting machines, but that wasn't true; he'd won fair and square through mass hypnosis.

Ibid.

3 That's always the way when you discover something new; everybody thinks you're crazy.

Ibid.

1333. Judy Syfers

1 The problems of an American wife stem from the fact that we live in a society which is structured in such a way as to profit only a few at the expense of the many. As long as we women tolerate such a capitalist system, all but a privileged few of us must necessarily be exploited as workers and as wives.

> "I Want a Wife," *The First Ms. Reader,*
> Francine Klagsbrun, ed.   *1972*

2 My God, who *wouldn't* want a wife?

> Ibid.

1334. Octavia Waldo

1 The rain fell like a cascade of pine needles over Rome. Rain—thirty days of it. It marked the interlude between winter and spring, and spring was late in coming. There was nothing to do about it but wait. There is nothing to do about most things that are late in Rome, whether it be an appointment, or a bus, or a promise. Or even hope.

> "Roman Spring," *American Scene:*
> *New Voices,* Don Wolfe, ed.   *1963*

2 ". . . Adam Maxwell, age twenty-four, husband to Ruth. A boy who wants to go to the top. As if the world had a top!"

> Ibid.

3 "Living," he had said, "like studying, needs a little practice."   Ibid.

4 But sleep had been taking a vacation from her; as if she were a pariah, it visited her too infrequently, and then only out of unavoidable duty.   Ibid., Ch. 2

5 The lazy pattern of living had reinstated itself, had returned an assuagement made of compromises and complacency. It had made things safe again between them.

> Ibid.

6 "The war has caved the very heart out of modesty and has left her rather bare."   Ibid.

Biographical Index

NOTES TO BIOGRAPHICAL INDEX

Every contributor is listed alphabetically and her contributor number given (these numbers will be found in page headings throughout the Quotations section). If a woman is well known by a name other than the one used at the heading of her entry in the Quotations section, that name is cross-indexed here. All co-authors are listed here except "as told to" authors.

Brief biographical information is given for each woman: her full name (those parts of her name not used at the heading of her quotations are in brackets), and any hereditary or honorary title she is known to hold; her nationality, and—if different—her country of residence (i.e., Am./It. indicates a woman was born in the United States but has lived most of her life in Italy); her profession; her family relationship to other well-known persons; any major awards or honors she is known to have received; any "firsts" or outstanding achievements for which she is responsible; any other names by which she is known.

Abbreviations (other than nationality) are: m.–married name; w.–wife of; d.–daughter of; s.–sister of; pseud.–fictitious name used specifically in her work; aka (also known as)—nicknames, aliases, and any other names by which she was known.

The term educator encompasses teachers, professors—whether full, associate or assistant—and other instructors; college administrators are specifically designated. The term composer is used in reference to classical music; composers of popular music are designated as songwriters.

The term (cont./no date) denotes contemporary/no date. This was utilized in the case of women who are alive but for whom no birth date could be found.

Biographical Index

Chesler, Phyllis (1940–   )   1207
  Am. psychiatrist, writer, educator
Chiang Ping-tzu (*see* Ting Ling)
Chicago, Judy (1939–   )   1188
  Am. painter, lecturer, writer; née Gerowitz; m.
  Hamrol; co-founder of the Woman's Building,
  Feminist Studio Workshop/College, Los Angeles
Child, Julia (1912–   )   868
  Am. chef, writer; née McWilliams; Emmy Award,
  1966
Chisholm, Shirley [Anita] (1924–   )   1000
  Am. educator, congresswoman, writer; née St. Hill
Clanmorris, Baroness (*see* Bingham, Madeleine)
Clarenbach, Kathryn (1925?–   )   1014
  Am. educator, feminist
Clark, Eleanor (1913–   )   880
  Am. writer; w. Robert Penn Warren; National
  Book Award, 1965
⊷Clingerman, Mildred (cont./n.d.)   1302
  Am. writer
Cochran, Jacqueline (1906?–   )   801
  Am. aviator; m. Odlum; head of U.S. Woman's Air-
  force Service Pilots (WASP); broke several world
  speed records
Cohen, Charlotte Bonny (1943–   )   1244
  Am. political activist
Collins, Judy [Marjorie] (1939–   )   1189
  Am. folksinger, songwriter
Conkling, Hilda (1910–   )   849
  Am. poet; d. Grace Conkling
Connolly, Olga (1932–   )   1105
  Czech./Am. athlete; née Fikotova; Olympic cham-
  pion, discus throwing
Conrad, Beatrice (cont./n.d.)   1303
  Am. educator, writer
Cookson, Catherine [McMullen] (1906–   )   802
  Eng. writer; aka Catherine Marchant
Craigin, Elisabeth (fl. 1930s)   1070
  Am. writer
Crane, Nathalia [Clara Ruth] (1913–   )   881
  Am. poet; m. Black
Crist, Judith (1922–   )   980
  Am. film critic; née Klein
Croce, Arlene (1934?–   )   1132
  Am. dance critic, writer, editor
Cross, Amanda (*see* Heilbrun, Carolyn)

E

F

Furness, Betty (1916–   )   908
    Am. columnist, government official, actress

G

Gabor, Zsa Zsa [Sari] (1921?–   )   972
    Hung./Am. actress, business executive; ex-w. Con-
    rad Hilton, George Saunders; Miss Hungary, 1936
Gallant, Mavis (1922–   )   981
    Can. writer
Gandhi, Indira [Priyadarshini] (1917–   )   924
    Ind. politician, Prime Minister of India, 1966–
    1977; d. Jawaharlal Nehru
Garbo, Greta (1905–   )   786
    Swed./Am. actress
Gardiner, Lisa (1900–1956)   716
    Am. dancer, choreographer, educator; founder of
    Washington School of Ballet
Garland, Judy (1922–1969)   982
    Am. singer, actress; née Frances Gumm; ex-w.
    Sidney Luft and Vincente Minnelli; mother of Liza
    Minnelli and Lorna Luft; Academy Award, 1939
Garthwaite, Terry (1939–   )   1195
    Am. singer, lyricist
Gearhart, Sally [Miller] (1931–   )   1094
    Am. writer
Gelpi, Barbara [Charlesworth] (1933–   )   1120
    Am. educator
Gibbons, Stella [Dorothea] (1902–   )   750
    Eng. writer, poet; m. Webb
Gibson, Althea (1927–   )   1041
    Am. tennis and golf pro; Olympic champion
Gillespie, Marcia [Ann] (1944–   )   1260
    Am. editor
Gilliatt, Penelope [Ann Douglass] (1932–   )   1107
    Eng. writer, film critic, scenarist
Ginsberg, Ruth Bader (1933–   )   1121
    Am. educator, lawyer
Ginzburg, Natalia (1916–   )   909
    It. writer; aka Alessandra Tornimparte; Premio
    Strega Prize, 1963
Giovanni, Nikki (1943–   )   1245
    Am. poet
Giroud, Françoise (1916–   )   910
    Swiss/Fr. politician, journalist, editor, French

531

Melanie (1947–   )   1281
   Am. singer, songwriter; née Melanie Safka
Mercouri, Melina (1929–   )   1063
   Grk. actress
Miles, Josephine (1911–   )   863
   Am. poet, educator, literary critic
Millar, Susanna (cont./n.d.)   1319
   Eng. psychologist, writer
Miller, Isabel (*see* Routsong, Alma)
Millett, Kate (1934–   )   1140
   Am. sculptor, writer, feminist
Milner, Marion (*see* Field, Joanna)
Mitchell, Joni (1943–   )   1252
   Am. songwriter, singer
Mitchell, Juliet (1940–   )   1213
   New Zeal./Eng. writer, lecturer, editor
Mitchell, Margaret (1900–1949)   725
   Am. writer; m. Marsh; Pulitzer Prize, 1937
Mitchell, Martha (1918–1976)   940
   Am. public figure; née Jennings; w. John Mitchell
Mitford, Jessica (1917–   )   928
   Eng./Am. writer, social critic; m. Treuhaft
Mitford, Nancy (1904–1973)   776
   Eng. writer, biographer
Moffat, Mary Jane (1938?–   )   1184
   Am. educator, writer, actress
Monroe, Marilyn (1926–1962)   1032
   Am. actress; née Norma Jean Baker
Moore, Grace (1901–1947)   741
   Am. opera singer, actress
Moore, Honor (1946–   )   1276
   Am. playwright, poet
Moore, Virginia (1903–   )   761
   Am. poet, biographer
Moreau, Jeanne (1929–   )   1064
   Fr. actress
Morgan, Barbara (1900–   )   726
   Am. photographer
Morgan, Elaine [Neville] (1920–   )   966
   Welsh writer, educator
Morgan, Robin (1941–   )   1224
   Am. poet, editor, writer, feminist
Morrison, Toni (1931–   )   1099
   Am. educator, editor, writer
Mortimer, Penelope (1918–   )   941
   Eng. writer; née Fletcher

Z

Subject Index

The numbers preceding the colons are contributor numbers; guides to these numbers are found at the top of each page in the Quotations section. The numbers following the colons refer to the specific quotations.

Entries are in the form of nouns, present participles, or proper names. Because of the amorphous nature of the English language, however, where the use of a noun might be confusing, "the" has been added for clarification (e.g., the obvious), or a noun is given in its plural form to clarify the author's use of the word (e.g., appearance has a different connotation than appearances, speech than speeches).

In subentries the symbol ~ is used to replace the main word; it is placed either before or after the subentry, whichever makes a whole phrase. For example, overpopulation is listed under population as over~, while marriage laws are listed under marriage as ~ laws.

Where there are two words in a main entry with a slash between them, the broader term appears first (e.g., barbarism/barbarian; nursing/nurse). This has been done when there were too few quotations under one or the other of such related subjects to warrant a separate listing.

For a statement on the purpose and style of the Subject Index, please see the Author's Preface.

Subject Index

704–1334

A

abortion, 730:3; 747:4; 913:9; 921:1; 944:1; 1121:2; 1144:16, 21; 1148:12; 1288:1; 1306:1, 2

absence, 1110:10; 1191:1

absolutes, 1034:2

absurdity, 795:25

abuse, 763:20

Abzug, Bella, 959:2

Academy Awards, 837:3; 1168:1

acceptance, 895:6

accomplishment (see achievement)

accusation, 804:36; 816:2

achievement, 740:16; 795:4; 1211:7

acting, 819:2, 4; 837:2; 863:1; 945:1; 1080:1; 1211:10; teaching of ∼, 866:5

action, need for, 859:4; 905:9; 913:8

activeness, 795:30; 799:10; 824:19; 882:6, 14; 1062:1; 1099:4; 1188:3

activity, 804:7; 866:3; 985:11

actor/actress (also see performer), 718:1, 4; 814:1; 853:1; 945:2; 1114:3; 1142:10; 1168:2; child ∼, 982:1; film ∼, 752:7; 1316:3

Adam and Eve, 705:1; 777:1; 988:13

adaptability, 971:10

admiration (also see adoration), 941:5; 1193:7

adolescence, 797:1; 859:2; 993:5; 1057:3; 1191:10

adoration (also see admiration), 981:6; 1126:3

adultery (also see infidelity), 764:7; 882:16

adulthood/adult, 733:4; 1124:5; 1233:6

adventure, 824:36; 829:1; 991:4; 1111:6; 1144:1; 1185:11; 1190:5

adversity (also see obstacle; trouble), 712:2; 724:5; 729:6; 1134:10; mastery of ∼, 731:4; 1115:3

advertising (also see merchandising; publicity), 715:9; 775:4; 819:1; 946:16; 1233:3; 1247:8; 1297:1; 1306:4

advice, 1159:6

affection, 1035:6

affluence (see wealth)

Africa/Africans, 1048:9; 1139:6

afterlife, 861:4

age/aging (also see men, aging; women, aging), 744:2; 758:1; 774:1; 824:44; 899:1; 993:4, 6; 1095:12; 1126:5; 1144:15; 1185:24; 1265:12; 1324:2; middle ∼, 807:9; 901:1, 5, 6; 949:20; 1323:1; 1324:2; old ∼, 755:1; 789:1, 3; 824:46; 888:4; 901:6; 942:1; 989:9; 1035:1; 1072:2; 1104:6; 1185:15; 1212:1

agism, 789:2

agitation/agitator, 1061:3; 1178:5

agreement, 1265:11

agriculture, 711:6

aimlessness, 811:6

airplane, 996:2; 1009:4

alcoholism (also see liquor), 996:10; 1162:2

556

alienation, 775:3; 789:4; 813:3; 904:1

alimony, 1241:4

aloneness (*also see* solitude), 985:11; 1144:20; 1188:2; 1276:2; 1321:5

altruism, 763:36; 795:6; 804:18; 816:4; 823:11; 850:17; 879:1; 897:4; 1016:14; 1024:7; 1190:8

ambition, 711:10; 776:1; 825:1; 840:16; 866:3; 948:3; 1032:4; 1041:1; 1106:4; 1124:4, 7; 1126:1; 1156:1; 1168:2; 1253:4; 1334:2

America (*see* United States)

Americans (*also see* United States), 760:11; 776:4; 874:14; 1126:7, 8; 1136:1; 1148:11; 1208:2

amorality, 799:11

analysis, 983:2; 1202:1

anatomy, 1101:10; 1160:10; 1256:3

ancestor, 724:6; 791:19

androgyny, 877:12; 936:3; 1025:2, 4, 8; 1033:3; 1034:13; 1050:1; 1120:1; 1192:2

anger, 804:52; 824:19; 986:2; 1013:2; 1034:10; 1057:1; 1108:11; 1137:2; 1138:2; 1185:3; 1224:6

Animal (*also see individual species*; wildlife), 750:1; 921:15; 1159:2; 1323:1; caged ~, 1177:1; fighting ~, 1159:7; play among ~, 1319:2

anonymity, 1060:7; 1098:1

answer (*also see* solution), 740:1; 921:4

anthology, 791:1, 3; 882:5

anthropology/anthropologist, 740:27; 971:7; 1224:4

anthropomorphism, 993:3

anticipation (*also see* expectation), 1202:1

antiquity (*also see* history), 1252:6

anti-Semitism, 719:5

anxiety (*also see* stress; worry), 763:45; 775:6; 1080:2

apathy (*also see* passivity), 815:4; 1126:4

appearance, physical, 767:5; 820:2; 826:3; 837:10; 1144:15

appearances, 725:11; 735:2; 901:3; 949:35; 1161:7; 1168:3

appeasement, 874:20

applause, 853:1

appreciation (*see* gratitude; respect)

apprehension (*see* dread; fear)

approval, 866:2; 1027:3

archeology, 1015:1

architecture, 731:7; 949:19; 1008:1; women in ~, 1028:1

argument (*also see* quarrel), 791:20, 21; 930:2; 941:7; 1175:4

aristocracy/aristocrat, 776:3

armed forces, 760:10; 878:5; 1254:2; discipline in ~, 878:11; enlistment in ~, 822:4; 1203:3; ~ during peacetime, 927:5

army (*see* armed forces)

arrogance, 804:22

art (*also see specific arts*), 715:6; 743:12; 754:1; 759:1; 855:39; 858:6; 859:7, 8; 867:3; 876:2; 890:15; 921:18; 946:6, 7, 13; 986:10; 1020:3; 1034:9; 1080:5; 1126:9; 1134:5; 1211:4; 1262:2, 4; 1271:2; ~ collector, 828:9; commercialization of ~, 1267:1, 2; feminist ~, 1262:1; government and ~, 818:2; Impressionist ~, 731:3; 828:8; modern ~, 1126:10; primitive ~, 1034:9; technology and ~, 828:8

artfulness, 974:1

artist, 748:4; 824:4; 828:4, 6, 7; 836:1, 2; 859:8; 931:15; 946:13; 1099:3; 1247:4, 15; struggle of ~, 752:1, 3; 1080:3; woman ~, 1247:22; 1271:4

Asia, 1181:6

aspiration (*see* ambition)

assassination, 1054:3; 1182:2

assertiveness, 1245:13

assessment, 968:1

assistance (*see* help)

astrology, 973:3; 1009:2; 1058:2, 3

athletics (*see* sports)

attention, need for, 877:11

attrition, 840:17

British, the (*see* the English)
budget, family, 888:2; national
  ~, 1007:1
bureaucracy (*also see* red tape),
  833:3; 874:12; 949:36; 1095:10
business, 795:20; 1269:4; 1296:6;
  1306:1, 2
businessman, 711:19; 1012:4, 5
butterfly, 717:6

C

Cabinet, U.S., 940:1
Cairo, Egypt, 1181:4
California, 820:15; 1185:29
Calvinism, 1253:3
cancer, 812:20; 1276:1
candor, 1104:3; 1162:3
capability, 1124:7
capitalism, 760:19; 799:17;
  874:17; 1113:3; 1159:9;
  1160:1; 1333:1; opposition to
  ~, 824:43
capriciousness, 948:3; 1124:1
career, 900:11; 1032:2; 1051:4
caring, 1148:3
cat, 763:24; 949:28, 29; 1150:2;
  ~ fancier, 981:10
catatonia, 1185:17
catharsis, 763:16
Catholicism (*see* Roman Catholic
  Church)
celebrities, 1104:2
celibacy, 820:14; 1247:5
cemetery, 993:14; 1074:1
censorship, 1049:1, 2
century, 20th, 824:39
certainty, 824:48; 882:18
challenge, 1064:1
champion, 1041:3; 1250:3
change, 728:6; 799:23; 804:46;
  863:8; 1066:17; 1101:12;
  1110:18; 1130:8; 1138:3;
  1139:19; 1148:7, 9; 1224:10;
  1234:3; 1244:4; 1272:2; social
  ~, 807:6; 867:1; 1005:2
chaos, social, 1034:1
Chaplin, Charlie, 1211:5
character, 943:4; 1057:6; 1273:1;
  ~ traits, 1048:4
charity, 720:5; 791:24; 855:43;
  952:2
charm, 949:30
cheerfulness, 1067:4

chemical, 812:11, 13, 14
Chicago, Illinois, 728:5
Chicano (*see* Mexican-
  Americans)
childbirth (*also see* birth), 720:6;
  725:9; 763:9, 10; 834:1; 971:9;
  1315:1
child care (*see* day care, children's)
childhood, 760:22; 763:7, 15, 24;
  764:2; 806:6; 859:1; 891:2;
  910:2; 1048:1; 1102:1; suppression of ~, 985:4
childlessness, 988:7; 1111:22
child rearing, 731:5; 788:2;
  825:4; 946:14; 971:3; 985:4;
  1033:2; 1034:6; 1139:14;
  1140:2; 1142:2; 1255:3
children (*also see* baby; boy;
  girl; offspring), 733:1; 760:2;
  791:17; 794:2; 858:7; 866:6;
  866:4; 902:1; 939:4; 952:1;
  968:4; 994:2, 8; 1048:3, 15;
  1059:2; 1095:14; 1097:6;
  1104:5; 1115:2; 1235:1;
  1249:2; 1296:3; 1319:4; illegitimate ~, 949:10; 1313:2; indulgence of ~, 797:6; 937:2;
  980:6; ~ in relation to parents,
  719:10; 804:52; 920:1; 1108:2;
  1124:8; learning and ~, 985:5,
  8; neglect of ~, 1167:1; obligation to ~, 852:2; psychology
  of ~, 824:27; sexism and ~,
  1103:1; work and ~, 982:1
China, 807:17; 810:3; 878:13, 16;
  931:2; 1139:14, 15; 1244:1, 3,
  4; agriculture in ~, 878:17;
  ~ army, 810:3; Chungking,
  ~, 931:2; family in ~, 810:1
Chinese, the, 1244:2; ~ women,
  971:5
chivalry, 850:9
choice (*also see* priorities),
  740:3; 890:9; 1099:1
Christ, Jesus, 822:6; 936:2;
  1016:2; 1216:2; 1245:12
Christianity/Christian (*also see*
  individual denominations; religion), 804:9; 918:1; 1098:5
Christian Science, 839:3
Chungking, China, 931:2
cinema (*see* film)

consciousness, 890:22; 973:4; 1120:2; 1265:1; historical ~, 1262:3; stream of ~, 731:8

consciousness-raising, 914:1; 1039:7; 1142:1; 1218:3; 1259:1

conscription, 878:3

conservation (also see ecology), 812:2, 3, 22

conservatism, 824:28

consistency, 820:12

consumerism/consumer, 760:20; 775:4; 988:4

contentment, 823:11

contents, 1158:5; 1233:4

contraception (see birth control)

contradiction, 890:10; 1294:1

conventionality, 1025:6

conversation, 743:4; 744:9; 776:5; 791:10; 1104:1; 1144:19; 1158:1; idle ~, 1144:14

cooking/cook, 817:3; 867:3, 5; 868:2; 932:5; 970:1; 1220:6

cooperation (also see harmony), 775:12; 795:20; 1050:12; 1156:3; 1188:5; 1191:11

corruption, 709:5; 719:4; 767:2; 768:7; 813:7; 928:8; 1005:1; 1133:1; 1155:5; 1161:4; political ~, 931:3; 1007:2

cosmetics, 1047:1; 1145:16; 1252:8

cost of living, 994:1

country life, 804:37; 882:7

courage (also see bravery), 804:26; 807:11; 921:7; 1190:3; 1297:5

court, law (see the judiciary)

courtesan (also see prostitution), 744:10; 817:2

courtesy, 744:8; 996:13; 1139:4; 1321:4

cow, 750:1

cowardice/coward, 874:19

coyness, 763:3; 813:6; 910:13

craftsmanship, 825:10; 942:9; 1211:5

Creation, the, 743:8; 1265:13

creativity, 717:7; 763:23; 828:9; 863:2; 882:6; 886:21; 926:6; 946:11, 14; 983:4; 1050:4; 1117:5; 1139:3; 1188:1; 1247:3; 1289:4

credibility, 1096:1

credit card, 1269:3

crime, 799:10, 22; 905:9; 928:6; 1097:1; 1130:1, 7; juvenile ~, 921:14; ~ of passion, 1176:2; political ~, 1217:1; premeditated ~, 1185:28; punishment of ~, 855:11; women and ~, 1130:1

criminology, 768:6

crisis, 719:9; 947:1; 1220:7

criticism/critic, 859:8; 874:2; 907:6; 945:1; 980:3; 1107:7; art ~, 1267:1; constructive ~, 1043:5; film ~, 980:2, 7; literary ~, 876:1; music ~, 804:29

crowd, 928:1; ~ psychology, 763:32

cruelty, 767:1; 1265:3

crying (also see tears), 763:3; 909:4; 987:8

culture (also see civilization), 740:4, 12; 799:3; 826:8; 1101:8

curiosity, 743:7; 1010:2; 1107:2; idle ~, 266:21

custom (also see habit; tradition), 910:10; 1256:10

cynicism, 715:15; 804:15; 815:3; 895:5; 916:2; 941:4; 1081:1; 1144:27; 1150:1; 1185:31; 1193:8

D

Dali, Salvador, 791:15

dance/dancer, 826:5, 6

danger (also see risk), 742:2; 1029:8

darkness, 841:1; 881:7; 1111:19

Darwin, Charles, 744:7; 812:21

daughter, 1183:3; ~ in relation to father, 1059:15; ~ in relation to mother, 995:1; 1027:9; 1059:13

day, 733:5; 809:2

day care, children's, 852:3; 1142:16; 1235:2, 3, 5

daydream, 783:1; 826:2; 982:4; 1098:5; 1189:2; 1248:4

dead, the (also see death), 767:7; 1110:22

deadline, 938:1

death (also see the dead), 725:9; 791:29; 804:20; 824:35, 46;

E

Earhart, Amelia, 742:1
earnings, 791:3; 900:12; 1037:4
earth (also see world), 812:10;
  872:1; 993:14; 1054:16;
  1190:4; 1224:9
East, the (see Asia)
East Bengal, India, 924:6
eccentricity, 963:6; 1107:6
ecology (also see conservation;
  pollution), 728:6; 740:30;
  812:2, 12, 15, 17, 19; 897:7;
  930:1; 1050:12; 1270:1
economics/economy, 747:2;
  799:17; 807:6; 888:1; 912:6, 9;
  1159:14
education (also see college;
  school), 784:2; 805:11; 826:6;
  942:7; 949:3; 985:9; 1142:6;
  children and ∼, 980:6; 1167:2;
  1200:2; liberal arts ∼, 900:13;
  methods of ∼, 985:7, 8;
  1308:1; public ∼, 1106:5;
  purpose of ∼, 1312:5; sexism
  in ∼, 1200:2; 1322:1, 2;
  women and ∼, 805:2; 971:18;
  1019:1; 1031:2; 1118:1;
  1188:4
educator (see teacher)
efficiency, 1086:1
ego, 715:3; 791:5; 795:18;
  1160:7; male ∼, 825:2, 9, 11
egotism/egotist, 823:9; 871:4;
  993:13; 996:8; 1007:7; 1099:2;
  1134:6; 1197:8
Egypt, 1181:3
Eichmann, Adolf, 799:7, 11
electricity, 1002:3
elegance, 1145:10; 1296:5
elitism, 722:1; 1096:2; 1160:2;
  1321:5
elusiveness, 874:8; 994:9
emotion (also see feeling), 760:9;
  1076:2; 1245:4; 1329:1
employment (see work)
emptiness (also see void), 997:2;
  1185:25; 1237:5
endeavor (also see struggle),
  811:2; 949:12
ending, 799:5; 840:20
endurance (also see strength),
  1193:5; 1247:19; 1318:3
enemy, 910:15; 1134:3; 1249:12

England, 749:3; 850:6, 12; 878:3;
  931:1; 1191:3; government in
  ∼, 959:5; women in ∼, 885:1
English, the, 776:4; 850:3, 4, 5,
  10; 870:6; 891:1; 916:1;
  949:4; 1107:6; 1191:13
enigma, 993:2
enjoyment, 709:2; 946:5; 1042:4
enlightenment, 1108:3
Enlightenment, Age of, 1071:1
entertainment (also see show
  business; theater), 799:3;
  980:4
enthusiasm, 925:5
environment, 795:36; 866:1;
  983:4
envy (also see jealousy), 921:8;
  949:20; 1012:2
equality, 968:3; 988:10; 1023:1;
  1059:1; racial ∼, 1174:3
Equal Rights Amendment,
  760:21; 1175:7
era, 863:8; 989:6, 9
ERA (see Equal Rights Amendment)
eroticism, 1140:6; 1211:3
escapism, 806:3; 824:34; 941:18;
  981:8; 1124:6; 1144:28;
  1228:2
Eskimo, 1221:1, 2
ESP (see extrasensory perception)
Establishment, the, 795:43;
  799:21; 913:12; 959:4; 1214:2
eternity, 1237:1
ethics, 795:34; 928:10
etiquette (see manners)
euphemism, 874:14, 17; 1095:9;
  1130:3
Europe/Europeans, 1183:2;
  1247:12
Evers, Medgar, 921:16
evidence, 1204:6
evil, 855:35, 41; 1016:8; 1050:8;
  1159:7
evolution, 743:8; 744:7; 1009:1;
  1101:12
exactness, 816:6; 996:12
exaggeration, 717:7; 910:14
excellence, 877:2; 898:1; 985:10;
  1009:3
excitement, 840:2; 881:1
execution, 1257:4
exhaustion (see weariness)
exile, 1237:2

existence (*also see* life), 824:2, 15, 45; 1101:1; 1111:13; 1237:1

expectation (*also see* anticipation), 716:1; 825:6; 855:31; 910:4; 1315:2

expediency, 777:3; 900:5

experience, 763:22; 846:2; 863:3; 866:1; 949:27; 991:5; 1191:4

exploitation, 709:6; 724:4; 804:33; 931:16; 1164:2; 1258:15; 1297:3; ~ in the arts, 980:9; sexual ~, 731:1

exploration, 823:7; 855:45; 1265:4; 1271:3

extinction, 812:12, 18

extrasensory perception, 869:2; 973:5

extravagance, 1144:12; 1265:10

extremism, 757:3; 989:1; 1002:4

eye, 828:2; 1054:17

F

face, human, 743:6; 1177:3, 4

fact, 820:17; 1066:1; 1101:9

factionalism, 981:4

failure (*also see* defeat), 813:5; 835:2; 996:6; 1100:3; 1247:15; 1328:1

faith (*also see* belief) 718:6; 854:5; loss of ~, 731:2; 1082:8

faithfulness, 763:28; 1246:5

Fall, the, 966:2

fame (*also see* stardom), 752:6, 7; 791:2; 837:7; 949:13; 950:1; 1041:1; 1114:3; 1124:2; 1127:4; 1134:5; 1256:5

familiarity, 944:3; 967:1

family, 797:3; 805:1; 823:18; 824:43; 888:2; 981:4; 1051:4; 1136:2; 1140:2; 1175:5; 1194:3; 1197:2; 1286:3; decline of ~, 1212:2; nuclear ~, 1164:4; woman's role in ~, 1289:3

fanaticism, 711:16; 816:6

fantasy, 728:8; 733:4; 1032:3; 1108:5; 1122:3; 1216:14; 1220:2

farming/farmer (*also see* agriculture), 860:1; 893:2; 956:1

fascination, 837:5

fascism/fascist, 804:27; 862:1; 1069:1

fashion (*also see* clothing), 756:3, 4, 5; 768:3; 817:1; 907:4; 1012:1, 3; 1145:10; 1287:2; 1296:4; 1316:4; ~ industry, 1012:2

fate (*also see* destiny; luck), 796:4, 5, 6; 863:1; 1095:20

father (*also see* parents), 719:7; 791:16; 949:10; 958:1; 1054:15; 1059:15; 1106:3; 1252:5; American ~, 850:13; unwed ~, 1313:3

fatherlessness, 1092:1; 1313:2

fatigue (*see* weariness)

fatness (*see* obesity; plumpness)

favoritism, 1059:21

fear (*also see* dread), 720:7; 770:2; 832:1; 841:1; 921:15, 16; 941:4; 975:7; 1139:5; 1190:3, 5

February, 963:7

feeling (*also see* emotion), 877:4, 10; 931:5; 1238:1; 1256:10; 1321:6; expression of ~, 1252:4; 1278:1; hurt ~, 1034:10; lack of ~, 840:15

female (*see* women)

femininity, 740:13, 28; 900:6; 910:7; 951:7; 985:2; illusion of ~, 929:4; loss of ~, 1060:1; 1316:4; repression of ~, 1289:2

feminism/feminist (*also see* liberation, women's; women's movement), 900:7; 1018:6; 1024:7, 8; 1026:2; 1231:7; 1249:1, 10; 1259:1; blacks and ~, 1297:4; decline of ~, 1125:1; ~ literature, 1253:2

fiction (*also see* novel; writing), 763:28, 35, 46; 820:21; 1107:7; 1112:4; 1178:4

fighting, 724:4; 1059:17

film (*also see* Hollywood; screenplay), 710:2; 754:3; 804:1; 939:3; 946:1, 2, 8, 10, 17, 18; 967:5; 980:2, 5; 981:16; 1107:11; 1178:2; 1211:3; 1240:1, 2, 7, 8; American ~, 946:6; ~ censorship, 1049:2; documentary ~, 754:2; foreign ~, 981:13; ~goer, 980:1; ~ industry, 926:2, 5; 1211:12;

~ making, 926:3; 946:9, 12; 967:6; 980:7; 1240:3, 6; 1010:1; 1056:1; 1261:1, 2, 3; propaganda ~, 1178:1; sex in ~, 865:3; 1178:3; violence in ~, 865:3; women and ~, 1056:2; 1080:4; 1089:5; 1107:11; 1211:3, 8; 1240:10; 1261:2
finality, 1066:18
First Lady, U.S., 1009:6
fish, 931:20; 949:28
Fitzgerald, F. Scott and Zelda, 911:7
flattery, 774:1; 1307:2
Fleming, Alexander, 835:3
flirtation, 775:5; 1218:5
flower (also see specific kinds), 822:5; 881:4; 1054:11; 1171:2; 1263:5; ~ arranging, 744:1
flying, 742:2; 807:1, 2, 4; 829:1; 1122:7
fog, 807:15
food, 817:5; 822:3; Creole ~, 1048:13; ~ faddist, 772:1
fool, 931:6; 1029:7, 9
foolishness, 949:14
foreign aid, 878:12; 932:7
foreigner, 1312:4
forgetfulness, 1170:1
forgetting, 706:2; 813:4; 823:15
forgiveness, 795:31; 813:4; 820:3; 895:6; 1083:2
foundation, weak, 921:11
fragmentation, 820:19
France (also see the French), Alpes-Maritimes, 1141:1; ~ in relation to Germany, 1075:1
freak, 991:3
free enterprise (see capitalism)
freedom (also see liberation; liberty), 725:2; 727:1; 729:8; 749:3; 778:2; 791:8; 799:12, 13, 17; 807:13; 823:20; 859:9; 890:21; 905:2, 10; 927:6; 968:3; 1068:2; 1122:7; 1139:8; 1197:1; 1224:3; 1244:4; 1328:4 ~ of thought, 818:2
free will, 974:10
French, the (also see France), 744:9; 981:9
Freud, Sigmund, 760:18; 763:40; 1213:4, 5; 1247:10
friend, 733:2; 957:1; 1223:5; 1247:16; choosing ~, 734:1

friendship (also see companionship), 763:38; 795:40; 830:1; 855:40; 878:15; 994:3; ~ between women (also see women, in relation to women), 1187:1; lasting ~, 1066:19
fulfillment, 823:4
funeral, 724:12; 775:1; 840:21; 921:2; 928:3; 1145:5; 1225:7
futility, 923:1; 1081:6; 1144:26
future, the, 724:13; 726:2; 738:2; 804:44; 807:5; 824:15, 29; 855:33; 897:1; 949:5; 1066:8; 1082:3; 1114:1; 1185:9; 1213:2, 3; 1220:4; 1247:17

G

games (see playing)
garden/gardening, 728:2; 949:11
Garland, Judy, 1040:1
geese, 728:1
gay liberation movement (also see homosexuality; lesbianism), 1146:7
generation gap, 820:7; 870:4; 1039:4; 1151:3; 1324:5
generosity, 804:50
genitals, male, 874:6
genius (also see greatness), 711:8; 824:47; 835:3; 877:12
genocide, 1228:2
gentleness, 1227:6
Germany, 760:10; 807:6; 863:7
ghetto, 994:3, 5
Gibson, Althea, 1041:3
gift (see presents; talent)
girl (also see children), 839:1; conditioning of ~ (also see women, conditioning of), 740:18; 820:9; 942:4; 1014:2; 1088:3; 1160:8; 1200:3
glamour, 744:3; 771:2; 1227:5
goal (also see purpose), 715:8; 804:41; 866:3; 886:5; 1062:8; 1124:4; 1135:2; 1280:1
God, 711:18; 721:2, 3, 4; 743:2; 791:26; 804:16; 815:3; 822:2; 854:4; 855:16, 36; 877:5; 879:2; 906:2; 907:2; 936:1; 986:5; 1015:4; 1029:9; 1050:4, 5, 6, 9; 1054:16; 1101:1; 1142:6; faith in ~, 915:1; 987:7

good and evil, 763:12; 855:14; 1139:10

goodness, 707:1; 764:4; 1220:4

gossip, 813:8; 986:2; 1107:9; 1247:13, 14; ~ columnist, 1107:9

government (*also see* nation), 711:13; 722:1; 912:8; 824:7; 1173:3, 5; 1235:4; duplicity of ~, 882:17; faults of ~, 1173:4; responsibility of ~, 824:13; 924:1; 1049:3; 1106:5; self-~, 1148:11; world ~, 897:6

grandparents, 1035:1

grass, 931:1

gratitude (*also see* appreciation), 719:8; 807:3; 921:5

graves (*see* cemetery)

Great Britain (*see* England)

greatness (*also see* genius), 795:7; 974:9; 989:4

greed, 768:7; 775:7, 8; 807:10; 1016:3; 1161:4

grief (*also see* sorrow), 719:6; 767:7; 941:9; 1038:2, 4; 1224:12

grooming, 744:3; 756:3; 859:3

group, encounter, 1146:1, 3; ~ therapy, 1146:1, 4

growing up, 730:1; 927:9; 1247:8

growth, 871:3; 1187:4; 1188:4

guarantee, 1108:4

guest, 870:1

guilt, 717:4; 799:9; 880:2; 1048:12; 1054:2

gullibility, 890:10; 1155:1

gun, 949:15; 1203:3

gynecology (*also see* medical profession), 763:9

H

habit (*also see* custom), 715:13; 1034:12; 1296:1

hairdresser, 1144:19

hand, 1185:37

handbag, 981:12

hand-holding, 1035:6

handicap, 811:4; 840:6; physical ~, 753:6; 1033:2

happiness (*also see* joy), 714:3; 719:1; 777:2; 793:1; 795:5, 16, 17; 824:14; 840:18; 873:1,

2; 980:8; 1057:4; 1067:4; 1218:1

hardship (*see* life, struggle of)

harmony (*also see* cooperation), 840:22; 1211:4

hatred, 717:2; 763:11; 824:23; 949:14; 1145:17; 1197:15; 1289:6

healing, 992:4; 1110:11

health, 731:3; 772:3; 1149:1

heat, 711:14; 776:5

heaven (*also see* paradise), 731:4; 881:5; 988:8; 1233:3; ~ on earth, 731:4

Hedda Gabler, 911:1

hell, 1265:9

help, 1180:2; 1321:4

here and now (*also see* the present), 1190:8; 1248:1

heredity, 1016:1; 1200:1

heritage, 724:6; 748:4; 855:44; 886:16; 1281:1

hero/heroine, 795:27; 911:3; 921:17; 1042:1; 1143:2; 1144:8; 1211:8; 1234:1; 1245:7

heroism, 911:3, 4

highway, '059:18

hill, 849:2

hillbilly, 1033:3

hippie, 795:43; 874:16; 1240:13

history (*also see* antiquity), 753:2; 791:23; 795:6; 804:21; 812:10; 855:28; 882:12; 924:10; 1174:2; 1185:8; cycles in ~, 731:1; oral ~, 1284:1; suppression of ~, 1266:3

Hitler, Adolf, 799:7; 998:1

Ho Chi Minh, 1208:6

Hollywood (*also see* film), 1033:1; 1139:11; 1144:6; 1211:2; 1240:6; 1272:1

home (*also see* house), 709:4; 715:13; 731:11; 760:24; 823:16; 963:10; comforts of ~, 840:7

homecoming, 1170:9

homeliness, 1048:7; 1177:3

homosexuality (*also see* bisexuality; gay liberation movement; lesbianism; sex), 719:12; love-making and ~, 975:4; 1210:2

honesty (*also see* truth), 711:1; 1062:7; 1139:4

honeymoon, 1151:1

honor/honored, 711:2; 717:8; 878:4

hope, 824:50; 855:17; 863:4; 886:7; 921:3; 974:8; 996:9, 15; 1110:15; 1245:10

hopelessness, 974:8; 1144:18

horizon, 962:4

horoscope (*see* astrology)

host/hostess, 870:1

hostility, 900:3; 924:3

house (*also see* home), 942:12; 1157:1; 1229:2

housewife (*also see* women, role of), 745:1; 785:1; 808:2; 951:8; 963:3; 966:4; 1032:3; 1043:1; 1051:2; 1111:16, 21; 1247:4; 1320:3

housework (*also see* women, work and), 805:10; 923:1; 1031:4; 1100:3; 1142:12; 1164:1, 3

human being (*see* humankind; people)

humankind (*also see* people), 711:21; 731:1; 753:1; 824:20; 882:8; 936:4; 949:3; 986:5; 1048:11; 1066:14; 1130:6; 1272:3; belief in ~, 987:7; dichotomy of ~, 744:5; 855:1; 1120:2; 1130:8; 1134:13; 1147:1; powerlessness of ~, 855:16; 1303:2

human nature, 1139:18

human potential movement, 1146:2

humiliation, 767:2

humility, 720:3

humor (*also see* comedy), 925:1; 1056:3; 1204:10; 1211:3

hunger, 931:4; 932:7, 8; 939:1; 1059:8

hunting, 870:2

hurry, 931:9

husband, 972:1; 981:15; 1027:5; 1113:2; 1170:4; rights of ~, 1246:1

hypocrisy, 709:5; 711:21; 763:4, 52; 777:4; 799:16; 802:3; 804:27; 874:4, 18; 951:8; 965:1; 996:13; 1050:8; 1081:3; 1140:10; 1159:5; 1245:9

I

iceberg, 858:3

idea, 719:3; 770:3; 910:14; 1025:1; 1039:2; 1101:9; 1103:2

idealism/ideals, 763:4; 945:5; loss of ~, 1252:6

identity, 743:1; 806:4; 1016:11; 1035:7; 1050:7; 1062:13, 15; 1097:8; 1098:3; 1144:11; 1148:4; 1154:1; 1185:26; 1245:15; lack of ~, 1209:2

ideology, 835:4; 928:9; 1244:1

idleness, 804:42; 1030:1

idolatry, 1024:4

ignorance (*also see* stupidity), 804:13; 858:7; 927:1; 945:5; 1148:13; 1220:1

illiteracy, 858:8; 1048:2

illness (*also see* disease), 767:8; 803:1; 840:1, 3; psychosomatic ~, 839:3; 1042:2

illusions, 763:39; 820:9; 920:2; 974:7; 982:3; 985:1; 1240:3; 1252:2

imagination, 756:2; 763:2; 855:28; 874:6; 1220:2; 1237:3; 1246:4; 1256:2; ~ of children, 753:8

imitation, 817:4; 874:21; 1145:1

immaturity, sexual, 1047:1

immigration/immigrant, 728:7

immortality, 799:6; 996:14; 1059:9; 1289:4

impairment, 725:16

impatience, 921:12

impeachment, 1253:5

imperialism, 931:16

imprisonment (*also see* prison), 981:18; 1258:7, 8, 9, 10

incentive, 801:1

indebtedness, 807:3; 855:27

independence, 795:10; 861:1; 902:1; 1036:3; 1097:5; 1127:1

indescribability, 715:6

India, 924:6, 8, 15; 1042:2, 5; 1139:7; 1247:18; corruption in ~, 924:17; government of ~, 924:13; overpopulation in ~, 924:16; women in ~, 729:5; youth in ~, 924:2

Indian, North American, 726:1; woman ~, 1228:2

indifference, 1005:1; 1152:2;
feigned ~, 977:2
indispensability, 1197:8
individuality, 725:10; 781:1;
795:17; 855:2; 902:4; 948:1;
985:5; 1139:3, 17; 1316:3
Indochinese War, 981:14; 1173:4
indomitability, 855:31; 890:20;
919:1
indulgence, 715:15; 971:3;
1043:5
industrialization, 924:19; 1164:2
inferiority, 981:3
infidelity (*also see* adultery),
921:13; 1145:3; 1324:3
influence, 730:2; 1011:3; 1144:2
information, 874:18; 1062:1;
1226:1; search for ~, 874:19
ingenuousness, 993:12
inheritance (*also see* legacy),
1233:2; 1276:2
injustice, 711:18; 874:2; 1249:11;
1258:14
innocence, 711:18; 767:2; 909:5;
911:4; 1095:18; 1159:1; loss of
~, 1144:5; 1211:1; 1245:11
innovator, 795:13
insect, 812:19
insecticide, 812:17, 21
insecurity, 967:2; emotional ~,
763:18; 1057:7
insight (*also see* perceptiveness),
824:33; 942:11; 949:31
insomnia, 1110:4; 1111:8;
1135:3; 1334:4
inspiration, 718:3; 1068:1;
1101:11
instinct, 899:2; 1169:1; fighting
~, 728:4
institution (*also see* mental institution), 824:30; 1246:3
integration, racial, 811:1; 861:5
integrity (*also see* principle),
795:39; 837:4; 1257:1
intellectualism/intellectual,
757:5; 795:38; 805:12
intelligence (*also see* the mind),
795:22, 29; 823:10; 854:4;
949:23; 1066:9; 1104:8;
1142:13; native ~, 1048:2
interaction, social, 1046:1;
1110:1
interdependence, 794:3; 1188:5
interior decorating, 850:7
interrogation, 1030:5

interruption, 1082:1
intimacy, 840:5; 927:14; 993:11;
1025:11; 1034:6; 1091:1;
1218:3; 1237:1
introspection, 1099:2; 1247:1
invention/inventor, 804:16;
1220:1
Ireland, in relation to England,
1217:1
Irish, the, 725:6
irony, 711:4
irrelevance, 1245:4
irresponsibility, 946:5; 950:3;
994:7
isolation, 789:4; 804:10; 927:15;
1110:12
Israel/Israelis, 782:2; 860:2;
sexism in ~, 782:2; women in
~, 782:1
Italy/Italians, 807:6; history of
~, 1321:2
itch, 966:3

J

Japan/Japanese, 736:2; 765:1;
1111:9; 1139:4
jealousy (*also see* envy), 740:26;
760:9; 804:55
Jerusalem, 1159:5
Jesus (*see* Christ, Jesus)
Jew (*see* Judaism)
Jewishness, 1225:5
Johnson, Lyndon B., 871:1;
1208:7; 1245:1
journalist (*also see* writer),
800:2; 896:2
journey (*see* travel)
joy (*also see* happiness), 953:6;
1062:9; 1228:3
Judaism/Jew, 1101:13; 1159:12;
1247:7; persecution of ~,
1129:3; image of ~, 719:2
Judas, 822:6
judge (*see* the judiciary)
judgment (*also see* opinion),
1117:1; value ~, 1252:7; pass
~, 949:39; 993:8
judiciary, the (*also see* jury),
913:4; 1030:6; 1185:32; sexism in ~, 1241:3
jungle, 931:10
jury (*also see* the judiciary),
1030:6

24; 872:3; 882:19; 910:8; 922:3; 951:1, 5, 6; 968:2; 1015:6; 1106:1; 1107:11; 1125:1; 1140:5; 1187:3; 1249:10; 1297:3

mankind (*see* humankind)

Mann, Thomas, 790:4

manners, 768:3; 804:31; 833:2, 3; 840:14; 870:5; 880:4

March, 820:16

Margaret, Princess, 994:11

marriage, 707:4; 709:6; 760:2, 3; 764:7; 776:2; 823:12; 882:25; 900:7; 923:2; 937:3; 941:1; 942:3; 949:24, 37; 972:2; 979:1; 981:7; 985:1; 996:3; 997:1; 1009:7; 1011:1; 1013:1; 1025:12, 13; 1035:4; 1051:3; 1106:2; 1107:3; 1111:6; 1144:13; 1174:4; 1247:16; 1325:2; children and ∼, 1185:13; ∼ contract, 1051:1; difficulties of ∼, 802:2; 886:11; dissolution of ∼ (*also see* divorce), 927:16; 1031:1; 1185:22; middle-class ∼, 1035:3; multiple ∼, 1226:2; reasons for ∼, 827:1; 990:1; sex in ∼, 820:13; women and ∼, 979:1; 1197:2

martyrdom/martyr, 903:1, 3; 924:4

marvels, 858:2

Marx, Karl, 763:40; 799:4, 14; 855:18; 927:3

Marxism/Marxist, 818:1; 855:26

masculinity, 740:13; 1015:2, 8; 1025:4; 1026:4; 1214:3

masochism, 922:3

masses, the (*also see* people), 1117:1

masturbation (*also see* the sex act), 780:2; 816:3

materialism, 795:32, 43; 824:5, 40; 931:17; 1012:2; 1020:4; 1106:3; 1164:1; 1317:1; dialectical ∼, 855:26; in U.S., 775:8; 904:4

mathematics, 808:3

matriarchy, 872:2, 3; 1015:3

maturity, 715:8, 14; 790:1; 902:2; 1039:8

McCarthyism, 712:7; 982:2

Mead, Margaret, 971:6

meals, 956:2

media, the (*also see* specific forms), 730:2; 763:19; 786:3; 946:4; violence in ∼, 980:9; women and ∼, 729:3; 901:5

medical profession (*also see* doctor; *specific branches*), 763:9; 874:7; 906:1; ethics of ∼, 1162:1; sexism in ∼, 906:1

mediocrity, 740:23; 945:6

meditation (*also see* prayer), 886:23

membership, 1234:5

memory (*also see* recollection), 725:16; 753:7; 763:25, 42; 806:2; 828:3; 840:9; 890:11; 949:27; 981:20; 1054:15; 1082:3; 1190:9; 1284:2

men (*also see* the sexes), 740:20; 760:24; 815:1; 824:10; 858:6; 953:7; 972:2; 1122:1; 1175:2; 1224:7; 1289:5; aging ∼, 760:1; competition and ∼, 1197:3; image of ∼, 1297:1; ∼ in relation to women (*also see* relationships, between men and women), 739:3; 744:11; 760:1, 17; 767:5; 773:1; 820:5; 1006:2; 1015:10; 1059:14; 1142:4; 1166:3; 1174:5; 1247:13; 1249:4, 7; physical size of ∼, 1152:1; power of ∼, 1196:2; 1249:3, 4; 1266:2; responsibilities of ∼, 986:6; role of ∼, 740:19; 1194:1

menstruation, 929:2; 1247:21

mental health, 1116:1

mental illness (*also see* madness), 942:17; 987:6; 1002:1; 1108:6, 8, 13; 1178:7; 1185:17; 1207:3; 1247:6; 1301:1

mental institution, 1054:13; 1207:4; 1301:1

mental retardedness, 1067:2

mental telepathy, 973:2

merchandising (*also see* advertising; publicity), 1029:3

mercy, 907:2; 1016:6; 1302:2

Mexican-Americans, 1317:3; women ∼, 1317:2

middle age (*see* age, middle)

middle class (*see* bourgeoisie; classes, middle)

militancy, 1197:1

military, the (*see* armed forces)

mind, the (*also see* intelligence; reason), 740:29; 1191:2; 1265:5; empty ~, 1185:10; limitations of ~, 1111:23; military ~, 804:32; state of ~, 949:25

miracle, 855:48; 1224:10

mirror, 763:24, 26; 1209:2

mischief, 771:1

misery, 744:5; 748:1; 941:5; 981:11; 983:3

misogyny, 1095:16; 1224:2

missionary, 910:12; 931:15; 993:1; 1081:2; 1265:9

mistake, 881:9; 907:7; 1104:7; 1191:4; 1245:5

mistress, 1329:3

moderation, 757:3

modesty, 887:1; 974:2; 1334:6

monarchy, 1159:8

money, 724:14; 725:3; 776:4; 839:2; 850:16; 855:12, 24; 859:5; 888:2; 943:2; 986:6; 996:9; 1020:4; 1101:2; 1145:8; 1161:7; 1164:1; 1185:12; 1234:6; 1264:2; 1277:5; acquisition of ~, 897:2; Americans and ~, 1269:5; evil of ~, 748:2; women and ~, 794:1; 1269:1, 2

monogamy, 1145:2; 1330:2

Monroe, Marilyn, 1142:10; 1211:11

monster, 1009:5

Montessori, Maria, 985:7

morality, 795:26, 37; 811:5; 1062:13; 1103:4; 1130:2; 1144:7; 1173:3; middle-class ~, 882:16

morning, 1252:3

mortality, 719:1; 901:7

Moscow, 729:4; 1011:2

motherhood/mother (*also see* parents), 731:5; 797:3, 5; 822:3; 824:50; 830:8; 838:2; 886:20; 992:3; 1001:1; 1031:3; 1043:2, 3; 1057:2; 1059:13; 1082:2; 1242:1, 2; 1252:5; 1264:3; 1327:3; glorification of ~, 1327:2; ~-in-law, 823:19; ~ in relation to children, 906:3; 1111:18; overbearing ~, 1027:9; stage ~, 894:1; unwed ~, 913:5; 1313:1; welfare ~, 913:5

mountain (*see* hill)

mourning (*see* grief)

movement, social (*also see* specific movements), 989:1; 1142:14

movie (*see* film)

mulatto, 1059:7

murder (*also see* killing), 784:1; 804:14; 1307:3

Museum of Modern Art, New York, 1020:3

music (*also see* opera; singing; symphony), 893:1; 909:2; 927:17; 1052:1; 1089:4; 1228:4; blues, 861:3; composing ~, 1199:1; gospel ~, 861:2, 3; recording of ~, 1045:1; rock ~, 1018:7; women in ~, 1283:1

music business, 902:4; 1087:1; sexism in ~, 1087:1

musician, 811:1; 999:4

mystique, 971:11

mythology, 872:3; 890:17; 910:4; Roman ~, 711:17

N

naiveté, 715:9; 768:5; 874:4

Napoleonic Wars, 878:2

narcissism, 816:7; 824:32; 946:14

narrow-mindedness, 949:16; 955:1

nation, 855:1; 1216:11; confidence in ~, 760:19; relations among ~, 760:12; 878:15; 924:5

national defense, 878:5; 1075:1

nationalism, 1011:1

National Organization of Women, 1018:2; 1024:8

national security, 924:7

naturalness, 892:2

nature (*see* human nature)

Nature, 715:19; 717:3; 753:1; 795:33; 812:10, 22; 849:3; 858:5; 881:5; 930:1; 956:1; 985:6; 1053:2; 1141:2; 1265:10; 1285:1

Nazi, 790:1, 2; Hitler Youth Organization, 790:2

neatness (*see* orderliness)

necessity, 855:45

needs, 855:30; 1145:17; 1281:1

negativity, 921:6; 1197:7

negligence, 764:3
Negro (*see* blacks)
Nehru, Pandit Jawaharlal, 924:14
neighborhood, mixed, 1193:1
Netherlands, the (*see* Holland)
neurosis, 763:23; 942:16; 1111:7
New England (*see* United States)
news, 906:5; 981:17; 1279:1;
  bad ~, 1110:7
newspaper, editor, 896:3; exaggeration in ~, 742:1
newspapermen (*see* journalist)
New Year, 980:8
New York City, 715:3; 884:3;
  942:18;   1134:8;   1144:1;
  1148:10; 1161:5; 1181:4
night, 856:1; 1185:21
nightmare, 790:5; 987:1; 1148:1
Nixon, Richard M., 965:1, 2;
  1000:7; 1218:6
Nobel Prize Committee, 1073:1
nonconformity, 711:15; 1257:4
nonviolence, 1216:8, 10
normalcy, 1067:3
North,   the/Northerners,   U.S.
  (*see* United States)
nosiness, 725:12; 786:3; 847:1;
  1159:3
nostalgia, 824:28
nothing, 804:42; 1107:5; 1110:13
novel (*also see* fiction; writing),
  731:4, 7; 1025:7; 1112:2
novelist (*see* writer)
NOW (*see* National Organization
  of Women)
nuclear power, use of, 976:1
nuisance, 733:1
nun, 720:4, 5; black ~, 1263:1
Nuremberg Trials, 799:11
nutrition, 772:1, 2, 4, 5, 6, 7

O

oath, legal, 820:18
obedience, 720:5; 878:11; 1002:1;
  blind ~, 1295:4
objectification   (*also   see*   dehumanization), 824:25; 901:3;
  1117:2
objectivity (*also see* detachment),
  763:49; 1160:6
obligation (*also see* duty; responsibility), 748:5; 855:9, 29;
  1193:3
obscurity, 1066:9

obsession (*also see* compulsion),
  763:6; 927:7
obstacle   (*also   see*   adversity),
  824:3
obstetrics (*see* medical profession)
obstinance, 824:3; 863:4
obvious, the, 1101:7
Occidentals, 880:4
ocean (*see* sea)
October, 949:9
offspring (*also see* children),
  797:1; 806:10; 988:16; 1066:11
old age (*see* age, old)
omnipotence (*also see* power),
  1276:1
oneness, 743:9; 795:15; 1120:4
opera (*also see* singing), 798:2;
  999:1, 2; ~ performer, 798:1;
  1036:2; 1067:1
opinion (*also see* judgment; viewpoint), 791:21; 799:18; 850:10;
  false   ~,   942:15;   slave   of
  ~, 816:1; 1027:3
opium (*see* drugs)
opportunism/opportunist, 725:3;
  1190:1
opportunity, 895:1; 1248:3
oppression (*also see* tyranny),
  724:2; 760:28; 824:22; 855:5;
  886:8; 913:1, 2, 6; 931:16;
  971:5; 1263:6
oppressor (*also see* tyranny),
  724:9; 748:3
optimism/optimist, 768:5; 855:31;
  953:5; 986:7; 1134:7; 1223:2
orderliness, 909:3; 912:2
orgasm (*also see* the sex act),
  763:33; 1249:5; 1264:1; female ~, 751:1; 1106:1; 1330:4
originality (*also see* uniqueness),
  795:13; 828:7; 874:16; 881:10
orphanage/orphan, 1003:1;
  1300:1

P

pacifism/pacifist (*also see* war,
  opposition to), 922:1
pain (*also see* suffering), 719:1;
  855:41; 931:21; 953:4; 996:7;
  1117:3
painting (*see* art)
panic, 873:5

paradise (*also see* heaven; utopia), 1101:5

paranoia, 873:5; 930:4; 1061:1

parasite (*also see* sycophancy), 703:1; 715:17; 731:12; 825:8; 1103:3

parents (*also see* father; mother), 788:2; 806:10; 866:6; 985:1; 1057:6; 1104:5; 1108:2; 1124:8; 1127:3; 1139:14; 1146:5; 1167:3; 1231:5; ~ in relation to children, 719:10; 788:1; 791:28; 825:4; 906:3; 1001:3; 1039:9; 1255:3; 1286:3; permissive ~, 1039:8; resentment toward ~, 1237:4

Paris, France, 878:7

participation, 763:47; 886:10

parting (*also see* separation), 820:8; 830:1

party (celebration), 827:2; 1104:9; 1144:14; 1182:1

passion (*also see* desire), 763:43; 895:4; 939:1

passivity (*also see* apathy), 750:1; 815:4; 855:25; 913:7; 1089:2; 1107:1

past, the (*also see* yesterday), 715:10; 795:33; 799:2; 806:7; 813:2; 824:9; 825:1; 859:10; 896:1; 909:5; 1082:7; 1088:3; 1193:8; 1321:1

paternalism (*also see* patriarchy; protectiveness), 722:2; 805:1; 1002:5; 1066:4; 1130:4; 1197:4

patience, 846:1; 1185:24; 1277:4

patriarchy (*also see* paternalism), 1136:4; 1181:1; 1213:5

patriotism (*see* nationalism)

peace, 717:5; 770:2; 890:7; 924:1; 1178:6; consequences of ~, 1208:9; domestic ~, 840:7; inner ~ (*also see* tranquility), 886:5; 1086:3, 4; 1180:1; ~-making, 924:3

peacock, 1016:10

pedantry, 731:13; 1095:9

penis, 806:1; 1122:1

people (*also see* humankind; the masses), 831:1; 934:1; 1111:5; 1231:2; primitive ~, 740:2, 26

perceptiveness (*also see* insight), 890:12; 927:10; 991:2; 1189:1; 1265:6

perfection, 828:4; 1107:2; 1110:5; 1116:2; 1148:16

performer (*also see* actor), 932:2, 3; 948:4; 984:2; 1127:4; 1139:19

permanence, 1066:5

permissiveness, 882:17

Peron, Juan, 952:1

persecution, 1159:8

perseverance (*also see* tenacity), 715:10; 883:5; 992:1

personality, 740:5, 13

personification, 763:27

persuasiveness, 942:10

Peru, education in, 1119:1

perversity, 1294:1

pessimism/pessimist, 1027:6

pet (*see* cat; dog)

philanthropy (*see* charity)

philosophy/philosopher, 795:42; 855:47

photography, 991:2

physical education, 1014:1; 1105:1

physician (*see* doctor)

physics, 808:1, 3

pimp, 709:3

pioneer, 819:5; 1218:2

pitfall (*see* trap)

pity (*also see* compassion), 799:15

plagiarism, 795:8

plant, 812:16

playing, 1221:2; 1235:1; 1319:2; children and ~, 866:6

plumpness, 784:3

poet, 882:4; 1158:5; 1177:2

poetry, 743:11; 811:4; 849:1; 882:4; 974:12; 1111:5; 1224:5

police, 907:5; 1018:9

Polish, the, 1191:13

politeness (*see* courtesy; tact)

politician, 768:2; 924:14; 959:7; 994:9; 1000:1; 1023:1; 1156:2; 1332:2

politics, 712:6; 729:8; 763:40; 776:4; 777:3; 799:4; 874:15; 1104:4; 1139:12; 1163:3; 1190:10; 1211:9; leftist ~, 1007:5; political party, 960:2; sexism in ~, 760:26; 959:8; women and ~, 760:13, 26; 1061:7; 1142:15; 1175:3

pollution (*also see* ecology), 775:8; 812:11, 13, 17; 908:1; 1275:1

polygamy, 1145:2; 1163:4

poor, the (*also see* classes, lower; poverty), 804:11; 854:1; 996:9; 1162:4; education of ∼, 1186:1

possessions, 763:5; 981:1; 1110:8; 1145:6; 1163:4

possessiveness, 779:3; 855:39, 42; 874:8; 992:3; 1111:1; 1181:6

posterity, 740:30; 1066:11

potato, 733:3

potential, 740:12; 743:9; 764:4; 1036:1; 1246:4

poverty (*also see* the poor), 799:14; 804:11, 31; 813:5; 858:7; 886:20; 902:2; 960:1; 1044:3; 1097:7; 1106:4; 1145:8; 1181:3; 1193:2; 1236:2; 1307:1

power (*also see* authority; omnipotence), 775:11; 789:5; 799:26; 855:42; 922:2; 950:5; 1018:2; 1062:16; lack of ∼, 886:20; 1040:2; 1081:5; political ∼, 1249:7

praise, 729:6; 820:6; 820:6; posthumous ∼, 931:8

prayer (*also see* meditation), 1190:4; 1193:4

preconception, 820:17; 897:5

prediction, 1062:2; 1183:1; 1213:2

pregnancy, 834:1, 2; 1153:2; 1236:3

prejudice (*also see* racism; sexism), 791:21; 824:12; 913:4; 1017:2; 1039:1; 1204:6; class ∼, 1176:3; 1168:1

premonition, 735:1

preoccupation, 1185:18

presence, 950:9

present, the (*also see* here and now), 806:7; 824:1, 9; 855:33; 896:1; 989:2; 1025:10; 1252:3; 1321:2

presents, 1017:1

President, U.S., 871:5; 944:2; candidate for ∼, 1000:4, 6

pretense, 725:1, 11; 743:3; 744:8; 763:14; 804:25; 813:3; 890:17; 917:1; 949:26; 1148:13

pride, 721:3; 723:2; 804:2; 863:6; 879:1; 951:5; 1030:3

principle (*also see* integrity), 712:4; 762:1; 791:20; 804:18; 903:3; 996:14; 1007:6; 1044:2

priorities (*also see* choice), 942:6; 1136:5

prison (*also see* imprisonment), 846:3; 928:8, 9, 10; 1232:1; 1258:8, 11, 12, 14; ∼ administrator, 928:4; homosexuality in ∼, 928:5; 1258:13

prisoner, 928:7, 9; 1258:7; political ∼, 720:1; 729:2; 835:5; 846:3; 903:1; 919:1

privacy, 725:12; 786:1, 2; 791:9; 795:2, 5; 804:45; 840:5; 927:2; 1008:1; 1029:6; 1031:1; 1062:10; 1082:4; 1140:9

privilege, 713:2; 805:6

procrastination, 725:14; 826:2

procreation, 740:18; 751:1; 763:29; 890:20; 1277:1

productivity, 795:3; 824:39; 901:2; 911:6

professionalism, 1160:3

professor (*see* teaching)

profit, 711:2; 1306:5

progress, 711:20; 724:3; 855:44; 897:1; 1044:1; 1081:6; social ∼, 1328:4; technical ∼, 855:20

proletariat (*see* classes, lower)

promiscuity, 775:2; 815:2; 820:14; 869:1; 877:13; 994:7; 1110:2; 1171:1; 1197:10

promise, campaign, 944:4; empty ∼, 1216:13

propaganda, 754:2; 855:13; 876:2; 882:13; 1007:5; 1211:2; 1224:5

prophet, 1016:8

propriety, 725:1; 1100:2

prosperity (*see* wealth)

prostitution/prostitute (*also see* courtesan), 709:1, 3, 5, 6; 779:1, 2; 881:6; 905:5; 1048:14; 1155:2, 3, 4, 5; 1161:1, 2, 4, 6; 1168:5; clients of ∼, 1155:3; earnings of ∼, 1161:3

protectiveness (*also see* paternalism), 870:6

protest, 1153:2; tactics of ∼, 1044:4

Protestantism, 711:3

Proust, Marcel, 1027:4
proverb, 791:14
psychiatry (*also see* psychology; therapy; 721:1; 763:16, 23; 856:3; 904:2; 941:3, 6; 943:5; 985:3; 1032:5; 1090:2; 1097:4; 1148:10; 1168:3; demystification of ~, 1090:1; limitations of ~, 731:6; 1108:13; 1319:15
psychoanalysis (*see* psychiatry)
psychology (*also see* psychiatry; therapy), 869:2; 1204:3; limitations of ~, 1204:2, 4; women and ~, 760:18; 1204:5; 1207:2
psychosis, 987:6
psychotherapy (*see* psychiatry)
puberty (*see* adolescence)
public, the, 768:2; 799:18; 939:3
publicity (*also see* advertising; merchandising), 1061:2
public service, 1022:1; 1096:2
punctuality, 1032:1
punishment, 717:4; 799:10; 804:53; 855:11; 981:17; 1016:4; 1033:2; 1258:10
pupil (*see* student)
purification, 1111:4
puritanism, 1140:7; 1211:7
purpose (*also see* goal), 795:17; 823:6; 1122:6; 1137:1; 1139:19

Q

Quaker, 820:18; 1253:1
quarrel (*also see* argument; bickering), 731:6; 886:11
question, 856:3; 925:3; 1247:7; 1256:7; hypothetical ~, 1216:3

R

rabbit, 1323:1
racism (*also see* prejudice; white supremacy), 740:14; 896:4; 924:8; 994:10; 1000:3; 1030:7; 1037:1; 1081:3; 1085:1; 1143:3; 1147:1; 1171:1, 3; 1174:1; 1194:2; 1258:15
radicalism, 893:1
radio, 1054:12
rage (*see* anger)
railroad, 931:22
rain, 820:15; 860:2; 1334:1

rainbow, 994:9
rape, 824:42; 967:3; 1143:1, 3, 4, 6; 1179:1; 1246:1; 1258:4; 1264:6; ~ laws, 1130:10; 1246:1
rationality (*also see* reason), 775:11; 874:20; 1318:1
rationalization, 705:2
reactionary, 795:13; 1000:2
readiness, 714:4; 824:49; 981:12
reading, 1012:4; 1030:2; ~ for children, 753:8
reality, 795:41; 855:3, 49; 856:1; 873:4; 962:1; 974:7; 996:11; 1062:17; 1108:4; 1159:7; 1193:12; 1208:7; 1320:2; facing ~, 735:3
reason (*also see* the mind; rationality), 795:41
rebirth (*also see* renewal), 905:2; 927:6; 953:1; 1054:5; 1224:9; 1247:20
recipe, 868:1; 1220:6
recognition, 763:50; 886:2; 967:2; 1061:2; 1066:14; 1320:1; 1328:5
recollection (*also see* memory), 813:1; 1216:14
red-baiting, 712:7
red tape (*also see* bureaucracy), 1228:6
reform/reformer, 791:27; 881:6; 1124:9
refuge, 1027:7
refugee, 924:6
regression, 813:2; 886:16
regret, 909:3; 1144:18; 1197:6
rehabilitation, 1272:2
reincarnation, 973:4
rejection, 854:3; 895:1
relationships (*also see* love), 805:4; 906:3; 1098:4; 1144:13, 26; 1163:4; 1185:1; 1213:1; 1228:1; 1303:1; 1334:5; ~ between men and women (*also see* men, in relation to women; women, in relation to men), 824:8, 31; 981:7; 1107:4; 1149:13; 1247:16; difficulty of ~, 856:2; 986:1; 1220:8
relaxation, 924:12
relevance, 1062:12
reliability, 882:9; 974:6
relief, feeling of, 966:3
religion (*also see* Christianity;

São Paulo, Brazil, 994:5
satisfaction, 855:34; 1330:1
scapegoat, 823:8
scholar, 988:3
school (see college; education);
  ~ administration, 1167:2
science, 740:1; 778:1; 795:23;
  805:12; 855:24, 32; 1256:2;
  experimentation in ~, 928:7
scientist, 740:27; 1332:1
screenplay/screenwriter (also see
  film), 926:1, 3, 4
sea, 723:1; 807:14; 812:1, 4, 6, 7,
  8; 815:5; 1054:14
seasons, the (also see individual
  seasons), 840:10; 963:7
secrecy/secret, 750:2; 763:35;
  844:1; 895:5; 1034:11;
  1191:12; 1197:10
secretary, 760:4; 900:4; 1224:11
security (also see safety), 724:10;
  1139:8; 1185:11; 1191:7;
  1197:11, 12, 13; false ~, 851:3
segregation, 905:8; 1000:3
self, the, 963:5; 1050:7; belief in
  ~, 1108:12; 1224:1
self-analysis, 850:8; 886:1;
  931:14; 1035:5; 1170:7; 1190:9
self-awareness, 804:25; 805:9;
  834:2; 932:4; 1050:3; 1110:12;
  1148:5
self-confidence, 508:21; 670:4;
  913:10
self-consciousness, 851:2; 1262:3;
  1265:7
self-control, 711:5; 924:12;
  949:25
self-deception, 1027:8; 1203:4;
  1256:1; 1324:3
self-defense, 1216:9
self-discovery, 1034:8; 1127:1;
  1139:13; 1313:1; 1304:1
self-hatred, 806:5; 824:34;
  1111:17; 1124:6; 1158:2, 4
self-image, 763:26; 1134:6;
  1247:6; 1292:1; 1302:1;
  1326:3
selfishness, 711:21; 725:15;
  847:1
self-justification, 1147:1
self-pity, 715:7; 804:4; 981:11
self-realization, 921:10; 971:15;
  947:7; 1035:4; 1068:2;
  1108:10; 1180:1; 1181:2;
  1256:6

self-reliance, 804:28; 1144:9
  1188:2; 1245:7
self-respect, 1144:5
semantics, 928:2
seniority, 1000:2
senses, the, 775:9; 945:7; 1108:14
separation (also see parting)
  823:3; 1139:1
servant, 988:9; 1059:11; 1110:16
sewing, 771:1
sex/sexuality (also see bisexuality; homosexuality; the sex
  act), 751:1; 874:5; 877:4;
  882:23; 942:19; 949:2; 975:6;
  1059:12, 21; 1126:12; 1225:3;
  1240:15; 1247:3; 1251:2;
  1330:3; adolescent ~, 804:51;
  1092:2, 4; children and ~,
  824:27; disinterest in ~,
  942:14; ~ fixation, 966:2;
  1211:6; 1247:10; ~ freedom,
  882:22; 1024:5; 1264:1; ~ in
  United States, 966:2; 971:12,
  14; 1134:4; 1211:6; men and
  ~, 951:5; objectification of
  ~, 1053:3, 4; 1161:2; pre-
  marital ~, 935:1; suppressed
  ~, 1140:7; women and
  ~, 901:8; 937:1; 1039:5;
  1132:1; 1165:2; 1330:2
sex act, the (also see masturbation; orgasm), 824:42; 825:7;
  949:22; 975:5; 1053:3, 4;
  1059:10; 1111:11; 1124:3;
  1140:4; 1145:11; 1185:23;
  1210:2; 1232:2; 1299:4; oral
  ~, 1247:18
sex appeal, 933:1
sexes, the (also see men; relationships between men and women;
  women); conflict between ~,
  889:1; differences between ~,
  740:6, 7, 10, 15, 20, 26, 29;
  820:4; 821:1; 824:31; 929:1,
  2; 958:2; 975:5; 988:19;
  1009:10; 1015:4; 1024:1;
  1052:1; 1089:1; 1112:3;
  1140:1; 1142:5; 1145:13;
  1160:10; 1185:12; 1192:2;
  1204:8; 1213:4; 1224:4;
  1245:15; 1266:1; 1289:2;
  1320:4; mistrust between ~,
  824:23; roles of ~, 740:4, 21;
  805:6; 889:1; 960:3; 971:20;
  988:2; 1157:2; 1320:4

fication of ∼, 729:3; 954:1; 1231:6; 1298:1; oppressed ∼, 715:4, 760:15; 910:8, 1007:7; 1015:7; 1037:1; passive ∼, 1140:8; power of ∼, 1158:5; 1195:1; repressed ∼, 1111:16; 1181:1; reproductive function of ∼, 1247:21; responsibilities of ∼, 1236:3; revolution and ∼, 834:3; role of ∼ (also see housewife), 740:8, 9, 25; 775:6; 805:2; 890:2; 910:5, 13; 971:13; 1019:1; 1024:4; 1038:1; 1147:2; 1188:4; 1194:1; 1207:2, 3; 1240:9; 1298:1; 1327:1; struggles of ∼, 738:1; 1061:6; suppressed ∼, 971:16; 1066:4; survival of ∼, 1000:5; 1231:7; war and ∼, 843:1; 938:2; 1240:9; work and ∼ (also see housework), 740:21; 824:25; 848:1; 877:3, 7; 964:2; 1020:1; 1037:3; 1118:1; 1142:12; 1269:1; working ∼, 506:3; 800:1; 852:1; 890:6; 938:1; 971:19

women's movement (also see feminism; suffrage, women's), 1055:1

Woods, Rose Mary, 1218:6

words, 763:41; 866:9; 881:8; 996:12; 1256:9; 1290:1; cruel ∼, 886:6; 986:1; 1054:18; fads in ∼, 870:4

work, 717:7; 724:7; 760:9; 790:4; 795:28; 823:11, 12; 837:9; 855:15, 37; 860:1; 874:10; 910:9; 974:9; 1057:5; conditions of ∼, 855:4; sexism in

∼, 740:11; 910:5; 913:11; 1107:10; 1164:3; value of ∼, 828:1

worker, 1268:2; 1296:6; domestic ∼, 1258:1; exploitation of ∼, 927:4; 1268:2

world (also see earth), 797:7; 863:3; 991:5; 1245:12; 1263:2; destruction of ∼, 636:24; 688:3; ∼unity, 463:4; 480:24; 528:42; 644:1

World War I, 878:8, 9

World War II, 770:3

worry (also see anxiety), 1059:14

writer (also see journalist), 718:3; 763:52, 53; 791:1; 812:9; 882:24; 926:2; 989:7; 1059:3, 4, 5; 1101:3; 1178:4; 1247:22; ghost ∼, 882:3; woman ∼, 806:11; 859:7; 946:15; 1196:1

writing (also see fiction), 731:6, 7; 753:9; 816:5; 820:10; 998:3; 1148:4

Y

Yangtze River, 807:17

yesterday (also see the past), 823:15

youth, 719:6; 764:1; 768:4; 820:7; 932:1; 946:13; 949:20; 963:2; 1010:2; 1252:9; cult of ∼, 789:1; ∼ in relation to the aged, 851:2; ∼ in wartime, 749:1; 796:3; rebellion of ∼, 1039:4; 1240:13; sex and ∼, 901:9